HOW THE
WORLD THINKS

HOW THE WORLD THINKS

A Global History of Philosophy

Julian Baggini

GRANTA

Granta Publications, 12 Addison Avenue, London W11 4QR
First published in Great Britain by Granta Books, 2018

A CIP catalogue record for this book
is available from the British Library.

1 3 5 7 9 10 8 6 4 2

ISBN 978 1 78378 228 4 (hardback)
ISBN 978 1 78378 483 7 (trade paperback)
ISBN 978 1 78378 229 1 (ebook)

Typeset in Caslon by M Rules
Printed and bound by CPI Group (UK) Ltd, Croydon, CR0 4YY

MIX
Paper from
responsible sources
FSC
www.fsc.org FSC® C020471

Dedicated to the East-West Center at the University of Hawai'i and the community of scholars in its orbit

Contents

Part One:
How the World Knows

PART FIVE:
CONCLUDING THOUGHTS

A NOTE ON NAMES

In China, Japan and Korea, the convention is for the family name to appear before the given name. However, many people of East Asian ancestry who live in the West refer to themselves by the Western convention of given name first, family name last. I have tried to follow the usage each individual customarily follows. This means most, but not all, East Asian names have the family name first. It should usually be clear in the context which is which. Chinese names are given in either pinyin or Wade-Giles romanisation.

INTRODUCTION

One of the great unexplained wonders of human history is that written philosophy first flowered entirely separately in different parts of the globe at more or less the same time. The early *Upaniṣads* – the foundational texts of Indian philosophy, of unknown authorship – were written between the eight and sixth centuries BCE. China's first great philosopher, Confucius, was born in 551 BCE, while in Greece the first notable pre-Socratic philosopher, Thales of Miletus, was born around 624 BCE. The Buddha's traditional birth date also places him in the sixth century BCE, although scholars now believe he probably wasn't born until around 480 BCE, about the same time as Socrates.

These early philosophies have had a profound impact on the development of distinctive cultures across the world. Their values and tenets have shaped the different ways people worship, live and think about the big questions that concern us all. Most people do not consciously articulate the philosophical assumptions they have absorbed and are often not even aware that they have any, but assumptions about the nature of self, ethics, sources of knowledge, the goals of life, are deeply embedded in our cultures and frame our thinking without our being aware of them. Evidence of their influence is even embedded in the fabric of the world's great monuments, which can be read like living books, expressions of the philosophies of the people who built them. The Forbidden City in Beijing is constructed on Confucian principles, the Alhambra in Granada is infused with Islamic thought, while even the cafés of the Parisian *rive gauche* testify to the existentialist vision of philosophy as a personal, everyday pursuit.

The process of cultural absorption of philosophical world views is sometimes called *sédimentation*. 'If it were possible to lay bare and unfold all the presuppositions in what I call my reason or my ideas at each moment,' wrote the twentieth-century French philosopher Merleau-Ponty, 'we should always find experiences which have not been made explicit, large-scale contributions from past and present, a whole "sedimentary history" which is not only relevant to the *genesis* of my thought, but which determines its *significance*.'[1] Just as a riverbed builds up sediment comprised of that which washes through it, values and beliefs become 'sedimented' in cultures. In turn, those values and beliefs begin to sediment in the minds of people who inhabit those cultures from birth, so that we mistake the build-up for an immutable riverbed. Through these channels of the minds our thoughts and experiences flow, not noticing how they are being directed. One value of comparative philosophy is that by exposing the different assumptions of others – their philosophical sediment, if you will – our own assumptions come to the fore.

Yet, for all the varied and rich philosophical traditions across the world, the Western philosophy I have studied for over thirty years – based entirely on canonical Western texts – is presented as the universal philosophy, the ultimate inquiry into human understanding. 'Comparative philosophy' – study in two or more philosophical traditions – is left almost entirely to people working in anthropology or cultural studies. This abdication of interest assumes that comparative philosophy might help us to understand the intellectual cultures of India, China or the Muslim world, but not the human condition.

In fact, Western philosophy is so parochial that it is Balkanised. When I lived in Manchester I attended senior philosophy seminars at both its universities in buildings on opposite sides of the same street, no more than half a mile apart. Because one department focused on Continental European philosophy and the other on anglophone philosophy, I was almost the only one to cross the road between the two, even though both claim a common ancestry through Descartes and Spinoza back to the ancient Greeks.

This has become something of an embarrassment for me. Until a few years ago I knew virtually nothing about anything other than *Western* philosophy, a tradition that stretches from the ancient Greeks to the great universities of Europe and America. Look at my PhD certificate or the names of the university departments where I studied, however, and there is only one, unqualified, word: philosophy.

Recently and belatedly, I have been exploring the great classical philosophies of the rest of the world, travelling across continents to encounter them first-hand. It has been the most rewarding intellectual journey of my life. I have discovered that to understand a culture's philosophical tradition better is to understand that culture better. To borrow an analogy from the Zimbabwean philosopher Joram Tarusarira, understanding the philosophical framework of a people is like understanding the software their minds work on: 'If you don't know their software there will always be this gap in terms of understanding in conversation.' Such gaps explain why, for example, so many development aid projects in Africa have failed. 'If you want that aid to be of effect, then you have to engage with the people; if you want sustainability, you have to engage with the people. But many a time we have had white elephant projects basically because the people bringing them have no understanding of the philosophy and religion of the people.'

The software analogy is neat, but the relationship between classical philosophical texts and the 'folk philosophy' of a people is clearly not a simple one. Ideas that are developed and analysed in depth by scholars do have their counterparts in the general culture, but in simpler, vaguer, broader forms. Most Americans and Europeans, for example, assert the value of individual freedom and liberty without any deep knowledge of how these concepts have been justified and explained by their philosophers. Millions of Indians live their lives according to principles of *karma* without an in-depth knowledge of the rich and complex literature articulating what precisely this involves. Ordinary Chinese assert the importance of harmony with little more than a cursory knowledge of the Confucian and Daoist texts that analyse and describe it. There is nonetheless a relationship between high scholarship and everyday living, which is why harmony, freedom and *karma* play very different roles in different parts of the world.

Even if we take the most sceptical view possible, that the folk versions of these philosophical ideas are diluted and bastardised beyond recognition, it is still important to understand how these concepts create the rhetorical space in which cultures think, explain and justify. When an American politician speaks in praise of freedom, it is because the culture demands that the value of freedom is upheld, just as in China it is harmony which must be defended. What is salient in the world's philosophies also tends to be salient in their host cultures, and in that way at least understanding philosophy is a window into culture.

Philosophies are important for understanding not just peoples but their histories. This is a view that became somewhat unfashionable in Western historiography, which has emphasised the actions of important individuals or economic and social forces. But until the mid-nineteenth century it was assumed that philosophies and religious beliefs were the primary causes of the major social and political upheavals of the epoch. Ideas not only mattered but could be deadly. 'There was once a man called Rousseau who wrote a book containing nothing but ideas,' said the nineteenth-century Scottish philosopher and essayist Thomas Carlyle to one who doubted this. 'The second edition was bound in the skins of those who laughed at the first.'[2]

The historian Jonathan Israel argues that we need to regain our sense of the importance of ideas in history. 'Without referring to Radical Enlightenment,' he argues, 'nothing about the French Revolution makes the slightest sense or can even begin to be provisionally explained.'[3] What Israel says of the Enlightenment 'revolution of the mind'[4] is true of history and historical change more generally. 'Although a philosophy is itself a cultural phenomenon, it can not only understand but also change a culture,' says philosopher Tom Kasulis.[5]

Kasulis reminds us not only that ideas matter but that they continually evolve. New forms of thinking are always being created to make sense of our changing aspirations and to give voice to our discontent. When we look at 'traditions' it is easy to overlook or downplay these changes. The temptation is always to look out for the continuities over time which make things seem to fit together. As a result, the dissident Chinese writer Xu Zhiyuan observes, people 'ignore intrinsic complexities and, having made their neat comparisons between present and past, or found a satisfying descriptive label, they sit back smugly to enjoy their understanding of things'.[6] Given that one of the oldest Chinese classics is the *I Ching* or *Book of Changes*, to deny the importance of change in the tradition it began would be a mockery. We need to be alert to the discontinuities within cultures as well as to the sometimes surprising commonalities between diverse societies separated by time and space. For example, Kasulis thinks that during Europe's Dark Ages the dominant mode of thought might well have been closer to that of the modern East.[7]

A proper understanding of philosophical traditions does not

efface all developments and differences over time, but it does appreciate how developments and dissent never emerge in a vacuum. Ideas and philosophies have histories that are constantly in the making. We have little chance of coming up with new ideas fit for new times unless we understand the ideas and times with which they are contiguous. Western democracy, for example, cannot simply be exported or imposed on countries with very different histories and cultures. For democracy to travel, it must adapt. Comparative philosophy should therefore be seen as the study not of philosophies set in stone like museum pieces but of dynamic systems. Understood properly, they give us insights not only into the present and past but also into potential futures.

As the relationship between philosophies and the cultures in which they emerge is a complex one, it is difficult to draw conclusions about cause and effect. Did Confucius shape the Chinese mind or did the Chinese mind shape Confucius? The answer, as it is to all these questions, is a bit of both and it is impossible to determine the actual weightings. 'A culture reflects or assumes a philosophy or set of affiliated philosophies even as it influences the framework within which philosophy takes shape,' says Kasulis.[8] For our purposes, it is enough to recognise that there is an intimate relationship here and every scholar I spoke to agreed that understanding the philosophical traditions of a culture helps us to understand that culture more generally.

My philosophical journey has also convinced me that we cannot understand ourselves if we do not understand others. In art and literature, this is little more than a truism. Novels, plays and films give us imaginative insight into the lives, thoughts and feelings of others, all of which enlarges and enriches our own hearts and minds. Philosophical traditions do the same. As the world shrinks, this kind of self-understanding is essential. If cultures are to meet rather than clash, we need to understand not just how others differ from ourselves, but how we differ from them.

We cannot pretend that we can understand the world's philosophies in a matter of a few years, let alone by reading one book. My more modest intention has been to find out *what we need to understand in order to begin to understand.* Searching for this philosophical entry point is like looking for the secret doors in an ethnographic theme park that allow us entry to the real thing. The Japanese might call this a *nyūmon.* Physically, a *nyūmon* is an entrance, such as the University of Tokyo's Red Gate. The *nyūmon* plays a dual role, both defining the boundaries of a space and inviting visitors in.[9] The word has been used by many Japanese writers for what in English we call 'introductions'. Taken more literally, that word also well describes the function of this book. When introduced to somebody, you are not told everything about them, rather you are given the opportunity to begin an acquaintance. This introductory book, then, is a prelude to closer examination, a first step in a longer, open and open-ended project.

Getting to know others requires avoiding the twin dangers of overestimating either how much we have in common or how much divides us. Our shared humanity and the perennial problems of life mean that we can always learn from and identify with the thoughts and practices of others, no matter how alien they might at first appear. At the same time, differences in ways of thinking can be both deep and subtle. If we assume too readily that we can see things from others' points of view we end up seeing them from merely a variation of our own. We are often told we should put ourselves in the shoes of others, but stepping into someone's footwear is not the same as getting inside their mind. We have to get beyond imagining how things would look to us from an unfamiliar viewpoint and really try to understand how they look to others for whom the landscape is home.

This book is a selective history of global philosophy, one which excavates the often hidden foundations of how the world thinks today. The archaeological metaphor also has another dimension.

The more visible, practical aspects of the world's philosophies appear last in these pages because to make sense of them we need to understand the foundations on which they are built. The most fundamental of these concern how the world knows: what justifies belief and claims to knowledge. This is the subject of Part One. Part Two looks at what the world believes about metaphysics and cosmology: the way the world works and is constructed. Part Three considers how different philosophies conceive of human nature, how we see ourselves. It is only after looking at how philosophies understand the basis of knowledge, the structure of the world and the nature of the self that we can make sense of how they think we ought to live, the topic of Part Four.

I do not claim to be fluent in all the forms of thinking I will be introducing you to. In many ways I am helped in this project by *not* being an expert on every tradition I've looked at. 'An insider is like a fish in a fishbowl,' says Xu Zhiyuan, 'unable to see the exact shape of its surroundings even though those surroundings are perfectly clear to everyone else.'[10] Having a certain distance makes the broad outline clearer than it is to those working close up, who in studying the unique features of every tree often forget that they are all of the same species, the one that gives the whole forest its distinctive character.

I have approached my task as a kind of philosophical journalist. The job of the journalist is to know enough about a subject to be able to track down those who know most, ask them the right questions and explain their answers. This is precisely what I have done, reading canonical texts alongside the words of experts, dozens of whom I have interviewed to find out what it is most helpful to know if we are to begin to really understand the philosophies of the world rather than simply memorise a list of their headline doctrines. Many of their names appear in this book, alongside those of other experts whose work I have read. Everyone I quote is a recent or contemporary expert in the topic under discussion unless described otherwise. All comments not referenced in the notes were made to me in conversation. Throughout I have also quoted extensively from the classical texts of each tradition which often make their points with unsurpassable elegance in distinctive voices, providing us with the opportunity for a direct encounter with these rich literatures.

In the seventeenth century, René Descartes wrote in his *Discourse on Method*, 'In my travelling, I learned that those who have views very different from our own are not therefore barbarians or savages, but that several use as much reason as we do, or more.' I hope that no one today would be so amazed. However, one conclusion Descartes drew is still pertinent, that wherever we live 'we are clearly persuaded more by custom and example than by any certain knowledge'. To travel around the world's philosophies is an opportunity to challenge the beliefs and ways of thinking we take for granted. By gaining greater knowledge of how others think, we can become less certain of the knowledge we think we have, which is always the first step to greater understanding.

PROLOGUE

A historical overview from the
Axial to the Information Age

Philosophy's birth between the eighth and third centuries BCE is described by the nineteenth-century German philosopher Karl Jaspers as the 'Axial Age'. It was a period of gradual transition from understanding the world in terms of myth to the more rational understanding of the world we have today.[1] Rational understanding didn't supplant early folk beliefs and myths so much as grow out of their values and tenets. World views, while shaped by the demands of cool reason, were not always led by it.

Although the classical philosophies of India, China and Greece differ in important ways, there are some highly significant commonalities. Each started with a basic assumption that everything is one. Whatever it is that explains human life must also explain the universe, nature, and anything else beyond. As William of Ockham would famously put it in his principle of the 'razor' much later, in the fourteenth century, it is never rational to postulate the existence of more things than are necessary. You start with the simpler explanation – that everything is governed by the same principles – and only complicate matters if that turns out not to work. The earliest philosophers were therefore implicitly following a rational principle that none had yet articulated.

Also, the project of understanding the universe only makes sense if the universe is understandable. If we thought that there was a motley collection of mechanisms and principles governing different parts of reality, with no connections between them, then the universe would be a less comprehensible place. Assuming a kind of unity is a prerequisite for any serious attempt at systematic understanding.

The unity of human knowledge was more evident in the Axial Age than it is today. For the Greeks, everything we consider the humanities or sciences was a part of philosophical study. Nor were there fundamental divisions of knowledge in China or India. As human inquiry grew, so different branches reached further from the trunk, but they are still fundamentally part of the same tree.

Another commonality was the assumption that a satisfactory account of the world must speak to reason. Attractive stories and myths are not enough: we need to articulate an intellectual case that supports the view we adopt. Reason – meaning rationality – is in essence the giving of *reasons*, ones which can be scrutinised, judged, assessed, accepted or rejected.[2] Humans have always had ways of understanding the world, but it is only since the dawn of philosophy that they have seriously attempted to provide and defend reasons for these.

What we see in early philosophy is an attempt to move from stories handed down and accepted on authority to more systematic explanations that could withstand the scrutiny of reason. In general, this led to an evolution of those old myths rather than the creation of entirely novel paradigms. In India, scholars generally divide the development of philosophy into four periods. The Vedic period preceded the Axial Age, roughly between 2500 and 600 BCE, and is described by Sarvepalli Radhakrishnan and Charles Moore as 'an age of groping, in which religion, philosophy, superstition and thought were inextricably interrelated and yet in perpetual conflict'.[3] It was during this period that four key *Vedas* considered by orthodox schools as revealed scriptures, *śruti*, were written: the *Ṛg, Yajur, Sāma* and *Atharva Vedas.*

The epic period followed (c. 500/600 BCE–200 CE), when the *Mahābhārata*, of which the *Bhagavad Gītā* is part, was written. Together with the *Upaniṣads* and the *Brahma Sūtras*, the *Bhagavad Gītā* forms the 'triple foundations' (*prasthāna-traya*) of orthodox Indian philosophy. Although not yet works of systematic philosophy, the doctrines which were developed in these earliest periods 'have determined the tone if not the precise pattern of the Indian philosophical development ever since'.[4] Chief among these is the idea that ultimate reality is *Brahman*, an infinite, unchanging, universal soul. The individual self, *ātman*, only has the illusion of independence. Our ultimate goal is to dissolve the ego and return to *Brahman*. It was also during this period that thinkers such as Gautama, Pāṇini and the Buddhist Nāgārjuna developed rich logics.

The schools of Indian philosophy that maintain the validity of the *Vedas* are known as orthodox or *āstika*. Those that do not are known as heterodox or *nāstika*. Although since around the turn of the late twentieth century this has been the standard classification of schools, it is not clear when the philosophies were first divided up along these lines, nor how straightforward the divisions are. With that caution in mind, the orthodox schools are Nyāyá, Vaiśeṣika, Sāṃkhya, Yoga, Mimāṃsā and Vedānta; and the heterodox schools are Buddhism, Jainism, Cārvāka, Ājīvika and Ajñana.

In China, in the absence of a strong religious culture featuring gods or other-worldly heavens, the new philosophies were more naturalistic than those of India. Confucius (551–479 BCE) based his teachings on the cultural norms of order, respect for elders and tradition. The other major tradition, Daoism, valued harmony with nature above all else and its foundational text, the *Daodejing*, was written between the fourth and third centuries BCE.

In contrast, Greece had to accommodate its gods. But since these were often portrayed as human superheroes in myths, interacting with mortals in the same physical spaces, there was no fundamental problem in explaining the universe in terms of principles that would apply to gods and humans equally.

These three philosophical traditions – Indian, Chinese and Greek – relied on different sources of knowledge. Only in Greece, with the creation of logic, was systematic reason developed to any great degree. In India, emphasis was placed on knowledge attained by seers in states of heightened awareness and on revelations in the sacred texts, the *Vedas*. In China, history and everyday experience provided the benchmarks for truth. The Buddha walked a middle path, arguing that the only evidence available to us is that of experience, which makes speculation as to the nature of 'ultimate' reality fruitless. Nonetheless, he shared the orthodox Indian assumption that ordinary experience was illusory and effort is required to see beyond it. In Greece, the power of reason took centre stage, with Socrates's maxim that we should follow the argument wherever it leads, letting 'our destination be decided by the winds of the discussion'.[5] Each classical tradition that emerged had its own ideas about the right methods for philosophising.

In the Axial Age, many foundational texts were produced which are placed at the centre of contemporary traditions. Indian philosophers still study the *Vedas*, Chinese philosophers the works of Confucius and Mencius, Western philosophers the works of Plato and Aristotle. Joel Kupperman observes that 'there are countries, India and China especially, in which a small number of philosophical texts are foundational, not merely to later philosophy but to the entire culture'.[6] While the ancient Greeks are just names to most Westerners, the Indian *Vedas* and the Chinese classics are familiar to most of the populations of these countries.

If the first phase of philosophy can be seen as an intercontinental move away from myth towards a more rational understanding of the universe, the direction of travel thereafter differed according to region. In the West, philosophy took a step back. The major challenge of medieval philosophy was to negotiate between the claims of Christian faith and the demands of rationality. Philosophy was no longer responding to folk myth but to doctrines established by ecclesiastical authorities in a systematic theology. In keeping with this, the most significant and influential philosopher of this period was the thirteenth-century priest St Thomas Aquinas. As in the ancient period, philosophy did not represent radical alternatives to the dominant religious culture, but rather worked with the grain of its doctrines. Natural theology provided a rational justification for faith, while the embrace of dualism, with its strict distinction between mind and body, fitted with the Christian stress on the superiority of the spiritual afterlife over the physical life here and now.

There are complications in this narrative as there are with that of the Middle East and North Africa, where religion rather than secular philosophy came to acquire the greatest authority. In the so-called golden age of Islamic philosophy, from the eighth to the thirteenth centuries CE, *falasīfa* translated and commented on ancient Greek classics, particularly the work of Aristotle. (This was critical for the transmission of Aristotle's philosophy to the West, where he became so significant that he became known simply as 'the philosopher'.) During this time there were fierce and learned debates between *falasīfa* such as Avicenna (Ibn Sīnā) and Averroes (Ibn Rushd) and more theologically inclined *kalām* thinkers such as al-Ghazālī, a tussle the latter eventually won, ending the prospect of the independence of Islamic philosophy from theology.

In India, the picture is yet more complicated. Philosophical attention turned to the interpretation of the ancient *sūtras*. *Sūtra* means 'string' or 'thread' in Sanskrit, referring to a genre of writing in which short, aphoristic teachings were collected together, most importantly in the *Vedas*. During the Sūtra period from the early centuries CE and the scholastic period which followed, a lot of commentaries on the ancient *sūtras* were written, subjecting their doctrines to rational analysis and justification. As Radhakrishnan puts it, 'Strenuous attempts were made to justify by reason what faith implicitly accepts.'[7]

An important divide also opened up in the Vedānta school. Śaṅkara founded Advaita Vedānta, which maintained a 'non-dualism' in which individual selves were illusory and all was in essence part of the ultimate one, *Brahman*. Thinkers like Rāmānuja and Madhva, however, rejected this and asserted a dualism in which selves are real and *Brahman* is a separate deity, Vishnu. Although Advaita Vedānta has been the dominant philosophical school since, this theistic Vedānta has arguably had more impact on wider society.

In the Far East, movement was steadier. In the absence of growth in religious authority, there was a gradual intellectual evolution, another example of the extraordinary continuity in Chinese thought and history. Confucianism was revived and revised by the Neo-Confucians, from the Northern Song era (960–1127 CE) through to the Qing dynasty (1644–1911), absorbing influences from Daoism and Buddhism.

The development of philosophy in the middle period illustrates how philosophy is in part led by developments in wider culture. The most obvious negative aspect of this is that women's voices are almost entirely absent from the world's classical traditions. This is only now changing. As recently as 2008/9, women held fewer than one in five of the most senior academic positions in British philosophy departments. Statistics in the USA and Australia are similar.[8]

As we enter the modern era, the increasing geopolitical power of the Western world means its philosophy has had impacts far beyond its boundaries. The growth of science and the Western emphasis on autonomy that arose in the eighteenth-century Enlightenment took the nascent naturalism of early philosophy to its logical conclusion, driving the last remnants of religious and mythological thinking from the philosophical mainstream. Many developments in global philosophy are a response to Western thought, not reciprocated in the same measure. Most influential have been the philosophies that suggested concrete action, which were seen by many as offering a challenge to traditional philosophies that were increasingly used to maintain the status quo. In India, both the Practical Vedānta movement and Mahātmā Gandhi were provoked by Karl Marx and the utilitarian John Stuart Mill to balance the traditional emphasis on spirituality with concerns for social justice. In China, European Marxism and Darwinism, along with American pragmatism, influenced both the reformist monarchist K'ang and the first communist leader of China, Mao Tse-tung. At the same time there have been reactions against Western thought, in particular in the Japanese Kyoto School's renunciation of individualism.

The power of the West to set the global agenda is reflected in the fact that the word 'philosophy' and its many translations only came to be used to describe all these divergent traditions relatively recently. The Japanese, for instance, did not have a word for philosophy until the nineteenth century, when Western philosophical ideas started to be discussed after the Meiji restoration, which lifted a 250-year ban on foreigners entering the country or Japanese leaving it. The word *tetsugaku* was coined, a compound of the words for 'sagacity' and '-ology'.[9] China too only got its word for philosophy (*zhexue*, literally 'wisdom learning') around the same time.

This raises the difficult question of what to count as 'philosophy' in the first place. Start with too narrow a definition and you end up excluding much or even most thinking from other traditions and 'philosophy' becomes nothing more than your own culture's version of it. Hence Richard Rorty's claim that 'the philosophers' own scholastic little definitions of "philosophy" are merely polemical devices – intended to exclude from the field of honour those who pedigrees are unfamiliar'.[10] Too loose a definition, however, and there is nothing that isn't let in.

Rather than narrowing the scope of philosophy, I think it is better to accept that it is a loose category, what Wittgenstein called a 'family resemblance' concept. We can't set out strict rules for what does or doesn't count as philosophy, but we can see that it has a set of shared features and that an intellectual tradition should be treated as philosophy if it shares enough of them. People are doing philosophy, badly or well, whenever they set their minds to a systematic investigation of the nature of the world, selfhood, language, logic, value, the human good, the sources and justifications of knowledge, the nature and limits of human reason. When such issues are dealt with purely by myth or dogma it is religion and folklore, not philosophy. When methods have been agreed upon to answer the questions empirically, inquiry becomes scientific, not philosophical. The borders between these two poles and the philosophy that lies between are not sharp, but they are clear enough for us to identify most of its territory and to see that what we call the world's great philosophical traditions all occupy parts of it. But none owns it and none has the right to deny others their share because it has come to its own conclusions about what philosophy at its best should look like. The nature of philosophy is itself a philosophical issue and so there must be a debate about this too.

This is most evident when we consider how, in addition to the great classical traditions, there are cultures in which something recognisably philosophical has been transmitted orally, with no historical thinkers credited with its creation. I'll refer to these collectively as 'oral philosophies'. There is a lot of academic debate as to whether these bodies of thought comprise 'philosophies' or are better described as mythologies or mere 'folk beliefs'. Whatever the ultimate answer to this (I'll consider this more later), these traditions contain too much that is clearly related to philosophy for the family resemblance to be dismissed. More importantly, they are sources of ways of seeing and understanding that can challenge and enrich the great written traditions.

Despite the rise of the West and its heavy influence, and no matter how tightly connected the philosophies and cultures of the world are in our global community, there remain clearly identifiable global philosophical traditions with their own distinctive characteristics. Ideas within these traditions do not stand in isolation. They form parts of wider wholes, networks of beliefs that mutually sustain and support each other, while sometimes also being in tension. It is this overall shape that gives each system its general character.

We must be careful, however, not to slip from the undeniable truth that these distinctive characters exist to the mistake of 'essentialising': thinking that each culture has a unique and homogeneous essence that all its members uniformly share. This exaggerates both the similarities within societies and the differences between them. For instance, 'Whatever Africans share, we do not have a common traditional culture, common languages, a common religious or conceptual vocabulary,' says Kwame Anthony Appiah, who as a British-born Ghanaian-American knows a thing or two about the complexities of cultural identity. 'Many African societies have as much in common with traditional societies that are not African as they do with each other.'[11]

However, we should not be so afraid of over-sweeping claims that we avoid making any generalisations at all. Mogobe B. Ramose, for instance, would probably agree with Appiah, but he also says 'a persuasive philosophical argument can be made that there is a "family atmosphere", that is, a kind of philosophical affinity and kinship among and between the indigenous people of Africa', albeit one with variations.[12] Generalisations are perfectly legitimate and accurate, so long as they are not mistaken for universal statements. 'Men are typically taller than women' is a true generalisation; 'all men are taller than all women' is a false universal statement. To say, accurately, that there are general characteristics of different philosophical traditions is not to say that every thinker or school in that tradition shares that characteristic. Generalisations have many exceptions, just as a mountainous country may have its plains or a serious person might be capable of great laughter. I have tried to provide gentle reminders of this throughout by the use of words such as 'often' and 'usually', but it would be tedious to press home the point too much too often, so it is up to the reader to keep this important caveat in mind.[13]

One good reason not to essentialise is that there is virtually no way of thinking which is unique to one culture. Whatever your cultural background, when we come to look at notions such as autonomy, harmony and insight, you will have some grasp of what they mean and why they matter. There may be differences in nuance of meaning which can throw you off course, but these are easily enough corrected. The main differences you will note will rather be about the different weight each idea carries in different cultures, 'what aspect of our humanness a cultural tradition tends to emphasise, enhance, and preserve as central', as Kasulis puts it. 'What is foreground in one culture may be background in another.'[14]

A philosophical tradition has a lot in common with a language. We can only communicate in a specific language: there is no universal human tongue. But that does not mean we should complacently assume that there is only one language – our own – that can express the truth. Without ever giving up our mother tongues, we can expand our understanding by learning others. Just as some can be bi- or multilingual, we can make ourselves culturally bi- or multi-orientational, making use of more than one philosophical tradition.[15] Research in social psychology suggests that the multicultural mind bestows many advantages and that bicultural people score higher on creativity.[16]

Today, there are signs that we are becoming more interested in improving our cultural literacy. The emergence of China as a global superpower has led to a flurry of books attempting to explain Chinese values and culture. Western academic interest in other philosophies is growing, albeit from a low base. Commonalties are recognised, such as those between Buddhist and anglophone conceptions of the self. In East Asian universities, there is interest in both indigenous philosophies and Western ones. We appear to be seeing less antagonism, less of a sense of having to choose which is superior, and more desire to learn from wisdom wherever it is found.

I was encouraged by a comment made to me by Leah Kalmanson, inspired by the work of postcolonialist thinker Dipesh Chakrabarty. As she says, 'When we read Aristotle we let him live in two times. He lives in his time and we understand him in a cultural and historical context and there's a kind of fidelity to his thought. But then he can speak to us today. We tend not to do that with non-Western texts.' My hope is that we can read the classical philosophies of the world and let them live in both two times and two places. If we forget when and where they wrote, we are doomed to misunderstand them. But if we fail to see how what they say applies to here and now, we are doomed to waste or misuse them.

PART ONE

How the World Knows

At an international school in Maastricht in the Netherlands, a pair of bright and precocious teenagers are going through the answers to a quiz they have set their peers. They admit they can't be 100 per cent sure they've got their facts right. But they can assure us that everything is correct 'according to the Internet'.

The question of what grounds our knowledge, what justifies the confidence that our beliefs are true, is one of the most fundamental in philosophy. That for a whole generation the answer might be 'the Internet' is frightening. It's one thing to have too much faith in Wikipedia, which is after all just one site with a pretty good record of integrity. To take the Internet, a motley collection of diverse sites with vastly different pedigrees, as an authority on truth en masse looks reckless.

Throughout history people usually haven't held their beliefs for philosophical reasons. People generally take on the beliefs that surround them, and only a minority rebel wholesale. That Pavel grew up in Krakow and Priti in Delhi better explains why Pavel believes in the resurrected Christ and Priti in *karma* than any theological justification either might give.

Nonetheless, at a societal level – if not the individual level – there are always some justifications for belief which carry more weight than others; reasons why some things are accepted as true and others rejected as false. Every culture has an implicit, folk epistemology – a theory of knowledge – just as almost every philosophy has an explicit one and these formal and informal epistemologies are connected.

The international students who cite the Internet as their source of knowledge provide one piece of evidence that folk and formal epistemologies are linked. Underlying the students' gullibility that the Internet is a trusted repository of truths is a set of assumptions about the nature of knowledge that is widely taken for granted today yet was not shared by others at different times and places in history. Their trust in the Web reflects a culture that has for several centuries understood knowledge as collectively produced by human beings with different areas of expertise. In their understanding, genuine knowledge is comprised of the most up-to-date true facts that can be listed and collected. If properly recorded, anyone with time and resource can discover this knowledge for themselves. Truth is not owned by elites, it has been democratised.

Ordinary people have not always been deemed competent to find out and understand truths for themselves. Human inquiry has not always generally been seen as the sole legitimate source of knowledge – divine revelation has often been taken to be far more reliable. Nor has being 'up to date' always been seen as a virtue. In fact, many traditions still assert that the deepest truths about human nature were revealed to ancient sages, prophets and seers.

This brief sketch outlines one example of how everyday ways of thinking are rooted in the rich soil of a philosophical tradition. If we want to understand why people believe the things they do, it is essential to start by asking what sources of knowledge the philosophical traditions they grew up in take to be valid.

INSIGHT

For someone like me, used to the rituals and traditions of modern, Western academic conferences, the 90th Session of the Indian Philosophical Congress was a strange affair. Some of the differences were more quantitative than qualitative. The failure to stick to a timetable and the tendency for speakers to talk for longer than their allocated time were merely exaggerated versions of familiar scholarly foibles. But in several respects the gathering differed more significantly from Western conferences.

Extreme deference was shown to invited speakers and grandees. The opening ceremony ran on for two hours, most of which was taken up with the feting of (mostly male) dignitaries, several of whom arrived late, delaying the start by half an hour. Each was honoured in turn, cloaked with a kind of golden shawl and handed a gift from a tray carried by a parade of young women students in elegant saris. This ritual respect-paying continued throughout the congress, with almost every speaker starting by thanking 'all the eminent scholars on the dais and off the dais'. People used the words 'humbly' and 'humility' a lot, a verbal corrective to the prouder reality.

The official fawning contrasted with the lack of any evident attention from the audience, who often chatted, wandered in and out, or played with their mobile phones. The audience applause at the end of each talk was generally perfunctory and involved fewer hands than were in the room. The rule seemed to be that everyone should speak but no one need listen, as long as all were given the necessary honour and the seats were filled.

In Europe and America, I would expect the keynote addresses to present an argument which was in substantial part new and original. At the IPC, the talks were more demonstrations of the erudition of the speaker, whose main job appeared to be to represent a traditional school of philosophy. As one of the invited speakers put it, 'Here, the thinker is not important, but wisdom is important.' So a Buddhist gave what sounded more like a sermon than a lecture, delivering a message familiar even to me, who knew little about Buddhism: if we live with good heart, good speech and good action, life will be good. (I was told this paper got a rave review in the *Hindustan Times* the following day.) In a similar vein, a Jain offered a paean to Aacharya Tulasi, a great Jain monk; the Gujarat Vidyapeeth Lecture on Gandhian Philosophy and Peace praised Gandhi as a philosopher, politician and saint who showed the way for a morally better world; a couple of speakers advocated Advaita Vedānta; another Saiva Siddhānta and so on. At the conclusion of each, the chair summarised and praised some combination of the eloquence, clarity, scholarship and profundity of the speaker. No questions were taken, which seemed fitting because no debate was going on. This feature of contemporary Indian philosophy not only frustrated a minority at the congress but irks a lot of scholars working outside the subcontinent too. One India-based philosopher told me that philosophy on the subcontinent has become all about repetition with no originality. One foreign speaker complained to me that most so-called philosophy in India today is reporting, not thinking. Ironically, even he gave a lecture endowed in the name of his teacher, whom he only praised.

At the congress, there was a strong current of animosity towards Western culture and philosophy, directed at both its manifest failings and its condescending sense of superiority to Indian culture, something I fear my sceptical comments might suggest I am guilty of. Several of these remarks were shameful reminders of the West's racist and colonial history. One speaker told the audience that the supposedly great liberal John Stuart Mill had dismissed the whole of India and Asia as the dark continent which needed civilising. That it was actually his father, James Mill, who talked of the 'feeble and half civilised people' of India and 'the darkness, the vagueness, and the confusion' of the 'Hindu mythology' in his 1817 *History of British India* hardly matters, since there are plenty of other examples the speaker could have used.[1] 'Humanity is at its greatest perfection in the race of the whites,' wrote Immanuel Kant in 1802. 'The yellow Indians do have a meagre talent. The Negroes are far below them and at the lowest point are a part of the American peoples.'[2] The racism of his near contemporary David Hume only differed in the degree of its certainty: 'I am apt to suspect the Negroes, and in general all other species of men to be naturally inferior to the whites.'[3]

Much of the dismissal of contemporary Western culture, however, was made on the basis of little more than selective anecdote. One speaker noted that looting took place after floods in the United States, but that after floods in Chennai the temple was left open around the clock to help victims. Another cited the suicide of a Harvard philosophy student as evidence of the nihilism of Western thought and its 'astounding failure in attaining a holistic vision of reality'.

It is tempting to explain these features of the Indian Philosophical Congress purely sociologically. It might be said that Indian society is more traditional and hierarchical than society in the West, and this – along with its colonial history – is all we need to understand the deference, the championing of traditions and the anti-Western rhetoric. However, this fails to take the philosophical setting seriously. To explain why Indian philosophers do philosophy in the way they do without paying attention to the philosophy reduces them to anthropological curiosities. To take them seriously as philosophers, we need to ask whether there are philosophical as well as sociological reasons for the way they conduct their intellectual lives.

This is surely only what Westerners would demand of their own tradition. Certainly there are matters of custom and etiquette which explain some of the peculiar goings-on at philosophy conferences in the West, such as why there is invariably a conference dinner that manages to be formally grand and gastronomically crummy at the same time. But to explain why philosophers at conferences advance arguments and take part in extended question and answer sessions you need to know how these fit the conception of philosophy they adhere to, in which individual thinkers present justifications for original conclusions in the form of rigorous arguments. In other words, to explain how philosophy is practised you need to explain the ideals such practice aims to exemplify. What, then, are the ideals behind the way in which the philosophers in India presented their ideas?

A clue is in the traditional word for philosophy in India: *darśana*. *Darśana* comes from the root *dṛś*, meaning 'to see'. It means both philosophy and to see, or to look at.[4] It has these dual meanings because to a large extent philosophy has been conceived in India as a kind of seeing. For instance, the original poets of the *Vedas* were the first *ṛṣis* (*rishis*), meaning seers.[5] It was believed that the route to understanding involved not so much reasoning as learning practices of *ānvīkṣikī* – looking at – which enable us to attain direct realisation (*sākṣāt-kāra*) of reality as it is.[6] That helps explain why one of the giants of Indian thought, Śaṅkara (sometimes Śaṅkarācārya), who is believed to have written in the eighth century CE, used the terms *māya* (illusion) and *avidyā* (ignorance) interchangeably. Ignorance is a failure to see correctly, the flip side of the view that seeing and knowing are identical.

This emphasis on a kind of subtle perception runs through the entire history of classical Indian philosophy, which identifies *pratyakṣa* as a valid source of knowledge. Although the original meaning of *pratyakṣa* was ordinary sense perception, it came to include all immediate apprehension, sensory, spiritual or intellectual.[7] Hence the *Upaniṣads*, for instance, say that knowledge of the great/universal self (*Ātman*) 'is not to be obtained by instruction, nor by intellect, nor by much learning'. Rather, 'He is seen by subtle seers with superior, subtle intellect.'[8] The kind of seeing required is not that of normal sense perception. 'Not by sight is It grasped, not even by speech, not by any other sense-organs, austerity, or work.' Only 'by meditating, one does behold Him who is without parts'.[9]

Radhakrishnan endorses this characterisation of the classical Indian tradition. Talking primarily of the orthodox schools, he says, 'Reason is subordinated to intuition. Life cannot be comprehended in its fullness by logical reason. [. . .] The philosophy of India takes its stand on the spirit which is above mere logic, and holds that culture based on mere logic or science may be efficient, but cannot be inspiring.'[10] More pithily, he says, 'Philosophy carries us to the gates of the promised land, but cannot let us in; for that, insight or realisation is necessary.'[11]

We have to be careful not to assume this means that *all* of Indian philosophy is a kind of mystical insight gained by meditation. The various schools of Indian philosophy take great care to enumerate and describe what they take to be valid *pramāṇas* (sources of knowledge). Although every school understands the *pramāṇas* differently, there are essentially six which they either reject or endorse. It's impossible to make sense of them by their names alone, but even a cursory overview shows that there is much more to Indian philosophy than mystical insight. The six *pramāṇas* are: *pratyakṣa* (perception), *anumāna* (inference), *upamāna* (comparison and analogy), *arthāpatti* (postulation, derivation from circumstances), *anupalabdhi* (non-perception, negative/cognitive proof) and *śabda* (word, testimony of reliable experts). Of these, *anumāna* is almost as ubiquitous as *pratyakṣa*, making it clear that for many schools at least forms of reasoning are as much a part of the Indian philosophical tradition as any insight.

Charles Moore warns that intuition, along with authority and scepticism about reason, tend to be overstated by both Western and indigenous commentators on Indian philosophy. The way to correct this overemphasis is to appreciate that intuition is not believed to trump all else but is simply an essential component of a system of understanding that involves all human capacities. As S. K. Saksena put it, the source of knowledge is 'neither sense, nor reason, nor intuition, but the whole of man'.[12] The point of difference is that in many schools *pratyakṣa* plays a much more important role than in other global traditions.

Pratyakṣa is intimately connected to another *pramāṇa*, *śabda*. The *Nyāya Sūtra* defines *śabda* as 'the instructive assertion of a reliable person'.[13] The two usually work as a kind of team in that we are to believe the testimony of *ṛṣis* because they had exceptional capacities to perceive reality for what it is. As Deepak Sarma puts it, sacred texts are taken as valid sources of knowledge because 'they are rooted in the *pratyakṣa* of *ṛṣis*'.[14]

Sometimes, these capacities are supernaturally extraordinary. Several biographies of Śaṅkara, founder of Advaita Vedānta, tell a story which begins with him arguing with a philosopher couple in favour of the renunciation of worldly life and hence of their marriage. When the wife points out that Śaṅkara is rejecting a life he has not himself experienced, he uses his yogic powers to enter the body of the recently deceased King Amaruka, brings him back to life and then proceeds to master the arts of lovemaking. When he is done, he returns to his own body able to confirm from first-hand experience that he had been right all along.[15]

In the hierarchy of sources of knowledge, the testimony (*śabda*) of the greatest seers (*ṛṣis*) usually trumps the perception (*pratyakṣa*) of even great minds, which in turn trumps the most impressive rational argument. Śaṅkara dismisses 'reasoning which disregards the holy texts' as resting 'on individual opinion only' with 'no proper foundation'. We cannot trust the reasoning even of 'men of the most undoubted mental eminence, such as Kapila, Kanâda, and other founders of philosophical schools' since they contradict one another.[16]

Anyone judged to have achieved a high degree of insight is treated with great deference and respect. The roots of the word *upaniṣad* reflect this: *upa* (near), *ni* (down) and *sad* (to sit). Groups of pupils would sit near their teachers to receive truth from them.[17] *The Laws of Manu* has a passage which stresses just how wicked it is to defy your teacher: 'By censuring his teacher, though justly, he will become in his next birth an ass; by falsely defaming him, a dog; he who lives on his teacher's substance, will become a worm, and he who is envious of his merit, a larger insect.'[18] Note the 'though justly': it is wrong to censor your teacher even if your teacher is wrong. This is deference in the extreme.

As my experience at the Indian Philosophical Congress suggested, deference to seers remains important in India today. One of the first groups I met were devotees of Dr Ramchandra Pralhad Parnerkar (1916–80), who, they told me with great enthusiasm, combined Vedic and Western philosophy, objective and subjective, mind and matter. They were so eager to spread his philosophy of *Poornawād* that they gifted me his book of the same name. At the front there is a series of colour plates with portraits not only of the author, but of 'our inspiration', his son and intellectual heir Adv. V. R. Parnerkar and his father, Vedmurti Pralhad Guru Ganesh Guru Parnerkar, to whom the book is dedicated. These portraits are an almost ritual honouring of great men in book form.

The deferential attitude towards the speakers made interviewing them difficult. They generally seemed to take my questions as invitations to preach their schools of thought. Our exchanges were not so much questions and answers as cues for monologues. Nor is this deference to authorities confined to academic conferences. Meera Baindur told me that the idea of insight as direct experience of ultimate reality remains mainstream in Indian culture, reflected in the saying 'One has to eat the sugar to know the taste.' India has many gurus presumed to have had direct experience of *Brahman*. They are taken as authorities to be trusted, so much so that their behaviour is often overlooked. 'There's a lot of blind belief,' says Baindur. In 2012, 'one of these fellows got caught having sex in a room with an actress. Someone put in a camera and they released it to the press.' His justification was that he was simply fulfilling a need, like a god, and his reputation didn't seem to suffer. It is as though once gurus achieve the status of *swamis*, recognised religious Hindu teachers, they are beyond reproach. As the *Vaiśeṣika Sūtra* says, 'Cognition of advanced sages, as also vision of the perfected ones, results from *dharma* [right conduct] or merits.'[19] The logic seems to be that to be a *swami* requires having insight; only the good have insight; therefore a *swami* is good, whatever their behaviour suggests to the contrary.

Baindur speaks with some authority on this since for several years she too was a *swami*, though not one who did 'anything of that sort', she stresses. Many people assumed that she had almost mystical powers. Once someone came to her and said, '*Swami*, explain to me this. You came to me in a dream and gave me a *gangajal* [holy water from the Ganges] and then I put a garland on the statue of Ganesh, who then turned into Krishna. How did you make that happen?' She told them she didn't make anything happen, it was just a dream. 'That's why I didn't succeed as a popular guru and had to come back to academics.'

Her devotee was not unusual in her belief in the reality of dreams. In the Nyāya school it is maintained that dream objects are real, for they too are perceived, and *pratyakṣa* is a valid *pramāṇa*.[20] Only the rigorously materialistic and empirical Cārvāka (or Lokayata) school, which is often the outlier in Indian philosophy, restricts *pratyakṣa* to sensory perception alone as the only valid source of knowledge.[21] Cārvāka hence has no time for the *ṛṣis* at all, claiming, 'The three authors of the Vedas were buffoons, knaves, and demons.'[22]

In the other schools, *pratyakṣa* is vitally important. Take Vedānta, one of the most important schools of Indian philosophy. One of the founding texts of its major subschool, Advaita Vedānta, is Śaṅkara's commentary on the *Vedānta Sūtras*. Śaṅkara wrote that although 'reasoning also is to be allowed its place', this 'must not deceitfully be taken as enjoining bare independent ratiocination, but must be understood to represent reasoning as a subordinate auxiliary of intuitional knowledge'.[23]

But how is *pratyakṣa* achieved? Sometimes, it comes as a kind of gift, from nowhere. The *Yoga Sūtras* say, 'The experience of extraordinary capacities may occur naturally (that is, as a result of inborn capacities at the time of rebirth).' If you're not lucky enough to be so gifted, taking herbal medications (*oṣadhi*, including elixirs and hallucinogens) or performing incantations (*mantra*) could achieve the same effect. More usually, however, *pratyakṣa* is the result of spiritual exercises such as ascetic practices (*tapas*) or *samādhi*, a form of concentration meditation in which practitioners enter a trance-like state.[24]

Other schools generally emphasise the need for a long spiritual practice. 'Cognition of advanced sages, as also vision of the perfected ones, (results) from *dharma* or merits,' says the *Vaiśeṣika Sūtra*.[25] Chief among these practices is meditation, which allows for a kind of understanding that goes beyond ordinary cognition. 'Meditation (*dhyāna*), assuredly, is more than thought,' as it says in the *Upaniṣads*.[26] There is too much variation between the schools for a simple account of what meditation entails, but many have in common an emphasis on practices of the body. Instructions for meditation always involve details of posture and breathing. This, suggests Sue Hamilton, is perhaps the most alien feature of Indian philosophy for Westerners in particular.[27] We see it most clearly in the classic *Yoga Sūtras*, written in the third century CE, but the general principle is accepted beyond the numerous yoga schools.

Outside India, these days yoga is often seen as little more than an exercise and relaxation technique. Its basic definition in the *Yoga Sūtras* sounds very calming, being 'the cessation of the functioning of ordinary awareness'.[28] However, the purpose of this mind-calming goes beyond mere relaxation. The basic principle behind it is that in daily life we are led astray by our senses and the mind is kept busy with ordinary, everyday things. By stopping this activity, we not only regain calm and control but can see things as they really are.[29] It is as though the world usually appears to us like a blur through the window of an express train and with practice we can slow time down and see what's really there. This is a view common to orthodox and non-orthodox schools. Hence, one Buddhist academic told me, 'A state of mind has extraordinary energies inside. If you clean your thought process, this causes a flowering of intuition in our minds, it is a source of knowing anything.'

All the classic texts give some guidance on the physical practices we need to follow to achieve this stillness and insight. In the *Upaniṣads*, the insight we are seeking is our unity with *Brahman*, the supreme self. To achieve this it advocates the 'sixfold yoga', which comprises 'restraint of the breath, withdrawal of the senses, meditation, concentration, contemplation, absorption'.[30] The *Bhagavad Gītā* also gives precise descriptions of the physical requirements of yoga:

> He should set in a clean place his firm seat, neither too high nor too low, covered with sacred grass, a deerskin, and a cloth, one over the other.

There taking his place on the seat, making his mind one-
pointed, and controlling his thought and sense, let him
practice *yoga* for the purification of the self.
Holding the body, head, and neck erect and still, looking
fixedly at the tip of his nose, without looking around. [...]
Verily, *yoga* is not for him who eats too much or abstains too
much from eating. It is not for him, O Arjuna, who sleeps too
much or keeps too much awaked.[31]

There is widespread belief in India that such practices lead not
only to insight but to almost supernatural powers. In the *Yoga
Sūtras*, there is a long list of what can be achieved with meditation, not just 'knowledge of what is subtle, concealed, or distant'.
With proper attention, you might achieve 'knowledge of various
universes' and 'the orderly arrangement of the stars', as well as
gain 'the strength of an elephant'. Almost miraculously, 'When the
base of the throat becomes the focus for comprehensive reflection,
cessation of hunger and thirst becomes possible.' And 'when the
relation between hearing and space becomes the focus for comprehensive reflection, celestial hearing (the "divine hearing") becomes
possible'.[32] Such beliefs persist today, especially in rural India,
where holy men and women are routinely ascribed magical powers.

Special powers aside, the idea of insight, both direct and via *ṛṣis*,
is clearly a potent and live one. What, then, is the role of reason
in all of this? The answer is partly historical. Although there was
little by way of systematic philosophy in the earliest Vedic and Epic
periods, certain key doctrines were fixed at these times and much
of the philosophical work of the Sūtra and scholastic periods was
to make rational sense of them.

A comparison could be made here between later Indian philosophy and the natural theology of medieval Europe. There too
faith and reason were seen as being in harmony, with reason's
role not to provide the foundations of faith, merely to explain

it. Philosophy was largely apologetics: the rational justification of revealed truths. Even as late as the seventeenth century, philosophers who by the use of reason reached conclusions that contradicted the Church's doctrines would be suppressed, even if they supported the existence of the Christian God. Such was the fate of Descartes, whose works were put on the Roman Catholic Church's list of banned books, the *Index Librorum Prohibitorum* in 1663, until its discontinuation in 1966.

The spirit of apologetics has for a long time been strong in India. One of the eminent endowment lecturers at the Indian Philosophical Congress, C. D. Sebastian, said that 'the main purpose of advaitic philosophy is to guard its revealed truth against all possible doubts and criticisms as well as to demonstrate its possibility to our reason. [...] By no amount of logical thinking about the facts of experience, you can ever come to the conclusion which denies all facts. The nature of ultimate reality is revealed by scriptures and accepted on faith.'[33] There is no neat separation between philosophy and religion in India. (As we shall see, this is also true in most other traditions.) In his presidential address to the IPC, L. N. Sharma said, '*Darśana* is the meeting ground of philosophy and religion, as it includes both of them. Those who hold that *darśana* is not philosophy only show their ignorance about the true nature of *darśana*.'[34] Religious themes were often addressed by speakers at the congress, one of whom was surely preaching to the converted when she titled her paper 'Indian Philosophy: The Ideal Combination of Philosophy and Religion'.

Another endowment lecturer, Chandrakala Padia, agreed that religion and philosophy are mixed in India and this is what makes Indian thought distinctive. This mixing reflects a wider permeation of religion in society. 'We can't just snatch religious feelings from persons,' says Padia. 'It is a deep-rooted, unconscious activity.' India may have a secular constitution but it does not keep religion and state separate, as in France or America. Rather, it is (or is supposed to be) even-handed on religious matters. In areas of personal law, covering issues such as marriage, each religion can operate under its own laws, so that Muslims, for instance, can live under sharia.

Advocates of the link between philosophy and religion tend to claim that there is no contradiction or conflict between the two, that they are in perfect harmony. 'The worlds of reason and religion do not turn in different orbits,' says Sarvepalli Radhakrishnan. 'Indian thought is firm in its conviction that religious propositions should be grounded in reason.'[35]

A vocal minority – more numerous off the subcontinent – challenges this interconnection of philosophy and religion. At the congress, P. George Victor said openly in his talk, 'We are preaching theology, teaching as philosophy.' He insists we must extract philosophy from theology to defend Indian philosophy against the attack that it is not philosophy at all. Another invited speaker confided privately that the IPC was the anti-philosophy conference, saying it represented a way of thinking about Indian philosophy which sought to differentiate itself from Western philosophy as much as possible by emphasising its deep links with religion, in contrast to the materialistic, unspiritual West.

The argument about how important religion is to Indian philosophy is very difficult for outsiders to present fairly. On the one hand, to emphasise its religious nature risks playing into tired stereotypes about Indian spirituality. However, to deny the links risks both contradicting what most Indian philosophers themselves say and forcing Indian philosophy into a foreign mould. One can stand accused of a colonial mindset by either setting Indian thought outside philosophy as the West knows it or making it fit philosophy as the West knows it. It's clear that the links between religion and philosophy are historically strong in both India and the West. Whereas they have weakened in the West, they remain firm on the subcontinent. But there remains much of interest in

Indian philosophy to secular thinkers, just as there is in the work of overtly Christian philosophers such as Aquinas and Descartes.

The paradox of Indian philosophy is that although it is rooted in the authority of ancient, sacred texts, for centuries commentators have interpreted them with such originality and creativity that philosophy has indeed progressed enormously. Moore calls these thinkers 'commentators only in what might be called the polite sense of the word'.[36] They 'claim for their views the sanction of the *Vedas* and exercise their ingenuity in forcing that sanction even when it is not spontaneously yielded', he and Radhakrishnan say. 'Besides, the very vastness of the *Vedas*, from which authors could select out of free conviction any portion for their authority, allowed room for original thought.'[37]

One of the endowment lecturers at the IPC, R. C. Sinha, thinks that this misunderstanding of originality lies behind a lot of the prejudice against Indian philosophy. 'Originality lies in interpretation,' he said. He recalled an international congress of Buddhist studies at the School of Oriental and African Studies at the University of London in which one professor declared Indian philosophy dead because, after Śaṅkara, it was merely repetition. 'I explained to him that originality in contemporary Indian thought is very remarkable,' said Sinha. 'Originality does not mean just constructing a system on original things, it means interpretations of the classical thought, of Indian thought. This is also original.' Contemporary Indian philosophers are well versed in both Western and Indian thought, contributing to this interpretive creativity. For instance, K. C. Bhattacharya created a new philosophy reconciling Kantian and Vedantic philosophy.

Śaṅkara himself provides a good example of originality rooted in the attempt at faithful interpretation. Although he is considered to be a great, creative thinker, he himself said that he was merely expounding what is contained in the *Vedas*,[38] offering as a conclusive argument for his position 'because it is directly stated in scripture'.[39] At the same time, he swept aside the conflicting accounts of the creation of the world in the *Vedas* 'since the creation of the world and similar topics are not at all what scripture wishes to teach'.[40] The *Vedas* provide such a rich list of philosophical ingredients that philosophers can cook up virtually anything from them.

India's emphasis on *pratyakṣa* is distinctive, but it is by no means the only philosophical tradition to allow a role for a kind of acute perception as well as reason. Indeed, the idea is not entirely alien even to Western philosophy. Aristotle, one of its founding fathers, wrote in the fourth century BCE that we should 'pay no less attention to the unproved assertions and opinions of experienced and older people than to demonstrations of fact; because they have an insight from their experience which enables them to see correctly'.[41] 'Practical wisdom' here is the standard translation for *phronēsis*, which is a kind of skilfulness in judgement which comes from long experience. (The concept of *zhi*, usually translated as 'wisdom', is used very similarly by the classical Chinese philosopher Mencius.[42]) Aristotle did not invent the word and it is likely that *phronēsis* was widely valued in ancient Greece. Western philosophy subsequently developed to emphasise forms of reasoning that are objective and capable of being broken down into discrete steps, leading to the sidelining of practical wisdom. Ironically, the whole edifice of logical philosophy was constructed on Aristotelian foundations, blocking the view of *phronēsis*.

Although the insight of the wise has no official status as a *pramāṇa* of Western philosophy, I think it has always had a large, and largely unacknowledged, role. It strikes me that many of the key moves in Western philosophy have not been arguments but acute observations. For example, when Descartes concluded in the seventeenth century that the one thing he could not doubt was his own existence, he did not offer an argument but an observation: 'I am, I exist.'[43] You cannot doubt your own existence without at the same time affirming it, by the mere fact that *you* doubt.

The major difference between this kind of insight and *pratyakṣa*, however, is that the latter demands a kind of trust. When Western philosophers use their insight, they invite you to attend in the same way and observe yourself. As one of the senior scholars at the Indian Philosophical Congress explained to me, in Indian philosophy too 'any individual can develop his own faculties and can acquire the power to see something, particularly the things that are beyond, to have a direct perception of those realities'. But before you can do that you need to trust the *ṛṣis* that you are on the right path. If you do not see what the superior mind sees, the response is that you are insufficiently developed in your wisdom and must practise harder, perhaps for years.

In that sense, Indian insight is unashamedly elitist, Western insight determinedly egalitarian. But it is not obvious which is more plausible. The idea that some talented and experienced people have better insight than others is no more shocking than the idea that some people are better than others at playing music, designing bridges or conducting scientific research, because they have a hard-earned combination of explicit learning and implicit skill. The idea that no one has better insight than others is arguably less credible than the idea that some do.

In other non-Western traditions, insight is valued more overtly. Robert E. Carter contrasts the Western tendency to make philosophy a 'purely cerebral affair' with the Japanese assumption that 'knowledge is also an experiential affair which can be achieved and honed through *practice* rather than reason alone'.[44] This is evident in the historical importance placed on martial arts, flower arranging, archery, calligraphy and the tea ceremony, all of which help us to achieve a kind of enlightenment by attending rather than ratiocinating.[45] Even in the highly technological Japan of today, this sensibility thrives. The Hakutsuru Sake Brewery Museum in

Kobe shows the visitor the traditional way in which the rice wine was made. One of numerous important stages in the process is steaming the rice, which should make the grains *gaiko nainan*: hard outside and soft inside. The narrator of the video explaining this is keen to point out that although the modern brewery is a high-tech operation, 'even today the condition of the steamed rice is checked in the same way. Sake production involves more than just science and theory. Human intuition and experience play a crucial role.'

The importance of human insight has been stressed by many Japanese philosophers. The early twentieth-century Kyoto School philosopher Nishida Kitarō wrote about *kenshō*, seeing into nature (*ken* being seeing or having a view and *shō* being the nature, essence, the 'suchness' of a thing). He argued that through pure experience one could have direct knowledge of reality as it is: 'To experience means to know facts just as they are, to know in accordance with facts by completely relinquishing one's own fabrications.' This is experience that is not 'adulterated with some sort of thought'.[46] 'This seeing is not a knowledge of the mind, analytically arrived at, but a direct, immediate view of it, as when the eye perceives an object before it.'

The parallels with *pratyakṣa* are obvious. One difference is that in Japanese philosophy perception is primarily aesthetic and this-worldly rather than spiritual and other-worldly. Nishida wrote, 'It is the artist, not the scholar, who arrives at the true nature of reality.'[47] The prestige of Zen poetry reflects this. Take this haiku by Bashō:

> The old pond
> A frog jumps in –
> The sound of the water.

For Nishida, the haiku evokes the sound of splashing without actually attempting to mimic it. The poem works because it conveys to the reader the pure experience of the frog entering the pond, perhaps even better than watching it without sufficient sensitivity.[48] Takeuchi Yoshinori interprets the poem differently, saying that what is evoked is not the sound of the water but the stillness that the splash disrupts. A similar effect is sought in an old Chinese poem which says 'A bird gives a cry – the mountains quiet all the more.'[49] (This is also perhaps the real meaning behind Hakuin Ekaku's famous eighteenth-century-BCE koan 'What is the Sound of the Single Hand?': it is an invitation to attend to the silence, the emptiness.[50]) These interpretations differ, but they share something more important in common: a belief that the purpose of the poem is to facilitate *kenshō*, a seeing into nature as it really is, by aesthetic rather than rational means. As D. T. Suzuki put it, 'We must accept the fact that the intellect has its limitations, and that things or facts belonging to our innermost experiences are altogether beyond its domain.'[51] Koans are 'to be meditated upon in order to break the hold of rationality on the self,' says Edward Slingerland, to 'fast away the mind'.[52]

One important way in which this kind of insight differs from intellectual understanding is that it breaks down the barrier between the known and the knower. 'To understand reality one must grasp it in one's own hands, or, better, one must *be* it,' says Suzuki.[53] Nishida's explanation of this is that 'the seeing in the experience of *kenshō* is not dualistic or dichotomous, because there is no separation here between the object of sight and the seeing subject, because the seer is the seen and the seen is the seer, the two are completely identical'.[54] Nishida believes this aspiration to dissolve the dualities of subject and object is typically Japanese. What Japanese people 'strongly yearn for', says Carter, is 'to become one with things and events',[55] collapsing the distinction between knowing and doing, thought and action. Nishida explored this idea in his late work through the concept of 'action intuition', the sense that we get to the heart of reality better by acting rather than by reflecting. True, complete awareness is not merely intellectual but actively experiential.[56]

The contemporary Japanese philosopher Kobayashi Yasuo described this experiential dimension as the 'aesthetic' character of Japanese thought, which contrasts with the Chinese ethical focus on right conduct, politeness, ceremony and so on. The 'charm of Japanese philosophical thought' is that it is about being touched by what is near. 'The most important thing happens not over there but in this present,' he told me. 'The important thing is to feel, not to conceptualise. Concepts always indicate something over there, it's very abstract.'

Time is a good example of this. 'Time is always present to us, not as a concept, but this feeling: cherry blossoms disappearing, something like that. We find out the truth of time in this sense. But we can't conceptualise this aesthetics.'

Achieving this kind of pure experience means accepting the limits of reason as well as language. Kyoto School philosopher Tanabe Hajime's take on this is metanoetics, which is giving up on the possibility of knowing through one's own efforts, one's own reason. Describing his own realisation of the importance of this, he wrote, 'In the thick of my distress, I let go and surrendered myself humbly to my own inability. I was suddenly brought to new insight! My penitent confession – metanoesis – unexpectedly threw me back on my own interiority and away from things external.'[57] It is noteworthy that he wrote about this autobiographically. Such a first-person approach is as natural in a philosophical culture that emphasises first-person experience as it is alien in a Western tradition that emphasises third-person objectivity.

Tanabe explicitly compares his experience to the one that led Shinran in the thirteenth century to establish Jōdo Shinshū, or Shin Buddhism, the most popular form of Buddhism in Japan. Shin is a school of Pure Land Buddhism, which teaches that enlightenment can be reached simply by the practice of *nembutsu*, reciting the phrase '*Namu Amida Butsu*' ('I take refuge in Amitābha Buddha'). (Amitābha, or Amida, is the principal Buddha of Jōdo Shinshū, not Gautama, the founder of all Buddhism.) The practice requires a worshipper to let go of the illusion that enlightenment can be achieved by oneself. Instead, one must give oneself over to 'other-power'.[58]

These Japanese takes on insight have roots which run through East Asia, back to the origins of Buddhism in India. The predecessors of Zen in Japan were the Chán Buddhists of China, who belong to the Mahāyāna tradition. From the Mahāyāna perspective, says Tom Kasulis, 'wisdom (*prajñā*) surpasses discriminating understanding (*vikalpa*)' and 'expressing an engagement with reality is of greater value than analysing it with detachment'.[59]

It is perhaps no coincidence that insight as a source of knowledge is stressed most in the traditions the West finds least philosophical. Western philosophy's self-image has largely been constructed by distancing itself from ideas of the philosopher as a sage or guru who penetrates the deep mysteries of the universe like some kind of seer. This distancing has blinded it to the obvious truth that all good philosophy requires some kind of insight. There are innumerable very clever, very scholarly philosophers who can pick apart an argument better than anyone but who don't have anything worthwhile to contribute to their discipline. What they lack is not an ability to be even more systematic in their analysis, but an ability to spot what is at stake, what matters. Insight without analysis and critique is just intuition taken on faith. But analysis without insight is empty intellectual game-playing. The world's philosophies offer not just insights but ideas about how to achieve them, and we would profit by sympathetically but critically engaging with both.

THE INEFFABLE

At Ikuta Shrine in the centre of Kobe, Japan, fashionably dressed young people are among the stream of visitors performing the simple Shintō rituals that have been a familiar sight here since its founding in the third century CE. Not all of them remember to bow as they pass through the *torii* gate marking the boundary between the holy space within and the secular world without. But all stop at the *temizuya* water pavilion to perform the *misogi*, a purification of body and soul. Scooping up a single ladle of water with their right hands, they first pour some over their left hand before transferring the ladle to their left hand and pouring over the right. Without touching the ladle with their mouths, they then take some of the water to rinse out their mouths before tipping any remaining water away. Thus cleansed, they are ready to greet Wakahirume, the female *kami* (spirit) housed at the shrine.

At the altar, they first make an offering of coins to the *kami*, then ring the bell to greet her. They bow twice and clap their hands twice to express joy at meeting the *kami* and respect for her, then bow once to pray. After the second clap, the hands remain together for a moment as the devotees silently express their feelings of gratitude before a final bow.

I found myself wondering how many of these worshippers actually believe in the *kami* they ostensibly come to honour. But perhaps that is the wrong question. As someone brought up in a Christian culture, I take religious belief to be primarily a matter of assenting to a list of doctrines. At the Roman Catholic Church I sometimes went to as a child, we would ritually repeat the Nicene Creed, beginning with 'We believe in one God, the Father, the Almighty, Maker of all that is, seen and unseen . . .' and concluding, 'We look for the resurrection of the dead, and the life of the world to come. Amen.' At Shintō shrines, however, the entire ritual is wordless, even the inner expression of gratitude, which is supposed to be more of a feeling than a thought. Since visitors to the shrine are not required to assert belief in anything, perhaps asking what they really believe is to miss the point.

The relative unimportance of asserting doctrine helps to explain the syncretic nature of religion in Japan, where a common expression is 'Born Shintō, live Confucian, die Buddhist'. When I visited the Buddhist temple of Kiyomizu-dera in Kyoto, for example, the Shintō shrine Jishu Jinja was so seamlessly adjoined to the site that it took me a while to realise they weren't part of the same complex. Japanese visitors performed rituals at both.

Doctrines are less important than they are in Western Christianity in part because it is believed that the purest knowledge of reality comes from direct experience and so the most fundamental truths cannot be captured in language. They are ineffable, literally unsayable. This is a common idea in East Asia, most evident in Chinese Daoism (or Taoism). Daoism has deep roots in Chinese culture and can be traced back to at least the fourth century BCE, when the earliest of the great Daoist teachers, Laozi, is said to have lived and written the *Daodejing* (or *Tao Te Ching*), one of Daoism's foundational texts. Whether Laozi was actually a historical figure or not is far from clear and matters little to most Daoists. Daoism's other key text is the *Zhuangzi*, named after its author and probably written a few centuries later. Every philosophical school has its *dao*, which simply means 'the way'. Where the *Dao* of Daoism most differs from that of Confucianism is that it emphasises naturalness and a kind of spontaneity rather than rules and rituals.

In China, Daoist thinkers often point to the inability of language to capture the true meaning of the *Dao*, which defies understanding and is always somewhat mysterious. 'The clearest Way seems obscure;/The Way ahead seems to lead backward,' says the *Daodejing*, in its typically paradoxical way.[1] It states, 'To know that one does not know is best; not to know but to believe that one knows is a disease.'[2] Because of its ineffability, the *Dao* is better understood by doing than by thinking.

> Look for it and it cannot be seen;
> Listen for it and it cannot be heard;
> But use it and it will never run dry![3]

The third-century-BCE classic *Lüshi Chunqui* says of the *Dao*, 'Forced to give it a name, I would call it "Great One".'[4] There is a very similar line in the *Daodejing* which reads, 'Forced to give it a proper name, I would call it "great".'[5] Both texts talk of being 'forced' to use language, the implication being that it would be better not to resort to words at all. 'Those who know do not talk about it;/Those who talk about it do not know.'[6]

If some of Daoism's paradoxical statements sound a little like jokes, that is no coincidence. Daoism celebrates humour and is often funny, which Joel Kupperman says is for a good reason: 'Because one never has a final truth, or a final "take" on anything, or a final adjustment to the world – Zhuangzi's philosophical training appears designed to encourage the ability to laugh at oneself. The philosophy is not intended to lead to a comfortable "complacency".[7]

There's a wonderful passage in the *Zhuangzi* which explains the limits of language in a typically wry way:

> A trap is for fish: when you've got the fish, you can forget the trap. A snare is for rabbits: when you've got the rabbit, you can forget the snare. Words are for meaning: when you've got the meaning, you can forget the words. Where can I find someone who's forgotten words so I can have a word with him?[8]

The mistrust of language in Daoism leads to a suspicion even of classical philosophical texts, which are dismissed in the *Zhuangzi* as 'leftovers'. In one passage a wheelwright named Slab explains this to his master by example of his skill:

> 'When I chisel a wheel, if I hit it too softly, it slips and won't bite. If I hit it too hard, it jams and won't move. Neither too soft nor too hard – I get it in my hand and respond with my hand. But my mouth cannot put it into words. There is an art to it. But your servant can't show it to his own son, and he can't get it from me. I've done it this way seventy years and am growing old chiseling wheels.'[9]

Slab has a skill that can be transmitted neither by words nor by mere showing. Rather, each new generation has to learn the craft anew, under careful tutelage. In the same way, Daoism asserts that philosophical wisdom can't be simply passed on in texts. The great sages develop their wisdom over a lifetime and it dies with them. 'The ancients died with what they could not pass down,' says Slab. 'So what M'Lord is reading can only be their leftovers.' His story also underlines the importance of practice over theory: Slab follows the way with his craft better than his scholarly master does with his learning.

Daoism puts greater emphasis on ineffability than China's other main indigenous tradition, although the limits of language are also often noted in Confucianism. For example, Confucius says 'Does heaven speak? The four seasons pursue their courses, and all things are continually being produced, but does heaven say anything?'[10] However, Confucius only advises silence on questions of ultimate reality, which he does not think we need to worry about in order to live well. For the things that matter, he emphasises the need to get words right. In one famous passage he says that if he were to administer a state his priority would be to rectify names, to return them to their true meaning and use. A ruler ought to be a ruler, a son, a son, and so on. People would do what they are supposed to do. Although he mentions this idea once only, 'the rectification of names' became an important idea in Confucian philosophy.[11]

In Japan, ineffability is in part why the indigenous Shintō religion has relatively little tradition of producing systematic philosophy. The eighteenth-century Shintō poet Kamo No Mabuchi wrote, 'To try to define things unequivocally in terms of principle is to treat them as dead objects.'[12] This is why we need poetry: to give us some sense of what we cannot precisely capture in language. Hence the Shintō scholar Fujitani Mitsue wrote, 'When I cannot take just what I am thinking and use either direct language or metaphor but I also cannot refrain from speaking, then of necessity I compose a poem.'[13]

The limits of language are most overtly and fully embraced in Zen Buddhism. Zen originated in Japan in the twelfth century as an indigenous version of the Chán school, which originated in seventh-century China. The founding myth of Zen is that the Buddha silently held up a flower, twirled it and winked.[14] It is the only major religious or philosophical tradition that didn't begin with an utterance of some kind. Buddhism in general is also notable for the number of passages which advise people to ignore the teachings of the Buddha, most starkly in the saying 'If you meet the

Buddha on the road, kill him.' As Shidō Bunan put it less violently, 'The teachings of the Buddha are greatly in error. How much more in error it is to learn them.' They are in error because no words can ever capture the truth, even the words of the Buddha. The best way to avoid error is therefore not to use words. 'If I would make any proposition whatever, then by that I would have a logical error,' wrote the second–third-century Buddhist philosopher Nāgārjuna. 'But I do not make a proposition; therefore I am not in error.'[15]

Words are like 'a finger pointing at the moon'. 'Guided by the finger, the other person should see the moon. If he looks at the finger instead and mistakes it for the moon, he loses not only the moon but the finger also. Why, because he mistakes the pointing finger for the bright moon.'[16] At their best words merely help us to get beyond words, to a place where they no longer stand between us and the world, but where we follow Bunan's injunction to 'See directly. Hear directly.'[17]

In Zen, language and rationality are both intellectual strait-jackets. 'Language is a product of intellection and intellection is what our intellect adds to, or rather, subtracts from, reality,' wrote Suzuki.[18] Language adds to reality in that it creates an extra layer on top of it, and this in turn subtracts from reality by obscuring its fullness. 'Meanings and judgments are an abstracted part of the original experience, and compared with the actual experiences they are meagre in content,' said Nishida.[19] One of the purposes of some paradoxical koans – such as 'What is the colour of wind?' or 'When you can do nothing, what can you do?' – is to draw our attention to the inadequacy of words and how apparently perfectly well-formed sentences can nonetheless be meaningless. 'Those who find Zen foolish are still under the spell of linguistic magic,' said Suzuki.[20]

Despite this disavowal of language, Zen teachers have left a lot of written words. Many see this paradox as an imperfect compromise. Musō Soseki says, 'If nothing was ever to be written down then the ways of guiding people would be lost. Thus the Zen school has resigned itself to publishing the records of the ancients, though this is not what they would have wanted.'[21] A similar rationale was perhaps behind Plato's decision to write his Socratic dialogues, even though Socrates himself refused to put ink to parchment, believing that ossified texts can never take the place of the practice of philosophising. When Zen masters did write, though, they chose their words carefully and sparingly. For Kazashi Nobuo, this shows as much respect for words as it does suspicion of them. He told me of the saying, which originated in China, 'The most important things can only be conveyed from heart to heart.' When a great Zen philosopher like Dōgen set things down on paper, he tried to use words to make this heart-to-heart connection.

You could say that it is because Japanese have such respect for words that their poets and thinkers use them so sparingly. It is not so much a mistrust of language as a reverence for it. Maeda Naoki, a junior priest from the Shingon sect of esoteric Buddhism, recently said, 'Speech is the silver medal. You get a gold medal for not speaking.'[22] But the very meaning of 'Shingon' is 'True Word', so it would make no sense for silence in Shingon to imply a disregard for language.

The deep respect for words in Japan is reflected in the Shintō belief in *kotodama*, a compound of 'word' and 'soul': the soul of a word. From this belief flow superstitions around words that sound like other, ominous ones. Four (四), for example, can be read as '*yon*' (よん) or '*shi*' (し), which sounds like the word for death, *shi* (死); hence the number four is considered unlucky. Something of the spirit of *kotodama* is found all over East Asia, where the sounds of words are imbued with powers and homophones are considered lucky or unlucky. In both Chinese and Korean, the number four also sounds like some words for death and is often avoided, with Korean hotels often missing room fours. In Chinese, the number three, *sān* (三), is propitious because it sounds like the word for birth, *shēng* (生).

Buddhism, of course, originated in India, and ineffability can also be found in the brahmanic tradition against which Buddhism reacted. In the *Upaniṣads*, *Brahman* is said to be inscrutable:

> It is conceived of by him whom It is not conceived of.
> He by whom It is conceived of, knows It not.
> It is not understood by those who [say they] understand it.
> It is understood by those who [say they] understand It not.[23]

Ultimate truth is beyond not just language but any rational understanding. 'Do not question too much, lest your head fall off,' warn the *Upaniṣads*. 'In truth, you are questioning too much about a divinity about which further questions cannot be asked.'[24] The supreme self is 'Incomprehensible [. . .] not to be reasoned about, unthinkable'.[25]

The ineffability of *Brahman* is perhaps most clearly expressed in a phrase found in both the *Upaniṣads* and the *Avadhuta Gītā* which describes *Brahman* as 'not this, not that' (*neti neti*). Another *Upaniṣad* passage says that *Brahman* is that 'wherefrom words turn back'.[26] Chakravarthi Ram-Prasad says that this is particularly emphasised by the Advaitains, who 'maintain that language cannot touch brahman; it is *ineffable*'.[27]

The deep appreciation of the limits of language and a refusal to confuse the world as it is with our conceptual categorisations are enduring strengths of philosophy all across Asia. In my experience, the West tends to see all limits to knowledge as an affront, a border to be crossed. The unknown presents the challenge 'to boldly go where no man has gone before'. Elsewhere, human limits are not just accepted but celebrated. At the Indian Philosophical Congress, Duvan Chandel quoted from the greatest poet of modern India, Rabindranath Tagore: 'Truth loves its limits, for there it meets the beautiful.'[28] It's a sentiment that has resonated in India for centuries.

The million-dollar question raised by an embrace of the ineffable is whether, having seen that the world is not the same as our linguistic conception of it, we can then see it how it really is. Many eastern traditions say we can. I remain unconvinced. Even if we can perceive reality unframed by concepts, it will still be framed by our perceptual and cognitive apparatus. You can take off the glasses of language, but our experience of the world still has to come through the lens of human nature. The idea that we can completely dissolve our human-specific ways of experience and see or become one with reality in itself is incoherent. There cannot be a view from either nowhere or everywhere: every view has to be from somewhere. To escape our human perspective altogether would be to cease to be human and thus cease to exist not only as we know it, but as we could know it.

My thoughts on ineffability owe something to the eighteenth-century Prussian philosopher Immanuel Kant. Kant, like many thinkers from the East, grappled with the idea that there was a distinction between the world as it is (the noumenal world) and the world as we perceive it (the phenomenal world). Reading the works of contemporaneous empiricist philosophers such as David Hume, he was worried that once we accept that all our knowledge of the world comes to us through our senses it would seem that we are trapped in the phenomenal world and can know nothing of the noumenal one. Rather than try to escape the trap, Kant embraced it.

Kant's starting point is the realisation that all the time we insist that our thoughts and concepts must conform to the way objects are, independently of us, we are doomed to failure. No matter how much we try to examine nature *as it is in itself*, we only observe nature *as it appears to us*. Even when we think we are getting close to nature itself, such as when we investigate the subatomic structure of the universe, we can only be looking even more closely at the world as it appears, not as it is. There is no escape from this:

we can only experience the world through the eyes, minds, ideas, models and constructs of humans.

Kant's solution was to question the basic assumption about what knowledge must involve: that we must conform our knowledge to the way objects are. Why not consider the possibility that objects must conform to the way we are? The world is only as it is because our minds frame it in a certain way. It is only because we experience the world in three spatial directions and in tensed time – with past, present and future – that there is a world in space and time. In other words, it is only because we perceive the world in the way that we do that the world that we know even exists. Rather than taking the thinker to the world, Kant brought the world to the thinker.

This might seem a cop-out: that Kant is solving the problem that we do not know the world as it is by saying it is just as good to know the world as it seems. But his argument is more subtle than that. He says that it is not a human tragedy that the noumenal world is beyond us, but a universal necessity for any conscious creature. For anything to have experiences, it needs to have a perceptual and cognitive framework. These can be radically different. Bats place themselves in space by echolocation; time passes four times more slowly for a fly than for a human being.[29] We don't know how extraterrestrial life forms might perceive the universe, but we do know that for them to be conscious at all they would have to see it *in some way*, and that would mean that they too were stuck in their own phenomenal universe, alienated from the noumenal one. In other words, for there to be any real world for any conscious life, there must be a phenomenal world. Such a world is real, for there is simply nothing else that could be more authentically real for any conceivable life form.

Kant does not deny that there is a world independent of human experience, the noumenal world of things-in-themselves. But he thought it senseless to believe we could ever know it. In that way, he is closer to Confucius and to the Buddha, both of whom advocated silence on the ultimate questions of metaphysics. From a Kantian perspective, all the other Asian philosophies that claim the possibility of concept-free, ineffable experience of the world as it truly is are clinging to an impossible dream of being able to escape our human cognitive apparatus. You can strip away language, but you can't strip away the human mind.

I think Kant's basic insight is very powerful. It explains to me why certain mystical or meditative experiences cannot be taken as reliable sources of knowledge of the world as it is. Many have believed that having an experience of the self as one with *Brahman*, or of the self as empty, or of past, present and future dissolving is some kind of evidence that this is how things really are. The Kantian response is that all such experiences are still just experiences. They tell you something about how things seem to you, but they cannot tell you about how things are. Feeling one with *Brahman* does not mean that you are one with *Brahman*; feeling yourself freed from the flow of time does not make you free from the flow of time. Most importantly, the fact that such experiences might feel more real to you than everyday experiences does not make them more real. Extraordinary states may be more powerful than ordinary ones, but that is not evidence that they reveal truth better than ordinary ones. 'Heightened' experiences may simply be ones where our feet lose touch with the ground, not ones that take us closer to the heavens. The irony is that the attempt to go beyond experience to how things really are depends even more on the particularities of personal experience than ordinary knowledge of the everyday world, which can at least be corroborated by objective, third-party observations.

I would even argue that concepts and language can help us get closer to reality, rather than stand in our way of such knowledge. To see why, we need to think more carefully about what objectivity means. There is a temptation to believe that objective knowledge transcends all points of view, all concepts, all language. Rather than objective knowledge being a view from somewhere it is a kind of view from nowhere. Such an objective account of the world has been the implicit or explicit goal of most Western philosophers. One of the clearest expressions of this came during the eighteenth-century French Enlightenment in d'Alembert's introduction to the *Encyclopédie*. He looked forward to a unified science in which 'the Universe would be only one fact and one great truth for whoever knew how to embrace it from a single point of view'.[30]

But as Kant suggests, a view from nowhere is no view at all. Hence the title of Thomas Nagel's contemporary classic *The View from Nowhere*, in which he criticises this notion of objectivity. But Nagel critiques objectivity in order to save it, not to bury it. He invites us to see objectivity as not an unachievable absolute but as a direction in which to aspire.

We all start with subjective experience. As babies, we are the centre of the universe and we don't even understand that others have different perspectives. We take our first step towards a more objective understanding when we realise that things still exist when they move out of sight. We begin to see that the way things are does not depend purely on how we happen to perceive them. We learn that some people are colour blind and so green for us is not green for all, or that a stick that looks bent in water is actually straight to the touch. This illustrates how objectivity for Nagel is a matter of degree. Our understanding becomes more objective the less it depends on the idiosyncrasies of our specific view-points, sense organs or conceptual schema. Nagel illustrates this with the image of concentric circles, the smallest at the middle the most subjective, the largest at the outside the most objective. Circles become larger as more people are able to share the same perspective.

The pinnacles of objective knowledge are found in maths and science, since these are ways of understanding the world that do not depend on which language you speak, where you live or even which of your senses are fully functioning. Even this kind of knowledge is not completely objective. We do not know whether extraterrestrials would be able to make sense of our science, or us of theirs. Nor can we ever know whether there is some fundamental limitation of human cognition that prevents us from achieving an even more objective understanding. Nonetheless, in science and maths we do reach very high degrees of objectivity, ways of understanding that transcend particular perspectives. This objective knowledge, however, requires concepts and language. Far from being obstacles to objective truth, they are enablers of it.

There is still value in the traditions that seek to get beyond words and symbols, in cultivating ways of relating to the world that are more rooted in direct experience, that set aside conceptual categories. At the very least, it is surely useful to remind ourselves that the way we currently experience the world might not exhaust all the possibilities that such a world has to offer. And there may be ways of knowing that can't be expressed in linguistic propositions. Anglophone philosophy tends to distinguish between know-how and knowing-that, arguing that only the latter generates real knowledge. But this seems to be an arbitrary stipulation. To deny that the wheelwright Slab has knowledge because he can't set it down on paper looks like moving the epistemological goalposts to fix the philosophical result.

Interestingly, in the early twentieth century, that most analytical of philosophers Bertrand Russell, no fan of the ineffable, distinguished between knowledge by acquaintance and knowledge by description. I know Bristol, the city I live in, by acquaintance, but I know Trieste only from descriptions I've read of it. Russell also claimed that all knowledge by description is rooted in knowledge by acquaintance, that experience of the world is primary. The people whose descriptions of Trieste I read are (hopefully) actually acquainted with the city. However, only propositions can be true or false, so although these *descriptions* of Trieste can be true or false, we cannot talk of their *experiences* of Trieste as being true or false. But what if some experiences cannot be adequately translated into language? We would then have knowledge by acquaintance without any associated knowledge by description. Could we not call that knowledge ineffable? Russell didn't consider this possibility, but it seems to me that this small twist makes a very Western philosophy suddenly look almost eastern. Some acquaintance with other traditions creates the possibility to redescribe our own in fruitful and fascinating ways.

THEOLOGY OR PHILOSOPHY?

At a conference on medieval Islamic philosophy, one of the leading academics in the field was fulminating in the cloakroom after a talk by an equally esteemed colleague. He was livid that his peer had basically dismissed most of what has been written in the Islamic intellectual tradition since Avicenna (also known as Ibn Sīnā, 980–1037) as theology, not philosophy. As he vented his spleen, his peer arrived unseen from behind to collect his coat, potentially overhearing some of the invective. Far from being embarrassed, the academic turned his fire on the object of his ire.

His peer defended himself, saying that he was simply asking whether the major thinkers were 'philosophising or simply recycling beautiful arguments to prove a mythological narrative'.

'You're talking about books that you haven't read,' accused the academic, adding that according to his peer's criteria one of the greatest thinkers in the history of Western philosophy, St Thomas Aquinas, is 'not a philosopher'.

'Of course he's not a philosopher!' said his peer, enthusiastically biting the bullet.

A peacemaker in the small throng that had gathered to witness these intellectual fisticuffs suggested a compromise. 'You can say it's a very philosophical theology. He's very philosophical but he's not a philosopher.'

The leading academic was having none of it, accusing his peer of restricting 'true' philosophy to what came in Europe after the Enlightenment.

'Go back to the Greeks, for heaven's sake!' his peer replied. 'That's our understanding of philosophy.'

'And there's no mythology that they want to explain?' retorted the academic. 'You're basically saying that if they employ philosophical arguments only for religious motives, then they are no longer philosophers. That cuts out the whole pre-Enlightenment philosophical tradition.'

It would have gone on but the melee was blocking the cloakroom and we had to vacate the building. Dinner beckoned. A temporary truce was tacitly called in what was clearly a long and bitter war.

I was glad to have witnessed this skirmish. It confirmed that one of the key debates concerning the history of Islamic philosophy is the extent to which it is philosophy and the extent to which it is theology. This debate is found almost everywhere that you find philosophy. It's certainly evident in the classical Indian tradition, where revelation and religion are deeply entwined with philosophical thought. The question also arises in East Asia, where Confucianism and Daoism are sometimes thought of as religions, and where Buddhism is a strong influence in many philosophical traditions. And one reason why many do not treat ancient oral traditions as philosophical systems is that they are assumed to be essentially religious in character.

Attempts to distinguish philosophy and theology are particularly difficult in Islamic philosophy, as the incident in the conference cloakroom illustrated. Even the way you describe the tradition is potentially controversial. To call it 'Islamic philosophy' is to suggest it all has a religious character, so some prefer the term 'philosophy in the Islamic world'. We don't, for example, call René Descartes or John Locke 'Christian philosophers', even though they were in fact both philosophers and Christian, identities that were not hermetically sealed from each other in the seventeenth century. Locke, for instance, praised toleration as 'the chief characteristic mark of the true Church' but insisted 'those are not at all to be tolerated who deny the being of a God' because 'promises, covenants, and oaths, which are the bonds of human society, can have no hold upon an atheist'.[1] However, for the sake of simplicity and nothing more, I will continue to call it Islamic philosophy on the understanding that that does not prejudge the extent to which it is all infused with theology.

The standard way of framing the debate about the religious nature of Islamic philosophy is to focus on the battle for supremacy between *falsafa* and *kalām* in the Middle Ages. *Falsafa* is usually translated as 'philosophy' while *ilm al-kalām*, to give it its full name (literally 'the science of the word/discourse'), represents the harder to translate idea of a kind of theological philosophy specific to Islam. The key protagonists in this historical dispute were Avicenna and Averroes, who spoke in support of the *falāsifa* (philosopher), and al-Ghazālī, whose *Incoherence of the Philosophers* attacked the pursuit of reason without revelation. The crude version of history is that al-Ghazālī won, and the decline of *falsafa* heralded the decline of secular philosophical thought in the Islamic world which has not been reversed to this day. '*Falsafa*' is a 'dirty word' in the Arab world, wrote Omar Saif Ghobash recently. 'It is seen as a distraction from the importance of keeping the faith pure and unsullied by questions that will only serve to divide and separate the Muslims.'[2] Religion claims priority over reason, which means that it has been difficult to reinterpret Islam in the light of contemporary science and to force its teaching to accommodate secular knowledge.

Although no serious scholar would entirely subscribe to the

simplistic narrative today in which theology drives out philosophy, in broad terms it does represent a received wisdom which is still a matter of dispute. Dimitri Guttas is foremost among the internationally respected scholars whose views are close to this default story. In his account, Avicenna marked the high point of Islamic philosophy. Avicenna was born during the time of the Persian Samanid dynasty (819– 999), when science and philosophy flourished. 'The Samanid rulers were not interested in having a hard line, sticking to the literal narrative of Islam as it expressed itself in the Qur'ān,' Guttas told me. 'The philosophers and scientists interpreted it metaphorically as almost everyone does anyway in social contexts in which religion is not being used by political agents for political purposes.' The openness of the early Islamic world contrasted with the more closed-minded Christendom of late antiquity, where 'the Hellenic scientific outlook on life was not allowed to continue because of the extreme adherence to the literal narrative of that kind of orthodox Christianity'.

During this period, ancient Greek philosophy, particularly that of Aristotle, was translated into Arabic and had a profound impact on thinking in the Islamic world. Guttas argues that Avicenna was basically doing science, by which he means 'open-ended inquiry into the nature of reality', which is also how he characterises classical Greek philosophy: 'In Avicenna we get the pinnacle of this scientific development because he puts together all the different sciences that were being developed and he creates an integrated system that is scientific and at the same time holistic.'

In one sense Avicenna was too successful and his system 'became itself a dogmatic outlook. Because he put together the scientific view of the world so consistently, with such integrity, the main purpose of philosophising after that became not so much doing more research science and finding out things as to try to criticise it or to defend it. The scientific system of Avicenna became frozen as *the* scientific outlook, and the rest tried to take it down.'

After Avicenna, however, Guttas argues that 'the theological motivations became paramount' as *kalām* came to dominate over *falsafa*. However, we have to be careful here, because *falsafa* does not mean philosophy in its modern, general sense. *Falsafa* is a transliteration of the Greek word *philosophia*, 'understood by everyone to be the works of Aristotle primarily, as well as of the mathematicians and astronomers, the Greek scientific literature'. In other words, *falsafa* referred to the sciences generally, as inherited from the Greeks, not just to what we would call philosophy today.

Guttas argues that *kalām*, in contrast, is 'what we would called theology, a kind of exercise of trying to understand religion in a rational way'. It had a 'double function to present religion in a more orderly, systemic way and also to argue against the people of the book, the Christians and the Jews'.

Initially, *kalām* and *falsafa* were not in conflict, as they were understood to be doing different things. This changed as much for political as for philosophical reasons, says Guttas. Rulers increasingly 'found it to their advantage to sponsor scholars and thinkers who would play the religion card' in part to get support from the people. The result was not so much *kalām* wiping out *falsafa* as subverting and subsuming it. The same pattern can be seen in scholastic philosophy in the medieval Christian world. The scholastics 'started using all the language, methods and arguments that the philosophers were using, but expunging it of the doctrinal aspects that they did not like, introducing their own so it seemed as though it was basically philosophical, but it wasn't. The skeleton of the arguments and the doctrines seemed to be philosophical, but the contents were Christian.' Likewise in the Islamic world, 'The arguments themselves seemed to be philosophical but the content was Islamic.' The difference is that around the seventeenth century in the Christian world, scholasticism started to decline and a more secular style of philosophy came to dominate, whereas in the Islamic world, *kalām* retained the upper hand.

To other scholars, there are many problematic elements in this account. A peak was passed simply because, as Richard Taylor put it, 'Avicenna was incredible. There would always be a decline in some sense after Avicenna.' But Taylor rejects the standard imperialist narrative of Islamic waning and Western ascendency which sees this decline as a form of degeneracy. 'The discourse of decline is rooted in European perceptions of the Islamic world which is generated out of Enlightenment ideas and the colonial context,' Frank Griffel told me. 'If you look for evidence of decline you find it on the battlefield. Islamic armies, starting in 1798, are regularly defeated and that increases in Europe the sense of a civilisation in decline.' From the point of view of someone living in say, Cairo, that looks less like an advert for the superiority of Western civilisation than a reflection of 'Europe as an aggressive culture, that aims at subjugating other cultures'.

For instance, in India and the Middle East there used to be very strong educational institutions and a high value placed on learning. Griffel says that 'there was an expectation that if you became a state functionary in the Moghul empire you needed to know your Avicenna. This was regarded as an intellectual exercise, not as something to be subscribed to.' Time and again it was the West that killed these institutions. For instance, after the 1857–8 uprising in India, 'the British basically took away the endowments from these institutions, and three years later they were all dead. The only real education that was offered was a school that would prepare you for the British Colonial Service.'

Another source of the perception of decline is that the Enlightenment gave birth to a strong idea that philosophy 'needs to be a secular discipline' while theology's 'premises are rooted in revelation. In Enlightenment discourse, philosophy comes up stronger. There is also this idea in France of the *philosophes*, like Voltaire, who are atheists. That shaped the expectation of what philosophy is, so when in the nineteenth century European observers looked into the Islamic world they found no Voltaire, no *philosophes*.' But they did see that in the classical tradition there were thinkers such as Avicenna and al-Farabi who did not talk much about religion openly. 'They called themselves *falāsifa*,' says Griffel, 'so the word is there as well. Everything matches. And we see that these societies are in decline, they are poorer than us, they are weaker than us. You put it all together and you get the narrative that once you had the great culture of the Islamic world and of course they declined because they had given up *falsafa*, philosophy.'

Griffel says that he struggles with this narrative because in some sense there does seem to be something of a decline in Islamic civilisation in the eighteenth and nineteenth centuries, as Islamic societies weren't as productive or as innovative as Western ones. 'Progress, innovation, material riches, the production of material wealth, the projection of military power overseas – all of this is something we connect to a successful society.' But is this the true measure of success and is decline its opposite? 'Decline?' asks Griffel. 'It depends on how you look at it. If you think of a success-ful society as one that aggressively pursues empires, yes.'

Others are even more outspoken. Yahya Michot says that when we judge the relative thriving of the Western and the Islamic worlds over recent centuries 'it's too early to compare. You will be dead, I will be dead. We will have the opportunity in fifty years, after climate change, which is knocking down civilisation every-where on this planet. Then it will be time enough to see what was more useful to mankind, so-called Western modernity or the more traditional civilisations that did not contribute or did not initiate that kind of climate change.'

He is insistent that the problems of the Islamic world come more from without than within. 'Instead of speaking of decline I speak of a fantastic capacity for survival. The Roman Empire fell for less than what the Muslim world had to go through in the thirteenth and the following centuries, starting with the Mongol invasions.' In more recent times, the West has been more dynamic, but do not assume that is a good thing, he warns. 'When you have a general cancer in an organism you can indeed speak legitimately of the dynamism of the cancer cells, but the result is what we know. And so you can say that compared to the cancer cells the healthy cells that are unable to resist are decaying, declining etc.'

Listening to leading scholars debate these issues with me and among themselves at the conference, it struck me that the disagreement was not as polarised as it might at first seem. The argument appears to be whether Islamic thought is truly philosophical or a kind of theology. This is often assumed to be an inherently value-laden disagreement: Islamic thought is 'proper' philosophy (good) or 'just' theology (bad). But of course the belief that proper philosophy has to be purged of all theological taint is itself an expression of a value that not everyone would agree with. In other words, it is possible to accept that Islamic thought has not been secularised in the same way as Western philosophy and to say it is all the better for it.

'Who says that a philosopher cannot be motivated by Church and God?' asks Griffel. 'You have major figures in the British tradition whom we consider philosophers, deeply pious people who didn't write about their faith, yet their motivation for understanding and explaining the world is still theological. Arabic authors are open about that.' Similarly, Luis Xavier Lopez-Farjeat says that 'you will have a very narrow conception of philosophy' if you insist it must conform to the strongly secular parameters of the Enlightenment.

All experts agree that there is no clear-cut distinction between theology and philosophy in Islamic thought and arguably in most other intellectual traditions in history. Talking of Cairo at the height of its intellectual vigour, for example, Griffel says, 'The distinction between theology and philosophy is something that these people in 1798 would have no idea of.'

Richard Taylor agrees, saying that there is 'absorption back and forth' between theology and secular philosophy in the Islamic world, 'parallel intellectual tracks which quite often come together and come apart, and they're watching one another to some extent'. An example of this is al-Ghazālī, often accused of destroying philosophy with his attack on Avicenna and *falsafa*. A much better way of looking at this, says Taylor, is to see that his study of Avicenna 'introduced philosophy to theology'.

Peter Adamson also thinks it unhelpful to see the *falsafa* and *kalām* distinction as a battle between faith and reason. 'Rather there was a struggle within *kalām* itself between more and less rationalist approaches to understanding the revelation brought by Muḥammad.'[3] The distinction is not really about two different ways of thinking. Rather, it is a division within a single body of Islamic-philosophical-theological thought. Al-Ghazālī, an archetypal proponent of *kalām*, not only argues philosophically but appeals to arguments by Plato and Galen, claiming that the *falāsifas* have misunderstood them.[4] Similarly, the *falāsifa* al-Kindī begins one of his philosophical treatises with 'May God grant you long life in the happiest of states and the purest of deeds, O son of noble lords and pious leaders. The beacon of faith, the precious gem, the best of both worlds!'[5] Even as he reaches his conclusion based on Neoplatonic reasoning, he does so in religious terms: 'Therefore, there are not many agents, but One without any multiplicity whatsoever (glorious and exalted is He above the descriptions of the heretics!)'[6]

Averroes (Ibn Rushd) is also keen to establish the theological licence of *falsafa*, arguing that the Qur'ān mandates it. He takes lines such as 'Reflect, you [who] have vision'[7] as Qur'ānic authority for the obligation to use philosophical methods.[8] He is also clear that philosophy cannot be done without piety and that its ultimate end is also piety:

From this it is evident that the study of the books of the ancients is obligatory by Law, since their aim and purpose in their books is just the purpose to which the Law has urged us, and that whoever forbids the study of them to anyone who is fit to study them, that is, anyone who unites two qualities, (1) natural intelligence, and (2) religious integrity and moral virtue, is blocking the door by which the Law summons them to knowledge of God, the door of theoretical study that leads to the truest knowledge of Him.[9]

Avicenna also uses scripture in his arguments, arguing against those who believe there was no being or time before God created the present being and time, saying, 'These opinions about the world do not conform to the apparent [i.e. evident] meaning of scripture' and 'It is not stated in scripture that God was existing with absolutely nothing else: a text to this effect is nowhere to be found.'[10] He also claimed that 'the purpose of scripture is simply to teach true science and right practice'.[11]

The struggle to find the right balance between revelation and reason continues across the Islamic world today. There have been times and places where the theological constraints on reasoning have been loosened and secular ideas have gained ground. For instance, Christopher de Bellaigue has chronicled what he calls the 'Islamic Enlightenment' of the nineteenth century, when creative Muslim thinking thrived in Cairo, Istanbul and Tehran. However, even de Bellaigue, a debunker of the idea that Islam and open-minded philosophy are incompatible, acknowledges that this was preceded by centuries in which free inquiry was almost impossible and much of the direction of travel in recent decades has been the same.

'If Islam engaged so successfully with modernity until the First World War,' he asks, 'why since then has reactionary revivalism been able to impose itself on ever larger swathes of the Muslim world?'[12] Much of the rest of the world has been too impatient to soberly try to answer this, demanding a more extensive Islamic Enlightenment along the lines of the European one (over-looking, among other things, the very long time it took for the Enlightenment to result in women's emancipation, racial equality and equal rights for homosexuals). However, we should know by now that urging the Islamic world to follow the same path as the West is more likely to spark resistance than enthusiasm. In the West, secular knowledge has been engaged in an ongoing tussle with religious authority, in a kind of zero-sum game. As de Bellaigue warns, we should not fall for the fallacy, promoted by 'progressives' and 'reactionaries' alike, 'that modernity is a fixed value to which there are only two possible responses – acceptance or rejection in favour of the status quo'.[13] The history of Islamic philosophy suggests that the Muslim world's accommodation of secular knowledge will have to be sui generis. There is little to no prospect of a rejection of the absolute truth of the Qur'ān or of a philosophy that fails to take religion into account. There is every prospect, however, of a distinctly Islamic philosophy which is open, tolerant and embraces secular knowledge by making it compatible with theology. It has happened in the past and it could happen again. Those who claim otherwise, that we are heading for an inevitable clash of civilisations, do not have history on their side.

However one resolves the dispute in Islamic philosophy, it is certainly true that in separating theology from philosophy the modern West is the global exception, not the rule. As we have seen, the same kind of intermingling of faith and reason is found in Indian philosophy, which in many ways echoes the natural theology of medieval Europe. But we ought to remember that this way of thinking is still mainstream in Christianity today. An Indian Catholic priest, Jose Nandhikkara, pointed out these parallels to me at the Indian Philosophical Congress: 'Pope John Paul II said faith and reason are like two wings with which the human spirit rises in contemplation of truth and both of them are gifts of God. So you should look more and more for the complementarity, and you should not be guided only by faith or only by reason. All branches of knowledge are important as they could contribute to the harmony of life.'

In East Asia, the picture is complicated by the fact that traditional vocabulary does not make the same kind of distinctions between religious and philosophical concepts as European languages do. For instance, there was no word to distinguish religion from superstition in Japanese until the late 1800s. Scholars of Japanese philosophy often note what Carter calls 'the lack of any sharp separation between philosophy and religion'.[14] Tanabe Hajime writes that 'religion and philosophy differ from one another and yet entail each other'.[15] According to Takeuchi Yoshinori:

> In Buddhism, religion and philosophy are like a tree that forks into two from its base. Both stem from the same roots and are nourished by the same sap. [...] There have been times in the long history of Buddhism in which a pruning of the philosophical branch has helped the trunk to flourish, and other times at which the philosophical branch stood in full bloom while the trunk had become hollowed out.[16]

Religion in the Japanese context has a different character from that in the West. 'Generally, religion in Japan is not about belief,' says Carter. 'Instead, religion in Japan is about consciousness transformation.'[17] It seeks to help people experience the world differently, not to change their beliefs about it. This distinction between belief and consciousness transformation is also found in Buddhism more generally. 'The Buddha himself often warned his disciples against confusing the religious search, the "noble quest", with philosophical and metaphysical questions,' says Takeuchi.[18] Hence philosophy and religion have a somewhat paradoxical relationship, 'inseparable yet distinct, complementary yet opposed, or in Nishida's words, self-contradictory and yet identical'.[19]

It can be very difficult for Western philosophers to deal with the broadly theological strands of other traditions. It seems to me that they often find themselves caught between a cosmopolitan enthusiasm for the unfamiliar and a parochial disdain for the dilution of pure philosophy with faith. The result is that they often play down or even deny the seemingly religious nature of the ideas they study. Leah Kalmanson recognises this. 'Some philosophers have a tendency to read all references to the supernatural out of the texts,' she says. As I noted earlier, I also saw something of this tendency at the Indian Philosophical Congress. There were those who felt that to defend Indian philosophy it was necessary to claim it was distinct from religion, even as others wanted to make their integration of philosophy and religion a matter of pride.

For those schooled in secular philosophy, it's a challenge to respond to other traditions in ways that fully acknowledge both their philosophical value and their religious or spiritual dimensions. Somehow, however, we must find a way to do this if we are to have an open dialogue across traditions. We must acknowledge that the strict secularisation of philosophy is itself a philosophical position that requires justification. To simply stipulate that faith separates you from philosophy is as deeply unphilosophical as stipulating that a sacred text must have the last word. Both positions need to be argued for as part of a shared philosophical enterprise.

LOGIC

The French Revolution of 1789–99 was fought in the name of *liberté*, *égalité* and *fraternité*. Standing unnamed alongside them – or perhaps supporting them from underneath – was the general of the campaign: *raison*. The new society the revolutionaries hoped to create would be a better one because it would be established on rational grounds.

This was evident in the manner in which they set about their work. After their victory, their priorities were not simply giving power to the people and removing the heads of the *ancien régime*. With revolutionary zeal they sought to rid society of its illogical quirks, without considering how these measures affected the plight of the ordinary citizen. Decimalisation was more important than nationalisation. 'The metric system is for all the people for all the time,' said the philosopher Condorcet, with a rhetoric more in keeping with social than mensural reform.

In 1795, out went the *livre*, the unit of currency for over 1,000 years, with its illogical subdivision into twenty *sous* (or *sols*), each of twelve *deniers*. In came the decimal *franc*, more pleasingly comprised of ten *décimes* or 100 *centimes*. In the same year, five decimal units of measurement were created: the *mètre* for length, the *are* for area, the *stère* for volumes of dry goods, the *litre* for volumes of liquid and the *gramme* for mass. These units could be magnified or shrunk by the addition of prefixes such as *kilo* (1,000), *hecta* (100), *deci* (a tenth) or *centi* (a hundredth). They were adopted nationally in 1795.

More radical but less enduring was a new calendar. Its weeks of ten days were divided into twenty hours of 100 decimal minutes, each comprising 100 decimal seconds. Introduced in 1793, the revolutionary calendar was used for only twelve years, and most gave up on revolutionary time after two.

These reforms reflected the importance revolutionaries placed on reason in general and logic in particular. The *Encyclopédie*, the defining text of the French Enlightenment, which was edited and largely written by Denis Diderot and Jean-Baptiste le Rond d'Alembert between 1751 and 1772, had the ambitious purpose to 'collect knowledge disseminated around the globe; to set forth its general system to the men with whom we live, and transmit it to those who will come after us'.[1]

In his introductory 'Preliminary Discourse', d'Alembert writes how important logic is to the acquisition of this knowledge. Logic

teaches how to arrange ideas in the most natural order, how to link them together in the most direct sequence, how to break up those which include too large a number of simple ideas, how to view ideas in all their facets, and finally how to present them to others in a form that makes them easy to grasp. This is what constitutes this science of reasoning, which is rightly considered the key to all our knowledge.[2]

There was little that the French enlightenment *philosophes* did not think could be improved by the application of logic. Writing about punctuation, for example, Diderot observed that 'the pause of a voice in discourse, and the signs of punctuation in writing, always correspond, indicate equally well the connection or separation of ideas, and complement countless expressions. Therefore,' he concluded, 'it will be useful to determine their number according to the rules of logic, and fix their value through examples.'[3]

Faith in the power of logic and reason was perhaps never as strong as it was during the French Enlightenment and Revolution. Arguably, however, the stress on logic has been the most distinctive feature of Western philosophy throughout its history and has shaped the entire culture. Logic is founded on the idea that reasoning should proceed by strict deductive steps, giving argument a kind of quasi-mathematical rigour. Aristotle first set out the basic principles of logic, and his rules would be followed until the emergence of symbolic logic in the nineteenth century. Defenders of Western philosophy argue that its emphasis on logic has given it a unique robustness, while critics say it has trapped the Western mind in crude, inflexible, dichotomous either/or ways of thinking. Ironically, sometimes this criticism itself betrays crude binary thinking. Tom Kasulis, for instance, once heard a Japanese scholar say, 'Unlike you Westerners, we Japanese are not dualistic.'[4] Western philosophers are not the only ones who make sharp distinctions.

'Logic' can look like an imposing, technical term but its essence is simple enough. Logic is simply the systematic working through of the implications of true statements. Its most uncontroversial principle is the Law of Excluded Middle. Put in its simplest form, it is the seventeenth-century philosopher Leibniz's 'principle of contradiction': namely, 'a proposition is either true or false', and hence there is no middle, third alternative.[5] Its first explicit articulation was probably in Aristotle. 'It is impossible, then, that "being a man" should mean precisely "not being a man", if "man" not only signifies something about one subject but also has one significance,' he wrote. 'And it will not be possible to be and not to be the same thing, except in virtue of an ambiguity.'[6]

This is the plain English meaning of what in contemporary symbolic notation can be rendered as ¬(p&¬p) or (p ∨ ¬p). Here 'p' stands for any statement that can be true or false (any 'proposition' with a 'truth value'). The symbolic '¬' is a negation, while 'v' is an exclusive 'or' (a 'disjunction') where it must be either/or and cannot be both . Hence ¬(p&¬p) expresses the principle that a statement cannot be both true and false, while (p ∨ ¬p) puts it another way: namely, a statement must be true or false and cannot be both. The common usage of such notation has deterred many a potential and actual student of logic, while attracting those of a more mathematical bent.

Although I said the Law of Excluded Middle was uncontroversial, many find themselves resistant to it, claiming that the world is more complicated than this. Some people are both very clever and very stupid, for example, while hermaphrodites are both male and female. But the Law of Excluded Middle does not deny this. Aristotle makes it very clear that for the either/or logic to work it is essential that there is no ambiguity, and that meanings are precise and have only 'one significance'. These conditions are not met when we colloquially say that something is true and not true. Someone who is both clever and stupid is clever in some ways or contexts and stupid in others. They are not clever and stupid in exactly the same way at the same time. For instance, someone can be a genius novelist and a complete fool in love. Even the precise same action can be clever in one way and stupid in another. A tactically brilliant military victory might be a strategic disaster, such as a successful operation to oust a dictator that creates a toxic power vacuum.

I would bet that it is impossible to come up with an example of something that appears to contradict the Law of Excluded Middle which on closer examination does not involve ambiguity (where the meaning is unclear) or equivocation (where more than one meaning is possible). The only real controversy about the law is how useful it is, given that the world *is* often ambiguous or unclear. This is the power behind traditions that might superficially appear to reject the principle. Both Daoism and Zen, for example, are replete with apparent paradoxes that assert that something is both true and not true. For instance, the *Daodejing* says, 'Sometimes diminishing a thing adds to it;/Sometimes adding to a thing diminishes it.'[7] You might parse this as meaning that losing can be not losing and gaining not gaining. But it doesn't take long to see that there is no logical contradiction here. There are two possible interpretations. One is that what first appears like a loss can actually turn out to be a gain. ('I have not so much lost a daughter as gained a son,' as the tired old father of the bride speech goes.) The other is that a loss might be part of a process that leads to a gain. (If I hadn't lost that job I wouldn't have got this much better one.) Neither means that an actual loss is in reality not a loss at all.

Or take the Zen saying 'The Bodhi tree is not a tree, and the bright mirror is not a mirror.' Here, the central idea is that there is a difference between ultimate reality and perceived reality. There is in one sense a Bodhi tree, but since nothing has a fixed essence, in another sense there is nothing that makes it a tree. Again, we have not a breach of the Law of Excluded Middle but a deliberate attempt to use the law to make us attend to the fact that there are different senses of 'exist'.

Remember also the description in Advaita of *Brahman* as 'not this, not that' (*neti neti*). This again might superficially appear to be an assertion that something both is and is not. But the point is to show how language cannot capture the nature of *Brahman*. We end up in a paradox when we try to describe the indescribable, not because ultimate reality is contradictory but because it defies the neat categorisations of our limited words and concepts. Indian philosophy does not embrace true contradiction, and even has something close to the Law of Excluded Middle in the concept of *vipratisedha*, defined by the third-century-BCE grammarian Patanjali as 'mutual prohibition'.[8]

The difference between the dominant ways of thinking in Western philosophy and in Asia is not that the West embraces a Law of Excluded Middle which the East rejects. Rather, the difference is the extent to which this law is foregrounded and taken to be practically important. There is plenty of what could be seen as logical argument in Chinese philosophy for example, but there is no development of logic as a specific discipline in the classical tradition. Perhaps the closest we get is the third-century-BCE White Horse paradox of Gongsun Long, in which it is argued that a white horse is not a horse since 'horse' names a shape, 'white' names a colour and 'what names the colour is not what names the shape'.[9] No substantive point seems to be made in this passage and Ram-Prasad suggests it is probably best understood as a 'refined joke'.[10]

The East has tended to stress the extent to which attempts to understand things in terms of exclusive either/or categories often fail, while the West has stressed the progress that can be made when we bring out contradictions in our common-sense ways of thinking and replace them with new distinctions that preserve logical consistency. Nicholas Rescher describes this as the *'aporetic'* nature of philosophy. An *apory* is 'a group of contentions that are individually plausible but collectively inconsistent'.[11] Philosophy exists because our pre-philosophical understanding of the world constantly generates such *apories*. In ethics, for example, the principle of impartiality seems compelling, but so does the apparent duty to put our families first. These two principles are 'individually plausible but collectively inconsistent'. In epistemology, it seems that we have knowledge and that knowledge implies certainty, but when we look for the grounds of our certainty there don't seem to be any. Again, it seems plausible both that we have knowledge and that we have none, and both can't be true. As a final example, take the apparent existence of free will and the belief that everything in nature operates according to strict laws of cause and effect. The claim that we both have free will and can't have it seems plausible, and only one can be right.

When faced with an *apory*, we could just throw up our hands and say it's beyond our comprehension. Western philosophy is based on the conviction that this is defeatist. We can't be sure that we will be able to resolve the *apory*, and indeed many of the problems of philosophy that persist have stubbornly resisted solution for millennia. But we have to try. Even if we can't entirely remove the contradiction, we might at least understand it more clearly or dissolve parts of it.

You could then summarise the modus operandi of Western philosophy as an attempt to remove from the world as many breaches of the Law of Excluded Middle as possible, leaving us with a clear distinction between propositions that are true and others that are false. This is the truth in the claim that Western philosophy is 'binary' or 'dichotomous', based on 'either/or' rather than 'both/and' thinking. It's a way of thinking that has clearly permeated the culture and is particularly evident in many political structures. Elites have been educated to be fierce debaters, adopting clear for and against positions, skilled at exposing flaws in opponents' arguments. As a result, parliaments are organised rather like university debating chambers, with laws debated as though they were motions and decisions reached by majority vote.

To Westerners, this seems so natural that it is hard to imagine alternatives, especially since the Western model has now been adopted by so many other countries. But whatever its philosophical merits, it is an approach that has several disadvantages. An antagonistic spirit of inquiry is antithetical to cooperation, compromise and seeking common ground. It is also more focused on winning arguments than achieving the best outcome. This dynamic can be seen in all corners of the culture, often with negative consequences.

For instance, as a legal process, divorce has tended to be even more antagonistic than it needs to be because it is conducted in adversarial terms, where one of the partnership must sue for divorce and attribute blame. Only relatively recently has the idea of 'no fault' divorce, with mediation rather than litigation, become popular.

The dichotomous mindset is also implicated in recent political problems. In Britain, America and several other countries we are seeing a new polarisation, with liberal, largely urban cosmopolitans pitted against conservative communitarians in smaller towns and villages. Such divisions were most evident in the US presidential election contest between Hillary Clinton and Donald Trump and in the referendum on EU membership in the UK, both in 2016. In each case the margin of victory was tiny but it is the nature of plebiscites with only two choices that all is given to the majority and nothing to the minority, even though they were very close to equal in size. The votes exposed the limitations of a dualistic culture which allows for only true or false, winner and loser.

Until recently, the flaws in the system appeared to be merely minor or theoretical, given how successful Western civilisation and its democracy had been. Churchill's quip about democracy could be complacently generalised to the whole culture: 'Western thinking is the worst form of philosophy except for all those other forms that have been tried from time to time.' It is not as though other models had generated prosperous, stable, peaceful civilisations. China, which has no philosophical tradition of formal logic, had given rise to a totalitarian state, while Africa, with its political values of consensus and agreement such as *ubuntu*, was the least developed continent on the planet. If rich and happy Europe, North America and Australasia were what you got from 'crudely dichotomous thinking', then it couldn't be all that bad.

Now political instability across the democratic West makes that attitude seem complacent. It turns out that only an unspoken spirit of compromise was tempering the tensions caused by the binary choices of two-party politics. For decades, there was a kind of tacit agreement that neither side would hold on to power indefinitely or undo everything its predecessor had done. In Britain, this took the form of the 'post-war consensus', which assured that from 1945 to the Thatcher government of 1979 both Left and Right supported a welfare state and a mixed economy of state-owned and privatised businesses and utilities. Once that consensus broke down, polarisation became inevitable.

The problems of Western democracy are a kind of allegory for the problems of Western philosophy. Its pursuit of the clear distinction between true and false creates a default either/or mindset. When only one thing can be true and we can know what it is, the distinction works. Science, for example, could not exist without the Law of Excluded Middle. Yet when we are dealing with values and preferences, different visions of the good life, even if there is some ultimate sense in which only one view is correct, in practice we cannot determine one and only one winner. A dualistic culture can get around this if it maintains an equilibrium between both opposites, granting as much to one as to the other. But there is always the risk that such an equilibrium will not be reached and that the logic of either/or turns into the logic of the zero-sum game, in which only one side can win. And when there are several plausible views, a binary mindset finds it hard to manage the complexity that creates.

Yet it would clearly be misguided to get rid of either/or logic entirely. The Law of Excluded Middle is implicit in all philosophies and the only difference is how much it is stressed. Although the West places the most importance on it, there is also a very strong role for logic in the classical Indian tradition. The tenth-century logician Udayana even set out an exact analogue of the Law of Excluded Middle in the wonderfully titled *Nyāya kusumāñjali* ('A Handful of Flowers of Logic'): 'Between a thing and its contradictory, there is no third way. And there cannot be also a unity of two contradictories, for the mere statements of them will cancel each other.'[12]

Udayana was a successor of Akṣapāda Gautama, the thinker who did the most to develop logic in India and was purportedly the author of the *Nyāya Sūtra*, the key text of the Nyāya school. The *Nyāya Sūtra* is a rich, detailed account of the forms of reasoning and their validity. Among its most interesting features is its taxonomy of the different kinds of dispute with its wonderful lexicon. *Discussion*, for example, is a sincere form of investigation where debaters adopt one of two opposing sides, defending them 'by the aid of any of the means of right knowledge' and assailing the opposition 'by confutation, without deviation from the established tenets'.[13] In contrast, *wrangling* simply aims at gaining victory, 'by quibbles, futilities, and other processes that deserve rebuke'.[14] Wrangling also comes in various forms. *Cavil*, for instance, 'is a kind of wrangling that consists in mere attacks on the opposite side. A *caviller* does not endeavour to establish anything, but confines himself to mere carping at the arguments of his opponent.'[15] We all know the sort.

Every term in these definitions is itself subject to precise specification. *Quibble* is a very specific fallacy of 'wilfully taking the term in a sense other than that intended by a speaker who has happened to use it ambiguously'. If I said a book was long and you said it wasn't, since it only measured twenty centimetres, you'd be quibbling. You can also quibble in respect of metaphors, by taking a word literally when it was meant metaphorically or vice versa.[16]

Written between the sixth and the second centuries BCE, the *Nyāya Sūtra* famously analyses the structure of sound arguments as a five-membered syllogism. The stock example is:

There is fire on the hill (the *pratijñā*, thesis).
Because there is smoke on the hill (the *hetu*, reason or *probans*).

Wherever there is smoke, there is fire; like a kitchen hearth
and unlike a lake (the *udāharaṇa*, illustration of concomitance).
This hill is likewise smoky (the *upanaya*, application of
the rule).
Thus, there is fire on the hill (the *nigamana*, conclusion).[17]

According to the *Nyāya Sūtra*, all other valid inferences have the
same general form. You start by stating the thesis you are seeking
to establish (the *pratijñā*). You then state the reason (the *hetu*) for
believing the thesis is true. However, the *hetu* alone is not enough
to establish that the thesis must be true. To do that you have to
state the general rule (the *udāharaṇa*), which if you apply it to the
hetu generates the conclusion, the *nigamana*. So, to take another,
non-traditional example:

This plate of tiramisu is fattening (the *pratijñā*).
Because it contains lots of fat and sugar (the *hetu*).
Anything that contains a lot of fat and sugar is fattening, like a
doughnut and unlike a carrot (the *udāharaṇa*).
The plate of tiramisu likewise contains a lot of fat and sugar
(the *upanaya*).
Thus, the plate of tiramisu is fattening (the *nigaman*).

The parallels with Greek logic are striking, despite the fact that
both appear to have developed independently. Aristotle introduced
the idea of the syllogism, an argument which proceeds deductively
from premises to conclusion. The premises are statements which
are taken to be true, either because they are evident by observation
or because they have been demonstrated as true in some other
way. A successful deduction takes premises and draws out the conclusion which results of necessity from them. Standard examples
are deliberately banal so that it is easy to see the movement from
premises to conclusion. For example:

John Kettley is a weather man.
All weather men are mortal.
Therefore John Kettley is mortal.

This is more concise than the five-membered syllogism, which can appear unnecessarily tortuous in comparison. In Aristotelian logic, the smoke and fire argument can be expressed in a simpler three-line argument:

Wherever there is smoke, there is fire.
There is smoke on the hill.
Therefore, there is fire on the hill.

Aristotelian logic analyses the structure of arguments to create a list of all valid deductions. This one is of the form called *modus ponens* or affirming the antecedent:

If P, then Q.
P.
Therefore Q.

Although this is indeed more economical than the five-membered syllogism, in practice Indian logic often uses a similar three-step process, one which has the same basic steps as the Aristotelian syllogism but in a different order. So the structure is

A is qualified by S,
because it is qualified by T
(whatever is qualified by T is qualified by S) like (Tb & Sb).

We can apply this to the example and also point out its parallel lines in the Aristotelian syllogism:

The hill is on fire (the hill is qualified by fieriness)
[Therefore Q]
because it is smoking (qualified by smokiness). *[P]*
Wherever there is smoke, there is fire (whatever is qualified by smokiness is qualified by fieriness), like a kitchen hearth and unlike a lake. *[If P, then Q]*

The advantage in the apparently convoluted formulation of the five-membered syllogism is that it combines two forms of argument that are traditionally separated in Western logic. The Aristotelian syllogism is an example of a deduction, in which the conclusion is supposed to flow from the premises with absolute certainty: if x, then y, by necessity. This is logic as mathematics. However, in practice most of the time we can't reason with such certainty. When we are trying to make sense of the world we have to generalise from experience in ways that are not deductively valid. If bread has always nourished and this is a piece of bread, it does not strictly follow that this bread will nourish me. The conclusion only follows if we take as a premise the fact that bread always nourishes, past, present and future. But we can't know that with certainty as we don't know what the future will bring, or whether this particular loaf is poisoned or adulterated. Of course, we all think it perfectly reasonable to assume that it will nourish, and so it is. But that form of 'being reasonable' is not the same as being strictly logical. Our reasoning is not *deductive*, by incontrovertible steps from premise to conclusion, but *inductive*, from past experience to general cases. The fact that this cannot be justified in logical terms creates what is known as the 'problem of induction'.

Indian philosophers were certainly aware of the problem, a version of which was developed by the fourteenth-century Cārvāka thinker Mādhavācarya.[18] He pointed out that the *udāharaṇa* contains a 'concomitance' (*vyāpti*) which grounds the inference: for example, 'Wherever there is smoke, there is fire.' But this can never be established by the senses, which in Cārvāka is the only way to establish any truth. This is simply because the senses only observe particular instances of the concomitance of smoke and fire but the *vyāpti* asserts a universal concomitance.

The five-membered syllogism marries the two forms of reasoning. As Ram-Prasad puts it, 'Indian logic combines the necessary certainty of deduction with the unavoidable need for induction.'[19] Its structure is deductive but in a way that explicitly acknowledges the inductive elements. In particular, a general rule is evoked (the *udāharaṇa*) which is clearly an observation from experience that cannot be counted as an absolute truth. The stock example seems designed to emphasise this, since the expression 'no smoke without fire' is one which we widely recognise to be not necessarily true. It is true often enough for us to make a provisional presumption of fire but not to be certain that there is one.

The application of the rule (the *upanaya*) is also inherently inductive, since the rule itself would only apply if there is a genuine instance of what the rule refers to. We do not establish this by pure logic but by observation and judgement. When we say, 'This hill is likewise smoky,' we could be wrong: we might be seeing steam or the synthetic output of a 'smoke' machine. So what might appear to be unnecessarily unwieldy in the five-membered syllogism could in fact reflect its strength in bringing together two features of argument – generalisations from observation and strict deduction – into one structure, when Western logic keeps them apart.

Where Indian and Western logic differ, however, is in how they fit into the wider philosophical system. For all its emphasis on logic, alongside inference (*anumāna*) and analogical reasoning (*upamāna*), Nyāya also accepts perception (*pratyakṣa*) and testimony (*śabda*) as legitimate *pramāṇas* (sources of knowledge). Hence, 'The *Veda* is reliable like the spell and the medical sciences, because of the reliability of their authors. [. . .] The sages themselves were reliable, because they had an intuitive perception of truths.'[20] This is why

Nyāya complains that a discussion with a Buddhist was 'considerably lengthened', not because he was reasoning badly, but because he 'does not admit the authority of scripture and holds that there are no eternal things, etc.'[21]

The antagonistic mention of a Buddhist here is probably not incidental. Classical Indian philosophy began with the largely mythical, religious teaching of the *Vedas*, in which logical argument was largely absent. During the Sūtra period and through the scholastic period, the tradition faced more challenges, particularly from Buddhism, which put greater emphasis on reason and argument. Nāgārjuna, for instance, often used logic, usually to show the inconsistency of positions. One example is an argument that there can be no ultimate proof that a source of knowledge is reliable because you would then have to prove that the method of proof itself was reliable and so on, ad infinitum. 'If by other sources of knowledge there would be the proof of a source – that would be an infinite regress.'[22] The mainstream then had to fight back, defending traditional doctrines with reason.

Because Nyāya maintains the authority of scripture, logic is often used as a kind of apologetics, as a tool to justify the *Vedas* rather than to question them. Take how the *Nyāya Sūtra* replies to the objection that the *Veda* 'is unreliable, as it involves the faults of untruth, contradiction, and tautology'. For instance, the *Veda* affirms that when the appropriate sacrifice for the sake of a son is performed, a son will be produced. But it is often observed that a son is not produced, even though the sacrifice has been performed. This would seem to be pretty conclusive proof that the sacrifices don't work and so the *Veda* is flawed. Not, however, if you start from the assumption that the *Veda* cannot be flawed. If you do that, it follows logically that 'the so-called untruth in the *Veda* comes from some defect in the act, operator, or materials of sacrifice'. By this logic, if 'a son is sure to be produced as a result of performing the sacrifice' but a son is not produced, it can only follow that the sacrifice was not performed correctly, however much it seems that it was performed properly. By such argument, the *Nyāya Sūtra* can safely conclude, 'Therefore there is no untruth in the *Veda*.'[23]

From the point of view of Western philosophy, this willingness to put logic in the service of revealed truth is a weakness. But as we have seen, the assumption that philosophy should be free of any theological commitment is peculiar to the modern West. As Ram-Prasad puts it, in Western philosophy, 'Logic is supposed to be about structures of reasons just as they are, regardless of who has them; it is potentially independent of human thinking.' This is a lofty aspiration but not necessarily a realistic one. It could also be thought of as a hubristic illusion of human beings who believe they can use a logic which transcends the human mind. In contrast, in the Indian tradition, logic is very much a tool of human beings, 'to do with the actual thoughts and cognitions people have'. It 'uses logic primarily to attain knowledge of the world, through debate and persuasion'.[24]

The difference in emphasis is perhaps most stark when we consider what it means to be human. For Aristotle and most of his contemporaries and successors, human beings are distinguished by their rationality. In Indian thought, we are differentiated by our capacity for *dharma*, the ability to distinguish right or wrong and live accordingly. An oft-quoted verse is 'Hunger, sleep, fear, sex are common to all animals, human and subhuman. It is the additional attribute of *dharma* that differentiates man from the beast. Devoid of *dharma*, man is like a beast.'[25]

Rationality lies at the heart of the West's conception of humanity. People are rational, autonomous individuals, and 'rational' is what holds the three characteristics together. It is because we each have the capacity and obligation to think for ourselves that we can be conceived of as individuals and have the freedom to direct our own lives. This underpins many Western values and practices: individual responsibility before the law; the belief in self-development, even if it takes you away from your family and community; confidence that Western values are universal values, because they are grounded in reason; the fetishisation of choice, giving individuals as much opportunity to exercise their powers of reason as possible.

The Western self-image is coming under threat. Many psychologists have argued that we are not usually as rational in our behaviour as we think we are. Far from being rational and autonomous, we are intuitive, emotional and heavily influenced by others and our environment. The best way to defend the importance of rationality is not to deny these findings but to look again at what it means to be rational. Comparative philosophy can help the West see that its conception of reason leans more heavily on logic than it needs to. It should hardly come as a surprise when psychologists point out that we do not behave like logical computers. But if we assume reason and logic are more or less synonymous, then that truism becomes a threat to our rationality. If reason uses a broader toolkit of cognitive tools, perhaps including insight and subtle perception, we might find that we are essentially rational after all.

SECULAR REASON

The Panthéon in Paris is often seen as a symbol of the rise of reason, and the fall of faith, in the West. Built by the great architect Soufflot as a Christian basilica, barely a year after its completion in 1791 it was transformed by French revolutionaries into a monument to the great men and women of France. The remains of the arch anti-cleric Voltaire were transferred there later that year, followed by those of numerous others, including Jean-Jacques Rousseau in 1794. The church was overthrown, usurped by a secular temple.

Even the most cursory look at the facts, however, belies this simple story of religion versus reason. Most of the Enlightenment thinkers whose ideas helped lead to the founding of the Panthéon, some of whom were interred there, were not atheists but panthe-ists, believing in a creator God who played no part in running the world. Nor were the religious elements of the building ever com-pletely removed. A cross still sits at the top of its dome, the interior of which depicts the apotheosis of Sainte Geneviève, to whom the original church was dedicated. Many more images of her and other religious frescoes cover several of its walls and the building has twice reverted to a church, its secular status only officially confirmed in 1885, when it was the scene of Victor Hugo's funeral.

The true significance of the Panthéon is embodied in the scientific demonstration that takes place sixty-seven metres under its dome. In 1851, the physicist Léon Foucault suspended a weight from a wire attached to the underside of the dome. On the floor beneath it was a circle divided like a sundial into the hours of the day, each number 11.3 degrees apart. The pendulum is released to start swinging from the position of whatever the time is. Over the day, the pendulum's swing appears to move along the dial, as though its swing is gradually shifting clockwise. In fact, the pendulum does not change the angle of its swing at all. It is the earth beneath it which is moving. The earth's rotation, usually imperceptible, is made visible.

Foucault's pendulum captures the spirit of the Enlightenment and the wider philosophical culture from which it emerged, characterised by a secularity which does not require a rejection of all religion. Rather, it requires an endorsement of the power of unaided human intellect. In this temple humanity, not God, comes first. Whereas in the Catholic Church of Saint-Germain-des-Prés, a mile down the road, images of God and Jesus are everywhere while the tomb of Descartes is difficult even to find, here the memorials to great mortals take pride of place. God may or may not be dead, but for the project of acquiring knowledge he is redundant. The human mind works without supernatural assistance to deliver an understanding of the world and ourselves.

I call this a belief in the power of *secular reason*. It is what almost all schools of modern Western philosophy endorse, implicitly or explicitly, and it unites them more profoundly than their differences divide them. Secular reason is built on the foundation stone of ancient Greek philosophy, which developed logic as an independent discipline, not dependent on insight, scripture or authority. In this world view, the natural world is scrutable and its operations can be described by laws which require no assumption of divine agency.

Belief in the power of secular reason lies behind the conviction that there is no human mystery that science should not try to penetrate. Between 1990 and 2003 the Human Genome Project mapped our complete DNA. Both the Human Brain Project and the Human Connectome Project seek to provide a complete map of the brain, unlocking the mechanisms behind all that we think, experience and feel. Physics searches for a complete 'theory of everything', which physicist Stephen Hawking said would let us 'know the mind of God'.[1] In the twenty-first century, we are creating new humans from three parents, genetically modifying organisms, looking at how to create life from inert matter, trying to freeze the dead to bring them back to life in the future, and starting to grow meat in a laboratory.

There is nothing natural about any of this. In many times and places, strict limits were put on what humans should study. The sacred was protected. Medical learning in the Islamic world, once the most advanced on the planet, was overtaken in part because of the prohibition on dissecting corpses. Astronomy was also prohibited. In Istanbul in 1580, the only remaining observatory in the Islamic world was razed because it was believed that the plague that had ravaged the city had been sent by God in response to astronomy's profanity.[2] Christendom was not much better. Galileo Galilei was allowed to study the stars, but after reporting back that the sun was at the centre of the universe, he was sentenced to indefinite imprisonment by the Roman Catholic Inquisition in 1633. Even today, virtually anything that pushes the boundaries of scientific understanding generates fears and doubts.

Secular reason is one reason why the West overcame these restrictions to lead the world in science for so many centuries. Modern science is the child of the West, born in 1620, when Francis Bacon set out its basic principles in his seminal *Novum*

Organum. Other societies also had the material resources to sustain scientific inquiry, so national wealth alone cannot explain the West's advances. Indeed, for centuries large parts of China were richer than the West. The difference has to be explained at least in part because of the nature of the Western mind, which can only be properly understood in the light of Western philosophy.

The validity of secular reason is widely assumed in the West, whether people have religious beliefs or not. The most religiously devout scientist trusts evidence and experiment and never seeks a scientific breakthrough through divine revelation. Standards of proof and probability are public and assessable by all. All human minds are capable of comprehending reality. There is no place for *ṛṣis* in secular reason. Nor is there any stress on the boundaries as to what the human mind can comprehend, as has been the case in much of the East. Although Chinese thought is largely secular, for example, it generally confines itself to questions of living and is agnostic about the nature of ultimate reality. Western secular reason has as its objective nothing less than a full description of the cosmos and how it works. To grant unaided human reason such a powerful role is historically the exception rather than the norm.

Secular reason was born in ancient Greece but many centuries passed before it became the default mindset of the West. Until the late Middle Ages, Christianity was the centre of gravity for all learning. Scholarship was largely biblical and confined to monasteries and all philosophy had to conform to the Church's teachings at the risk of excommunication or even death. Gradually, however, through the Renaissance and especially into the seventeenth–eighteenth-century Enlightenment, philosophy became more autonomous from theology. Science – then called natural philosophy – gave precedence to experiment and observation over scripture and creed. This emerging form of secular reason was not inherently opposed to religion, merely independent of it. Many of the philosophers of this era were religious and believed that secular reason would and could only confirm the teachings of the Church. The Bible was read as theology, not as science or even always as history.

During its long gestation, secular reason had two wings. One was empirical, examining the world itself and basing conclusions on careful observation. Empiricists are broadly scientific in their reasoning. The other wing was rationalist, looking at what reason alone demands and assuming that the world must conform to it. Rationalists are caricatured as 'armchair thinkers', but the implication that they have no need to go out and study how the world actually works is accurate enough.

It is tempting to overstate this distinction as absolute, dividing Western philosophers into empiricists (Aristotle, Locke, Berkeley, Hume) and rationalists (Plato, Descartes, Spinoza, Leibniz), and this is indeed how countless textbooks carve up the canon. There is some sense in this. In particular, there does seem to be a fundamental difference between those who believe it is possible to discover truths about the way the world is by reason alone, without reference to experience, and those who believe that pure reason can only tell us about abstract mathematics and the relations between concepts, and that all knowledge of the real world must be rooted in experience. The technical names for these two types of knowledge express this difference neatly: knowledge can be gained either prior to experience (a priori) or post-experience (a posteriori).

Take cause and effect. The rationalist Spinoza believed that we could know that every event is the effect of some cause a priori. The third axiom in his *Ethics* is: 'From a given determinate there necessarily follows an effect; on the other hand, if there be no determinate cause it is impossible that an effect should follow.' From such self-evident truths he quickly reached substantive conclusions about the fundamental nature of the universe, so that by the eighth proposition he claimed to have proved the remarkable

HOW THE WORLD THINKS

assertion: 'Every substance is necessarily infinite.'[3] Similarly, Descartes thought it 'manifest by the natural light that there must be at least as much reality in the efficient and total cause as in the effect of that cause. For where, I ask, could the effect get its reality from, if not from the cause?'[4] This sounds like common sense, but it is in fact a bold claim to know something about the fundamental laws of the physical universe by armchair reasoning alone.

Empiricists are not persuaded that such arguments can work. To use David Hume's terminology, Spinoza and Descartes are merely analysing the 'relations of ideas'. The concept of cause implies an effect, but that doesn't tell us anything about what we think of as causes and effects in the real world. For all we know, some things that happen just happen without any cause whatsoever, or from causes that have random effects. So a priori reason cannot deliver us knowledge of the real world. For that we need a posteriori knowledge based on experience.

That too has its limitations. Hume argued that we can't even observe causation in action: 'When we look about us towards external objects, and consider the operation of causes, we are never able, in a single instance, to discover any power or necessary connexion; any quality, which binds the effect to the cause, and renders the one an infallible consequence of the other.'[5] All we can observe is one thing after another, not the causal connections between them.

The distinction between rationalist and empiricist approaches is real and important. However, it would be misleading to think that the division is clear-cut. So-called rationalists make use of a lot of the data of experience and so-called empiricists appeal to principles of logic and argument that are established by reason not observation. It is better to think of an empiricist–rationalist spectrum, with different philosophers giving more weight to observation and reason respectively.

Taking a long view of the history of Western philosophy, empiricism has been in slow but uneven ascendency and rationalism in similar decline. In the early days of Western philosophy, empirical methods didn't extend beyond everyday observations. The earliest forms of science were little more than armchair speculation, with Thales proposing that everything was made of water and Democritus suggesting that everything was made up of discrete atoms. Much later many philosophers continued to see an important role for a priori reasoning even as they embraced empirical methods. Likewise, some of the most rationalist philosophers spent a lot of time on empirical inquiry. Descartes, for example, was a keen experimenter who dissected carcasses, Leibniz wrote on chemistry, medicine, botany, geology and technology, while Spinoza was not only a lens grinder but a pioneer in experimental hydrodynamics and metallurgy.

Nonetheless, over time the empirical branch of secular reason, which began with Aristotle observing the plants and animals of a lagoon on the island of Lesbos, gradually became more dominant. By the twentieth century, secular reason had established itself as common sense and science took pride of place at its heart. Consider, for example, the rousing speech that concludes Charlie Chaplin's masterpiece *The Great Dictator* (1940). Chaplin's character, a Jewish barber, finds himself mistaken for the Hitleresque dictator Adenoid Hynkel (also played by Chaplin) and required to give a speech. In it, he attacks the 'greed' which 'has poisoned men's souls' and 'goose-stepped us into misery'. In many ways, his speech is an attack on the ills of modernity. 'We have developed speed, but we have shut ourselves in,' he says. 'Machinery that gives abundance has left us in want. [...] More than machinery we need humanity.' Yet Chaplin ends by reasserting his faith in the bedrocks of the secular reason on which modernity was built. 'Let us fight for a world of reason,' he pleads, 'a world where science and progress will lead to all men's happiness.'

This sentence contains all three elements that make modern secular reason distinctive: belief in science, reason and the progress which will inevitably result if we follow both. 'Science and reason' are so often uttered in the same breath that it is tempting to think either that they always go together or that they simply mean the same thing. In fact, for large parts of history reason has been anything but scientific. Few in the West today, however, would accept as truth anything established on the basis of any combination of insight, logic, tradition, authority or revelation. We also demand facts, based on observation and experiment, empirical evidence that can tested.

Of course, other traditions have not been blind to the benefits of observation. Around the same time as Aristotle, Gautama in India was arguing in the *Nyāya Sūtra* that knowledge must be based on observation and that we should not waste time on abstractions such as mathematical logic. His logic combines inductive and deductive methods: logic without evidence is empty. However, his empiricism was highly qualified by his acceptance of the *śabda* of the authors of the *Vedas* as a valid *pramāṇa*.

In China, the fourth-century-BCE philosopher Mozi was also distinguished by his advocacy of a kind of empiricism, based on 'the gauges of precedent, evidence, and application'. One looks 'up for precedent among the affairs and actions of the ancient sage-kings, [. . .] down to examine evidence of what the people have heard and seen' and then 'implements it as state policy and sees whether or not it produces benefit for the state, families and people'. Although the Mohists had a strong influence on the development of Chinese thought, their ideas have never become dominant.

For all their strong empirical leanings, Aristotle, Gautama and Mozi did not share the modern idea that nature should and could be investigated for its own sake, not only to help us live better.[6] This 'autonomy of reason' is arguably the most distinctive feature of secular reason. Philosophy and science have broken free not only of religion and culture, but of everything. Rational inquiry must not be hindered by anything other than the demands of self-preservation.

The idea that understanding was good for its own sake emerged in the West as part of the growth of science, which was still often known as natural philosophy until the late nineteenth century. Henri Poincaré, for example, advocated 'science for its own sake', saying, 'Science has wonderful applications; but the science which would have in view only applications would no longer be science – it would be only the kitchen. There is no science but disinterested science.' He argued that all the hard work of scientists was 'for seeing's sake; or at the very least that others may one day see'. In this Poincaré was self-consciously evoking a tradition in Western thought of knowledge for knowledge's sake, which he perhaps incorrectly thought was fully formed in antiquity. 'The spirit which should animate the man of science is that which breathed of old on Greece and brought there to birth poets and thinkers.'[7]

Belief in the autonomy of science entails that the scientist belongs in the laboratory and it is for society to decide how to best use its findings. 'Science has nothing to be ashamed of even in the ruins of Nagasaki,' said the scientist and broadcaster Jacob Bronowski. 'The shame is theirs who appeal to other values than the human imaginative values which science has evolved. The shame is ours if we do not make science part of our world.'

For some, the strength of science is that it is solely concerned with truth, remaining free of ethics and ideology. For others, this is its problem. The contemporary Islamic philosopher Seyyed Hossein Nasr argues that modern science, premised on a 'secularised view of the cosmos', not interested in whether its fruits are used for good or ill, is an aberration. Far from being a glory of civilisation, it is decadent and amoral, responsible for catastrophic climate change, pollution and weapons of mass destruction. 'Finally, one can at last ask not only why Islam and China, with their long and rich scientific traditions, did not produce a Descartes or Galileo,' he writes, 'but rather why Europe did.'[8]

Nasr is a strong critic of the West, but many within the tradition have also had misgivings about the moral neutrality of science. 'Science is a magnificent force, but it is not a teacher of morals,' said the lawyer William Jennings Bryan at the Scopes Monkey Trial in 1925. Most scientists would agree and see this as no problem. For Bryan, this was a failing. Arguing against teaching the theory of evolution, he said that science

> can perfect machinery, but it adds no moral restraints to protect society from the misuse of the machine. It can also build gigantic intellectual ships, but it constructs no moral rudders for the control of storm-tossed human vessels. It not only fails to supply the spiritual element needed but some of its unproven hypotheses rob the ship of its compass and thus endangers its cargo.[9]

Even Winston Churchill said, 'It is arguable whether the human race have been gainers by the march of science beyond the steam engine.' Pondering 'the consequences of entrusting a human race so little different from their predecessors of the so-called barbarous ages such awful agencies as the atomic bomb', he pleaded, 'Give me the horse.'[10]

The physicist Fritjof Capra resisted the idea that science and ethics must be kept separate. 'Scientists,' he said, 'are responsible for their research, not only intellectually but also morally.' Discoveries in his own field 'may lead us – to put it in extreme terms – to the Buddha or to the Bomb, and it is up to each of us to decide which path to take'.[11] Similarly, the science fiction writer Arthur C. Clarke saw the need for a moral compass in science. 'As our own species is in the process of proving, one cannot have superior science and inferior morals,' he wrote. 'The combination is unstable and self-destroying.'[12]

The debate about the right relationship between science and ethics reveals a tension in secular reason. On the one hand, the autonomy of reason implies that we should go wherever our thought takes us, without concern for the practical uses. On the other, it assumes a link between science, reason and progress. But how can we be sure that secular reason will benefit us if it is ethically neutral? Why assume 'science for science's sake' will work for humanity's sake?

The assumption that autonomous reason will inevitably lead to progress also fosters a dangerous complacency among academics, who often baulk if asked to say how their work benefits wider society. The logic of secular reason would answer that if learning has no practical effect, it doesn't matter because inquiry is good for its own sake. If it does have an effect, it is bound to be good because learning leads to progress. But it surely makes sense to question whether the right people are studying the right things in the right way, and we cannot answer this unless we have some idea of what 'right' is. Is it right, for example, if an academic community breeds a kind of consensus that stifles dissenting voices? Excessive belief in the autonomy of secular reason stops us asking these questions, raising the spectre of academic 'censorship'.

Secular reason has been a powerful tool for scientific and intellectual development. But complacency about its benefits needs to be challenged, perhaps by traditions that have maintained that philosophy and science exist only to serve human flourishing. If our ultimate goal is human good, the autonomy of reason cannot be absolute. Who would want to build and stock the finest libraries in the world without caring if they stand amidst desolate streets?

PRAGMATISM

The USA is a curious outlier when it comes to religious belief. The pattern in the rest of the developed world is that as economies develop and education becomes more widespread religious belief declines. Although there is some evidence that this is belatedly beginning to happen in America, religious belief has been unusually resilient there. One recent survey showed that 56 per cent of Americans describe themselves as religious compared to 27 per cent in the UK, 22 per cent in Sweden and 37 per cent in Spain. Only 7 per cent are convinced atheists, compared to 21 per cent in France, 14 per cent in Germany and 11 per cent in the UK.[1]

There are many theories as to why this is so. One of the most credible is that religious belief correlates less with average levels of wealth than with economic security. America is the world's richest country but it lacks a European welfare state. Many people feel economically vulnerable, one pay cheque away from poverty.

It would be foolish to ignore such evidence, but it would be equally simplistic to ignore the values and beliefs that have shaped the American mind. If we want to know why Americans tend to be more religious, we might learn something from their home-grown philosophical tradition: pragmatism.

Pragmatism's philosophical lineage extends back to British empiricism. The nineteenth-century philosopher and psychologist William James explicitly linked pragmatism to 'the great English way of investigating a conception' which is 'to ask yourself right off, "What is it *known as*? In what facts does it result?"'[2]

James's definition echoes those given by the two other great founders of pragmatism, John Dewey and Charles Sanders Peirce. Peirce defined the central principle of pragmatism as follows: 'Consider what effects, that might conceivably have practical bearings, we conceive of our conception to have. Then our conception of these effects is the whole of our conception of the object.'[3] Similarly, Dewey wrote that 'knowledge is always a matter of the use that is made of experienced natural events'[4] and that 'knowing is a way of employing empirical occurrences with respect to increasing power to direct the consequences which flow from things'.[5]

Both the truth and the meaning of beliefs are to be understood in terms of not abstract ideas or the inner workings of the mind but the practical difference they make. 'Grant an idea or belief to be true,' says James, and pragmatism asks, 'what concrete difference will its being true make in anyone's actual life? How will the truth be realized? What experiences will be different from those which would obtain if the belief were false? What, in short, is the truth's cash-value in experiential terms?'[6]

Pragmatism takes abstractions such as truth and meaning and links them to human action. 'The essence of belief is the establishment of a habit,' wrote Peirce, 'and different beliefs are distinguished by the different modes of action to which they give rise [...] and that whatever there is connected with a thought, but irrelevant to its purpose, is an accretion to it, but no part of it. [...] What a thing means is simply what habits it involves.'[7]

James put it even more clearly: 'Beliefs, in short, are really rules for action; and the whole function of thinking is but one step in the production of habits of action. If there were any part of a thought that made no difference in the thought's practical consequences, then that part would be no proper element of the thought's significance.'[8]

One consequence of adopting the pragmatist viewpoint is that many philosophical problems are not so much *solved* as *dissolved*. 'Intellectual progress usually occurs through sheer abandonment of questions together with both of the alternatives they assume – an abandonment that results from their decreasing vitality and a change of urgent interest,' wrote Dewey. 'We do not solve them [philosophical problems]: we get over them.'[9] James made much the same point more figuratively: 'The true line of philosophic progress lies, in short, it seems to me, not so much *through* Kant as *round* him to the point where we now stand.'[10] Once you have understood the practical implications of any belief, there is nothing else left to understand. Old philosophical questions are seen to be artefacts of muddle-headed ways of thinking and are simply abandoned, as redundant as asking what phlogiston is made of or how many leeches are needed to cure dropsy.

Hence many traditional metaphysical problems about the fundamental nature of time, being or mind just disappear. They are shown to be pseudo-problems that arose only because philosophers got lost in dust clouds of confusion thrown up by concepts that they had erroneously detached from the world of lived experience. The search for ultimate causes and explanations is a futile one. Peirce, for example, wrote, 'In a recent admired work on Analytic Mechanics it is stated that we understand precisely the effect of force, but what force is we do not understand! This is simply a self-contradiction.'[11]

As Dewey wrote, 'Philosophy recovers itself when it ceases to be a device for dealing with the problems of philosophers and becomes a method, cultivated by philosophers, for dealing with the problems of men.'[12] There is perhaps no clearer example of the former than radical scepticism, doubting that the external world even exists. This can be played as a philosophical game but only at the price of detaching words like 'world' and 'existence' from their practical usage. 'We cannot begin with complete doubt. We must begin with the prejudices which we actually have when we enter upon the study of philosophy,' wrote Peirce. 'Let us not pretend to doubt in philosophy what we do not doubt in our hearts.'[13]

Pragmatists were bullish about their capacity to transform philosophy but realistic about the difficulty of the task: 'Old ideas give way slowly; for they are more than abstract logical forms and categories.'[14] Dewey knew that telling philosophers that most of what they have worked on all their lives is a waste of time and space was hardly the way to win friends and influence people.

Pragmatism's non-metaphysical bent perhaps explains why it has had some impact in China and Japan. Chinese admirers included the late nineteenth–early twentieth-century reformist monarchist K'ang and Sun Yat-Sen, the first president of the Republic of China in 1912, whose philosophy, like that of the pragmatists, emphasised action. Traditional Chinese philosophy was generally focused on the practical issues of living and many felt that Buddhism had exerted a bad influence by concentrating too much on spiritual matters. Hence Hu Shih, who studied under Dewey, returned to his own country critical of 'eastern spirituality'. 'What spirituality is there in the old beggar woman who dies while still mumbling the name of Buddha?' he wrote in the 1920s.

In Japan, Nishida was influenced by reading James's *Varieties of Religious Experience*, which encouraged him to follow an empirical method that took as data the phenomenology of experience, in accordance with Zen tradition. In Nishida's philosophy, the pragmatic emphasis on experience was linked with the Japanese emphasis on the limits of language. 'Meanings and judgments are an abstracted part of the original experience,' he writes, 'and compared with the actual experience they are meager in content.'[15]

The problem many critics have with pragmatism is that it appears to be *too* pragmatic. That is to say, it gives up the traditional conception of absolute truth and replaces it with a 'whatever works' model instead. The negative move is certainly there. Dewey rejects the idea that philosophical knowing involves 'an alleged peculiarly intimate concern with supreme, ultimate, true reality', an assumption he took to be central to the mainstream Western tradition. Such is its ubiquity that even a thinker as radical as Dewey's contemporary Henri Bergson 'does not find it in his heart to abandon the [. . .] search for the truly Real'.[16]

The closest we get to the 'absolute', says James, using scare-quotes, is 'that ideal vanishing-point towards which we imagine that all our temporary truths will some day converge'. He took this idea of truth as convergence from Peirce, who wrote, 'The opinion which is fated to be ultimately agreed to by all who investigate, is what we mean by the truth, and the object represented in this opinion is real.'[17] The arbiter of truth is therefore the community, not the individual. 'To make single individuals absolute judges of truth is most pernicious,' said Peirce.[18] The twentieth-century pragmatist Richard Rorty reiterated this, writing, 'For pragmatists, the desire for objectivity is not the desire to escape the limitations of one's community, but simply the desire for as much intersubjective agreement as possible, the desire to extend the reference of "us" as far as we can.'[19]

Given that most convergence on truth is in a hypothetical future, in practice this means what we now call truth is somewhat provisional and relative. 'We have to live to-day by what truth we can get to-day, and be ready tomorrow to call it falsehood,' wrote Peirce.[20] The worry is that if we take this seriously we are left with a dangerous relativism in which anyone can claim as true whatever they happen to find useful. Truth becomes a matter of expediency and it is then impossible to dispute the truth claims of others, no matter how wild. For the pragmatist, says Rorty, '"knowledge" is, like "truth", simply a compliment paid to the beliefs that we think so well justified that, for the moment, further justification is not needed'.[21]

However, pragmatism, properly understood, is not as permissive as it might at first seem. It shares with empiricism an insistence on careful examination of the evidence and deference to what that evidence requires of us. 'Really valuable ideas can only be had at the price of close attention,' wrote Peirce. 'But I know that in the matter of ideas the public prefer the cheap and nasty.'[22]

Rorty argues that pragmatism does not endorse the kind of relativism which says that what is true is simply what is true for us: 'The pragmatist does not have a theory of truth, much less a relativistic one.' Pragmatism for Rorty is driven by the value of solidarity, which means that 'the value of cooperative human inquiry has only an ethical base, not an epistemological or metaphysical one'.[23] The function of belief is to bind us together, to make collective endeavour possible. It simply doesn't matter whether those beliefs correspond to some absolute reality.

The misconception that pragmatism reduces to 'whatever works for you' comes from a panicked reading of statements like James's 'You can say of it then either that "it is useful because it is true" or that "it is true because it is useful". Both these phrases mean exactly the same thing, [. . .]' This can sound so permissive that readers fail to pay attention to how the sentence is completed after that final comma: 'namely that here is an idea that gets fulfilled and can be verified'.[24] The pragmatic conception of 'useful' is not what is merely locally expedient, but what most fully integrates with our wider understanding and the evidence. James's qualification is frequently missed. As Dewey put it, 'James's statement that general conceptions must "cash in" has been taken (especially by European critics) to mean that the end and measure of intelligence lies in the narrow and coarse utilities which it produces.'[25] What James in fact maintains is that 'true ideas are those that we can assimilate, validate, corroborate and verify. False ideas are those that we cannot.'[26] For example, we can say that his critics characterise his view falsely because their version of what he said simply cannot be validated, corroborated and verified by looking closely at what he actually wrote.

Given pragmatism's British empiricist roots, we might ask why it was that it emerged as a distinctively American movement. It does not seem fanciful to suggest that full-blown philosophical pragmatism reflects a more general cultural pragmatism. Peirce, Dewey and James seem to be in tune with their compatriots in several respects. The British are noted for their 'common sense' and distrust of intellectualisation, but in the USA this seems to go further. Americans, with their frequent paeans to the common man, appear to have more faith in ordinary people than in experts and elites. After all, populist discontent with elites is a phenomenon across the Western world, but only America gave a vulgar property developer the presidency.

Pragmatism also seems to dovetail with America's historical sense of certainty, which at its most extreme takes the form of a belief in its 'manifest destiny' as leader of the free world. This claim might sound odd given pragmatism's lack of interest in absolute truth. But it is precisely by eliminating the obligation to provide absolute justification that conviction can be gained. Hence Dewey's claims about philosophical certainty seems to apply equally to certainty in society: 'After [agreement] is reached, the question of certainty becomes an idle one, because there is no one left who doubts it.'[27]

If pragmatism has any relevance to the broader culture it cannot be because its principles are explicitly endorsed. Most people want their beliefs to be true and think that they are. However, if we look at what people do rather than what they might say when asked to justify their beliefs, we can detect a strong pragmatist character to the American mind. We should remember, as Carlin Romano says, that the enduring impact of pragmatist philosophers on the American people 'rests predominately in the headlines they communicate to us, not the footnotes'.[28] This is perhaps most evident when it comes to religion. 'What keeps religion going is something else than abstract definitions and systems of logically concatenated adjectives, and something different from faculties of theology and their professors,' claimed James. 'All these things are after-effects, secondary accretions upon a mass of concrete religious experiences, connecting themselves with feeling and conduct that renew themselves in *saecula saeculorum* in the lives of humble private men.'[29] In other words, people trust their own sense of the divine more than any theological or scientific arguments. Given that outside big cities most communities are religious, these feelings are dignified by the pragmatic justification of convergence.

What's more, having a religious belief appears to work. It has a cash-value in terms of giving people meaning, purpose, values and a sense of belonging. 'Religion says essentially two things,' wrote James. 'First, she says that the best things are the more eternal things, the overlapping things, the things in the universe that throw the last stone, so to speak, and say the final word.' This is 'an affirmation which obviously cannot yet be verified scientifically at all', but this does not matter because 'the second affirmation of religion is that we are better off even now if we believe her first affirmation to be true'.[30] In other words, religion is true because it is useful, and since that is the same as saying it is useful because it is true, it is true, period.

I am not suggesting that a rigorous application of pragmatist philosophy justifies the everyday religious belief of millions of Americans. Dewey argued that traditional religion was being pushed out by our increasingly scientific outlook, while neither Peirce nor James defended Christian fundamentalism. The point is simply that a more broadly pragmatist outlook can help explain the persistence of religious belief.

Even harder for many academic pragmatists to swallow is the fact that a lot of the most notorious utterances in politics over recent years are too close to pragmatism for the connection to be ignored. Take, for example, the then unnamed aide to President George W. Bush, later identified as Karl Rove, who in 2004 told Ron Suskind that journalists like him belonged to 'the reality-based community' where people 'believe that solutions emerge from your judicious study of discernible reality'. That sounds like common sense, but 'That's not the way the world really works anymore. We're an empire now, and when we act, we create our own reality. And while you're studying that reality – judiciously, as you will – we'll act again, creating other new realities, which you can study too, and that's how things will sort out.'

For many this was outrageous, but pragmatism does not need to be distorted very much to get to beliefs like this. Rorty argued that we should 'employ images of making rather than finding', rejecting the idea that we simply study 'discernible reality', and suggested that we create reality with our concepts.[31] If there is no absolute reality, only truths we converge on, then why not direct that convergence to the truths we want to believe? Advocates of pragmatism will see this as a gross distortion of their philosophy, but this misses the point, which is that there is something in the American psyche that if considered carefully and intellectually gives rise to philosophical pragmatism, but if left to express itself more loosely gives rise to something much less rigorous and opportunistic. Folk pragmatism is not the abuse of academic pragmatism, rather academic pragmatism is a refinement of folk pragmatism.

This folk pragmatism has in many ways served America well. Its 'can do' attitude is the clearest expression of a mindset that is unconcerned with intellectual niceties and focused on solutions. More dangerously, it can lead people to take less interest in

'discernible facts' than they should. The most egregious manifestation of the dark side of folk pragmatism is surely President Trump.
Take just two of innumerable examples. His first press secretary,
Sean Spicer, said, contrary to all objective facts, that Trump had
'the largest audience to witness an inauguration, period', while
Trump himself tweeted, 'Any negative polls are fake news.' Many
around the world and in the USA were flabbergasted at these
outrageous refusals to accept reality. Why were so many Trump
supporters not equally disgusted? Part of the explanation must be
a deep-seated small-p pragmatism in America that places greater
value on efficacy and solidarity than on more objective measures
of truth. The solution is not to get Americans to think less like
Americans, but to get them to appreciate better the virtues of their
indigenous pragmatic philosophers.

TRADITION

We find it natural to talk about different philosophical traditions. Yet there is something about that phrase that might seem odd: philosophies have histories but surely they need to be justified ahistorically? You can appeal to the insight of sages, the power of logic, the evidence of experience, but never to the mere fact that a belief belongs to a tradition. Yet, in practice, tradition exerts a strong influence on all cultures, including philosophical ones. Nowhere is this more evident than in China. A visit to the Shanghai Museum, the country's pre-eminent collection of ancient art, brings home just how old this civilisation is. There I found myself admiring a remarkably ornate bronze *fanglei* (a wine vessel) and saw that it was made in the early Zhou period, from the eleventh century BCE. The Zhou dynasty ruled a large area of what is modern China, a culture so developed that written Chinese was already close to its modern form. Northern Europe, in contrast, was in its pre-literate tribal Iron Age.

I was impressed, and soon discovered the collection delved back in time yet further. I came across an equally remarkable bronze pig-shaped *zun* (another kind of wine vessel) from the late Shang dynasty (thirteenth–eleventh century BCE), another highly developed culture with a written script. The oldest object I saw was a *yue* (a kind of axe weapon), inlaid with a coloured tile pattern, from the Xia dynasty (eighteenth–sixteenth century BCE).

It is difficult to overestimate the depth and force of China's sense of its own long history. In Athens, I saw artefacts as old as those in Shanghai, but the Greeks are the exception in a Europe where most nations are merely hundreds of years old and where few feel any connection with the ancient past. In Confucius's hometown of Qufu, in contrast, not only are a great many people direct descendants of the philosopher, but they know exactly how close that relationship is. A hotel chambermaid, for example, told me she was seventy-fourth generation Kong, the family name of Confucius. My guide, who used the English name Frank, was seventy-fifth generation. The past is vividly present to the Chinese in a way that is astonishing to foreigners. Although it is probably not true that the Chinese premier Zhou Enlai told Richard Nixon in 1972 that it was 'too early to say' what the impact of the 1789 French Revolution was, the story stuck because it accurately reflected something about China's long view of history.

The power of tradition is as potent in philosophy as elsewhere. As Wen Haiming put it to me, 'For Chinese people the ancient philosophical classics are the foundation of Chinese thinking, thinking paradigms, the Chinese way of understanding the world, how we should behave. China has such a long, historical culture, a tradition of over 3,000 years. Everything we have today is not from nowhere, it is from a deep, very thoughtful tradition.'

Even the most ancient Chinese philosophers saw themselves as doing little more than recording the wisdom of their ancestors. 'The tendency in China, as in India,' says Charles Moore, 'is for later thinkers to consider themselves as mere commentators upon or followers of the major classical schools or of the great early think-ers.'[1] Confucius said on several occasions that all he was doing was passing on and protecting the principles of the great sage-kings of his own antiquity. He described himself as 'a transmitter, not a maker, believing in and loving the ancients'.[2]

However, this reverence for the past should not be mistaken for slavish, unthinking devotion to it. Chan Wing-Tsit stresses, 'I have not found a single case in which a philosopher asserted that reading the classics is the only or chief way of obtaining knowledge or that a thing is true simply because the classics say so. Knowledge is always one's own adventure.'[3] That's why, as in India, 'interpreters' of classical texts are often highly original and innovative.

The emphasis on tradition is not essentially conservative and anti-rational. As Chan explains, it is a logical consequence of accepting that 'truth is not understood as something revealed from above or as an abstract principle, however logically consistent, but as a discoverable and demonstrable principle of human affairs. In other words, the real test of truth is human history.'[4]

Traditions evolve but ways of thinking that have been embed-ded in a culture for centuries, even millennia, continue to shape the way we think around the world today. Kobayashi Yasuo is as aware as anyone of the impact of Westernisation in Japan but still believes that 'the mind, the sensitivity, doesn't change in one hundred years'.

This is as true in the West as it is in the East. Since the Enlightenment the West has stopped venerating tradition and has if anything turned against it. The apotheosis of this came during the French Revolution, when, as we have seen, there was an attack on tradition the likes of which the West has not seen before or after. Reverses in France and less successful attempts at reform elsewhere show that the old ways have endured more than many expected. Nonetheless, respect for tradition has never been restored to its pre-Enlightenment levels.

Perhaps influenced by Christian eschatology, the Western imagination is framed by ideas of progress towards a final goal. The West honours progress, innovation and novelty. As John C. H. Wu points out, 'The East generally puts the Golden Age at the beginning, the West at the end.'[5] This is in part why, to the Western mind, the philosophical traditions of China and India often seem primitive, stuck in their pasts. But it would be a mistake to dismiss them on these grounds. As we have already seen, tradition does not prevent innovation and can even enable it. 'Novelty is received not by dismissing old traditions but by coexisting with them,' writes Shimomura Toratarō, adding, 'Such a mentality may be hard to understand for the kind of critical, decisive thinking we see in the West.'[6]

The dismissal of a body of thought as 'mere tradition' is most overt when it comes to the philosophies transmitted orally in Africa, by first peoples and by nations such as the Māori who have no deep history of great thinkers writing canonical works. Historically, it was not even acknowledged that these cultures had philosophies worthy of the name. Only written languages, claimed Walter Ong, enabled the emergence of more analytic, logical discourses, which in turn enabled innovation and greater objectivity. In contrast, oral cultures have more concrete concepts and their transmission is more conservative. As Eric Havelock put it, 'Without modern literacy, which means Greek literacy, we would not have science, philosophy, written law or literature, nor the automobile or the airplane.'[7] When this view is prevalent, the belief systems of oral cultures are studied purely anthropologically as 'folk beliefs' akin to primitive religions, lacking sophistication or rigour.

It should by now be evident that to restrict philosophy only to that which falls under the purview of Western philosophy is hopelessly narrow. 'To deny the existence of African philosophy is also to reject the very idea of philosophy,' writes Mogobe B. Ramose.

'It is to foreclose in advance the doors of communication with what we do not know.'[8] However, it can be difficult to get over our preconceptions of what philosophy must look like. As Hirini Kaa put it, even to ask what Māori philosophy is 'would be trying to get the triangle and fit it into the square of European philosophy'.

In the case of African philosophy, some argue it requires an engagement with the continent's philosophical traditions and others insist that any African doing philosophy today is doing African philosophy. For Pieter Boele Van Hensbroek, this debate is silly. European philosophy isn't one thing, so why should African philosophy be any different?

African philosophy can come in many forms. One of them is ethnophilosophy, which analyses the way philosophy is embedded in a people's set of shared beliefs, values, categories and assumptions that are implicit in the language, practices and beliefs of African cultures. An interesting corollary is that ethnophilosophy assumes the 'philosopher' in such cultures is not an individual but the whole community, which reasons as a collective.[9] Another form is hermeneutic philosophy. As Joram Tarusarira explains, 'You investigate the language that is spoken by people in Africa and you distil philosophical ideas and concepts from the way people speak.' The key idea here is that philosophies are implicit in the way people talk and, with careful attention, these implicit ideas can be made explicit.

One danger with ethnophilosophy is that it usually in effect 'translates' indigenous ideas into the discourse of Western philosophy. This was explicitly recognised by early ethnophilosophers. Placide Tempels wrote, 'We do not claim, of course, that the Bantu are capable of formulating a philosophical treatise, complete with an adequate vocabulary. It is our job to proceed to such systematic development. It is we who will be able to tell them, in precise terms, what their inmost concept of being is.'[10]

Unsurprisingly, many objected to the apparently colonial nature of this enterprise. Paulin Houtondji argued that in ethnophilosophy 'The black man continues to be the very opposite of an interlocutor; he remains a topic, a voiceless face under private investigation, an object to be defined and not the subject of possible discourse'.[11] One consequence, says Tarusarira, is that 'even among African scholars themselves, people who have studied African philosophy have taken the categories from the Western tradition and started to work with them'. For instance, when looking at African philosophy of religion, they think about gods in a Christian or Greek sense and then look for these kinds of gods in Africa. There is also the now familiar problem that 'categories of the religious and secular wouldn't make much sense' in Africa.

Another objection to ethnophilosophy was raised by the Kenyan Henry Odera Oruka, who saw it as 'derived not from the critical but from the uncritical part of the African traditions', when 'philosophy proper is always found in the critical'. To locate that critical part one has to look for 'the expressed thoughts of wise men and women in any given community'. These reveal 'a way of thinking and explaining the world that fluctuates between popular wisdom (well-known communal maxims, aphorisms and general common-sense truths) and didactic wisdom, an expounded wisdom and a rational thought of some given individuals within a community'.[12] Oruka sought to capture such 'sage philosophy', as he called it, by taking tape recorders into villages and discoursing with those considered by the communities themselves to be wise. He did not uncritically document everything he heard as sage philosophy. Only those who were able to answer questions and objections rationally were deemed true sages, while those who simply reiterated ideas without being able to analyse them were classified as mere vessels of popular wisdom.

Whether we use the tools of sage philosophy or ethnophilosophy, those serious about African philosophy should see it in its own terms, not through the lens of Western categories and concepts.

One way to do this is to attend to how African languages 'structure reality differently, maybe better, for some questions', says Pieter Boele Van Hensbroek. He recalls the Ghanaian philosopher Kwasi Wiredu recommending that a good way to gain a new perspective on a philosophical problem is to translate it into your indigenous language, try to deal with it there in that language and then translate it back.

Western philosophers, who do not present themselves as carrying a torch for their ancestors, are in fact working within a tradition as much as thinkers elsewhere in the world. Anyone who stepped into a Western department of philosophy would be struck by just how much of what is taught there is historical. Undergraduates study the ancient Greeks, universally lauded as the founders of the discipline. Reproductions of Raphael's *School of Athens* decorate walls of many departments, while Socrates's line 'The unexamined life is not worth living' is still the most common marketing tool to recruit students. All across the West, no philosophical education is complete without study of Plato, Aristotle, Descartes and Kant, supplemented by a slightly different cast of pre-twentieth-century modern thinkers depending on whether they are seen as predecessors of contemporary, mainly anglophone 'analytic' philosophers or predominantly European 'continental' thinkers. That contemporary Western philosophy is less shaped by its traditions than philosophies elsewhere in the world is as deplorable an idea as it is laughable.

Indeed, it is striking that non-Western traditions are more open to Western philosophy than vice versa. While Indian philosophy has synthesised many Western influences (the Indian Philosophical Congress programme was peppered with references to the likes of William James, Wittgenstein, John Passmore, G. E. Moore, Kant, Descartes and Hegel), the programmes of the American Philosophical Association's meetings refer to very little outside the Western tradition. Japanese philosophy has also absorbed a lot from both continental phenomenology and American pragmatism. Western philosophy, officially the most contemptuous of the value of tradition, is arguably the most chauvinistic and tradition-based of all.

CONCLUSION

'Imagine,' said the Buddha, 'there were a man struck by an arrow that was smeared thickly with poison [. . .] the man might say, "I will not draw out this arrow so long as I do not know whether the man by whom I was struck was of the Brahman, Ruler, Trader, or Servant class [. . .] whether he was tall, short or of medium height [. . .] whether he was black, brown or light-skinned [. . .]"' The list goes on, hammering home the point that just as these questions are pointless, so are the enquiries of the person who demands to know the answers to metaphysical questions about the nature of ultimate reality that are 'not relevant to the spiritual life' and that do not lead to 'disenchantment, to dispassion, to cessation, to peace, to direct knowledge, to full awakening, to nirvana'. Whatever view one takes on questions such as whether the universe is finite or infinite, 'there is still birth, ageing, death, grief, despair, pain, and unhappiness – and it is the destruction of these here and now that I declare'.[1]

As we have seen, the Buddha, like Confucius, was explicitly not concerned with ultimate questions of metaphysics, reflecting a fault line that runs through the world's philosophical traditions.

David Hall and Roger Ames describe this as the difference between 'truth-seekers' and 'way-seekers'. Western philosophy is characteristically truth-seeking. It seeks to describe the basic structure of reality, logic, language, the mind. One example of this is the Western emphasis on science for science's sake. For truth-seekers, disinterested learning is the best kind, while for way-seekers to be disinterested is as nonsensical as driving a car without caring where you end up.

The Chinese are predominantly way-seekers, who, according to Chenyang Li, 'typically do not see truth as correspondence with objective fact in the world; rather, they understand truth more as a way of being a good person, a good father, or a good son. For them, truth is not carved in stone, and there is no ultimate fixed order in the world.' Whereas Western truth is 'absolute, eternal and ultimately true', the Chinese *dao* 'is not present; it must be generated through human activity'.[2]

Way-seeking chimes with Robin Wang's idea that the concepts of *yin*, *yang* and *qi* are not so much descriptions of ultimate reality as part of a '*shu*, a strategy or technique that enables one to function effectively in any given circumstance'.[3] The centrality of technique or strategy in thought is reflected in the contemporary Chinese word for academic learning, *xue shu*, which is the *shu* of study or learning: 'All philosophy is assumed to be an art [*shu*].'[4] That translation of *shu* is useful because the way- and truth-seeking distinction reflects the difference between seeing philosophy as an art or as a science. Philosophy in the West has always aspired to be more of a science: rigorous, precise, describing reality as it is. In the East it is more of an art of living.

Is philosophy fundamentally about pinning down the world or attempting to navigate through it? These two projects are related, of course. You understand the world at least in part to get around it, and you can't have an interest in getting around it without also knowing something about the way it is. But the difference of emphasis is important. If you are a truth-seeker fixed on getting your understanding of the world right, you are not going to be satisfied with conceptual vagueness, unclarity or ambiguity. If you are a way-seeker more concerned with how you live, you might not only accept such limitations but embrace them. You might find that engaging in the world with less reliance on concepts or language helps you to feel closer to it, more engaged.

Both way- and truth-seeking have their downsides. The risk for truth-seekers is that the pursuit of knowledge becomes something valued purely for its own sake, with no concern for its practical effects or benefits. Arguably this has been the fate of much Western philosophy, which has attracted a lot of people with 'Rubik's cube-type minds', as Owen Flanagan colourfully puts it.[5] However, truth-seeking has been remarkably fruitful for science and technology. There has been plenty of academic head-scratching and speculation as to why modern science emerged in the West rather than in China, which was for a long time better educated, richer and more advanced than the West. Edward Slingerland suggests one plausible reason was China's 'deep-seated suspicion of abstract thought for its own sake and a corresponding failure to develop a disembodied, instrumental stance toward the world'.[6]

The way-seeker/truth-seeker distinction was devised with China and the West in mind. But how does India fit in? Perhaps it doesn't. Chakravarthi Ram-Prasad suggests a different way to distinguish between global traditions, between those who use language as a guide and those who use it as reference. He argues that in India, as in the West, language is understood chiefly as referential: words pick out aspects of reality. In China, language is primarily a guide. It is there to tell us how to live, not what there is.[7] He says, for example, that 'Mozi appears at no point to use language to refer to things in the world, and confines himself to using it for guidance alone. In this, too, he is no different from Confucius.'[8]

Ram-Prasad's distinction would seem to portray India as a truth-seeking tradition, although in many other respects Indian philosophy is more of a way-seeking tradition than philosophy in the West. 'The intimacy of philosophy and life in India is so fundamental to the whole Indian point of view,' says Charles Moore, summing up a widely shared sentiment which notes the closeness of philosophy to life.[9] It would seem that although there is a strong truth-seeking strand in Indian philosophy, the truths sought are always ones that relate to the way we ought to live. To put it another way, Indian philosophy uses language as reference but philosophy as a guide. If we see way and truth as poles on a spectrum rather than either/or opposites, India seems to occupy an intermediate position, but one closer to the way-seekers. Correspondingly, at least in its self-conception, it balances aspects of art and science. Yogic practices, for example, are in part spiritual algorithms that guarantee results if followed but which can only be executed with a skill that comes from practice and can't be simply conveyed by instructions.

Distinctions between way- and truth-seeking, between language as guide and reference, between art and science are not neat, and there are aspects of each in all cultures. 'Any philosophical tradition will in some measure seek both knowledge-that and knowledge-how,' says Ram-Prasad, 'but there are differences in emphasis.'[10] We should remember that way-seeking and truth-seeking are not incompatible. It should be possible for us to see the strengths of both and give both due emphasis. Your chances of finding the right way are improved if you are willing to see the world as it is, independently of your values. And your chances of making the most of the truths you discover are higher if you constantly try to bring those truths to bear on what most matters for human life. Truth is useless unless it allows us to move forward and we cannot move forward unless truth illuminates the way.

These broad differences in approach are a warning that

differences between the world's philosophical traditions run deep. It is easy to assume that each tradition offers a different answer to the same question, when often they are asking different questions. For example, the nature of the question of how we know, how we define knowledge, is changed within different traditions because their interests in asking this question are quite different. For some, 'How do we know?' is always 'How do we know what we need to know in order to live well?' For others, the question is essentially about 'How can we best understand what we know to be true by the revelations of gods or *ṛṣis*?' For yet others, it is about how we can establish objective facts. Some assume knowledge is always effable, others that it is not. Not everyone believes that unaided human reason has much chance of telling us anything important about the world or how to live in it. All these versions of 'How can we know?' are asked in all traditions, but some with greater emphasis than others.

I hope it is now obvious why I have started this book by asking how the world knows. It might at first look like an abstract question, but if we want to understand how the world thinks, it is fundamental. It helps us to be better prepared to understand ideas about how the world is, which we can turn to now.

PART TWO

How the World Is

The Mahabodhi Temple complex in Bodh Gaya, northern India, is a strange combination of stillness and spiritual industry. Around the complex, people sit meditating and praying, often in large, similarly dressed groups, reflecting the diversity of Buddhisms around the world. There is much chanting and little chatter, and parades of people move from one part of the site to another, to pray in front of a descendant of the Bodhi tree under which the Buddha is supposed to have gained enlightenment, or to queue to offer prayers and gifts before the statue of the Buddha situated at the heart of the fifty-five-metre-high temple.

Down one pathway a stream of laypeople and monks in maroon robes run their hands over a long row of vertical rotating cylinders, spinning them clockwise. These are prayer wheels, wrapped in *mantras*. Each turn of the cylinder has the same meritorious effect as reciting the *mantras* on them.

Everything that happens here reflects a particular way of understanding the fundamental nature and structure of reality – a *metaphysics*. Belief in the efficacy of prayer wheels, chants and offerings reflects a belief that there is more to the universe than is revealed by the laws of physics. As well as physical cause and effect there is karmic cause and effect. Actions and intentions have consequences, not just in this life but for the cycle of rebirth that can only be escaped by achieving enlightenment.

This metaphysical picture is strange and exotic for those outside the tradition, but for those within, it is often little more than a common-sense assumption about how the world works. The same is true of any metaphysical picture. Indeed, most people would be flummoxed if asked to spell out their metaphysical framework, not even aware they have one. As is the case with all our deepest assumptions, we're not conscious of making them and we're even less aware of how they have been shaped by centuries of philosophical reflection. By bringing these assumptions to the surface, we can better understand how we and others see the world, which in turn will help us to understand why we do what we do in it.

TIME

In the beginning was the end.

Around the world today, time is linear, ordered into past, present and future. Our days are organised by the progression of the clock, the short to medium term by calendars and diaries, history by timelines stretching back over millennia. All cultures have a sense of past, present and future, but for much of human history this has been underpinned by a more fundamental sense of time as cyclical. The past is also the future, the future is also the past, the beginning also the end.

The dominance of linear time fits in with an eschatological world view in which all of human history is building up to a final judgement. This is perhaps why it has become the common-sense way of viewing time in the largely Christian West. When God created the world he began a story with a beginning, middle and end. As the Book of Revelation puts it, while prophesying the end times, Jesus is this epic's 'Alpha and Omega, the beginning and the end, the first and the last'.[1]

Cyclical time offers an alternative view: that alpha and omega, beginning and end, are and have always been the same because time is essentially cyclical. This is the most intuitively plausible way of thinking about eternity. When we imagine time as a line we end up baffled: what happened before time began? How can a line go on without end? A circle allows us to visualise going backwards or forwards forever, at no point coming up against an ultimate beginning or end.

Thinking of time cyclically makes especial sense in pre-modern societies, where there were few innovations across generations and people lived very similar lives to those of their grandparents, their great-grandparents, going many generations back. Without change, progress was unimaginable. Meaning could therefore only be found in embracing the cycle of life and death and playing your part in it as best you could.

Perhaps this is why cyclical time appears to have been the human default. The Mayans, Incans and Hopi all viewed time in this way. Many non-Western traditions contain elements of cyclical thinking about time, perhaps most evident in classical Indian philosophy. Sarvepalli Radhakrishnan says, 'All the [orthodox] systems accept the view of the great world rhythm. Vast periods of creation, maintenance and dissolution follow each other in endless succession.'[2] For example, a passage in the *Ṛg Veda* addressing Dyaus and Pṛthvī (heaven and earth) reads, 'Which was the former, which of them the latter? How born? O sages, who discerns? They bear themselves all that has existence. Day and night revolve as on a wheel.'[3]

East Asian philosophy is deeply rooted in the cycle of the seasons, part of a larger cycle of existence. This is particularly evident in Daoism, as is vividly illustrated by Zhuangzi's surprising cheerfulness when everyone thought he should have been mourning for his wife. At first, he explained, he was as miserable as anyone else. Then he thought back beyond her to the beginning of time itself: 'In all the mixed-up bustle and confusion, something changed and there was *qi*. The *qi* changed and there was form. The form changed and she had life. Today there was another change and she died. It's just like the round of four seasons: spring, summer, fall, and winter.'[4]

In Chinese thought, wisdom and truth are timeless, and we don't need to go forward to learn, only to hold on to what we already have. As the nineteenth-century Scottish sinologist James Legge put it, Confucius did not think his purpose was 'to announce any new truths, or to initiate any new economy. It was to prevent what had previously been known from being lost.'[5] Mencius similarly criticised the princes of his day because 'they do not put into practice the ways of the ancient kings'.[6] He also says in the penultimate chapter of the eponymous collection of his conversations, close to the book's conclusion, 'The superior man seeks simply to bring back the unchanging standard, and, that being correct, the masses are roused to virtue.'[7] The very last chapter charts the ages between the great kings and sages.

A hybrid of cyclical and linear time operates in strands of Islamic thought. 'The Islamic conception of time is based essentially on the cyclic rejuvenation of human history through the appearance of various prophets,' says Seyyed Hossein Nasr. Each cycle, however, also moves humanity forward, with each revelation building on the former – the dictation of the Qur'ān to Muḥammad being the last, complete testimony of God – until ultimately the series of cycles 'ends finally in the eschatological events identified with the appearance of the Mahdī'.[8]

The distinction between linear and cyclical time is therefore not always neat. The assumption of an either/or leads many to assume that oral philosophical traditions have straightforwardly cyclical conceptions of time. The reality is more complicated. Take Australian Aboriginal philosophies. There is no single Australian first people with a shared culture, but there are enough similarities across the country for some tentative generalisations to be made about ideas that are common or dominant. David Maybury Lewis has suggested that time in Aboriginal culture is neither cyclical nor linear; instead, it resembles the space-time of modern physics. Time is intimately linked to place in what he calls the 'dreamtime' of 'past, present, future all present in this place'.[9]

'One lives in a place more than in a time,' is how Stephen Muecke puts it.[10] More important than the distinction between linear or cyclical time is whether time is separated from or intimately connected to place. Take, for example, how we conceive of death. In the contemporary West, death is primarily seen as the expiration of the individual, with the body as the locus, and the location of that body irrelevant. In contrast, Muecke says, 'Many indigenous accounts of the death of an individual are not so much about bodily death as about a return of energy to the place of emanation with which it reidentifies.'[11]

Such a way of thinking is especially alien to the modern West, where a pursuit of objectivity systematically downplays the particular, the specifically located. In a provocative and evocative sentence, Muecke says, 'Let me suggest that long-sightedness is a European form of philosophical myopia and that other versions of philosophy, indigenous perhaps, have a more lived-in and intimate association with societies of people and the way they talk about themselves.'[12]

Muecke cites Tony Swain's view that the concept of linear time is a kind of fall from place. 'I've got a hunch that modern physics separated out those dimensions and worked on them and so we produced time as we know it through a whole lot of experimental and theoretical activities,' he told me. 'If you're not conceptually and experimentally separating those dimensions, then they would tend to flow together.' His indigenous friends talk less of time or place independently but more of located events. The key temporal question is not 'When did this happen?' but 'How is this related to other events?'

That word 'related' is important. Time and space have become theoretical abstractions in modern physics, but in human culture they are concrete realities. Nothing exists purely as a point on a map or a moment in time: everything stands in relation to everything else. So to understand time and space in oral philosophical traditions we have to see them less as abstract concepts in metaphysical theories and more as living conceptions, part and parcel of a broader way of understanding the world, one that is rooted in relatedness. Hirini Kaa says that 'the key underpinning of Māori thought is kinship, the connectedness between humanity, between one another, between the natural environment'. He sees this as a form of spirituality. 'The ocean wasn't just water, it wasn't something for us to be afraid of or to utilise as a commodity, but became an ancestor deity, Tangaroa. Every living thing has a life force.'

The Ngarinyin David Mowaljarlai from Western Australia called this principle of connectivity 'pattern thinking'.[13] Pattern thinking suffuses the natural and the social worlds, which are, after all, in this way of thinking, part of one thing. As Muecke puts it, 'The concept of connectedness is, of course, the basis of all kinship systems [...] Getting married, in this case, is not just pairing off, it is, in a way, sharing each other.'[14]

The emphasis on connectedness and place leads to a way of thinking that runs counter to the abstract universalism developed to a certain extent in all the great written traditions of philosophy. Muecke describes as one of the 'enduring Aboriginal principles' that 'a way of being will be specific to the resources and needs of a time and place and that one's conduct will be informed by responsibility specific to that place'.[15] This is not an 'anything goes' relativism but a recognition that rights, duties and values exist only in actual human cultures, and their exact shape and form will depend on the nature of those situations.

This should be clear enough. But the tradition of Western philosophy in particular has striven for a universality that glosses over differences of time and place. The Western university, for example, even shares the same etymological root as 'universal'. In such institutions, 'The pursuit of truth recognises no national boundaries,' as one commentator typically observed.[16] Place is so unimportant in Western philosophy that when I discovered it was the theme of the quinquennial East-West Philosophers' Conference I seriously wondered if there was anything I could bring to the party at all. (Eventually I decided that the absence of place in Western philosophy itself merited consideration.)

The universalist thrust has many merits. The refusal to accept any and every practice as a legitimate custom has bred a very good form of intolerance for the barbaric and unjust traditional practices of the West itself. Without this intolerance, we would still have slavery, torture, fewer rights for women and homosexuals, feudal lords and unelected parliaments. The universalist aspiration has allowed the West to transcend its own prejudices. At the same time, it has also legitimised some prejudices by confusing them with universal truths. Kwame Anthony Appiah argues that the complaints of anti-universalists are not generally about universalism at all, but *pseudo-universalism*, 'Eurocentric hegemony *posing* as universalism'.[17] When this happens, intolerance for the indefensible becomes intolerance for anything that is different. The aspiration for the universal becomes a crude insistence on the uniform. Sensitivity is lost to the very different needs of different cultures at different times and places.

This 'posing' is widespread and often implicit, with Western concepts being taken as universal but Indian ones remaining Indian, Chinese remaining Chinese, and so on. To end this pretence, Jay L. Garfield and Bryan W. Van Norden propose that those departments of philosophy which refuse to teach anything from non-Western traditions at least have the decency to call themselves departments of *Western* philosophy.[18]

The 'pattern thinking' of Māori and Aboriginal philosophies

could provide a corrective to the assumption that *our* values are the universal ones and that others are aberrations. It makes credible and comprehensible the idea that philosophy is never placeless and that thinking which is uprooted from any land soon withers and dies.

Mistrust of the universalist aspiration, however, can go too far. At the very least, there is a contradiction in saying there are no universal truths, since that is itself a universal claim about the nature of truth.[19] The right view probably lies somewhere between the claims of naive universalists and those of defiant localists. There seems to be a sense in which even the universalist aspiration has to be rooted in something more particular. T. S. Eliot is supposed to have said, 'Although it is only too easy for a writer to be local without being universal, I doubt whether a poet or novelist can be universal without being local too.'[20] To be purely universal is to inhabit an abstract universe too detached from the real world. But just as a novelist can touch on universals of the human condition through the particulars of a couple of characters and a specific story, so our different, regional philosophical traditions can shed light on more universal philosophical truths even though they approach them from their own specific angles.

We should not be afraid to ground ourselves in our own traditions, but we should not be bound by them. Gandhi put this poetically when he wrote, 'I do not want my house to be walled in on all sides and my windows to be stuffed. I want the cultures of all lands to be blown about my house as freely as possible. But I refuse to be blown off my feet by any. I refuse to live in other people's houses as an interloper, a beggar or a slave.'[21]

In the West, the predominance of linear time is associated with the idea of progress which reached its apotheosis in the Enlightenment. Before this, argues Anthony Kenny, 'people looking for ideals had looked backwards in time, whether to the primitive church, or to classical antiquity, or to some mythical prelapsarian era. It was a key doctrine of the Enlightenment that the human race, so far from falling from some earlier eminence, was moving forward to a happier future.'[22] Kenny is expressing a popular view, but many see the roots of belief in progress deeper in the Christian eschatological religious world view. 'Belief in progress is a relic of the Christian view of history as a universal narrative,' claims John Gray. Secular thinkers, he says, 'reject the idea of providence, but they continue to think humankind is moving towards a universal goal', even though 'the idea of progress in history is a myth created by the need for meaning'.[23]

Whether faith in progress is an invention or an adaptation of the Enlightenment, the image of secular humanists naively believing humanity is on an irreversible, linear path of advancement seems to me a caricature of their more modest hope, based in history, that progress has occurred and that more is possible. As the historian Jonathan Israel says, Enlightenment ideas of progress 'were usually tempered by a strong streak of pessimism, a sense of the dangers and challenges to which the human condition is subject'. He dismisses the idea that 'Enlightenment thinkers nurtured a naive belief in man's perfectibility' as a 'complete myth conjured up by early twentieth-century scholars unsympathetic to its claims'.[24] Nevertheless, Gray is right to point out that linear progress is a kind of default way of thinking about history in the modern West and that this risks blinding us to the ways in which gains can be lost, advances reversed. It also fosters a Whiggish sense of the superiority of the present age over earlier, less 'advanced' times. Finally, it occludes the extent to which history doesn't repeat itself but does rhyme. (This aphorism is often attributed to Mark Twain. In fact, it doesn't repeat what he said, but it does 'rhyme' with it: 'History never repeats itself, but the Kaleidoscopic combinations of the pictured present often seem to be constructed out of the broken fragments of antique legends.'[25])

The different ways in which philosophical traditions have

conceived time turn out to be far from mere metaphysical curiosities. They shape the way we think about both our temporal place in history and our relation to the physical places in which we live. It provides one of the easiest and clearest examples of how borrowing another way of thinking can bring a fresh perspective to our world. Sometimes, simply by changing the frame, the whole picture can look very different.

'IF A MAN SPEAKS OR ACTS WITH AN EVIL
THOUGHT, SORROW FOLLOWS HIM EVEN AS THE
WHEEL FOLLOWS THE FOOT OF THE DRAWER'

KARMA

Bodh Gaya is in Bihar, one of the poorest regions of India. I had never been to the subcontinent before and arrived primed to expect a country that had come a long way from the old clichés of squalor. Sadly, what I saw fitted the stereotypes all too well. The taxi drive from Patna airport gave me a front-seat view of this deprived region and plenty of time to take it in, since the roads were so bad that the 115-kilometre journey took three and a half hours. Statistics tell us there is a growing Indian middle class, but once I left the airport car park I saw none of it. The only homes I saw ranged from shabby brick houses to small concrete shacks to makeshift shanty-like camps. The most opulent shops were small concrete units, with most traders operating from huts or from the side of the road. Scrawny chickens were at best packed loosely into cages. Fish were laid out on the ground without ice or refrigeration. We passed people collecting water and washing from hand pumps, and lots of what looked like foraging. One recurrent sight was flattened discs of cow dung drying in the sun, for use as fuel. There were pools of stagnant water and litter was scattered everywhere, even more on the rural roads. I've been to places at least as poor in East Africa, but none were as dirty.

Any romantic notion that this is a simpler way of life that the 'spiritual' Indians enjoy living is contradicted by the endless posters and billboard adverts for schools, many emphasising maths and preparation for jobs in banks and teaching. There is a widespread aspiration for a more materially comfortable life for the next generation.

I soon discovered that the most important part of the car is the horn, as this is used to tell other drivers that you are coming through, whether they like it or not, and that they should take evasive action. *Not* constantly beeping is ruder than doing so: Indian trucks almost all bear the sign 'Horn Please' on their backs. The drive followed the logic of a race, where the only concern was to get ahead. Oddly, though, it wasn't terrifying, as the potholed roads restricted top speeds and it was obvious everyone knew the rules. The people most at risk were the cyclists and motorbikers.

There are certainly more godforsaken places, but has anywhere been forsaken by so many gods? The *Vedas* name thirty-three deities and it is popularly believed by Indians that there are in fact 330 million. If these gods were real, you might have thought they would have given more divine assistance to the nation of a billion people that worships them. In another way, however, belief here in deities makes perfect sense. When life is harsh, it is no surprise that so many look for salvation in a life to come.

I'll come back to salvation later, but first we need to understand the basic mechanism which makes salvation both necessary and possible: *karma*. This is one of the earliest philosophical concepts in human history and it still exerts a powerful influence. The principle of *karma* emerged in the Brahminical tradition as early as the fifth century BCE. The original meaning concerned getting the mechanics of rituals right so that they worked. *Karma* had no moral connotations.[1] It soon evolved, however, into the idea that all actions have not only consequences, but *moral* consequences, which by some law of the cosmos means that over time people are repaid for their actions: good with good, evil with evil. *Karma* has developed in various ways and remains important in the Hindu, Sikh, Jain and Buddhist worlds today. 'While it is differently interpreted by different schools of thought,' says Sue Hamilton, 'it is nevertheless a fundamental part of the Indian worldview as a whole.'[2]

Interestingly, even among the heterodox schools of classical Indian philosophy that reject the *Vedas*, all bar Carvākā accept *karma*, including the Jains, who believe that each *jīva* (sentient being) is omniscient and pure, but corrupted by accumulated *karma*. By ridding oneself of this, one can return to the pure state of *kevala* (unlimited and absolute knowledge).[3]

Buddhism imported the idea of *karma* pretty much fully formed, but added a twist, as is evident at the start of the *Dhammapada*, one of the earliest and most read collections of the Buddha's teachings: '(The mental) natures are the result of what we have thought, are chieftained by our thoughts, are made up of our thoughts. If a man speaks or acts with an evil thought, sorrow follows him (as a consequence) even as the wheel follows the foot of the drawer (i.e. the ox which drives the cart).'[4] Note that *karma* is the result of *thought*, not just of action. Intentions, mental and spiritual purity, matter more than deeds.

One of the most important consequences of *karma* is the nature of your rebirth. In the ancient Hindu *dharmaśāstra* (treatise) *The Laws of Manu*, it is explained, 'In consequence of (many) sinful acts committed with his body, a man becomes (in the next birth) something inanimate; in consequence (of sins) committed by speech, a bird, or a beast; and in consequence of mental sins he is re-born in a low caste.'[5]

Although the concept of *karma* is specific to the religions and

philosophies that grew out of India, some kind of similar principle is found elsewhere and could even be thought of as a kind of
common sense. Westerners only started saying 'What goes around,
comes around' in the 1960s, as hippies borrowed promiscuously
from Buddhism. But nearly two millennia before, St Paul wrote in
his Letter to the Galatians, 'Whatsoever a man soweth, that shall
he also reap.'[6]

There are also hints of something *karmic* in classical Chinese
philosophy, where some kind of cosmic regulative principle often
seems to be at work. This is *tian*, usually translated as 'heaven'
but not a kind of transcendental place where gods live or we are
destined to go. It is more like a kind of divine power, something
that we should try to emulate but will also bite us if we don't.

We can see an example of how this works in a passage from
Mozi, which tells us that 'The ancient sage-kings of the Three
Dynasties, Yu, Tang, Wen, and Wu, were those that obeyed the
will of Heaven and obtained reward. And the wicked kings of the
Three Dynasties, Jie, Zhou, You, and Li, were those that opposed
the will of Heaven and incurred punishment.' The sage-kings
revered *tian*, worshipped the spirits and loved the people. As a
result, *tian* enriched them with an empire that ruled for 10,000
generations. The wicked kings, in contrast, blasphemed against
tian and the spirits and oppressed the people. The will of Heaven
saw to it that 'they did not finish out their natural span of life, and
their line did not even span a single generation'.[7]

Karma differs from these more general ideas about cause and
effect because it works across and not just within lifetimes. It
places our actions in a much larger timescale and so makes them
of much more consequence. It would not therefore be surprising if
this affected the way people think about their current misfortunes.
I've always been suspicious of the idea that *karma* makes people
more sanguine about their problems, but the Indian philosopher
Meera Baindur suggests there is something to this. As ever,

however, we have to appreciate that there is a difference between the full philosophical concept and its popular analogue. The *karma* that the person in the Indian street believes in is 'a kind of watered-down, general, popular version,' she says, 'like how people quote Nietzsche here and there, everywhere'.

The popular version of *karma* places more emphasis on the external playing out of cosmic mechanisms and less on the internal influence of our choices and motivations. It's therefore more fatalistic than true *karma* arguably should be. Baindur says, 'People sometimes don't come to the doctor because they think it's *karma*.' Similarly, she says Indians are more likely to blame the government or external circumstances than they are in countries like the USA. 'It's the conditions that cause the person and not the person's internal motivations.' Baindur sees that this can function as a kind of psychological coping mechanism but that 'it also makes people a little laid back'. So, for example, 'When you look at a person who's suffering there's empathy, but you could also say, "It's just *karma*."' You can see how that might be helpful when you are surrounded by too much suffering to fully empathise without becoming emotionally overwhelmed.

The kind of resigned fatalism that belief in *karma* generates sounds to me a little too close to the comforting 'poor but happy' stereotype of the 'spiritual' Indian. Fatalism stands in the way of increased social justice. S. K. Saksena, for instance, claims that Indian philosophy is extremely practical but that Westerners misunderstand what 'practical' means in this context. It concerns 'the inner transformation of man rather than to any socialized transformation of his style of living'.[8] That sounds laudable, but it could breed too much acceptance of the status quo, which makes people put up with all sorts of nonsense. Baindur shares this concern, but points out that 'People in that nonsense don't see it as putting up.' *Karmic* sanguineness only becomes a problem when it's used as an excuse to keep people in their difficulties. Take, for example, the increasing problem of farmer suicides in India, numbering 12,000 a year. 'The reason farmers are killing themselves is not because their crops are not growing, it's because they can't repay the loan they have taken because the seeds that they've bought are GM seeds that they can't regrow. It's not about your *karma*, it's about economics.'

Perhaps the most pernicious effect of the *karmic* world view is the way it has been used to support the rigid caste system in India. Most scholars today agree that castes were never meant to be hermetically sealed and that movement between them was possible. The *Vedas* talk of four *varnas* (the word 'caste' is not an Indian one): *brāhmin* (priests), *kṣatriya* (rulers, administrators and warriors), *vaiśya* (artisans, merchants, tradesmen and farmers) and *śūdras* (labourers). Although it is explicitly said that there is no fifth *varna* there is an implicit category of those who fit into none of the four: the *dalit* or 'untouchables'.[9]

The castes were 'assigned separate duties and occupations' and have been treated differently for centuries. The *Vedas* explicitly advocate some strict separation. 'Adultery is caused by a mixture of the castes among men', warns *The Laws of Manu*.[10] However, it is also clear that movement between castes was possible and that merit, not birth, should be the ultimate determinant. 'A twice-born man [*brāhmaṇa*] who, not having studied the Veda, applies himself to other (and worldly study), soon falls, even while living, to the condition of a Sudra and his descendants (after him),'[11] says *The Laws of Manu*. And 'a *śūdra* attains the rank of a *brāhmaṇa*, and (in a similar manner) a *brāhmaṇa* sinks to the level of a *śūdra*; but know that it is the same with the offspring of a Kshatriya or of a Vaisya'.[12]

However, at some point the *varnas* became rigid castes with ever more subdivisions. Different scholars blame different factors. One told me that *varnas* were fluid until British imperial rule, when Indians were obliged to state their caste on their identity cards. But this cannot have been the start of the ossification, which intriguing genetic studies show began seventy generations ago. Researchers from the National Institute of Biomedical Genomics (NIBMG) at Kalyani, West Bengal, found that the vast majority of Indians today descend from five different ancient populations that freely mixed and interbred for thousands of years until some point in the sixth century CE. Then a prohibition on intercaste marriage abruptly put a halt to the mixing, erecting caste barriers that still stand, entrenched by the sanction of a selective reading of scriptures.[13]

When India gained independence its constitution banned discrimination on the basis of caste, but few would deny that it still exerts a huge influence and that a lot of prejudice remains. I was surprised to note that even the personal ads in the *Times of India* are arranged by caste, suggesting that many of India's educated middle class still want to marry within their own.

India is changing and Somini Sengupta argues in *The End of Karma: Hope and Fury Among India's Young* that the young no longer believe in *karma* and that ideas of free will and aspiration have come in its place. Given the median age in India is now seventeen, that could signal a huge shift. But even Sengupta's stories present a mixed picture. Monica and Kuldeep are an example of a couple from different castes who defied family and married. Although it seemed to be going well, three years after their marriage Monica's brother shot them both in the head.[14]

Baindur gave me reason to believe that the old ideas are persisting in younger generations. I spoke to her at the East-West Philosophers' Conference in Hawai'i. Knowing she was going there, her students would say she was lucky. 'They may not see that I work very, very hard to write a paper and self-sponsor and stay in a hostel,' she says. 'Using the word "lucky" they're saying "You're karmically benefited and we can't be like you."'

Baindur does see a shift from a default kind of acceptance to a striving for more, one that is not all good: 'The craving for things has never been there, it's been generated, unfortunately. It's coming now, it's changing things. There's more dissatisfaction. People are being told they should buy a car, they're being told you should own your own house.'

In Bodh Gaya, my own cravings and dissatisfactions drew me to Barista, the only Western-style café in town. Going in was like passing through a portal to a suburban British high street. I joined six other customers: three Buddhist monks with an Asian woman, another Buddhist monk and a single young Japanese man who had a big slice of cake, then a chicken sandwich, then a chicken burger, accompanied by two iced coffees. The clientele suggested that the choice between spiritual and worldly values is not as stark as many who either romanticise Indian spirituality or demonise Western materialism suggest. *Karma*, coffee and cake can coexist. Belief in *karma* is very deeply rooted in India, but we can perhaps expect it to lose some of its fatalistic edge as people embrace Western ideas about the possibility of fulfilling individual potential in this world, not the next.

EMPTINESS

The Japanese aesthetic is known for its simplicity and purity. So it should be unsurprising that more than a century before abstract minimalism took off in the West the Zen abbot and artist Gibon Sengai was painting canvases featuring only simple shapes. His most famous work is known as *Circle Triangle Square*. The circle represents the infinite, out of which comes form, in the shape of a triangle. The triangle doubled creates a square, and thus begins the process of the multiplication of forms which fill the sensible universe. The painting is a beautiful example of the Japanese marriage of the intellectual and the aesthetic.

I first encountered Sengai's work at the Idemitsu Museum of Arts in Tokyo, where I was taken by his *ensō* painting: a circle drawn in what looks like a single stroke with two lines of calligraphy to one side, all in black apart from the red of the artist's *hanko* signature-stamp. A Westerner encountering an *ensō* will probably see easily enough how the circle, with its wholeness and symmetry, represents the universe and enlightenment. More puzzling, however, is its third symbolic meaning: emptiness.

Emptiness is a concept as alien to Western philosophy as it is central to many East Asian traditions. Nor is it merely some obscure scholastic idea. Whereas the Western mind focuses its attention on things, in East Asia there is also a natural focus on the space *between* things. The psychologist Richard Nisbett has conducted a memory test in which Americans and East Asians are asked to look at a picture of a fish tank and then try to spot any changes when it is presented back to them. Americans tended to notice only changes in the fish, while East Asians were sensitive to changes in the background. This fits in with other tests and cultural observations which suggest that East Asians (for cultural, not genetic reasons) are more attuned to the relationships between things and their 'backgrounds'.

It's not difficult to see how this relates to viewing an *ensō*. A Westerner sees first and foremost a circle, the round line. A Japanese sees at least as immediately the space contained within the circle. It is not that Westerners don't notice empty spaces. It's simply a matter of primacy of attention.

Once you see this, you see Japanese art differently. Kobayashi Yasuo alerted me to this when I asked him about the aesthetic minimalism of Japan. This seemed a natural way to put it, but Kobayashi corrected me, or at least added a necessary clarification. 'It's not only minimalism,' he said. 'It's a core idea of sensitivity to "between".' So in a painting, for example, you might have a large white space and only one flower, 'but the important thing is the tension of powers or energies between this space and the flower. You have to appreciate not the flower itself but the relationship between the space and the flower. Flower arranging is the same thing. It's not the beauty of each flower but the arrangement.'

You find this aesthetic of betweenness in every Japanese art form. *Ma*, the Japanese concept of the space between, is important in traditional *gagaku* music. For Westerners *ma* is dismissed 'as mere silence', wrote one critic. However, in the playing of a contemporary ensemble, Reigakusha, 'that silence is made to speak volumes'.[1]

This betweenness is evident in the haiku, another art form which we think of as essentially minimalist, not noticing the importance of the in-between. 'A haiku must be absolutely divided in two parts,' says Kobayashi. 'You must have a kind of separation. This separation is the key. The last letter of the first part is the *kireji*, the cutting word. It's a kind of "Oo!", "Aaa!"' There is a double meaning to this. The actual sound of the *kireji* is often an 'Ooo' or an 'Aah', but the intention is also to evoke a kind of "Ooo!" or "Aah!" from the reader as the connection is made. For example, take this haiku from the seventeenth-century poet Bashō:

Lonely silence
a single cicada's cry
sinking into stone

The *kireji* here is the fourth character, や, pronounced 'ya'. It doesn't really add any meaning but it comes at the end of the first line in the English translation and marks the cut between the stillness and the cry of the cicada that disturbs it. The haiku evokes not just the contrast but the transition between the two, the 'Aah!' moment when your attention is suddenly taken from the quiet to the animal.

The importance of betweenness in Japanese culture is reflected in the fact that one of the Japanese words for human being is *ningen*, which is made up of *nin*, meaning 'human' or 'person', and *gen*, meaning 'space' or 'between'. The twentieth-century Kyoto School philosopher Watsuji Tetsurō emphasised this etymology in his account of how human beings are essentially defined by their relations to others. *Ningen* are both individuals and interdependent. As Kobayashi put it, in Japan there is 'no separation between interiority and exteriority, everything goes in this between. It's a kind of intimacy which constitutes a very intimate world.' This 'intimacy', as Tom Kasulis calls it, is for Kobayashi 'the kind of Japanese soil of all the culture'.

Kasulis's concept of 'intimacy' involves the idea that in Japanese thought, every part contains the whole. Many thinkers have expressed something like this idea. Nishida says, 'In a painting or melody [...] there is not one brush stroke or one note that does not directly express the spirit of the whole.'[2] Dōgen says, 'There are myriad forms and hundreds of blades of grass in the entirety of space, but you should also realise that the entirety of space is within each single blade of grass, each single form.'[3] Takuan Sōhō wrote, 'If your mind does not stop on any one leaf, thousands of leaves are visible. Someone who achieves this mind is exactly like the thousand eyes and thousand arms of Kannon.'[4]

As we have seen, betweenness is a way of seeing emptiness as a presence as well as an absence. Such positive conceptions of emptiness have long, deep roots through Buddhism to ancient India. Take this striking passage from the *Upaniṣads*: 'Then they said to him: Brahman is life (*prāṇa*), Brahman is joy. Brahman in the void. [...] Joy (*ka*) – verily, that is the same as the Void (*kha*). The Void – verily, that is the same as joy.'[5]

There is also a central role for a kind of emptiness in Vaiśeṣika, one of the six Indian orthodox schools. Vaiśeṣika maintains that reality has seven categories: substance, quality, action, universality, particularity, a relation on inherence, and absence or negation. Absence in turn comes in five kinds: 'there is no rose here (absence); a rose is not a cow (difference); there is no flower yet on the rosebush (non-existence prior to existence); the rose is no more (non-existence following existence); roseness is never found in a cow (something that never exists).'[6] This highly developed taxonomy of kinds of absence shows an interest in nothingness and emptiness that was much more developed than in the West.

Similarly, one of the six *pramāṇas* – sources of knowledge – is *anupalabdhi*, usually called non-perception, negative or non-cognitive proof. The key feature of *anupalabdhi* is that it assumes we can perceive non-existence just as well as existence. The fact that there is no butter in the fridge is as evident to you when you look in as the fact that there is cheese.[7] It is often said in the West that absence of evidence is not evidence of absence, but often the best evidence of absence is indeed the observation of absence.

In Indian philosophy emptiness came to the fore in Buddhism, in particular in the writings of Nāgārjuna, one of the most influential Buddhist philosophers in history. In the second to third century CE, Nāgārjuna founded the Madhyamaka ('Middle Way') school, a part of Mahāyāna Buddhism, the branch which most Buddhists today follow in one of its varieties. Mahāyāna teaches that enlightenment can be achieved in one lifetime and those who achieve it become *bodhisattvas* who choose to remain on earth rather than to escape the cycle of rebirth, to help others attain enlightenment.

Nāgārjuna's main philosophical contribution, however, is his development of the concept of dependent origination, building on an idea that is central to all Buddhist thought. The essence of dependent origination is that 'all phenomena are devoid of inherent existence and are empty'.[8] 'Inherent existence' here means a kind of existence which does not depend on anything else. Anything which exists inherently for Nāgārjuna would need to have a permanent, unchanging existence: 'If actions were to have inherent existence then they would not be impermanent, but would have the nature of permanence.'[9] The word used for permanent here (*mi 'gyur*) literally means 'unchanging' or 'unchangeable'.[10]

Once defined in this way, it is quite easy for Nāgārjuna to show that nothing has this kind of perfect autonomy. 'Time', for example, 'does not exist inherently because the three periods of time [past, present and future] do not maintain continuity by themselves but are dependent on each other.'[11] Similarly, colour and shape do not have inherent existence because if they did we would be able to conceive of them independently. However, every colour we think of has a shape and every shape a colour.[12] Everything is like this: dependent on other things for its own existence. This 'being dependent nature' of existing things Nāgārjuna calls 'emptiness'.[13] As should now be clear, this emptiness is not non-existence. Things are empty of *inherent existence*, they are not *non-existent*.

There is much debate within Buddhism about the precise meanings of 'dependent origination' and 'inherent existence', but the broader truth these concepts try to explain is simple enough to accept: everything is impermanent. As an early Buddhist Hīnayāna text puts it, 'It remains a fact and the fixed and necessary constitution of being that all its constituents are transitory.'[14] In Buddhism this is not a merely theoretical point, it is the cause of all suffering. Since nothing is permanent, our state of being entails *dukkha*, best translated as 'unsatisfactoriness' but often rendered as 'suffering'. Seeing reality as it really is, devoid of inherent existence, is the path to enlightenment. It is what enables us to see the futility of grasping for an existence which is empty. 'With the elimination of wrong views,' writes Nāgārjuna, 'they will have abandoned attachment, broad-mindedness and hatred and therefore attain *nirvāṇa* unsustained by wrong views.'[15]

Impermanence is a major theme in all Buddhist thought, but it is also central to Chinese philosophy, where the *I Ching*, or *Book of Changes*, is a deep part of the culture, possibly dating back to as early as the ninth century BCE. Although often seen by foreigners as something of a mystical work concerned with divination, it is also a work of philosophy. The first commentary on the *Book of Changes* was supposedly written by Confucius and to some extent almost all Confucian scholars since have interpreted the work.[16] Change is an even bigger theme in Daosim. One of Laozi's most famous poems has the refrain 'All things pass', concluding with the advice, 'Take things as they come.'

The idea of emptiness arguably reached its highest development in the early twentieth century with the philosophers of Japan's Kyoto School, who wrote both of *śūnyatā*, emptiness (*ku* in Japanese), and *mu*, nothingness. Each thinker in the school (which was never a formal group) had a distinctive view, but what united them was a belief that neither *ku* nor *mu* signifies an absence of being. As Suzuki put it, 'To say that reality is "empty" means that it goes beyond definability and cannot be qualified as this or that. It is above categories of universal and particular. But it must not therefore be regarded as free of all content, as void in the relative sense would be. On the contrary, it is the fullness of things, containing all possibilities.'[17]

Again, surprising though it may seem, this does reflect aspects of everyday Japanese culture. John Krummel grew up in Japan and told me, 'You can find this talk of nothingness in a lot of spheres of Japanese culture, in sports and in martial arts. For example, when I was studying at a martial arts school, we would meditate and the teacher would say "put your mind into nothingness" to think of nothing, and he would use the same terminology that the Zen Buddhists use: *mu* (nothing), *mushin* (no mind). They'd say, "When you're practising the movements with the sword, don't think, just keep your mind in no mind." Even in modern sports, the way they approach high school baseball often seemed Zen Buddhist. They would meditate, the coaches would tell the players not to think about it, to put your mind into no mind.'

The idea that nothingness is at the centre of being might sound absurd, but in some sense it is extremely rational and scientific. Suzuki talks of nothingness as the 'beginning of the world' on the basis that if we postulate that the world came from something, you have to then ask where that something came from, and so on, in infinite regress. It seems to me that nothingness as the basis of all being can be understood as the simple materialist common sense that the universe rests on nothing other than itself. This is not mystical but rational and empirical.[18]

A nothingness that is the origin of all things is not an inert absence but a generative power. Kazashi Nobuo emphasises the dynamic, creative feature of nothingness in Kyoto School thinking. He cites a favourite phrase in Dōgen: 'You should not regard time's flying as its sole activity.' The quote continues, 'If time were exclusively dependent on flying, there would be an interspace (between time and the self).' The Buddhist idea of the impermanence of everything is not merely a negative statement about absence of unchanging essence. Because everything is related, there can be creation. Kazashi says, 'Because everything is empty, something new, something novel can come out of these networks and relations.'

This helps explain one of the paradoxes of the Japanese emphasis on transience, in that it also involves an awareness of the eternal. Kazashi explained this to me in terms of the seasons. The constant change of seasons is a sign of impermanence but of course the seasons return. The process has a permanence its parts do not.

An example of both change and continuity is found in the poet Bashō's *Narrow Road to the Interior*, published in 1694. He writes about coming across the ancient monument Tsubo-no-ishibumi in Ichikawa, built in 714, with moss growing over its inscription. It is a scene of transience, decay, impermanence, but also one of connection, of the past kept alive. 'The past remains hidden in clouds of memory. Still it returned us to memories from a thousand years before. Such a moment is the reason for a pilgrimage: infirmities forgotten, the ancients remembered, joyous tears trembled in my eyes.'[19]

Kazashi also talks of the trend to be buried under a *sakura* (cherry blossom tree) rather than a traditional stone pillar. This is driven in part by the increasing cost of traditional burials, since temples require annual fees or else bodies are exhumed. *Sakura* is a national symbol of transience. Watsuji Tetsurō says, 'It is of deep significance and highly appropriate that [...] the Japanese should be symbolised by the cherry blossoms, for they flower abruptly, showily and almost in indecent haste, but the blooms have no tenacity – they fall as abruptly and disinterestedly as they flowered.'[20] Nothing could be more apt to symbolise the fleeting, brief nature of life. At the same time, says Kazashi, 'people want to bury their family members' cremated remains under the cherry blossom because the beauty of the cherry blossom comes back year after year. There's trust in the recurrence of nature. It's not really thoroughgoing transience.'

At the Kabukiza Theatre I got a glimpse of some of the complexities and contradictions around attitudes to impermanence. The kabuki play I saw, *Meoto Dojiji*, was full of references to transience. At one point the chorus sings about the fickleness of love, comparing it to how the cherry blossom falls, celebrating its beauty at the same time as lamenting its temporariness. This is the bitter-sweet melancholy of the aesthetic principle of *wabi-sabi*. But we need to be careful not to romanticise. The bitter has as much prominence as the sweet. At the very start of the play the chorus sings of hating the temple bell because it reminds them of impermanence. People naturally feel attached to what doesn't last and there is no culture where sanguine acceptance is entirely second nature. To me it seemed that the action of the play provided a kind of catharsis. In their desire for each other, the two lovers embrace attachment and we empathise with their passion. But ultimately the story reinforces the orthodox view that we should not cling to that which does not last, since the love, and the lovers, are doomed. In its art and philosophy, Japan offers a lesson in how to appreciate ephemeral riches in the emptiness of existence.

NATURALISM

Walk around a museum of Western art that is organised chronologically and you'll find many centuries are represented only by religious scenes, apart from portraits of the great and (as it often turns out) not so good. Only in the nineteenth century did landscape painting really take off, after which secular themes increasingly became predominant.

In China, however, the most popular subject has always been nature. Not the idealised, untouched nature of Western Romanticism, but one where small signs of human life, like a hut or a farmer, are often tucked away in the corners.[1] At the Shanghai Museum, I saw a painting by the Ming dynasty artist Jin Dai (1388–1462), *Dense Green Covering the Spring Mountains*, which is dominated by steep, tree-lined mountains; two small figures walk along a path in the bottom left-hand corner and two roofs discreetly peek from above the treetops. In Yuan dynasty painter Wang Meng's (c. 1308 –85) *Secluded Dwelling in the Qingbian Mountains*, a small retreat hut is easy to miss unless you examine the picture closely. Where the West tends to contrast natural with 'human-made', in

China humanity does not stand apart from nature but is fully part of it, albeit a tiny part dwarfed by mountains and forests.

To anyone familiar with classical Chinese philosophy, this would come as no surprise. At least since the time of Confucius, in China there has been no God or focus on the afterlife. 'For the Chinese, philosophy takes the place of religion,' says Charles Moore.[2] All the important questions are about the here and now, our duties on earth, hence Chinese philosophy is often characterised as practical and humanistic. There are none of the sharp divisions between mind and spirit, heaven and earth, that are found in many other traditions. Mencius reminds us, 'All who speak about the natures of things, have in fact only their phenomena to reason from, and the value of a phenomenon is its being natural.'[3] Chinese philosophy is profoundly non-dualistic: *yin* and *yang* represent two aspects of the same whole, not two things that need to be reconciled.

This account might appear to contradict the recurring centrality of heaven, *tian*, in Chinese thought. Confucians talk about following the 'way of heaven', while legitimate emperors are said to govern under the 'mandate of heaven'. But 'heaven' is a loose and misleading translation of *tian*, even though it has come to be the standard one, for lack of a clearer alternative. As Philip Ivanhoe and Bryan Van Norden explain it, 'Heaven is not primarily thought of as a place, and is not connected with any explicit views about an afterlife.' It does seem to be about a kind of 'higher power', but this is not generally personal or purposeful. *Tian* literally means 'sky' and is a part of the whole world, *tiāndì*, the sky and the earth (*dì*). 'In ancient Chinese philosophy,' says Yao Xinzhong, '*tiāndì*, heaven and earth, is the origin of everything, of human beings, human knowledge, human law, human morality, everything.'[4] In the Axial Age, only the Mohists talked about *tian* as a personal being with will and emotion, but Mohist philosophy didn't have much influence over later developments.

Following heaven's way is more like living in accordance with nature than adhering to some supernatural purpose.[5] A nice passage in the *Analects*, the main collection of Confucius's teachings, captures something of this. 'The superior man is quiet and calm, waiting for the appointments of heaven,' says Confucius, 'while the mean man walks in dangerous paths, looking for lucky occurrences.'[6] The difference is not that one looks beyond the world while the other looks within it, but rather that the superior man follows the grain of the world, looking for indications of what is timely, while the mean one wanders haphazardly, seeing no patterns and responding randomly.

One problem with accurately characterising this Chinese emphasis on the natural world is that the categories 'natural' and 'supernatural' do not easily fit Chinese philosophy. There are many aspects of Chinese thinking that would be characterised as supernatural in the Western schema. For example, *tian* needs to be respected and if you offend it you will be punished. This is not the indifferent nature of Western science, but nor is it the purposeful, conscious will of Western theistic religion. *Tian* is a fundamentally natural force but has a moral dimension.

Confucianism also emphasises the importance of ancestor worship. For Confucians, it often seems that dead ancestors are not just exemplars for later generations but continue to exist in some sense, influencing the world. From a Western materialistic perspective this is supernatural, but traditionally in China it was considered perfectly natural. However, how literally people took the powers of ancestors is not clear. The third-century-BCE Confucian Xunzi suggests that the purpose of many of what we would call 'supernatural' rituals is to give shape and order to life, not to actually influence the way the world works. 'One performs the rain sacrifice and it rains. Why?' he asks. 'I say: There is no special reason why. It is the same as when one does not perform the rain sacrifice and it rains anyway. [. . .] One performs divination and only then decides on important affairs. But this is not for the sake of getting what one seeks, but rather to give things proper form.'[7]

It would also be wrong to suggest that Chinese 'naturalism' means the Chinese have always been entirely satisfied with the here and now. Many argue that part of the appeal of Buddhism in China is that it offered the promise of a life to come and another, higher world that was absent in the indigenous traditions. However, the forms of Buddhism that became most popular in China, and also in Japan, are the ones that focus on the living world. The early twentieth-century Buddhist Taixu emphasised the possibility of becoming a Buddha in your lifetime. The most popular Buddhist deity in China, observes Chan Wing-Tsit, has been Kuan-yin (Avalokiteśvara), who has become much more humanised than in Japanese and Indian versions, portrayed as a mother figure from the Tang Period (618–907) onwards. Pictures portray her offering worldly blessings of health, wealth, long life and children, not transcendental *nirvāṇa*.[8] This chimes more with Daoist ideals of everlasting life here on earth and immortals who inhabit not the heavens but the high mountains. It also has echoes in the common Chinese aspiration to 'leave behind a fragrance lasting for millennia' in this world.[9]

Chinese thought is therefore not typically naturalistic in the Western sense of the word. Rather, it does not distinguish between the natural and the supernatural and is focused on the needs of humans here and now. It is not that it has a naturalist metaphysics – a theory of the nature of ultimate reality – but more that it doesn't much concern itself with metaphysics at all. As Legge put it, Confucius 'did not speculate on the creation of things or the end of them. He was not troubled to account for the origin of man, nor did he seek to know about his hereafter. He meddled neither with physics nor metaphysics.'[10] Zigong in the *Analects* says, 'One does not get to hear the Master expounding upon the subjects of human nature or the Way of Heaven.'[11]

Similarly, when Chî Lû asked him about serving the spirits of the dead, Confucius replied, 'While you are not able to serve men, how can you serve their spirits?' The disciple insisted, 'I venture to ask about death', and was told, 'While you do not know life, how can you know about death?'[12]

Xunzi discards ultimate questions even more firmly, saying, 'Only the sage does not seek to understand Heaven.'[13] For him, the only true way for humans is the human way: 'The Way is not the way of heaven, nor is it the way of earth. It is that whereby humans make their way, and that which the gentleman takes as his way.'[14] And 'If one rejects what lies with man and instead longs for what lies with Heaven, then one will have lost grasp of the true disposition of things.'[15]

Chakravarthi Ram-Prasad echoes this, describing classical Chinese thought as '*a*metaphysical'. It 'simply does not concern itself with ultimate reality; but it does ask questions of the most fundamental significance. It poses ultimate questions without ever concerning itself with ultimate realities.' Even when the Neo-Confucians later developed a more overt metaphysics of 'pattern' this was only in the service of understanding the nature of goodness and virtue.[16] Here Chinese philosophy contrasts with both Indian and Western philosophy, which are 'cosmogonic' (from the Greek *cosmos*, 'universe/order', and *gonia*, 'creation'). 'In a cosmogony, understanding the world requires an account of the first principles behind its structure.'[17] Cosmogonic traditions tend 'to be driven initially by the question "What is there (really)?"' while 'Chinese philosophy tends to ask "What should be done?"'[18]

The distinctive nature of Chinese naturalism is perhaps even more evident in Daoism. On the one hand, no major global philosophy is more associated with nature than Daosim; on the other, many of its teachings appear to invoke forces that are beyond nature, most obviously the *Dao* itself. Take this passage:

The Way has an essence and can be trusted. But it takes no action and has no form. It can be passed on but not received, gotten but not seen. It is its own trunk, its own root. Before Heaven and earth existed, it spiritualised the ghosts and gods, and gave birth to Heaven and earth. It is above the supreme ultimate but not high, below the six limits but not deep. It was born before Heaven and earth but does not age.[19]

The *Dao* here is said to exist before either heaven or earth and would therefore appear to be outside nature. However, its connection with nature is more intimate than this. It is after all a principle of how nature works, not something invoked to override nature. It is not before or underneath nature but a life force that creates and sustains nature. It is difficult to be more precise than this because the ultimate nature of the *Dao* is beyond language.

This way of thinking about the *Dao* has parallels with how we should think about *qi*. *Qi* is often thought of as a kind of ghostly force or energy, real but unmeasurable by science, a kind of rival force to those described by the laws of physics. In this account, *qi* is part of an alternative metaphysics to the modern Western, naturalistic one. As such it could now be dismissed as nothing more than an obsolete, pre-scientific guess at the ultimate nature of reality.

However, there are ways of understanding *qi* that still make sense even within the contemporary scientific paradigm. *Qi* refers to what Robin Wang calls the 'fundamentally dynamic' nature of reality, something that Chinese philosophers appreciated before empirical science described more fully the actual structure of this reality.[20] To see the world in terms of *qi* is not to commit yourself to beliefs about the fundamental forces or building blocks of reality but to see the world in terms of its dynamic interrelations. For instance, Wang says that 'In art, the movement of *qi* is what weaves together the painter, the painting, and the viewer into a single unified experience.' This does not require us to think of *qi* as some kind of ethereal substance. Rather, it invites us to focus on the aesthetic experience that brings viewer, creator and artwork together in ways that are not supernatural but that cannot be captured in scientific terms alone.

The value of thinking in terms of *qi* is the effect it has on how we live, not on what we believe metaphysically. This is exemplified by those who attain *wu-wei*, a kind of effortless action we achieve when we live in perfect harmony with the flow of nature. In the *Zhaungzi*, a butcher, Ding, wields his cleaver so skilfully that the meat appears to fall from the bone as the blade touches it. Ding says, 'I encounter then with spirit and don't look with my eyes. Sensible knowledge stops and spiritual desires proceed. I rely on the Heavenly patterns, strike in the big gaps, am guided by the large fissures, and follow what is inherently so.'[21] Through practice, Ding has gone beyond intellectual knowledge to intuitive mastery. He sees and hears, but not as lesser-skilled butchers see and hear. As Zhuangzi later says, 'Do not listen with your ears but listen with your mind. Do not listen with your mind but listen with your *qi*.'[22] The language sounds mystical but the sentiment is comprehensive in naturalistic terms. Think of a top tennis player in action. It is not possible to react quickly enough and choose the right shot by thinking things through rationally and consciously. Rather, through years of effort and practice, the goal is to intuitively sense where to be and how to hit the ball. Looking with your *qi*, you become so sensitive to the dynamics of the situation that you can tune in and harmonise perfectly.

Daoism shares the metaphysical agnosticism of Confucianism. This is the moral of the famous story of Zhuangzi, who awakens from a dream unable to tell whether 'it was Zhuangzi who had dreamt the butterfly or the butterfly dreaming Zhuangzi'. The author, reputedly Zhuangzi, says, 'There must be some difference between them!'[23] The implication is that, even if there is a difference, it doesn't matter. Earlier he said, 'If after ten thousand generations we encounter a single sage who knows the solution, it would be no different from what we encounter every morning and evening.'[24] What matters is how we encounter existence, not what might be ultimately true of it, which is in any case beyond our comprehension. Nature is the only reality we need to consider, whether or not it is in fact the only reality there is.

Japanese naturalism is very close to that of China. Its art, like that in China, has always taken nature as its main subject. One of the most famous Japanese styles is the *yamato-e* seasonal painting from the Muromachi period (1392–1573). An extraordinary example of this is the *Landscape of the Four Seasons*, a scroll over ten metres long attributed to Sesshū, on display at the Kyoto National Museum. Like Chinese Daoist paintings, it includes signs of human life, but the scenes are dominated by nature. Zen ink paintings are also mostly of nature and depictions of the Buddha are comparatively rare. The painting of Zhongfeng Mingben meditating pays more attention to the detail of the tree than to the man sitting under it, who is almost a sketch. Contrast this with many other Buddhist artistic traditions which focus almost exclusively on Buddhas. Nature is ubiquitous, and while some Japanese art portrays supernatural or superstitious ideas – like the paintings of Amida Buddha descending to earth, and the ten kings of hell, and scenes of punishment on display at the Idemitsu Museum – these are only a small fraction of classical art. The issue, as ever, is about emphasis.

Many consider the idea of Japanese reverence for nature as hopelessly out of date. Japan is, after all, a society where vending machines are ubiquitous, robots are increasingly popular, toilets routinely have built-in electric bidets and a nuclear power plant at Fukushima was the scene of a major environmental disaster. However, this is only alienation from nature in Western terms. Kobayashi Yasuo told me that Japanese nature is not European Nature with a capital letter, something almost divine. It is nature 'very near to you, this mountain in my village, this forest in my village, the nature of my community'. In Shintō, the indigenous religion of Japan, the shrine you should worship at is always your local one. If you're travelling you might visit another, but that's very much second best.

'Nature is not a paradise,' says Kobayashi, as it is for occidental romantics. 'We have no idea of paradise. Nature may be bad, may be disturbing, violent, like tsunamis, like volcanoes.' Japan has around 1,500 earthquakes every year. Showing respect and gratitude to nature is in part a way of trying to ensure it doesn't disturb us too much. It also means that what in the West is often disparagingly called trying to 'tame' nature is no more than good sense. Of course nature has to be tamed. This isn't a battle between humanity and nature, though, but a struggle for humanity within nature. We don't do things *to* nature, from the outside, but *with* nature, from the inside. As Kasulis explains it, 'If we join Shintō in considering human beings as part of nature instead of separate from it, even human inventiveness can be natural.' A *tatami* mat, for example, 'is not natural in that it is not found in nature [...] yet much of the sensory experience of straw remains.'[25] There is no distinction here between the natural and the artificial because everything is a part of nature.

Similar ideas are held by many Aboriginal Australians, with surprising consequences which challenge the thinking of Western environmentalists. Stephen Muecke describes a car journey with the Aboriginal philosopher Paddy Roe in which his companion threw empty cans out of the car window, much to Muecke's dismay. To the Western mind, this is despoiling nature; to Roe, the can is just another part of nature and it will find its place in it.[26] Of course, Aboriginal Australians generally now see as much reason to dispose of waste carefully as anyone else, but these reasons do not include any injunction to protect nature from humans: how could it, when humans are already part of nature?

Similarly, there is nothing in the Japanese embrace of the disposable culture that is essentially anti-nature. In Japan, the popularity of the disposable is due to its associations with purity, not convenience or consumerist fetishisation of the new. In Shintō, shrines are dismantled every twenty years and fresh ones are erected to maintain purity. For the same reason, before the eighth century, each new emperor or empress had a new palace built.[27] The moist paper towel in a little plastic sack that comes with any meal, even a takeaway, is a continuation of ancient rituals of purification before eating, not an ultra-modern extra.

Kasulis provides another telling example of how nature and human endeavour dovetail in an apocryphal story about two chefs, one Chinese and one Japanese, boasting about their skills. The Chinese chef said that he had such control over his sauces, spices and the texture of his food that he could make chicken taste like duck. 'The Japanese retorted,' says Kasulis, 'he could make a carrot taste more like a carrot than any other carrot anyone has ever eaten.'[28] Natural qualities require supreme human talent to be fully expressed.

The interplay between human ingenuity and nature is most striking in the development of advanced technology. Kobayashi sees this 'total negotiation with nature' reflected in the making of robots. To the traditional Japanese mind, everything is alive, and this animism is arguably reflected in their fascination with robots. 'We apply our principle of animism to machines,' says Kobayashi. 'We are not going to make a machine but a humanoid robot, an android.'

I heard similar things from Nakajima Takahiro, who claims that 'the Japanese way of thinking about nature has been closely connected to that of technology. We do not see wild nature as it is. It's a domesticated nature, it's a hybridity of wild nature and technology.' Even the famous *sakura* – cherry blossoms – reflect this. Before the Nara period, which began in 710 CE, the plum tree was a much more widespread plant in Japan. The spread of cherry blossom was the consequence of very deliberate planting by certain Japanese rulers.

While naturalist currents of thought exist outside East Asia, none have been so central or dominant for so long. In the West, naturalism first emerged in ancient Greece in the thinking of Thales of Miletus, often considered the father of science for his insistence that the material world is all that there is. His ideas didn't take strong hold, as for most of its history Western thought was under the influence of a combination of Platonism and Christianity, both of which asserted the existence of some kind of non-physical realm, more real than the world of perception. Even during the Enlightenment, when naturalism became more prominent, a residual separation of humanity and nature, mind and matter, persisted. Even now Westerners who accept a naturalistic world view find themselves distinguishing humanity and nature, mind and body, far more sharply than those in China or Japan.

This 'dualism' is often taken to be a distinctive feature of Western philosophy. If so, then it would be yet another mistaken kind of dualism to think that there is one alternative to it, in the Far East. Elsewhere in the world there is yet another way of thinking, which accepts a plurality of substances, of minds, bodies and spirits, yet which avoids sharp dualism. 'The distinction between the material and the spiritual has no place in African thinking,' say Lebisa J. Teffo and Abraham P. J. Roux.[29] Instead, there is a kind of vitalism in which everything is seen to be alive; perhaps even a panpsychism in which everything is conscious. This would also seem to be true of most oral philosophies. 'What we have in common with most of the world is that we don't separate out the spiritual from the physical,' the Māori Hirini Kaa told me. 'I think that's what makes Europe different. You're the ones who have separated it out, you're the ones who are abnormal.'

This separation is at the root of one of the most enduring

puzzles in Western philosophy, the 'mind-body problem': how can inert matter give rise to conscious thought and subjective experience? Galen Strawson, one of the most eminent contributors to the contemporary debate, sees panpsychism as the most credible solution on the table.[30] The idea that everything has at least a spark of mind could yet gain traction in Western philosophy.

For all its dominance in the East, naturalism is practically unheard of in classical Indian philosophy. Of the heterodox and orthodox schools, only Cārvāka embraces materialism, arguing that the four elements – earth, fire, water and air – are 'the original principles; from these alone, when transformed into body, intelligence is produced. [...] therefore the soul is only the body distinguished by the attribute of intelligence, since there is no evidence for any soul distinct from the body'.[31] Cārvāka, however, is the least influential of the six orthodox and five heterodox schools.

Dualistic thinking is a hard habit to break, but if it is ditched distinctions assumed fundamental disappear. Take away the mind/body distinction and you also take away the interior/exterior distinction, because there is no matter for the immaterial mind to be housed in. Muecke told me that in indigenous Australia, 'Nobody's interested in what goes on in the mind, because the mind may not even be a concept. Any notion of psychological interiority or souls is not part of their vision. Everything is exterior, that's what matters.'

In the modern secular West, most of us are officially naturalists, reflected in the constant calls to 'seize the day', to live 'the one life you have'. That we need reminding points to naturalism's historical novelty. Nor have Westerners yet learned how best to follow their own advice. Too often, living for today becomes a shallow pursuit of fleeting pleasure that always leaves us starting each day empty, needing another 'experience'. We are constantly dissatisfied, forever grasping at moments that elude us. Instead, we need to learn to savour without grasping, to caress the moment rather than to grab it. If we look east, we might find models for living as mortals in a natural world from cultures that have been doing just that for millennia.

UNITY

In the Middle Ages, there were palaces scattered all over the Muslim world. Today, only one remains, but as any visitor to the Alhambra will testify, posterity could not have chosen a better sole survivor. Its location is magical, situated on a hill opposite the undulating old part of the Spanish city of Granada, where every turn of the corner affords a new, breathtaking view. At dawn and dusk it glows like a dying ember, a consequence of the ferruginous dust that has stained its walls and given it its name, derived from *al-hamra*, Arabic for 'the red'.[1]

The Alhambra is not a single building or even a complex, but a settlement that expanded and evolved over several centuries. At its glorious heart are the Nasrid Palaces, built by the Muslim rulers Yusuf I (1333–53) and Mohammed V (1353–91). Not only are the decoration and design of these buildings extraordinarily harmonious and intricate, but they also bring to life some key Islamic ideals. This is because, not despite the fact that, the palaces are not religious buildings, at least as we would usually understand that term. In Islamic thought, there is no distinction between the sacred and the secular. There is an 'ubiquitous presence of the sacred in all forms of architecture in such a way as to remove the very notion of the secular as a category,' says Seyyed Hossein Nasr.[2] Allah is everywhere, even in the homes of wealthy secular rulers, because 'the soul is much more affected by what it experiences every day than by a painting that one might see on a Sunday in a museum or church'.[3]

Most explicitly, the building is decorated with tens of thousands of Arabic inscriptions. It is, says Robert Irwin, an 'inhabitable book'.[4] The motto of the Nasrid dynasty, 'There is no victor but Allah', recurs hundreds of times on walls, arches and columns. Qur'ānic texts are placed in the highest spaces, where God but not humans can read them. All that is good in the building reflects the glory of God. The fountain in the Court of the Lions bears the inscription 'Allah the exalted one desired that it should surpass everything in wonderful beauty.'

The geometric shapes and patterns that dominate the decoration signify more than the mere absence of representational figures, prohibited by Islam. They represent a cosmic order that is divinely ordained. For example, Nasr sees the recurring patterns of intertwined polygons and arabesques as symbolising the masculine and the feminine, which represent 'the rhythms of life itself'.[5] For Irwin, the whole point of the complexity and detail of the Alhambra is that they defy all attempts to take them in. Rather, this is an exploration of infinity that we are supposed to 'drown in', aware of our limitations as finite beings.[6] Tourists who marvel at the building's beauty but do not recognise its religious significance fail to appreciate that the building is 'a machine to think in'.[7]

The Alhambra is a material expression of spiritual and intellectual ideals of oneness, wholeness, unity, of the presence of the divine in every aspect of the secular and of the infinite in everything finite. Islam proposes not just a fundamental unity of all things, but the perfect divine transcendental unity of God. John

Renard writes, 'At the heart of all Islamic theological reflection and debate is an intense interest in articulating the manifold mystery of God's perfect transcendent oneness.'[8] Nasr says that 'the several enduring intellectual perspectives that have been cultivated in the Islamic world all conform to the doctrine of unity (*al-tawḥīd*)'.[9]

Some idea of oneness or unity is found in many great philosophical traditions. All the major schools of Indian philosophy, for instance, assert a basic oneness of all being. This was first clearly articulated in the early *Upaniṣads*, which state that *ātman* is *Brahman*, that our own individual selves are part of the universal self, the 'One':

> It moves, It moves not.
> It is far, and It is near.
> It is within all this.
> And It is outside of all this.[10]

There are a couple of key phrases that express this oneness in telegraphic form, one of which is *tat tvam asi* in Sanskrit, usually translated 'this is that' or 'that art thou'. For example, 'That which is the finest essence – this whole world has that as its self. That is reality. That is *Ātman*. That art thou [*Tat tvam asi*].'[11] (Note that *Ātman* is capitalised when it refers to the universal self which is identical with *Brahman* but is lower case when referring to the manifestation of that self in the individual.) The phrase echoes another famous formulation that *Ātman* (and hence also *Brahman*) is *neti neti*: not this, not that. In other words, it is nothing in particular but it is everything. 'It is unseizable, for it cannot be seized; indestructible, for it cannot be destroyed; unattached, because it does not attach itself; is unbound, does not tremble, is not injured.'[12]

The notion of unity came to greatest fruition in the non-dualism of the school of Advaita Vedānta, developed in the work of Śaṅkara. Advaita literally means non (*a-*) duality (*dvaita*). Śaṅkara maintained that there are two levels of reality, the absolute and the conventional level of ordinary perception. In conventional reality, there is the appearance of plurality, but at the absolute level, there is only unity. Everything is *Brahman*.

If everything is one, there is no difference between self and other, no subject and object, and hence no individual consciousness or intentionality. The world of ordinary experience is nothing more than a powerful illusion. Only if there is a duality of self and other can one see another, smell another, hear another, speak to another. When we realise the absolute unity, we realise there is no one to smell, speak, think or understand. 'Whereby would one understand him by whom one understands this All? Lo, whereby would one understand the understander?'[13]

Similarly, the concept of *dharma*, which concerns a harmony between the cosmic order and your own personal duty, draws on an assumption of fundamental unity. *Dharma* refers to the cosmic order as a whole (*ṛta*) but also to the duties of the individual. Right action is therefore that which upholds the fundamental unity and oneness of the whole.[14]

Chinese thought has elements which stress unity as well. In Daoism there is a belief that distinctions are created by thought and language and that beyond these artificial divisions everything is in a sense one. 'No matter how diverse or strange, the Way comprehends them as one,' says the *Zhuangzi*. The mistake we make when we fail to see this is called 'three in the morning', after a story about a monkey trainer who tells his monkeys they will get three peanuts in the morning and four at night. They become angry at this so he gives them four in the morning and three at night and they are pleased. They fail to see that it's all the same.[15]

Unity is less of a theme in Confucianism, but more than once Confucius uses the image of a single thread to capture the unity of his teaching. 'All that I teach can be strung together on a single thread,' he said. Master Zeng later explained to the disciples, 'All that the master teaches amounts to nothing more than dutifulness (*zhong*) tempered by sympathetic understanding (*shu*).'[16] Another way of expressing the wholeness is 'When I have presented one corner of a subject to any one, and he cannot from it learn the other three, I do not repeat my lesson.'[17]

However, unity and oneness find their fullest realisation in Islamic philosophy. Oneness, or simplicity, *tawḥīd*, is first and foremost a property of God. Al-Ghazālī wrote, 'God is the witness who makes known to His chosen people that in His essence He is one, without partner, alone and without any like, enduring and without opposite, unique and without equal.'[18] Ironically, although this is taken to show the timelessness of Islam, it seems clear that the idea itself was borrowed from the Neoplatonists and is therefore both historical and non-Islamic in origin.[19]

In what Peter Adamson calls the 'formative period' of Islamic philosophy, *tawḥīd* was central to the thinking of the Mu'tazalites, a *kalām* movement founded by Wāṣil ibn 'Aṭā (d. 748). They were known as the 'upholders of unity and justice'.[20] But it was also a key element of *falsafa*: al-Kindī, the first *falāsifa*, 'portrayed God as "the True One", free of all multiplicity', while Avicenna argued there can only be one necessary existent.[21]

In the minority mystical Sufi tradition (to which no more than 5 per cent of Muslims belong), this unity extends to the whole of existence (*waḥdat al-wujūd*), with the idea that, as Adamson puts it, 'all created reality is a manifestation of the one true reality, namely God'.[22]

Although the emphasis on the unity of all things is most explicit in Sufism, unity and oneness are a recurring theme in Islamic thought as a whole. First and most obviously, the Qur'ān is taken to be complete and perfect. Al-Ghazālī wrote, 'The Qur'ān is recited by the tongues, written in the copies, and remembered in the hearts, but despite this it is from eternity subsisting in God's essence'.[23] One of the many names for the Qur'ān is *umm al-kitāb* (the mother of all books), because, as Nasr puts it, 'all authentic knowledge contained in "all books" is ultimately contained in its bosom'.[24] Nasr is not always representative of Islamic philosophy today, but he certainly speaks for almost all Muslims when he says, 'Traditional Islam accepts, of course, without any ifs, ands, or buts, the Noble Qur'ān in both content and form as the word of God.'[25] He acknowledges the existence of some recent reformers but downplays their influence, saying that 'a figure such as al-Ghazālī [. . .] is still a much more powerful and influential religious authority in the Islamic world than all the so-called reformers taken together'.[26] Even the contemporary reformist Tariq Ramadan agrees that for Muslims the Qur'ān was 'revealed without human intervention and modification' and is 'the last word of God, revealed in its entirety, and will remain the ultimate reference for all time'.[27]

The completeness of the Qur'ān does not mean that it must always be read as literal truth. Avicenna says clearly, 'We the Muslim community know definitely that demonstrative study does not lead to conclusions conflicting with what Scripture has given us; for truth does not oppose truth but accord with it and bears witness to it.'[28] But he also accepts the authority of 'demonstrative reason', drawing conclusions from accepted premises by rational methods. Accepting both the authority of demonstrative reason and the Qur'ān entails that 'if [the apparent meaning of scripture] conflicts with [the conclusions of demonstration], there is a call for allegorical interpretation of it'.[29] It is more than possible that Islam will in the future emphasise these metaphorical readings more. After all, it was not until the 1940s that the Catholic Church accepted that the first eleven chapters of Genesis were not 'history in the classical or modern sense'.[30]

Second, for Muslims, there is no part of life which is outside Islam and unaffected by it. Even the sounds of nature, says Nasr, should be 'heard as the invocation (*dhikr*) of God's Blessed Names and as His Praise according to the Qur'ānic verse, "All things hymn the praise of God"'.[31] The distinction between the secular and the sacred is non-existent. To many outside Islam, this gives the religion a seemingly totalitarian character. Nasr prefers the term *intégrisme*, which he thinks equally applies to 'traditional Catholics who wish to integrate all of life into their religion and, conversely, their religion into all aspects of life'.[32]

Yahya Michot stressed to me how vital it is to recognise that in an Islamic society this 'doesn't mean that this framework will have a coercive influence on every aspect of your life'. It will have an impact on public life but 'inside of your house you do whatever you want', which is one of the reasons why traditionally 'within Muslim society non-Muslims are welcome'. Indeed, Michot believes that true Islam (not necessarily manifest in Muslim-majority countries) grants more individual freedom than Western liberal regimes. 'In the West today,' he says, 'in some countries you can't buy *Mein Kampf*, or *Das Kapital*, have them in your home, or display in your home some Nazi or Communist symbols. In the Netherlands, some politicians now speak of forbidding copies of the Qur'ān. In Islam a judge, the authorities, have no access to the home. Inside the home that's a separate space, it doesn't belong to any authority.'

Michot cites a well-known passage in the *hadith* collection *Al-Mustadrak alaa al-Sahihain* that sets out this principle. (A *hadith* is a non-Qur'ānic report of the words, actions, or habits of Muḥammad.) Two men, Abdur Rahman ibn Awf and Umar ibn Al-Khattab, were patrolling the streets one night when Umar realised that a Muslim neighbour was drinking wine at home. Abdur Rahman replied, 'I think we have done what Allah has prohibited for us', quoting the Qur'ānic injunction 'Do not spy.'[33] So the men left the neighbour alone.[34]

For a Muslim, however, Islam determines how you should live in every aspect of your life, from how you wash and what you eat. Education is therefore inherently religious too. 'The goal of education is to perfect and actualise all the possibilities of the human soul, leading finally to that supreme knowledge of the divinity that is the goal of human life,' says Nasr. In most of the Muslim world, education still starts with the teaching of the Qur'ān.[35] 'The general aim of the educational system should be to make its intellectual perspective and worldview totally Islamic,' says Nasr.[36]

This helps explain why, as we saw earlier, there is no clear distinction between philosophy and theology in Islam. The *falāsifa* thought that *falsafa* would supplant *kalām*, but instead, in the Mongol period, they increasingly became fused. As Nasr puts it, the Islamic philosophical tradition 'lives in a religious universe in which a revealed book and prophecy understood as sources of knowledge dominate the horizon'. The intellect is a divine gift which if used correctly will lead to the same truths as those revealed in scripture. 'Islamic philosophy is therefore concerned above all with the doctrine of unity (*al-tawḥīd*), which dominates the whole message of Islam,' says Nasr.[37]

Given the completeness of the Qur'ān and the oneness of all things, there is no possibility of progress in the modern, Western Enlightenment sense. Truth is unchanging and its essence can be known. Al-Ghazālī wrote, 'Know that true demonstration is what provides necessary, perpetual and eternal certainty that cannot change.'[38] Of course Islam accepts that there are many facts about the world that were not known at the time of Muḥammad and many more still to be discovered. But these new facts are in an important sense mere details. The growth of knowledge is like colouring in and embellishing a canvas rather than expanding the picture. The Qur'ān expresses a complete world view and nothing that comes after it can alter those fundamentals.

Nasr states this view more forthrightly than anyone. For him, the 'esoteric' truth contained within Islam always has priority over any other 'exoteric' truths discovered independently of it: 'The esoteric comprehends the exoteric, but the exoteric excludes and does not comprehend the esoteric.'[39] For example, esoteric Islamic metaphysics is 'the science of Ultimate Reality', while secular 'so-called cosmology' presents only 'theories based upon certain questionable, far-fetched extrapolations and usually empirically unprovable assumptions'.[40]

Such a world view is in complete contradiction to Western modernity, as Nasr is happy to emphasise. While there is diversity within contemporary Islamic thought, Nasr's views are within the mainstream of the classical tradition. For those like him, there is little prospect of adopting modern views on issues such as gender roles and homosexuality. Masculine and feminine are divinely pre-scribed distinctions with complementary roles and so 'to reject the distinct and distinguishing features of the two sexes and the Sacred Legislation based on this objective cosmic reality is to live below the human level; to be, in fact, only accidentally human'.[41] Even those who take a far less extreme view do not waver on the funda-mental sexual morality of Islam. Although the reformist Ramadan is against punishment of homosexuality, he says that 'the Qur'ān itself [. . .] leaves very little room for interpretation [. . .] meaning that homosexuality is considered a sin and forbidden in Islam'.[42]

A striking consequence of the fundamental oneness of the Islamic cosmos is that everything that happens has already been written. Predestination features heavily in Islamic thought. One *hadith* talks about an individual's 'recorded destiny', which has the power to alter the direction of a life in an instant. A person might 'behave like the inhabitants of paradise until he is barely an arm's length from it, when his recorded destiny overtakes him so that he [suddenly] behaves like the people of Hell-fire and therefore enters it [instead]'. The converse might also happen, with a sinner starting to behave like the inhabitants of paradise just in time to enter it.[43]

Such passages are not rare. Another *hadith* tells us:

When the drop of (semen) remains in the womb for forty or fifty (days) or forty nights, the angel comes and says: My Lord, will he be good or evil? And both these things would be written. Then the angel says: My Lord, would he be male or female? And both these things are written. And his deeds and actions, his death, his livelihood; these are also recorded. Then his document of destiny is rolled and there is no addition to and subtraction from it.[44]

In the Qur'ān itself numerous passages suggest God decides in advance who is good and bad, who is saved or damned. 'Indeed, Allah leaves astray whom He wills and guides to Himself whoever turns back [to Him].'[45] 'And when they deviated, Allah caused their hearts to deviate.'[46] 'Allah keeps firm those who believe, with the firm word, in worldly life and in the Hereafter. And Allah sends astray the wrongdoers. And Allah does what He wills.'[47]

Theologians have debated over the centuries how predetermination is compatible with just punishment and reward. On the face of it, it seems outrageous that God should punish those whom he has preordained to sin and reward those who were only ever going to be good. Most outside the faith are unconvinced that this issue has been resolved. Still, to understand the Islamic world today we need to recognise that Muslims typically see all events as being the will of God but nonetheless hold people to be culpable and praiseworthy.

For example, after the Asian tsunami that killed around a quarter of million people in 2004, many Muslim voices expressed the view that it was God's will, inscrutable though that might be. Iqbal Sacranie, secretary general of the Muslim Council of Britain, told the BBC, 'It is our firm belief that any such disaster, anything of that nature happening, is through the will of God Almighty. Allah knows best.' This would have been an almost universal view among Muslims.

Not as universal, but nonetheless common, is the idea that God's will in such disasters is to punish. In an analysis of responses to the tsunami, two academics reported, 'Many Acehnese Muslims believe that the tsunami was divine punishment for lay Muslims shirking their daily prayer and/or following a materialistic lifestyle.'[48] Similarly, after the Japanese tsunami of 2011, the website Islam21C.com quoted the Qur'ānic verses: 'And if the people of the towns had believed and had the *taqwa* (piety), certainly, We should have opened for them blessings from the heaven and the earth, but they believed (the Messengers). So We took them (with punishment) for what they used to earn (polytheism and crimes, etc.).'[49] These modern-day interpreters say the Japanese paid the price for 'the lack of submission to Allah and refusing to admit that all of the favours they are blessed with are given to them by their Creator'.[50]

The completeness of the Qur'ānic revelation has another implication: that reason is of limited use. Take the twelfth-century poetry of Sanā'ī, from what is now Afghanistan.

> No one can understand Him unaided; His essence one can
> know only through Him.
> Reason desired the truth of Him but did not fare well [. . .]
> Reason is a guide but [only] to his door; only his favour
> brings you to Him.
> You will not make the journey with the evidence of reason;
> do not make this error like other fools.[51]

In *Deliverer from Error*, al-Ghazālī wrote about his escape from sceptical worries. For Adamson, 'Al-Ghazālī was freed from the impasse only thanks to "a light cast in his heart" by God. This experience taught him that human reason cannot provide the highest form of insight and certainty. [. . .] The problem is not using reason, but thinking that reason can do too much.'[52] Adamson says that even according to the *falāsifa*, 'prophets are individuals who have attained more completely, and without effort, the same kind

of understanding that other humans must acquire through laborious enquiry'.[53] Avicenna says that both prophets and philosophers
have a capacity for intuition (*ḥads*), which is required to find the
middle term in a syllogism, something that might happen out of
the blue. 'The prophet is simply a more extreme case. He has
intuition to a maximum degree and receives the intelligibles from
the agent intellect either "all at one or nearly so", as Avicenna puts
it.'[54] Reason is not always necessary.

Muslims believe the oneness of Islam is a great strength. Nasr
argues that Islam is a traditional philosophy based on a 'supra-
individual' intellect, a collaboration of many minds over history,
superior to the philosophy dominant in the West, which relies
on individualistic reasoning. Its superiority, he claims, explains
Islamic philosophy's constancy and longevity compared to other
philosophies that go in and out of fashion.[55]

For those outside the tradition, oneness makes philosophy a
mere handmaiden to theology, and results in stasis and inertia.
Yet although ossification of thought is a risk in Islamic intellectual
culture, it is far from inevitable. The idea that the Islamic world
is trapped within a medieval world view is belied by history.
There have been several periods when various Islamic societies
have made great advances in knowledge, most notably during
the so-called Golden Age from the eighth to the thirteenth
centuries, when 'Houses of Wisdom' were established in cities
such as Baghdad, Damascus, Cairo and Córdoba.[56] Christopher
de Bellaigue has also written extensively about what he calls the
'Islamic Enlightenment' in which free thought flourished in Cairo,
Istanbul and Tehran in the nineteenth century.[57] Although the
Qur'ān is considered complete, it leaves much unsaid or in need
of interpretation. There has always been an important role for *itjihād*, independent reasoning, to fill the space 'between the silence
of scripture and the specificity of the context', as Ramadan puts
it. Although all Muslims agree on the pillars of Islam, there is and

always has been great diversity of interpretation as to what that singular faith requires of believers.

Oneness in Islam does not preclude it from changing or accommodating itself to the modern world. It is rather that no one can expect the Muslim world to embrace a non-Islamic, secular notion of modernity. Islamic modernity is emerging from within the tradition and will not involve shedding anything of central importance to the faith. When reformists like Ramadan call for 'Islamic renewal' and 'an intellectual and psychological revolution', they are not calling for Islam to conform to secular ideals. Islamic modernity is a particular vision of Islamic principles at their best, a 'rediscovery of the way', not the taking of an alternative path.[58]

REDUCTIONISM

The idea that each part contains the whole may be a character-istically eastern one, but the most common example of its use is occidental. It has been said that everything good, but more usually bad, about Western culture can be found at a McDonald's. When people complain of Western cultural colonialism, they point to the globally ubiquitous golden arches. When people talk of poorly paid, menial work, they talk of 'McJobs'. When health campaigners lament the poor Western diet, a Big Mac and fries is Exhibit A.

Such observations are often somewhat unfair, simplistic and lazy. In another less-noticed way, however, the fast-food giant does exemplify a quintessentially Western way of thinking. On the McDonald's website, you can find a complete list of its products' ingredients and nutritional values. Take the Big Mac. Many are surprised to learn that the patty itself is 100 per cent pure beef with a little salt. The bun, on the other hand, contains wheat flour, water, sugar, sesame seeds, rapeseed oil, salt, yeast, wheat gluten, emulsifiers (mono- and diacetyl tartaric acid esters of mono- and diglycerides of fatty acids), improver (monocalcium phosphate), preservative (calcium propionate), antioxidant (ascorbic acid), wheat starch, calcium, iron, niacin (B3) and thiamin (B1). It would take several more lines to detail what's in the sauce, pickle and cheese slices. You'll also find a breakdown of calories, fat, carbohydrate, fibre, protein and salt alongside the recommended daily intakes (RDI) for each of these. You can even use a calculator to discover that a Big Mac and medium fries gives you 42 per cent of your daily calorific needs, around half your fat and salt, and only 10 per cent of your sugar allowance – which can be splurged instead on a large chocolate milkshake (25 per cent of RDI calories, 67 per cent of RDI sugars).

Behind this information is a deep philosophical assumption that has informed Western ways of thinking for centuries: reductionism. This is the idea that the best way to understand anything is to break it down into its constituent parts, emphasising these over wholes. Tom Kasulis sees this approach manifested in pretty much every corner of Western thought: 'The ethicist places ultimate responsibility on the smallest unit of ethical integrity (the individual agent); the physicist breaks down the universe into its smallest invisible units and their relations; the geneticist looks for the connections between the smallest genetic unit, the genes, and their relations to each other.'[1]

'Reductionism' became an established concept only in the second half of the twentieth century, but as a method it has been with us since the advent of modern science, as d'Alembert makes plain in his 'Preliminary Discourse' to the *Encyclopédie*. 'In our study of Nature, which we make partly by necessity and partly for amusement, we note that bodies have a large number of properties,' he wrote. 'However, in most cases they are so closely united in the same subject that, in order to study each of them more thoroughly, we are obliged to consider them separately.' This is an advantage, not an inconvenience. 'Indeed, the more one reduces the number of principles of a science, the more one gives them scope, and since the object of a science is necessarily fixed, the principles applied to that object will be so much the more fertile as they are fewer in number. This reduction which, moreover, makes them easier to understand.' So much easier, in fact, that 'it is perhaps true that there is hardly a science or an art which cannot, with rigour and good logic, be taught to the most limited mind, because there are but few arts or sciences whose propositions or rules cannot be reduced to some simple notions and arranged in such a close order that their chain of connection will nowhere be interrupted.'[2] Only by first breaking down can we build up a complete and systematic account of the world, as found in the 'encyclopedic tree which will gather the various branches of know-ledge together' that Diderot and d'Alembert were attempting to construct in their *Encyclopédie*. D'Alembert was describing nothing less than the scientific method, as revealed by his declaration that 'we owe principally to Chancellor Bacon the encyclopedic tree'.

The reductionist method has resulted in many remarkable advances in the physical sciences and, fuelled by this success, has been applied far beyond. Indeed, it is more difficult to think of a non-reductionist paradigm than a reductionist one. For example, when I began my training in philosophy, concepts were routinely analysed in terms of 'necessary and sufficient conditions'. Concepts were boiled down to a checklist of what must be true in order for it to be correctly applied. Plato's definition of knowledge as justified true belief was the classical inspiration for this approach. To have knowledge it is both necessary and sufficient that you believe something that is true and justified. Ironically, in Plato's dialogue *Theaetetus*, the attempt to specify the necessary and sufficient con-ditions of knowledge was ultimately judged to be a failure. Later philosophers concluded not that the method was flawed, but that we need a better list of conditions.

Similarly, when I wrote my PhD on personal identity, the issue was standardly framed as the question of what the necessary and sufficient conditions are for a person at two different times to be the same person. I argued that this was the wrong question, but the fact I had to make that case at all is testament to the dominance of the necessary and sufficient conditions paradigm.

When Harry Frankfurt applied the method of seeking necessary and sufficient conditions to the concept of 'bullshit' in an essay that ended up as an international bestseller, I wondered whether he had in fact pulled off a kind of postmodern joke, showing how silly it was to try to analyse everything this way. 'Any suggestion about what conditions are logically both necessary and sufficient for the constitution of bullshit is bound to be somewhat arbitrary,' he admitted, but then shrugged this concern aside, adding 'nonetheless it should be possible to say something helpful'.[3]

Reductionism even extends to ethics. Utilitarianism reduces the rightness and wrongness of actions to the consequences they have with regards to happiness, preference satisfaction or welfare, depending on the variant of the theory. The godfather of utilitarianism, Jeremy Bentham, proposed what came to be called a 'felicific calculus' that would enable us to calculate which actions are better according to this principle.[4] Even most contemporary utilitarians scoff at this today, but the basic idea is entirely within the spirit of an approach to ethics which reduces morality to a single dimension.

Many see a connection between this broad reductionist tendency and the individualism which has flowered in the West. Society has been broken down into its constituent parts, individual human beings, the basis for all thinking about how we ought to live, individually and collectively. But it is not obvious that we are primarily individuals and only secondarily part of a wider society. After all, we come into the world as someone's child, we grow up as siblings, peers, members of a community, perhaps a religion, and become parts of other communities of interest.

Reductionist approaches are now so aligned with common sense that we fail to notice that they rest on contested philosophical assumptions. As we have seen, there is a much greater emphasis on holistic understanding elsewhere. Even in Western science, the home of reductionism, there is an increasing acceptance that it is only one tool. Biology often progresses by analysing systems rather than simply isolated parts. Complexity and chaos theory are premised on the notion that the behaviour of systems is not predictable from the behaviours of their constituent elements.

Nutritional science has not abandoned its commitment to the value of the kind of reductionist lists printed on food packaging, but increasingly people understand their limits. So, 20g of added refined sugar does not affect the body in the same way as 20g of sugar from whole fruit. Credible research even suggests the same amount of saturated fat from a diary source might have a different effect on cholesterol depending on whether it comes from cheese or cream. The reductionist response is that we must reduce further, to be more specific in what we analyse. While there may be some truth in this, it seems certain that without looking at the context in which food is ingested, including the specific features of the individual eater, the reductionist picture will always be incomplete at best and misleading at worst.

It is perhaps in the field of semantics that reductionist necessary and sufficient conditions are most in retreat. There may be some philosophical value in specifying the precise meanings of technical terms, but ordinary language certainly doesn't work that way. We are all competent language users yet few of us are easily able to come up with good, clear definitions of the words we use. As Eleanor Rosch argues in her prototype theory, the way we actually learn what words mean is first to see how they are most commonly applied ('chair' refers to those four-legged items of furniture we sit on, for example), then to feel our way to their extended meanings (using a tree stump as a chair) and finally to become able to use them in ambiguous (is a sofa or a stool a chair?) or metaphorical (chair of the meeting) senses. All of this is done without ever formulating a set of necessary and sufficient conditions, breaking down meaning to a precise definition.[5]

Scientific progress has depended on reductionism, but it creates weaknesses in a culture where it becomes the default frame of mind. The reductionist tendency blinds people to the complex effects of whole systems and leads to an overconfidence that the key to solving problems is identifying discrete elements. For example, the discovery of a link between the serotonin levels in the brain and depression led many to advocate the 'serotonin hypothesis' – that an imbalance in the neurotransmitter serotonin *causes* depression and that so-called second-generation antidepressants such as selective serotonin reuptake inhibitors (SSRIs) could treat depression by correcting this serotonin imbalance. As almost always happens when someone tries to reduce a complex phenomenon to a single factor, however, we have subsequently found that it is more complicated than this simplified model suggests. Many now believe that low serotonin does not cause depression and that in many cases, if not all, SSRIs are of little or no help.

There are many reasons why people put too much faith in the serotonin hypothesis. Pharmaceutical companies had vested interests: one of the earliest, Prozac (the brand name for fluoxetine), became the biggest-selling antidepressant in history within two years of its release. Depression is both debilitating and hard for doctors to treat, so the promise of a wonder cure was always going to be attractive. The least-noticed factor is that the cultural assumption of reductionism made the hypothesis much more credible than in retrospect it ever was.

Reductionist explanations are too often taken to be the only ones that count. For example, most of us accept that our brains are in a sense the hardware that enables us to be conscious. So whenever anything conscious happens it is in theory always possible to describe what is going in on neuronal terms. For instance, when you make a decision, some kind of neuronal event occurs. But it does not follow that what you did is best understood by that reductive, neuronal explanation and that whatever you were consciously thinking is now irrelevant. If reductive explanations were the only true ones, then nothing would be explained except in the terms of fundamental physics. This can't be right: there is a very real sense in which the explanation for why your car doesn't start is that the battery is flat, even though there are no batteries and cars in fundamental physics.

The philosopher Janet Radcliffe Richards explains this confusion by distinguishing between debunking and non-debunking explanations.[6] A debunking explanation replaces one explanation with another. For example, when the physician Barry Marshall discovered that up to 90 per cent of peptic ulcers are caused by a bacterium called *Helicobacter pylori*, he was debunking the rival theory that ulcers were commonly caused by stress. A non-debunking explanation, however, can leave other explanations intact. Sailors discovered that eating citrus fruit prevented scurvy long before we understood the reason for this, which was that scurvy was caused by vitamin C deficiency. The medical explanation in no way debunked the theory that eating citrus fruit prevented scurvy, it merely explained the mechanism that made this true.

Radcliffe Richards points out that too often reductive explanations are assumed to be debunking when they need not be. Brain studies show the neural mechanisms behind decisions, not that we don't make them. Similarly, depression is bound to show up in changes in the brain, but events in life can be causes of depression and talking therapies can often help. 'Explaining is not the same as explaining away,' as Radcliffe Richards pithily put it.[7] Often, when Western reductionism is criticised, the reductionism itself is not the problem, it's the way in which it is taken to be debunking.

Once we become attuned to the reductionist assumption it is

evident everywhere in Western culture. Its peculiarity is no reason to reject it. Reductionism is a source of many of the strengths in Western thinking as well as its weaknesses. The important thing is simply to notice that there is indeed a reductionist assumption being made and to ask whether or not, in this particular case, thinking more holistically might either enrich our understanding or be preferable to the reductionist analysis. When reductionism becomes the only way of thinking, we reduce too much.

CONCLUSION

In 2011 Stephen Hawking caused a stir by declaring that 'philosophy is dead'. He said that scientists 'have become the bearers of the torch of discovery in our quest for knowledge' and are now the ones answering the big questions such as 'Why are we here?' and 'Where do we come from?' Philosophers have been left behind because they 'have not kept up with modern developments in science, particularly physics'.[1]

These were grand assertions, but came without supporting evidence or further explanation – curious from someone who champions the scientific method. What Hawking seemed to mean was that philosophical metaphysics was dead, replaced by scientific physics. This would fit a familiar story about the advance of human knowledge, the first iteration of which was put forward in *The Golden Bough* by the anthropologist Sir James George Frazer in 1890. First, we tried to understand the world mythologically. Then, we applied our reason and tried to make sense of it philosophically. Finally, we developed the experimental and theoretical tools which enabled us to study it scientifically. In this view, the mythological and the philosophical are merely stepping stones on the way to the scientific. Even some philosophers have agreed with something like this. Karl Popper, for example, lumped metaphysics together with 'pre-scientific myths' that are not open to empirical testing.[2]

It might indeed be true that some traditionally metaphysical issues, such as the nature of space and time, really are best studied scientifically. But to call this the death of philosophy is an overstatement, not least because a great many philosophical questions do not belong in the domain of science. Problems in moral and political philosophy, for example, can't be solved by scrutinising them with Large Hadron Colliders or fMRI scanners.

More fundamentally, there is no reason why we should consider philosophical metaphysics to be amateur physics. Even if we completely gave up the idea that metaphysics explains the world as it really is (which many philosophers have believed), there is still work to be done explaining the world as it appears to us, in lived experience. This is in effect what Kant proposed as the proper object of metaphysical inquiry.

We might call this *phenomenological metaphysics*: the study of the structure of the world of experience. Phenomenological metaphysics would remain a proper subject of inquiry even if our scientific physics were to be complete. Nor would physics and phenomenological metaphysics necessarily be in competition. For example, according to many physicists, there is no 'now' in nature, nor any past or future. But human beings certainly do live in tensed time and phenomenological metaphysics should have something to say about this.

However the philosophers of the great world's traditions viewed their metaphysics, it is most fruitful now to consider their ideas through the lens of phenomenological metaphysics rather than a scientific one. When we consider time philosophically we are concerned with how we must fruitfully think about and relate to its passage. The value of the concept of emptiness has nothing to do with whether or not it corresponds to the findings of quantum theory. The value of metaphysics is existential, not scientific. That is why it is possible to learn from more than one metaphysical system, because the way we structure experience is in part due to the innate structure of our minds and in part because of the way our minds and societies structure each other. Although Kant said that 'the time for the collapse of all dogmatic metaphysics is undoubtedly here' he was right to add, 'There will always be metaphysics in the world, and what is more, in every human being, and especially the reflective ones.'[3]

PART THREE

Who in the World Are We?

The opening of Beethoven's Fifth Symphony is one of the most famous in Western musical history. You can almost certainly imagine it in your head or hum it right now: 'da-da-da-*daaaaaa*'. You'll have no problem identifying the fourth note, which is an E. What is it, however, that makes it that *particular* E?

There are at least three ways to answer that question. One is that it is that E rather than another E because of where it stands in relation to the opening three Gs and the rest of the symphony that follows. In a different sequence of notes, it would be a different E. This defines the nature of E *relationally*.

Another is that it is the E it is simply because it is a particular instance of E and that's all there is to be said about it, just as a particular pound coin is simply one minting of the general type. This defines the nature of the E *atomistically*.

A third, more radical answer is that the question is misguided. Nothing makes it the particular E that it is because it has no essential nature at all. We can call it E and refer to it on a score but that creates the illusion that there is something really there. In reality, the note is an ephemeral event that comes and goes, and is slightly different every time it is played. The belief that there is an E, the nature of which can be defined, is an illusion.

Which of these answers is correct? Perhaps all and none. Each describes a way of thinking about the note which captures a truth, but none is the only right way of thinking about it. However, which description we choose will affect the way we think about the note:

as part of a wider whole, as it is in itself, and as it manifests itself in the impermanent flux of perception.

This is a useful analogy for how we can think about ourselves. There is a sense in which we all exist atomistically. Each of us is a biological unity and when we die there is one less such individual in the world. But we also exist relationally: we are someone's son or daughter, neighbour, colleague, compatriot, comrade. At the same time it is arguable that there is no essence that makes us who we are. We come into existence as a bundle of cells which grows, ever-changing, the locus of a stream of experiences, until the bundle falls apart at physical death.

The first two of these ways of thinking about ourselves are universal. No culture has existed that hasn't both recognised the individuality of every member and the extent to which their identity is connected to others. What varies across cultures is the emphasis placed on the relational or atomistic aspects of self. The third way of thinking is not universal. The idea that there is no essence of self contradicts the widespread idea that human beings are ensouled creatures with some non-material essence that survives death. It also challenges the intuitive sense that many have that there is some kind of personal essence, a unique 'me-ness'.

The world's classical philosophical traditions all have views on which of these ways of thinking should be foregrounded, views which are reflected in the cultures to which they belong. Understanding these philosophical views is therefore a powerful way of understanding what it means to be a person in another culture, and in our own.

NO-SELF

Freud's phrase 'the narcissism of small differences' could be used to describe many intracultural philosophical debates. From the inside of any tradition, differences that look merely technical to outsiders take on tremendous importance, reminding me of the line in *The Blues Brothers* movie where a bar owner assures the nervous band that they like all kinds of music here, 'country *and* western'. In this caricatured rural corner, two styles which sound like two sides of the same coin to outsiders are placed at opposite ends of the musical spectrum.

In the classical Indian tradition, there is a pair of concepts that seems from within to present a choice between two radically different alternatives. The Vedic tradition has the concept of *ātman* (Sanskrit, *attā* in Pāli): a kind of personal essence of being that makes each individual who he or she is. Buddhism's great break from this tradition is captured in the concept of *anattā*. This is literally no (*an-*) *ātman* (*attā*). The difference seems as clear as that between night and day, especially since the name of the Buddhist position is the negation of the Vedic one.

However, from this outsider's perspective, the similarities between the theories of *ātman* and *anattā* are more striking than the differences. They both contradict the classical Western idea that the essential self is a personal self, rooted in the psychological individuality of the person. Both subscribe to theories of rebirth, but of a form which is radically non-personal.

In classical Indian philosophy (with the exception, as usual, of Cārvāka), everything – including the self, *ātman* – is ultimately part of *Brahman*, the universal self, the 'One'. Salvation, *mokṣa*, is achieved when *ātman* realises its real nature and so returns to its true state of oneness with *Brahman*. In this cosmology there is ultimately no difference between the macrocosmic and microcosmic: the whole is the part, the part is the whole. *Tat tvam asi*, That art thou. In the *Upaniṣads*, it is stated:

> This Self of mine within the heart is smaller than a grain of rice, or a barley-corn, or a mustard seed, or a grain of millet, or the kernel of a grain of millet; this Self of mine within the heart is greater than the earth, greater than the atmosphere, greater than the sky, greater than all these worlds.
>
> Containing all works, containing all desires, containing all odours, containing all tastes, encompassing the whole world, the unspeaking, the unconcerned – this is the Self of mine within the heart, this is Brahman. Into him I shall enter on departing hence ...[1]

In subtly different ways, all the major Vedic traditions assert that this 'entering into' *Brahman* entails a cessation of our consciousness as individuals. The ultimate goal is the dissolution of the ego, something that L. N. Sharma suggests is a central theme in many images of Indian mythology: 'Kali beheading and carrying in her hand the head of her beloved devotee, the image of Siva adorned with the garlands of severed heads, and numerous symbols, such as the dance of Nataraja suppressing the demon of self-forgetfulness, vividly bring out the significance of ego-dissolution.'[2]

It might seem paradoxical that to achieve this state of selfless-ness, you need to realise that in a deep sense the self already does not exist. How can you strive to achieve something that is already the case? The paradox can be lessened, if not removed, by remembering that the individual self is an illusion, so what you need to do is not change reality, but escape your distorted vision of it.

That's why *mokṣa*, liberation, is achieved by attaining a full recognition of the truth. For example, in the Vaiśeṣika school, you need to realise that *ātman* 'cannot belong to the mind'[3] to attain what Deepak Sarma calls 'the desired state of existence with-out consciousness'.[4] Similarly, the Sāṃkhya school says that the ultimate wisdom one attains is the truth 'I do not exist, naught is mine, I am not.'[5] And in the Nyāyá school: 'Birth is the connec-tion of soul [*ātman*] with body, sense-organs, mind, intellect and sentiments, while death is the soul's separation from them.'[6] If we can escape this cycle, then *ātman* will exist without possessing any consciousness.

The same basic dynamic is found in Yoga, where the means to liberation is disciplined practice, in the form of physical practices of concentration or meditation. Through yoga you achieve altered states of awareness (*samādhi*) and eventually isolation (*kaivalya*).[7] The *Yoga Sūtras* teach, 'When there is cessation of even that spe-cial cognition, inasmuch as there is the cessation of everything (that is, all contents), there is a concentration without content (that is, a concentration "without seed" or content (*nirbīja*).'[8]

It should now be clear that the usual translation of *ātman* as 'self' or 'soul' is extremely misleading, since in Western termin-ology selves and souls are usually thought of as personal. Self or soul is the core of the person, and a person is, as John Locke defined it in the seventeenth century, 'a thinking intelligent being that has reflection and can consider itself as itself, the same thinking thing in different times and places'.[9] However, *ātman* is a *depersonalised* self or soul. That is to say, what defines it is not what we usually take to define ourselves: our personalities, memories, desires, beliefs and so on. 'This is somewhat paradoxical,' observes Chakravarthi Ram-Prasad. 'The self [*ātman*] of the human person is truly and really what that person is, but that is precisely because the true self is more than – and lasts beyond – that person!'[10] The price we pay for returning to union with *Brahman* is a loss of all our individuality, of what we ordinarily think makes us who we really are. *Mokṣa* 'does not bring immortality, in the sense of making the individual person who gains knowledge live forever.'[11] The karmic cycle brings rebirth, but it is not a personal rebirth.

Buddhism also sees salvation in escaping the cycle of rebirth and suffering and thus attaining *nirvāṇa*. The exact characterisation of this varies, but it is striking how often the general idea is very close to that of the orthodox Indian schools. In Yogācāra Buddhism, one seeks the state of *śūnyatā* (emptiness), where there is no distinction between subject and object.[12] This is much closer to the Indian orthodox views it supposedly rejects than anything in the Western tradition.

What appears to make Buddhism radically different is that it denies the existence of an enduring, eternally existent and immutable self, *ātman*. It asserts instead no-self, *anatta*, saying that what we think of as the self is nothing more than five *skandhas* (aggregates): the form of matter or body (*rūpa*), sensations and feelings (*vedanā*), perceptions (*saññā*), mental activity or formations (*sankhāra*) and consciousness (*viññāṇa*). There is no *ātman* that *has* physical form, sensations, thoughts, perceptions of consciousness. Rather, what we think of as the individual person is merely an assemblage of these things.

Anatta is famously explained in a discourse in the first-century-BCE *Milindapañha*, *The Questions of King Milinda*. The priestess Vajira explains it by analogy to a chariot:

Even as the word of 'chariot' means
That members join to frame a whole;
So when the groups appear to view,
we use the phrase 'a living being'.[13]

Just as there is no chariot other than the sum of chariot parts, there is no self other than the sum of 'self' parts, the five *skandhas*. This is certainly radical in the context of a tradition that asserts the fundamental reality of *ātman*, just as it would be in any tradition that asserts the existence of any kind of immortal, immaterial, indivisible soul. For anyone who takes a broadly scientific, naturalistic world view, however, it should be obvious. After all, can you think of anything at all in the universe, apart perhaps from the most fundamental elements of physics, that is not 'merely' the sum of its parts? Water is H_2O: it is made up of two parts hydrogen and one part oxygen, it is not a thing that has two hydrogen atoms and one oxygen atom attached to it. We say a book 'has' pages and a cover, but we don't think there is a strange, immaterial thing called a book to which pages and a cover are attached. Ink is printed onto pages which are bound between covers and that just is what a book is.

If *anattā* seems more radical a view than it is, that is in large part because its usual translation is 'no-self'. But all it really means is no-*ātman*: no eternal, immaterial, indivisible self. This is very different from denying there is any kind of self at all. In the *anattā* view, there is something which is *myself*, but there is no such discrete entity as *my self*. Indeed, the Buddha often talks about paying attention to ourselves. In the *Dhammapada*, for instance, he says, 'Engineers (who build canals and aqueducts) lead the water (wherever they like), fletchers make the arrow straight, carpenters carve the wood; wise people fashion (discipline) themselves.'[14] All the Buddha would avoid saying is anything that suggested that the 'selves' wise people fashion are simple, unified souls.

So although in one respect the doctrine of *anattā* is the exact contradiction of that of *ātman*, most branches of Buddhism and the orthodox Indian schools agree on the arguably more fundamental point that the personal selves we take ourselves to be in conventional reality are an illusion and that liberation comes only when we detach ourselves from this and enter into a kind of depersonalised existence.

However, in practice, it is not entirely clear that the true self really is so different from the conventional one, even in Buddhism. Sometimes, the distinction seems clear, such as in these lines from the fifth-century Sri Lankan text the *Visuddhi-magga*: 'Nirvāṇa is, but not the man who seeks it./The Path exists, but not the traveller on it.'[15] Here it seems unambiguous that the conventional self does not exist. Yet on other occasions, the personal self is not so easily dispensed with. 'The evil-doer grieves in this world, he grieves in the next, he grieves in both,' says the *Dhammapada*; and 'The righteous man rejoices in this world, he rejoices in the next, he rejoices in both.'[16] What progresses from one life to the next seems to be a kind of person in the conventional sense.

In Indian conceptions of the self, there is a deep tension between an insistence that our sense of personal self is an illusion and the persistence of the idea that what is reborn in future lives is nonetheless a version of me. This became evident in two encounters I had with Tibetan lamas several years ago while working on a book about personal identity. In Buddhism, everyone is a reincarnation, but lamas are supposed to know exactly who they are reincarnations of. How, then, I wondered, do these people think of their relation to their earlier selves? The answer seemed to fluctuate between thinking of that relation in impersonal and personal terms.

Akong Tulku talked about the reincarnated self as the empty space contained within a building. At death, the building is demolished and a new one is built, but the space it contains remains the same, continuing the karmic habits that are the consequence of past actions. What doesn't continue is memory, knowledge, belief, or presumably personality, since it is a matter of historical record that different incarnations have different personalities. The thirteenth Dalai Lama, for example, was a shrewd political operator who built up Tibet's armed forces and police. He advised near the end of his life that 'Efficient and well-equipped troops must be stationed even on the minor frontiers bordering hostile forces. Such an army must be well trained in warfare as a sure deterrent against any adversaries.'[17] He had a reputation for being tough and hard-headed, feared by officials he would often punish. The fourteenth and current Dalai Lama is a much more mischievous, playful, pacific character who knows full well how different he is from his predecessor. 'Even if I felt I wanted to act like the 13th Dalai Lama, I couldn't have done it at all,' he once told an interviewer. 'A person's personality is important. Without such a personality, one couldn't act like that.'[18]

On some occasions, however, Akong lapsed into ways of talking that suggest a continuation of the personal self. Although he said he had no memories of his previous lives, he was keen to stress that others do. He also thought we could inherit learning from previous lives. 'Some people, six or seven children, can read, write books or poetry, from their past development,' he told me in his broken English. But if reincarnation has nothing to do with the continued existence of the personal self, why would this be important or likely?

Similarly, Ringu Tulku embraced the idea that there is no abiding self, 'So you don't have to be afraid of your destruction because there is nothing to destroy.' The only thing of him that will continue will be 'my habitual tendencies, the way I react, the way I think'. He also acknowledges he doesn't remember anything from past lives. 'That's why I'm thinking in my case it's a mistake,' he said of his identification with a laugh.

But the best description he could come up with of passing from one life to another is to compare it to going to sleep and waking up in a different body. He stressed the fact that many people do claim to remember past lives. Here again is the tension between denying the personal in reincarnation and maintaining that aspects of our individual personalities and memories will continue.

Understanding this tension brings us closer to Indian conceptions of self in everyday life. Buddhism and the orthodox schools accept that we have to live our daily lives as though we were personal selves. The illusion is deep and so we should not be surprised that in a culture where officially there is no personal self we see people living as persons just as much as we do anywhere else in the world. Day-to-day life is lived in the world of appearances, not absolute reality.

However, we would expect it to make some difference if people believed their true self was not to be identified with the temporary, finite person living in this biological life. In practice, the depersonalisation of self has less impact than the more comprehensible and comforting belief in reincarnation. Take Meera Baindur. She finds that *karma* means 'There's no sense of regret. I've seen this happen time and again and it happens to me too. So I've just heard all this brilliant Chinese philosophy and I'm like "I wish I could do Chinese philosophy." I'm not left with a sense of dissatisfaction at the end of it because I think, "OK, next lifetime." It's so automatic for me. So my mum has never travelled abroad and she's not dissatisfied. She's content because she says, "If I need to travel abroad I'll do it in another lifetime and maybe it's not in my *karma* to travel abroad."'

More importance is placed on the cycle of rebirth than on the depersonalisation of self. Put in abstract terms, the ultimate goal of dissolving the self and entering into union with *Brahman* sounds like a beautiful vision. The idea that we are all part of *Brahman* probably also gives people a reassuring sense of their own significance in what would otherwise appear to be a harsh world, indifferent to their welfare. But it seems people are rather attached to *ātman* and more pleased by the thought of lives to come than they are by the prospect of eventual extinction.

Perhaps the clearest sign that India and Buddhist cultures have been selective in what they have taken to heart from their philosophies is the extent to which they glorify individuals. Buddhists venerate *bodhisattvas*, Buddhas and lamas. In Bodh Gaya, one of the main pilgrimage sites is the twenty-five-metre-high Giant Buddha statue, and at almost every shrine people bow down in front of Buddhas. We've already seen India's deference to authorities, *ṛṣis* and *swamis*.

Although philosophical theories form complex wholes where one idea entails another, the ways they percolate down to wider society tends to be more pick and mix, with little regard for consistency. Philosophical theories and religious doctrines either adapt to fit societies or remain the idle thoughts of thinkers and theologians, doomed to wither and die. Hence *anattā* found a different form in Chinese Buddhism, more suited to that culture. Chinese thought is orientated towards engagement in this world. Many believe that Buddhism took off in China in part because it offered the prospect of an other-worldly existence to come that indigenous traditions did not. Yet to be credible to the Chinese mind, it had to meet the local culture halfway, by marrying the metaphysical emptiness of no-self with the pro-social selflessness of Chinese ethics. The purpose of realising *anattā* in Chinese thought is therefore less about escaping the cycle of rebirth and more about attainment in this life of the Buddha-nature – defined by Ram-Prasad as 'a principle of ethical and mental purity exemplified in and remaining potent through the life of the Buddha. [. . .] Realising this principle in one's thoughts, feelings and actions allows the person to lead a proper life of selfless engagement with everything in the world.' He notes that 'this doctrine plays little part in Indian Buddhism'.[19]

If recognition of *anattā* is supposed to lead to greater selflessness, it is arguably more evident in the Chinese iteration than in the original Indian ones. *Anattā* fell on fertile soil because historically in China individuals are not of prime importance. Indeed, even the emphasis on Confucius is a Western way of thinking about the school of philosophy he founded. The term 'Confucianism' was introduced by sixteenth-century Jesuit missionaries who named the philosophy after its founder, following their own convention. In China, Confucianism is still known as Rujia, or the school of the *ru* (*ru* means 'scholar' or 'learned man', and *jia* is literally 'house' or 'family'). It is not tied to any one person. It would be more in keeping with the Chinese way to talk not of Confucianism but of Ruism.[20]

A kind of no-self view is found also in Sufism, the mystical strand of Islam that seeks a unity with God requiring annihilation (*fanā*) of the self. Many expressions of this view are found in the works of the thirteenth-century Persian poet Rumi. In the *Masnavi*, he writes, 'The only way to be safe from one's internal enemies is to annihilate self, and to be absorbed in the eternity of God, as the light of the stars is lost in the light of the noonday sun.'[21] Sufis, however, only comprise a small proportion of the world's Muslims and the no-self view is a minority one in Islam.

There is one other major philosophical tradition in which *anattā* appears in a different guise: modern Western anglophone philosophy. The same core idea that there is no unchanging essence of self, only a collection of experiences, thoughts, sensations and so on, appeared to emerge in the eighteenth century completely independently from Buddhist *anattā*. Intriguingly, there is a real possibility that David Hume, one of the most important developers of the idea, could have come across *anattā* in a book about Buddhist philosophy written by the Jesuit missionary Ippolito Desideri in 1728. The book was deemed unsuitable for publication by the Vatican and the manuscript was archived. But Desideri had been a visitor to the Jesuit Royal College at La Flèche at around the time that Hume was living nearby, and Hume had met and talked with some of the monks there. This was just before Hume began working on *A Treatise of Human Nature*, which includes his own account of self and identity.[22]

Delightful as the story is, the evidence for Hume's vicarious encounter with Buddhism is purely circumstantial and there is a more obvious and uncontroversial source for his theories: those of the seventeenth-century philosopher John Locke. Locke used a powerful thought experiment to disentangle the ideas of soul and self. Let us suppose, he said, that we each have an immaterial soul that sustains thought and enables us to continue to exist over time. Now suppose that this soul was exactly the same as the one that was in Nestor or Thersites at the siege of Troy. If you remembered nothing of this, would you be the same person as either of them? Locke assumed that his readers would answer no.[23] We distinguish between whatever substance – material or immaterial – sustains our identity and our identity itself. What makes you *you* is the unity and continuity of your mental life, not the stuff that you are made of. That's why we can imagine waking up in a different body or living on after the death of our own. We might well (indeed do) need a body or soul in order to exist, but that is just the vehicle of the self. The clearest modern analogy is that we are software that runs on the hardware of the brain and body. If you move a file from a desktop to a memory stick, the file continues to exist even though it is now being sustained by completely different chunks of matter.

Hume developed this idea, clarifying its repercussions. He saw that if our identity resides in our thoughts, feelings, memories, beliefs and so on, then we are not abiding, single things at all, merely 'bundles' of perceptions. Hume made his case by inviting us to introspect. Observe yourself, your own consciousness. What do you find? A thought here, a sensation there, a catchy tune that you can't get out of your head, a desire for some of that cake you can see out of the corner of your eye and so on. What you observe are particular thoughts, perceptions and sensations. 'I never catch my *self*, distinct from some such perception,' wrote Hume, assuming he was not peculiar. What we call the self is 'nothing but a bundle or collection of different perceptions, which succeed each other with an inconceivable rapidity, and are in a perpetual flux and movement'.[24]

Not only does this sound remarkably like *anattā*, but even the method for establishing its truth is essentially the same. In Buddhism, one of the purposes of meditation is to attend carefully to the nature of your consciousness so as to see that there is no abiding self, merely thoughts and feelings that arise and fade. (In Buddhism this is only one particular instance of the broader theory of *Pratītyasamutpāda*, 'dependent origination', which maintains that nothing has any independent existence.) The main difference between Humean and Buddhist introspection is that for Hume you only needed to do it once or twice to establish the absence of the abiding, permanent self, whereas for Buddhists you should do it often to cultivate awareness of this absence and so lessen your attachment to your sense of self.

This difference is an intriguing one. Even in cultures where all major philosophies deny the reality of the personal self, attachment to it remains strong. For Buddhists, the solution is dedication: try harder. An alternative response says there is no need to undermine completely the conventional sense of self. Hume is not saying the self isn't real, just as the priestess Vajira doesn't show that a cart isn't real. As long as we realise that there is no permanent unchanging essence of self, what's the problem with continuing life on a day-by-day basis more or less as we have always done? It might, and perhaps should, make us more sanguine about our own impermanence and therefore less attached to the sense of self we feel at any given point. But it doesn't, and needn't, undermine the value of our selves and our continued existence.

The bundle view is now the most popular one among academic

philosophers, and even more prevalent among psychologists and neuroscientists who study the sense of self and where it comes from.[25] Our knowledge of brain circuitry supports the essential Humean and Buddhist insight that there is no central control centre of the self, no single locus of consciousness. Rather, the brain is constantly engaged in parallel processes, most of which are unconscious and others of which jostle for conscious awareness. In fact, the distinction between conscious and unconscious is problematic. When driving, for example, we are often shocked to realise that we don't have any recollection of what we've been doing, as though we were driving on auto-pilot. However, had a deer jumped in front of the car during that period we would have been aware of it, showing that we were indeed conscious. What we call 'auto-pilot' is not truly unconscious. It seems rather to be a state in which nothing is retained by the conscious mind, which is why in retrospect it seems we were not conscious at all.

The bundle view, however, is only dominant among academics, while wider culture is still dominated by the atomistic view, which we will look at shortly. That is not to say that the bundle view has had no impact on wider society. A growing awareness of the consensus in psychology, combined with the reductive outlook described in the last chapter, has led to the increasing popularity of the idea that the self is an 'illusion'. Scientists have encouraged this interpretation, publishing books with titles and subtitles such as *The Self Illusion* and *The Science of the Mind and the Myth of the Self*.[26] But as we have seen, it is only the singular, unified essence of self that is an illusion, not the self that is the sum of its parts.

More widespread than this, however, is the increasing sense in the West that identity is fluid, malleable and not defined at birth for life. Younger people in particular are shunning essentialised identities, believing that they are free to define who and what they are, or to choose not to define themselves at all. A striking example of this was a 2015 survey which suggested that only half of young people identified as heterosexual, even though most of these did not follow bisexual or homosexual lifestyles.[27] It was not that they felt 'not heterosexual', in the sense of something other than heterosexual, rather that they did not want to be 'pigeonholed' with any sexual orientation. In the West, *anattā* increasingly looks less exotic and much closer to common sense.

The relational self

On the plane out of Tokyo I noticed that a lot of the Japanese passengers had selected the same movie on their personal inflight entertainment systems. Curious, I settled back to watch it myself. *Orange* is a Japanese teen fantasy drama based on the highly successful manga comic book series by Ichigo Takano. The film was also a hit, number one in the Japanese box office on its opening weekend. The clever plot sees a teenage girl, Naho, receive letters from her future self encouraging her to do what she can to stop the death of her new classmate, Kakeru. His original death can't be undone, but if she acts differently she can create another, parallel future in which she and Kakeru marry and live happily ever after.

The film showed how many aspects of Japanese philosophical thought are part and parcel of mainstream culture, not simply academic speculations. Their fascination with the turning of the seasons, for example, was evident from the opening shot, which showed the heroine walking along a tree-lined road, a letter from her future self reminding her '6th April. You're almost late for school as you're mesmerised by the cherry blossoms.' Later in the film, the teenage chat among her friends is how 'in spring we'll go see cherry blossoms at Mt Kobo, Kamikochi in the summer, and Alps Park in the autumn'. Not forgetting winter: 'Matsumoto castle looks good in the snow too.' Add to that the two suicides central to the plot and it's clear this was no typical American teen movie.

Most striking was the way the central romance developed. The focus was hardly ever on just the couple, who were alone only a handful of times. Rather, the film centred around the group of friends of whom the couple were a part. When Kakeru is saved, all the friends are there, as they are in the concluding shot in which they watch the sunset, a scene which surely would have been reserved for the romantic couple in a western movie. True love found a way because the wider social group made it happen.

The emphasis in the film is on acting for others. Early on, Naho makes Kakeru lunch as she notices he doesn't bring any to school. Seeing his happiness when he accepted it almost made her cry. When Kakeru's mother commits suicide, she reveals in a video message that it was to relieve him of the burden of her depression. Even her classmate Hiroto, Naho's husband in the future she writes from, wants her to get together with Kakeru in an alternative future because, despite loving her and being the happy father of their child, he sees that Kakeru is a better match. Everyone feels responsible for the welfare of each other. The future Hiroto, Naho and their friends express regret at letting Kakeru die, taking responsibility for his suicide. The future Naho implores her younger self, 'I want you to share his burden.' All the characters seem eager to do this, as illustrated in a scene in which the friends help Kakeru and Naho carry a large gym crash-mat. 'If the load gets too heavy, don't carry it alone,' one says. In case the metaphor hasn't been made clear enough, he adds, 'We'll help you carry the load.'

Orange provides a great insight into how the self in Japan, as in the rest of East Asia and in many traditional societies, is essentially understood as it relates to others. This is not a form of collectivism which eradicates the differences between people. When

Westerners see films of daily life in a Japanese city like Tokyo, the sense they often get is of a conformist mass following the herd. People with expressionless faces move in an extraordinarily punctilious fashion, crossing streets or getting into impossibly crowded subway trains. This fits the stereotype of Japan as a conformist society, where individuality is subsumed under the identity of the group, where discipline and politeness repress emotion.

When I went to Japan, this is not how it felt. Most people I dealt with I found extremely warm. They were not so much conformist as *pro-social*. The reason they board trains in such an orderly fashion is because everyone behaves in the best interests of everybody else, not because they are trying to 'fit in'. This way of behaving began to rub off on me, even though I was only there a matter of days. I realised that my default way of walking around a city is with my shoulders slightly out, not exactly barging people aside but ready to compete in a subliminal battle for space and priority. I loosened up and paid more attention to whose space I might be infringing upon.

John Krummel, a philosopher whose mother is Japanese and who grew up in the country, recognised this. 'When you ride the subways in New York City, often you see people spreading their legs out,' he told me. Even New Yorkers have belatedly seen the problem with this, with signs on the subway discouraging 'manspreading'. 'In Japan people are mindful of the person sitting next to them and if there's a little bit of space they'll make room for you, inviting you to sit next to them.'

One sign at a Tokyo subway station captured this ethos beautifully. It showed two outline figures next to each other, one with a personal stereo, the other without. 'Any masterpiece just becomes noise disturbance when emanating from earphones,' it said, with a musical score behind the listener and a jagged series of parallel lines behind the other, labelled 'masterpiece' and 'noise' respectively. The sign did not command or even ask passengers to turn their music off and down, it simply reminded them of the antisocial consequences of headphone leakage.

It seemed to work, because in Japan I was never bothered by the irritating rattle of other people's iPods, as I almost invariably am on British public transport. Back home, it is those who don't want their ears to be molested who have to make the special effort of finding the 'quiet carriage', if there is one. Even then, should you kindly remind someone that devices which disturb the peace with their irritating tinny rhythms are not allowed, it's common for them to look at you as though you are an uptight maniac with no right to interfere in their enjoyment, even if it ruins yours.

'Collectivism' seems the wrong term to describe this pro-social culture, which is evident in some form all over East Asia. It's better understood by examining the very way in which selves are conceived of in the region, something most scholars describe using the concept of 'relationality'. The nature of any individual is determined by how that individual stands in relation to others. Take away those relations and you are left not with a self stripped down *to* its essence, but a self stripped *of* its essence.

Japan is a syncretic culture in which different philosophies and religions meld. In the saying that a Japanese is born into Shintōism, lives as a Confucian and dies a Buddhist, it is significant that it is in living that Confucianism takes priority, since in that philosophy social relations are paramount. Yet relationality is not a Chinese import into Japanese culture. More likely, when Confucianism arrived in Japan in the sixth century it brought 'a deepening of what was already common practice in Japan', as Robert E. Carter puts it, evident in the importance placed on ancestors, family and *kami* spirits in Shintō.[1]

Japanese relational thinking is deeply rooted in the culture and is reflected in the language, which usually dispenses with pronouns and has no need to express who the subject of a verb is. Whereas English says 'I went shopping', in Japanese it is more common to use a construction literally translated as 'went to shopping'. English says 'I feel cold', but in Japanese people usually just say the adjective *samui*. The literal translations for some Japanese equivalents of 'excuse me' are '[indebtedness] does not end' (*sumimasen*) and 'This way [goes the indebtedness]' (*kochirakoso*).[2] 'Usually "I" is not necessary and not welcome,' philosopher Kazashi Nobuo told me.

At the same time, Japanese is very sensitive to the relations between speakers. 'In most social situations, a conversation between strangers can hardly begin until there has been an exchange of business cards or an introduction by an intermediary so that each party is aware of the other person's relative status,' says Tom Kasulis.[3] 'We differentiate between at least two or three levels of respect through language all the time,' says Kazashi. When you do refer to 'I' or 'you', different words are chosen depending on your relationship to the person you're talking to. For instance, *watashi* is used to mean 'I' in formal situations, whereas *boku* or *ore* is more informal, although the latter can sound aggressive if not used among close friends. In European languages these relational indicators tend to be completely absent or less complicated. In French you can use the informal *tu* or the polite *vous* for 'you', in Spanish *tu* or *usted*, but that is all the variation possible and you only have the option of 'I' for yourself.

One further linguistic clue to Japanese thinking about selves is that although there is a word for the self as an individual, *kojin*, when considering the nature of persons it would be more usual to use *ningen*, which emphasises the relational aspect of selfhood, combining *nin*, 'human', and *gen*, 'space' or 'between'.

These linguistic features reflect a way of thinking about the self in which there is less emphasis on the 'I' and more on the context in which that 'I' exists. Virtually every aspect of Japanese life and culture reflects this relational thinking. At the kabuki theatre the most dramatic moments were typically collective actions, such as the rapid costume changes, which involved several actors. Solo dances were understated, displaying precision and grace over virtuoso action. At one point the audience roundly applauded what sounded remarkably like a rock guitar solo but was in fact a passage performed by a dozen or so players on traditional string instruments in a remarkable feat of coordination.

Carter gives numerous other examples. The system of law is consensual rather than adversarial, as it is in the West.[4] In aikido, the indigenous martial art, you have partners, not opponents.[5] Even in business, a former CEO of Ricoh, Hiroshi Hamada, says that at the heart of the company is *oyakudachi*: helping others, being of mutual assistance, doing what is useful for others.[6] In traditional homes, in place of fixed walls and doors are movable screens that indicate 'division within unity' based on 'mutual trust and the lack of a strong need for division'.[7]

As ever, it is important not to overstate this. Differences in emphasis in self-conception do not add up to completely different selves. That's a lesson Nakajima Takahiro learned when he travelled to the West, full of preconceptions. 'Before I went to the Western countries – the United States, France, Great Britain and so on – I imagined that they were very much individualistic persons, so I had to fight against them. But actually speaking I didn't have such an experience at all. They are very polite. They focus on family values much more than I expected. They are not egoistic, individualistic persons in their behaviour.'

Just as Westerners are not the raging egotists their reputation as 'individualists' suggests, the Japanese are not devoid of a sense of individuality as their 'collectivist' reputation suggests. In his 1930s essay 'Regarding the Japanese Character', Kuki Shuzō gave the example of a scene at the 1931 Olympic Games when 'a certain victorious Japanese athlete was standing at the awards podium, listening to "The Emperor's Reign" and looking up at the Rising Sun Flag – and he was crying'. A publication of the German Olympic

Committee subsequently explained that 'he cried with the deep, moral emotion of getting to carry out his responsibility to Japan'. Kuki does not deny that this was probably one factor in his emotion. But another is that he was an athlete who had just broken a world record and won an Olympic gold. The exotic explanation for his emotion might supplement the more familiar one, but it should not displace it.[8]

The relational self was a central theme of the so-called Kyoto School of early twentieth-century Japanese philosophers. One of its leading lights, Nishida Kitarō, stressed that nothing in this philosophy is against individualism and that 'individualism and egoism must be strictly distinguished'. Indeed, he argues that the greatest human beings display the greatest individuality and that 'a society that ignores the individual is anything but a healthy one'.[9] Indeed, all the characters in *Orange*, my in-flight movie, were very distinctive. Their sense of belonging to the group did not so much inhibit their individuality as license it.

If Japan does not from the outside look like a culture that deeply appreciates individuality, that could in part be because individualism has come to be associated not with genuine individuality but with the *assertion* or *expression* of individual identity. In the West, the strident assertion of individualism does not necessarily reflect real individualism. For example, when I asked the Japanese philosopher Kobayashi Yasuo if he noticed any difference between Japanese and American academics, he said, 'American professors are always trying to make themselves individual, always. "I'm not like these guys. I am special." Maybe Japanese are also diverse, but they think that we must behave a little bit like others.'

David Wong wonders whether cultures that encourage more overt expressions of individuality are actually more deeply conformist. He had this thought after reading the reflections of the anthropologist Arlene Stairs. She spent some time with the Inuit, who like the Japanese feel comparatively little need to assert their individual identity in public. When she got to know them, however, she found they were much more diverse than most Westerners, who went to great lengths to express their individuality but were all remarkably similar in their tastes, political views, even shopping habits. Whether such an inverse correlation exists or not, the observation certainly shows that we should not conflate assertions of individuality with the possession of individuality, a point made with great comic concision in *Monty Python's Life of Brian*, when a crowd of people are told they are all individuals and they respond as one, 'Yes, we're all individuals!' (The joke has an even better second punchline when one person pipes up, 'I'm not.')

Japanese philosophy both reflects and develops this relationality. The word for ethics, *rinri*, is a compound of *rin*, meaning 'follows' or 'company', and *ri*, meaning 'principle'. Hence, says Carter, *rinri* is 'the rational ordering of relations with our fellow human beings'. Relationality is built in to the very idea of ethics.

Japanese philosophy has generally analysed the nature of this relationality as being rooted in the lack of a fundamental distinction between self and other, subject and object. Take this encounter between two 'Zen men' in the *Blue Cliff Records*, a twelfth-century collection of Chán (Chinese Zen) Buddhist koans:

> Kyōzan Ejaku asked Sanshō Enen, 'What is your name?'
> Sanshō said, 'Ejaku!'
> 'Ejaku!' replied Kyōzan, 'that's my name.'
> 'Well then,' said Sanshō, 'my name is Enen.'
> Kyōzan roared with laughter.

This story shows how by taking Kyōzan's name, Sanshō symbolically collapses the difference between them. Nonetheless, they retain their distinct identities. There is both oneness *and* difference. This is the basis of ethics. If you recognise yourself in another, treating the other as yourself becomes not an abstract duty but second nature.[10] For example, the intense loyalty of the Samurai – the noble military class which endured from medieval times until the nineteenth century – was not so much rooted in allegiance to a principle as in a sense of oneness with their fellow warriors.[11] This is a good example of the aesthetic nature of Japanese philosophy: it is rooted more in experience than in abstract cognition.

Cognition, of course, is indispensable when philosophising. But as we have observed, because intellect is seen as in some sense inadequate for grasping reality, East Asian philosophy often wilfully exposes the limits of reason by appealing to paradox. Perhaps the most head-scratching examples come in discourses on the nature of subject and object: the perceiver and the thing perceived. The idea of relationality is philosophically linked with the idea that the subject–object distinction belongs only in the realm of appearances, not ultimate reality. The distinction between self and other is only apparent. Rinzai (Lin-Chi), a ninth-century Chinese Chán master, said enlightenment required:

(a) to let the subject (man) go and the object (environment) remain;
(b) to let the object go and the subject remain;
(c) to let both subject and object go;
(d) to let both subject and object remain.[12]

This is a very Zen way of thinking in that it affirms all permutations, even though they contradict each other. It is nonetheless coherent because the contradiction is only at the level of intellect or appearance. If we relate this to experience, we can see the truth in it. Take the example of archery. First (a) you focus on the target, forgetting yourself. Then (b) you focus on your task, forgetting any desired outcome. Then (c) you forget both yourself and the target, losing yourself in the task. If you do that, then (d) self and target fuse effortlessly and you hit the bullseye, successfully performing the task.

Another paradox is that it is an ethical imperative to work on your self but your self does not exist. 'Person is an appearance with nothing at all behind it to make an appearance,' wrote the Kyoto School philosopher Nishitani Keiji.[13] Versions of this idea have recurred over centuries of Japanese philosophy. As Kazashi Nobuo summed up the teaching of Dōgen, quoting the first fascicle of his magnum opus, *Shobogenzo*: 'to study the way is to study the self; to study the self is to forget the self; to be enlightened is to be enlightened by all of the things in this world.' It is by attending to your self that you come to see its emptiness and so see that what you are attending to is not a discrete self at all but a microcosm of the whole world. Realisation of this emptiness is enlightenment.

That is perhaps why Kobayashi didn't like the characterisation of Japanese philosophy as concerned with 'interiority', which might seem like a fair way of describing this attention to self and experience. 'Interiority isn't separated from exteriority,' he told me. 'Everything goes in this between.' A better term is perhaps one coined by Kasulis, *intimacy*, which we'll look at in more detail shortly.

Japan offers the clearest example of the relational self in theory and in practice. But as I've mentioned, relationality features in conceptions of self all over East Asia. In Chinese Confucianism, every individual is defined by where they stand in the five relationships or 'bonds': ruler to ruled, father to son, husband to wife, elder brother to younger brother, friend to friend. Importantly, all but the last of these relationships is a hierarchical one. Neo-Confucianism also stresses the relational nature of selves as part of a broader idea that 'nothing exists alone'.[14]

The dissident writer Xu Zhiyuan made an intriguing connection between the relational self in China and its historic absence of theism. 'In the Western tradition individuality is part of your relationship between you and God,' he said. This is a point which has often been made by Christians who argue that supposedly secular enlightenment values are in fact deeply rooted in religion. Individualism starts with Christianity, which stressed personal salvation, the individual's relationship with God, the fact that God cares for each one of us. For the Chinese, the sacred is found in society and your peer group, says Xu. That's what defines Chinese individuality and also in a sense its religiosity. Religion is usually thought of as a set of creeds, but perhaps more fundamentally it is a source of transcendence: something which takes us beyond our mundane lives and allows us to partake of something greater. Westerners transcend themselves through belief in a God; transcendence for the Chinese comes from wider society, the group.

Again, this must not be confused with a subsuming of individual identity in the group. Yu-Wei Hsieh goes so far as to claim, 'Confucian ethics considered the individual even more important than the community.'[15] As it says in the Confucian classic *The Great Learning*, 'From the emperor down to the common people, all, without exception, must consider cultivation of the individual's character as the root.'[16] Only then can the branches and leaves of the family and wider society flourish. The good society starts with good selves.

The deep connection between individual and group in East Asia has a consequence that many Westerners find puzzling: the way families and communities share responsibility for the wrongdoings and failures of their members. This is not simply a matter of feeling shame, for which the person bringing the shame is blamed. Rather, it is a deeper sense of really sharing responsibility. For example, in April 2014, the South Korean ferry MV *Sewol* capsized en route from Incheon to Jeju, killing 304 passengers and crew members, mostly students from Danwon High School. The school's vice-principal, who organised the trip, survived but hanged himself soon afterwards, leaving a note in which he said,

'I take full responsibility.' Even people unconnected with the trip expressed shame and shared responsibility. One volunteer assisting the relatives of the victims told a reporter, 'When we look at this disaster, it's clearly man-made. I'm ashamed.' As a newspaper commentator put it, 'Our nation has run headlong toward the goal of becoming wealthy for half a century, but we turned a blind eye to the goal of being a civilized and safe society.'[17] The South Korean people viewed the tragedy as a failing of society as a whole, not of any particular individual or ferry company. Under a relational concept of self, this makes perfect sense, since those we are most closely related to do in a very real sense form parts of our own identities. Strangely, Westerners do seem to appreciate this, but in a lopsided way: families feel pride in the achievements of their members, sharing the glory, but rarely take any responsibility for their failures.

Relational thinking also features in many oral philosophies. Stephen Muecke gives as an example the central character in Donald Stuart's novel *Yaralie*, known simply as the 'growing girl', her individual identity not as significant as her social position.[18] This does not mean people lack individuality in traditional societies. 'In indigenous Australia the quirkiness of the person is very much noticed, remarked upon, even made fun of,' says Muecke.

What makes these philosophies distinctive is that relationality often extends beyond the human domain. Muecke cites Deborah Bird Rose's view that Aboriginal understandings 'incorporate a non-human-being centred view of the world, which also tends to be an ecological one. "Man" is just one living being among plants, animals, even the inanimate environment – all are kin.'[19] One practical manifestation of this was when the Tūhoe Māori were given management rights of their ancestral land, Te Urewera, in 2014. One condition of the deal was that they were not granted ownership of the land, but this was not a problem because they never believed it was theirs to own. Instead the land was granted legal personality, effectively owning itself, a legal arrangement that better matched the sense of kinship between the Tūhoe and Te Urewera.[20]

The default conception of self in Africa is also a relational one, as many writers have pointed out.[21] 'The "I" is just a "we" from another perspective, and persons are therefore not construed as atomic individuals,' says Segun Gbadegesin, explaining the Yoruba concept of a person.[22] An Akan maxim captures this: 'A person is not a palm tree that he should be self-complete or self-sufficient.'[23] One manifestation of this is the southern African concept of *ubuntu*. This word defies translation but means something like 'humanity towards others' or 'the universal bond of sharing that connects all humanity'. As Michael Onyebuchi Eze put it, *ubuntu* asserts that 'a person is a person through other people'.[24] Its relational aspect is emphasised by the fact that it is a gerundive, a verbal noun. *Ubuntu* implies movement and action; it is not a static '-ism' and is thus also opposed to any kind of dogmatism.[25] It is a humanistic concept which, like relationality in China, sees society, not God, as the transcendent source of value. It has political and ethical repercussions, not least that in most African cultures important decisions are ideally reached by consensus in the whole group rather than by majority opinion.[26]

The relational self is far from being entirely alien even in the West. The opening words of the United States Constitution are 'We the People . . .', emphasising the relations of citizenship rather than the individuality of citizens. Western identities are often tied up with relations, to community, locality, faith group, sporting team, political party. The world is not fundamentally divided between collectivists and individualists but simply differs in the degree to which it emphasises relationality and individuality.

THE ATOMISED SELF

The Areopagus in Athens commands excellent views of the glorious Acropolis above and the sprawling, shambolic modern city below. The 115-metre-high rocky outcrop itself is devoid of any significant sign of human construction. It was here, however, that one of the most significant events in the history of Western philosophy almost certainly took place. As a discreet information board tells the visitor, 'A judicial body, the Areopagus council, met on this hill to preside over cases of murder, sacrilege and arson.' One such case would have been the trial of Socrates, the founding father of Western philosophy, condemned to death by drinking poison for corrupting the youth of Athens and refusing to recognise its gods. It seems that he accepted this verdict rather than fleeing into exile.

The information panel doesn't mention this. Perhaps the Athenians don't like to point out to visitors that they killed their city's most famous son. Nor is there any indication at the Temple of the Winds in the Roman Agora that this was the site where he might have been held before his trial and execution. The only reminder of his execution is a picturesque little cave off the path to Filopappou Hill which a sign identifies as 'Socrates' prison', albeit with scare quotes that hint at the truth that it was probably no such thing.

One of Montaigne's most famous essays is called 'That to Study Philosophy is to Learn to Die'. If this rings true, then it is probably due to the example set by Socrates cheerfully accepting his fate, confident that he had nothing to fear. We don't really know the details of his last hours, but his student Plato wrote three dialogues that dramatised his trial and death. These root Socrates's imperturbability in his belief that his soul was immortal and would be glad to get rid of its cumbersome body with its annoying pains and distracting desires. For Socrates, the 'soul is a helpless prisoner, chained hand and foot in the body, compelled to view reality not directly but only through its prison bars'. The body is 'mortal, multiform' but the soul is 'divine, immortal, intelligible, uniform, indissoluble'. The soul is easily 'drawn away by the body into the realm of the variable', but when it confines itself to pure reason it 'passes into the realm of the pure and everlasting and immortal and changeless'. The soul of a philosopher understands this and 'secures immunity from its desires by following Reason and abiding always in her company'.[1]

This view of the soul – 'uniform', 'indissoluble', 'immortal', 'divine' – arguably shaped the Western conception of self for the millennia that followed. Its impact is most striking on Christianity. It was no mere detail that Christ's resurrection was a bodily one. Jesus's soul didn't ascend to heaven; he did, body and all. The idea that the soul was separate from the body was a later Platonic corruption of original Christian thinking but one which had a profound influence.

Two thousand years later, a French philosopher defended a conception of self and souls which was in all its central respects identical to that of Plato's Socrates. René Descartes claimed to know that 'nothing else belongs to my nature or essence except that I am a thinking thing' and that 'my essence consists solely in the fact that I am a thinking thing'. This self or mind is 'non-extended' and 'utterly indivisible'. 'I understand myself to be something single and complete,' wrote Descartes, with a mind that is 'really distinct from my body, and can exist without it'.[2]

Mind–body dualism has become such a natural way of thinking in the West that it is easy to think it is a human universal. But although all cultures have separate words for mind and body, they are not always seen as two essentially different things. We can distinguish between a flute and the wood from which is made, for example, but we do not conclude that a flute is a different kind of substance from wood. Mind and body could be as intimately linked as this. That certainly seems to be the understanding across East Asia. For instance, Nakajima Takahiro suggested to me that the core concept in Japanese philosophy is *kokoro*, heart-mind. 'We have a very long tradition of animism but it's not a primitive animism,' he says. Similarly the Chinese word *xin* can mean both 'heart' and 'mind'.

The Platonic–Cartesian version of the self never received unanimous support in the West. Plato was countered by his junior Aristotle, who saw the 'soul' as the proper functioning of the human being, not a separate, immaterial entity. David Hume directly challenged Descartes when he opened his discussion on personal identity by saying, 'There are some philosophers who imagine we are every moment intimately conscious of what we call our *self*; that we feel its existence and its continuance in existence; and are certain, beyond the evidence of a demonstration, both of its perfect identity and simplicity.' In contrast, he found that 'For my part, when I enter most intimately into what I call myself, I always stumble on some particular perception or other, of heat or cold, light or shade, love or hatred, pain or pleasure. I never can catch myself at any time without a perception.'[3]

However, it is the Platonic–Cartesian self that has done most to shape the Western philosophical imagination, in its elite and popular forms. It is not just that belief in an immaterial soul arguably became folk common sense. More importantly, the self has been assumed to be simple, indivisible, unchanging. The adjectives used by both Descartes and Plato are the kinds of adjectives used to describe atoms, in the original sense. We know now that atoms can be split, but their name derived from the belief they could not, *atomos* meaning 'indivisible'. The earliest atomic theory was posited in the fifth century BCE, first by Leucippus, then by his student Democritus, who believed everything was made up of tiny, solid, invisible, indestructible elements.

Interestingly, the metaphor of the 'atomic individual' became more common only when people started to worry that Western individualism had gone too far. There has been much talk of an 'atomised' society, in which people have become radically isolated from each other, living in their own private bubbles. But arguably the fundamental atomisation happened as soon as selves were conceived in Platonic terms. Unlike the relational selves of East Asian thought, such selves are discrete, self-contained. They may interact and cooperate with others but each is a separate unit, entire unto itself.

In the West, this is reflected in the way in which individuals are always placed at the heart of intellectual, political or social history. Christianity is the only major world religion named after its founder. (A Buddha is anyone who has achieved enlightenment and 'the Buddha' is simply an honorific shorthand for Siddhartha Gautama, the founder of the religion.) In philosophy, you can be a Platonist, an Aristotelian, a Kantian, Spinozist, while in other cultures schools like Daoism, Rujia, Sāṃkhya, Yoga, Nyāyá, Vedānta, Kalām and Falsafa are typically not named after people. In Islam, much as the prophet is revered, he is explicitly not to be worshipped – one reason why it is forbidden to depict him. In China, for all Confucius's importance, his hometown has been little-visited for most of its history and is only now being promoted as a tourist destination. Even his tomb is simply an earth mound with a modest stone in front of it paying homage to the 'teacher of ten-thousand generations'.

The atomistic way of thinking about selves may have its root in Plato and Descartes but it has become free-floating, independent of any commitment to immortal and immaterial minds. Westerners who long ago stopped believing in souls often still maintain a sense of self that is fundamentally atomistic. We see this in the Western conception of rights. That human rights is a uniquely Western concept is an exaggeration at best, a falsehood at worst. When the UN drew up its Universal Declaration of Human Rights after the Second World War, many non-Western countries were among its greatest champions, with the likes of Afghanistan, India, Iran, Iraq and Syria voting in favour of its adoption. The Chinese philosopher Chang Peng Chun was one the key drafters of the text and the only countries to abstain were South Africa, Saudi Arabia and six Soviet bloc nations. However, in the West rights have a stronger and more individualistic emphasis than in many other parts of the world. So when the then prime minister Tony Blair declared 'no rights without responsibilities' in the late 1990s, even its advocates saw it as controversial rather than a statement of the obvious. Anthony Giddens, one of the main philosophical shapers of the 'Third Way' politics pursued by Blair in the UK and Clinton in the USA, described it as requiring a 'redefinition of rights and responsibilities'.[4] Rights were generally assumed to be unconditional, inviolable and absolute, possessed simply by virtue of being a human being or a citizen. The suggestion that they were conditional on fulfilling responsibilities was considered a dilution of our individual rights.

Such is the pervasiveness of atomistic thinking that it penetrates even philosophies that explicitly reject any notion of a Platonic–Cartesian self. Most notably, the French existentialist Jean-Paul

Sartre claimed that there is no such thing as a given fixed human essence. His famous slogan 'Existence precedes essence' captures the idea that human beings are born into the world without any unchanging core of being and we must create our own identities for ourselves.[5] Yet this denial of essence if anything puts even more focus on the individual than the *Cogito ergo sum* (I think, therefore I am) doctrine it replaces. Value, meaning, purpose, identity – all are determined by individuals for themselves.

Not many people consciously follow Sartre's theory, but it is enacted every day in the ways in which people think that they can and should be the sole authors of their own lives.[6] Take religious belief. Western liberalism is permissive about religious belief, or a lack of it, as long as it does not infringe on the rights and liberties of others. (Current hostility towards Islam might seem to be the exception, but it is precisely due to its being widely perceived as a threat to other ways of life.) However, it is important that whatever you believe, you choose to believe for yourself. Even when people have an identity that binds them to a wider group, that identity has to be chosen by the individual alone, autonomously. The value of the group is secondary to the value of the individual choice, and so the idea of people adopting the religion of their community without questioning it is considered worrying and wrong.

Owen Flanagan has collated various findings in comparative psychology that suggest there is an overemphasis on the individual in the West that leads to real, demonstrable mistakes.[7] Americans are more prone to self-serving bias, believing that their own abilities are higher than they are. For instance, 94 per cent of American college professors believe their work is above average, which means at least 44 per cent are overestimating themselves.[8] Similarly, Americans are more susceptible than Indians, Chinese and Koreans to 'fundamental attribution error' – attributing more of what happens to us to our own personality and character traits than situational factors. Explaining why we give money to, say, a homeless person, Americans are more likely to point to their own generosity or compassion, Indians to the behaviour or apparent need of the recipient. Americans are also more likely to believe they have more control than they do over things such as the sex of their children, avoiding cancer or winning lotteries. To some extent, all these biases are by-products of an excessive emphasis on our capacity to be the authors of our own lives.

There seems little doubt that the Western imagination has too much faith in our capacity to direct and control our own destinies. It is bad faith to deny or even play down the respect to which we are the products of our societies, epochs, families, localities. It is hubris to believe that all that we are, all that we have and all that we believe is the result of our actions alone. If we see others in this way it also makes it much harder to achieve an empathetic acceptance of difference. When we look at others with different beliefs that we think are clearly wrong, for example, we do not have the sense that if life had been different we could have ended up believing the same thing. In contrast, when we understand that there is a deep contingency in who we have become, a kind of modesty is fostered.

The problems associated by belief in sole self-authorship can be avoided without entirely rejecting the ideas behind it. At its root is the true belief, expressed most explicitly in existentialist philosophy, that we must take responsibility for our own lives and create our own meanings. The likes of Sartre, de Beauvoir and Camus would have been horrified to see how their ideas have mutated into the individualism that flourishes today. In the cafés and streets of Paris's *rive gauche*, where the French existentialists once met, worked and talked, there is little sign of their moral seriousness. In their old haunts such as the Café de Flore, La Palette and the Café de la Mairie a constant churn of tourists drink overpriced coffees and eat mediocre food with little time or inclination to discuss the problems of human existence. Around them are upmarket boutiques and expensive private galleries, catering to a consumerism that the left-wing intellectuals would have abhorred.

Even setting aside the shallower forms of materialism associated with individualism, a less-noticed wrong turn has been to over-estimate both how much of our life story is down to our authorship and the extent to which we can write unaided. The idea of absolute freedom, popularised by Jean-Paul Sartre, is exhilarating but false. It remains the case, however, that no one else can hand us our meanings and values on a plate; that we become who we are by what we do and do not come into the world with fully formed, unchanging essences; and that we ultimately must take responsibility for our choices and actions.

It should be possible to avoid the excesses of atomism without adopting wholesale an eastern-style relational conception of self. While Aristotle did not share Plato's belief in the indivisible, immortal soul, he did write about human beings as discrete individuals. But that does not make him a modern-style individualist. Aristotle repeatedly presented being in relation to others as the best way to live. 'Man is a social animal,' he famously wrote.[9] Ethics, according to him, is really a part of politics, because it does not concern how individuals live alone but how we best live together. 'While it is desirable to secure what is good in the case of an individual,' he writes, 'to do so in the case of a people or state is something finer and more sublime.'[10] These are sentiments many live by. 'Even Americans – so individualistic – are on familiar terms with this group called "the people",' observes Leif Wenar, pointing to its appearance in numerous key documents and speeches, not least the US Constitution.[11] The West has as proud a record of taking collective action for the good of others as any other part of the world. People march in protest, volunteer and buy fair-trade bananas and coffee as individuals for the greater good. Aristotle's 'soft individualism' reminds us that the West's foregrounding of the individual does not condemn it to isolating atomisation.

CONCLUSION

The contrast between relational and atomistic selves reflects a much broader, more fundamental distinction between Western and East Asian cultures, described by Tom Kasulis as a distinction between an orientation towards primarily intimacy or integrity. Although I think this choice of labels is unfortunate, in that they do not immediately suggest what Kasulis makes them stand for, his distinction is a profound and helpful one. The best way to get a sense of it is not through words, but with images.

Think of intimacy in terms of overlapping circles. When the world is seen from an intimacy perspective, nothing is entirely distinct from anything else. Self and other, objective and subjective, rational and emotional, mental and physical: these are not discrete opposites but parts of the same whole. For that reason it is best not to even think of them as having solid edges.

Now think of integrity as non-overlapping circles with solid edges. Everything is clearly distinguished from everything else. Each item does of course stand in relation to other things, but their individual identity and essence is primary.

Intimacy

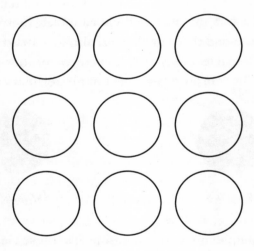

Integrity

It should be clear how this relates to conceptions of self. The nature of the 'relational self' (intimacy) is bound in with the other selves (and lands, cultures, languages etc.) so much that it is not even possible to conceive of it as a discrete unit. The atomistic self (integrity) is fundamentally just such a unit.

Another vivid way of visualising this difference is to think of what happens when two selves 'overlap' in a close, long-term relationship, something that is possible from both an integrity and an intimacy perspective.

In every culture we understand this kind of intimate bond and that it does not entail a loss of individual identity. As Kasulis beautifully puts it, 'When I share myself in the intimacy of love, I do not lose my identity into my lover, but the part I share reflects all of me.'[1] But what happens if one of such a pair dies? From an integrity perspective, the loss leaves the other individual intact. From an intimacy perspective, the one that remains has also lost a part of itself. 'To dissolve an internal relationship would not merely disconnect them: it would actually transform an aspect of the relatents themselves.'[2]

Integrity   *Intimacy*

Even many people in integrity cultures use idioms such as 'it was like losing an arm' or 'a piece of me died' to describe such a loss. Thinking in relational, intimate ways is far from alien. We see it reflected in different ways of talking about belonging. Think about losing a photo with great sentimental value or simply losing money. The money merely belongs *to* you, the photos belong *with* you. This difference is real even though you cannot detect it by putting the items lost under a microscope.[3]

Cultural anthropologists have observed how Japanese culture privileges intimacy over integrity in personal and professional relationships. If you ask someone about their occupation, Japanese typically say, 'I work for the such-and-such corporation', whereas Americans specify their role. Japanese instinctively think of their part in the whole, whereas Americans just as automatically think of their discrete function.[4] Kasulis finds that whereas Americans studying for MBAs are looking to learn principles, Japanese students who go to the USA to get an MBA are looking to meet people and to form business relationships for the future.[5]

When it comes to child-rearing, Japanese parents tend to concentrate on bringing up their children to be *responsive to others*, 'coordinating oneself to the behaviour and concerns of others'. American parents raise children to be *responsible for themselves*. It is more important for Japanese to learn to be sensitive to context, more important for Americans to uphold universal principles.[6]

Kasulis persuasively argues that this pattern of *interdependence* or *independence* recurs in every aspect of a culture, not just in conceptions of self. He chose the word 'intimacy' to describe the pattern of interdependence because intimacy denotes a lack of separateness, a deep sharing, a profound bond. We talk of intimate links, intimate understanding, intimate relationships. The word 'integrity' describes the pattern of independence because it denotes keeping something whole, untouched by anything else that might dilute its essence. Kasulis stresses that every culture contains examples of both intimacy and integrity. The difference is which is dominant.

There are numerous ways in which orientations towards intimacy and integrity manifest themselves. In the West, an integrity culture, objective truths or judgements are those that can be made publicly and impersonally. 'The truth cannot depend on who discovers it or articulates it.'[7] In intimacy cultures, it is common for even objective judgements to be personal. In the West, that would be a contradiction in terms, since the personal is subjective. Kasulis explains why this is not necessarily so, giving the example of a gymnastics judge. The scores such a judge gives are not merely subjective opinions; they require expertise and taking an objective perspective. But, says Kasulis, 'no publicly accessible videotape can prove the performance was a 5.8 rather than a 5.7'. This kind of intimate objectivity 'is accessible only to those within the appropriate intimate locus, those who have achieved their expert knowledge through years of practical experience'.

Similarly, a doctor who knows a patient personally is 'able to make medical judgements drawing on their intimate knowledge of the patient as well as the empirical knowledge gained from lab reports'. Even in a dominantly integrity culture, 'people often justifiably trust intimate forms of knowing that cannot be publicly verified but are still, in a significant sense, objective'.[8] We wouldn't value experience if we really thought that the grounds of all knowledge could be set out objectively in a manual that anyone could follow.[9]

The intimacy–integrity distinction is the most useful one I've come across in my foray into comparative philosophy. What makes it so valuable is that it doesn't only help us to understand our differences, it points us to similarities which enable us to see those differences in more nuanced and sympathetic terms. Even more importantly, it allows us to reflect on our cultures and values and ask whether we need a little more or a little less intimacy or integrity.

It seems to me that a lot of what is going wrong in the West is a breakdown of a stable equilibrium between intimacy and integrity. Consider the distinction in terms of autonomy and belonging. More of one inevitably leaves us with less of the other, and in the West the autonomy culture has become so dominant it has squeezed out belonging.

There are countless examples of where a desire to promote

autonomy has undermined belonging. The sale of social housing in Britain gave more power to individual homeowners but broke down the solidarity of estates where everyone was on the same footing. Educational opportunity has divided towns and cities into those where there are large graduate populations and those that have been deserted by people who went to university and never went back. I'm one of those who has advanced personally at the price of losing any sense of belonging in his hometown.

Autonomy has also been relentlessly promoted in a consumer culture where doing things your way, making your own choices, is always best. The promotion of these values is subtle and all-pervasive. At the same time, belonging has been undermined by the collapse of traditional industry and the fragmentation of the class system. Former coal and steel towns are among the most depressed in Britain, economically and psychologically. Even those who went on to get well-paid work lament the decline of community.

Belonging has been exoticised. For many decades, Western liberals celebrated minority communities but looked at patriotism with suspicion and sneered at local pride as parochialism. A person who had no aspiration to live anywhere other than where they were born was seen as lacking in vision and ambition. And yet all over the West many people are stubbornly immobile and proud of it. In Britain, 60 per cent still live within twenty miles of where they lived when aged fourteen.[10]

At the same time, non-belonging, in the guise of cosmopolitanism, has been festishised. Ironically, citizens of the world delight in visiting places whose distinctive local character is preserved only by their residents being very much citizens of one place.

Much of the rise of populism and nationalism in the West is a backlash against the gradual erosion of belonging. What I find powerful about this way of understanding the problem is that it suggests the deep causes are cultural, a matter of the West becoming too

'Western'. What allowed it to rise is now what is making it weak. A creative energy was released when we unshackled ourselves from the constraints of class and culture, but after years of wandering we find ourselves too alone.

Western culture needs rebalancing. Greater intimacy or belonging can be created if the gap between the left-behinds and the prosperous is narrowed, if local and regional identities can be more expressed without excluding outsiders, if common values can be asserted and shared. Should this sound like trying to square a circle, then ideas about individuals and society in China and Japan can help us make sense of it. Individuality is not opposed to intimacy. We are who we are because of our relations to others. We do not subsume our identities into the whole, but rather express our identities by finding our own place in that whole. The individual needs the group, autonomy needs belonging.

PART FOUR

How the World Lives

Adrian Wooldridge, the political editor of *The Economist*, is a cosmopolitan man of the world, sensitive to differences in values and ethos around the globe. So he was not surprised to find that as soon he arrived at a hotel in Bengal 'the Indian genius for service kicked in'. A charming personal valet arrived outside his room and took all the clothes he wasn't wearing to be cleaned and pressed. The next day, however, the valet did not return them as scheduled. That's because the hotel did not have any such service. The man was a scam artist.[1]

This is a cautionary tale not just for the traveller but for the ethnophilosopher, who also needs to avoid overgeneralising about a culture's values and beliefs. It is indisputable that cultures have very different ideas about ethics and politics. But it is equally indisputable that every nation displays every virtue and every vice. As ever, what we need to look for is not defining, essential characteristics but tendencies, trends and emphases.

Clues to these are everywhere. In Athens, you can visit the ruins of the Agora, the marketplace where philosophers and statesmen talked and debated openly. A democratic spirit was on display there, albeit a deeply imperfect one that was restricted to free men and denied to slaves and women. In China's Forbidden City, in contrast, you can stroll around an inner court that was so closed to ordinary people that the public were not even allowed access to what is now Jingshan Park, as it would have enabled them to overlook it. When the emperor left the palace, no one was allowed to cast an eye upon him. There are no slaves now in Athens and no emperors in Beijing, but the ways in which contemporary political values reflect these historical precedents is clear.

But because values also straddle continents, seeing how other cultures live is a way of reflecting on our own. Each provides a kind of living experiment in what would happen if we valued this a little less and that a little more. Given that no culture can claim to have cracked how to live, the lessons we can learn from our varying histories and philosophies are more precious than ever.

HARMONY

Travelling from Shanghai on one of China's new bullet trains, part of what is already the largest high-speed network in the world, I passed countless modern, high-rise cities seemingly being built from scratch, interspersed with the towns and villages they were designed to replace, comprised of single-storey concrete shacks. My destination, Qufu, was until recently a quiet backwater of 60,000 souls. Now East Qufu is emerging as yet another new city, an appendage larger than the body to which it is attached.

China is living through a period of massive disruption and change, which made the sign advertising the sprawling Sincere Garden housing development seem somewhat incongruous: 'Live in Confucianism, Life is Harmony'.

The first step to dissolving the incongruity is to realise that Qufu was the birthplace of Confucius and a large proportion of its population (at least before the new influx) still carries his family name, Kong. China is a country with a remarkably deep historical memory and so it should come as no surprise that contemporary developers invoke the name of ancient ancestors. Confucianism was officially suppressed after the communist revolution, but its values never entirely vanished and more recently the regime has embraced its national philosopher once more. In 2004, the Chinese government opened its first Confucius Institute in Seoul to promote Chinese language and culture, along similar lines to the Institut français, the Goethe-Institut and the British Council. At the time of writing there were over 500 Confucius Institutes worldwide, with a target of 2,000 by 2020.

The relevance of 'harmony' to modern apartment living is less obvious, but a visit to the Forbidden City in Beijing makes it clear that it is nothing new for developers to build with Confucian principles in mind. As one of the guidebooks sold within its walls says, 'Every aspect of its design, and the design of the administration it housed, reflected the tenets of the Confucian thought which had become the inspiration and model for Chinese society and government continuously since the time of the Han dynasty in the second century A.D.'[1]

Take the names given to the key buildings. To enter the outer court you pass through the Gate of Supreme Harmony, which has two lions guarding the stairway, one male with a ball under his foot, the other female with a cub under her paw, expressing the balance of *yinyang*. If this did not emphasise the importance of harmony enough, to proceed to the inner court you pass through the Halls of Supreme Harmony, Central Harmony and Preserving Harmony.

There is arguably no more important concept than harmony (*he*) for understanding how China thinks and lives. 'If we were to choose just one word to characterize the Chinese ideal way of life, that word would be "harmony",' says Chenyang Li, opening his book on the subject.[2] Similarly, John C. H. Wu writes, 'The most deep-rooted desire of the Chinese people is for harmony.'[3] I had been reading about harmony before visiting the country and was somewhat suspicious that it might be something of an academic construction with little relevance to daily life. What I found was the exact opposite. The term was ubiquitous in every-day discourse, even that of property developers. One woman told me about her five years spent in Edinburgh, which she greatly enjoyed. When I asked what the biggest difference she noticed between her Scottish colleagues and people back home was, she said that the Chinese wish always to please other people while Brits please themselves. The word she used unprompted to describe this value was 'harmony'.

Daniel Bell says that social scientists support the notion that the Chinese typically strive for harmony. 'Even in Hong Kong – supposedly the most individualist part of China – 55.3 per cent of people surveyed by the Chinese University of Hong Kong in 2012 agreed that harmony should be the goal of development, compared to 17.8 per cent that saw democracy and freedom as goals.'

Harmony is a value that straddles the domestic and the civic, private and public, taking on a slightly different character in each case. When Mencius described the 'five relations' or 'bonds' of humanity, he stressed how each should achieve harmony in a different way: 'between father and son, there should be affection; between sovereign and minister, righteousness; between husband and wife, attention to their separate functions; between old and young, a proper order; and between friends, fidelity'.[4]

The meaning of *he* (and the related term *xie*), however, is easily lost in translation. Westerners often confuse it with compliance and conformity. The nineteenth-century translator of the Chinese classics, James Legge, was guilty of this when he wrote, 'The love of order and quiet, and a willingness to submit to "the powers that be," eminently distinguish them [the Chinese]. Foreign writers have often taken notice of this, and have attributed it to the influence of Confucius's doctrines as inculcating subordination.' Legge only challenges this misconception in so far as he claims that Chinese docility pre-dated the Master: 'The character of the people moulded his system, more than it was moulded by it.'[5]

Legge is not entirely wrong, in that the desire for harmony can lead to an arguably excessive toleration of bad rule. But this is not inevitable, in part because harmony is not desired at any price. Nor is harmony the same as refusing to countenance any conflict or disagreement. It is not bland uniformity but balanced diversity. The *Analects* of Confucius clearly state, 'The exemplary person pursues harmony rather than sameness; the small person does the opposite.' Consider the extant Chinese expression 'a pool of dead water', which refers to 'a lifeless state of uniformity'.[6] Indeed, the most famous images representing harmony have difference at their core. In the fifth–fourth-century-BCE classic *Gouyu*, the politician-scholar Shi Bo says, 'A single sound is not musical, a single colour does not constitute a beautiful pattern, a single flavour does not make a delicious dish, and a single thing does not make harmony.'[7] A piece of music, for example, needs different instruments playing different notes in order for the whole composition to be harmonious. A soup requires a variety of ingredients with different but complementary flavours, or else it is bland and unwholesome. The right and left hands both have their own strengths, and so 'merging them into a "middle hand" does not make one better off', as Li puts it.[8] Whenever anyone promotes uniformity in the name of harmony, they are getting harmony wrong.

Harmony actually depends upon division. 'Seeing creative tension as a necessary manifestation of diversity in the world,' says Li, 'Confucian philosophy takes it as the driving force towards harmony.'[9] The problem is not just that the English word 'harmony' is 'usually understood as accord and agreement'.[10] The misunderstanding has also arisen within China. Mozi, the great dissenter of Chinese classical philosophy, criticised Confucian harmony precisely because he thought that it required people to share and follow the same idea.[11] Ironically, the same Mozi emphasised the importance of harmony by another name: order. Mohism promotes three basic goods: the wealth, order and population of the state.[12]

If Westerners are more likely to mistake harmony with uniformity, it is perhaps because, as Li points out, ideas of 'an underlying fixed cosmic order' or 'a transcendent, static foundation' have been dominant in Western thinking.[13] Li calls this 'innocent harmony' and traces it back to the Pythagoreans of sixth-century-BCE Greece, who were the first to use the word 'cosmos', meaning order, for the universe. Pythagoreans also thought that harmony required us to live in accordance with the pre-existing ratios of the underlying cosmic order, an idea strongly echoed in Plato, who canonised the notion of innocent harmony.[14] This also seems to be true in Indian thought, with its idea of *ṛta*, a cosmic order or harmony.[15]

Things might have been different in the Western tradition if the rival Heraclitean view of harmony had won out. Heraclitus said, 'Harmony consists of opposing tension, like that of the bow and the lyre.'[16] Aristotle quotes three Heraclitean maxims: 'Opposition unites', 'From the different comes the fairest harmony' and 'All things come from strife.'[17] Ironically, the etymology of harmony is more Heraclitean than Platonic, even though its current meaning is more Platonic than Heraclitean. In both Latin and Greek *harmonia* means 'concord of sounds'.[18]

Because harmony involves a kind of tension it is not always easy to create. 'Harmony cannot be achieved unless all sides are willing to give up something,' says Yao Xinzhong. If everyone holds out for everything they want, the result can only be conflict. Harmony requires compromise and patience. There is a famous story of a prime minister, Chang Kung-ni, in the Song dynasty who lived with nine generations of his family in the same house. The emperor, Tang Kao-chung, wondered how such a household could be harmonious and asked him for his secret. Chang Kung-ni asked for pen and paper and wrote *jen* ('patience' or 'endurance') over a hundred times. This has been taken as a model for family life in Chinese society ever since, where 'hundred patience' (*po jen*) has become a common idiom.[19]

Whether it is because of or despite the fact that harmonious families are hard to maintain, one of the best-known manifestations of harmony in Confucian ethics is in the virtue of filial piety (*xiào*). Almost every culture has placed a high value on family ties and their corresponding duties. For instance, 'A son may not disown his father, although a father may disown his son,' wrote Aristotle. 'For a debtor ought to repay his debts, but nothing that a son can do is a due return for what he has received, so he is permanently in his father's debt.'[20] Today, people all around the world often say they owe their parents everything. In China, however, family ties are at the very heart of virtue and ethics.

Xiào is easily assumed to require slavish obedience, but as the fourth-century-BCE Confucian text *The Classic of Filial Piety* clearly states, 'When the father is not right, the son must remonstrate with the father [...] Hence, if the son follows the father without remonstrating with him when the father is not right, how can this be filial?'[21] But if obedience is overstated, loyalty certainly is not. For a son to report a crime committed by his father was actually a crime for much of China's history.[22]

Xiào concerns more than just fathers and sons. It is about everyone standing in the right relation to one another, so that the whole family unit works organically and harmoniously. Of the five bonds (or relations) in Confucian ethics, three concern the family: father to son is just one, alongside husband to wife and elder brother to younger brother. The older brother must be *liang* (*xian liang* or *wen liang*, good-natured and caring), the younger *ti* (respectful and agreeable).[23] This is in part why Roger Ames prefers 'family reverence' to the more traditional translation of *xiào*. It gives a greater sense of the importance of all familial ties, not just those of sons to fathers, or siblings to parents, which receive the most emphasis in classical texts, later commentaries and Chinese culture. The wider scope of *xiào* is reflected in the proverb 'When the family is harmonious, everything thrives.' Or as the twentieth-century philosopher Yu-Wei Hsieh put it, 'If anyone does not like his ancestors, how can he like the man in the street?'[24] That is why when Mencius wrote, 'Let careful attention be paid to education in schools', he singled out the inculcation of filial and fraternal duties as its prime goal. Only this would ensure that 'grey-haired men will not be seen upon the roads, carrying burdens on their backs or on their heads', a stock Chinese image of societal breakdown.[25]

Family harmony is is also crucial for the development of personal virtue, whereas in the Western philosophical tradition, Li points out, it's almost the opposite. Nietzsche dismissed the married philosopher as something that belonged in comedy.[26] On his deathbed, Socrates had nothing to say to his family, who weren't even present and whom he didn't mention (his last words were an instruction to offer a cock to Asclepius, the god of healing).[27] 'To some extent, freedom for Socrates implies freedom from the family,' says Li. Few major Western philosophers in the male-dominated canon discuss family or give any impression that such a mundane, domestic concern would distract them from the serious business of thinking.

How relevant is *xiào* in today's China, after decades not only of a one-child policy but also of communist rule? When Mao launched the Cultural Revolution in 1966, he waged a head-on assault on traditional Confucian values, aiming to wipe out the 'Four Olds': Old Customs, Old Culture, Old Habits and Old Ideas. Prime among these was loyalty to family. From a traditional point of view, nothing could have been more un-Chinese than the Maoist encouragement of children to denounce their own parents.

Certainly there are young Chinese who have embraced more Western, individualistic values and so find the old family ways odd. 'I don't think they love each other,' one woman told me about Chinese parents and children. 'I feel I've been looked after but not truly loved or respected as a person.' Younger Chinese like her want to forge their own way in the world, not just continue the family line. 'Parents want you to be successful in their values, instead of yours, and they're willing to spend all their money, all their lifetime's savings, to ensure the success of their children to fulfil their parents' dreams instead of doing what they want to do.'

However, there are many other signs that *xiào* lives on, albeit in modified form. Everyone I spoke to, including the young staff at a go-ahead publishing company in Beijing, said that they felt a sense of responsibility to their parents and would look after their welfare as they grew older. These could just be fine words, of course, but the very fact that people felt they were fine shows the value itself is still there.

Even more anecdotal, but more striking still, is a story told to me by a French philosopher, Yves Vende, who has spent some time living in China. When he first arrived he met a Chinese artist who told him that once she thought about suicide. He asked her why she didn't go ahead. She answered, 'Because if I committed suicide nobody is going to take care of my parents.' Vende found himself thinking, 'No French artist would give this answer.'

At the same time as people uphold the value of *xiào*, they also talk of it breaking down, in much the same way that people in many Western countries eulogise community but believe it is in decline. Yet paradoxically, even some of the signs of weakening family ties reflect its enduring importance. For example, China has made it a legal requirement to visit elderly relatives, which shows both how the spontaneous fulfilment of filial duty is declining and how important it is still considered to fulfil it. This also illustrates the Confucian point that if you have to resort to the law to enforce virtuous behaviour, society has already failed.[28]

David Wong thinks that there are several reasons for the decline of *xiào*, including the experience of communism and the encounter with the more individualistic West. But there are also more social-structural reasons, not least the one-child policy. 'Particularly in the cities, families have been so small, the relationship between parents and children has changed. I think it's also true that with a sense of increased economic opportunity there is less stress on family to the extent that it's become less economically essential, especially to have a large family. That's not to say that was the only reason to have it in the first place, but when a moral ideal is working it is reinforced by institutional structures, or sets of practices that give people multiple motivations to adhere to it. I think that's what's breaking down.'

One further pressure is that in some respects traditional Confucian ideals of familial harmony are patriarchal and out of date. Even most Confucians today accept that their tradition has not had a great record on equal rights for women.[29] Optimists, however, believe that the basic framework is robust and can contain something more progressive. Key to this are the twin facts that, as Li puts it, 'Confucian harmony requires differences' and 'Differences can exist without oppression.'[30]

Nonetheless, it would be disingenuous to pretend that Confucian harmony can be entirely divorced from any sense of hierarchy, even if we reject misogynistic hierarchies of gender. The third-century-BCE Confucian Xunzi, for instance, clearly appeals to hierarchical ideals when he talks of the need for 'differentiation', for 'noble and lowly to have their proper ranking, for elder and youth to have their proper distance, and for poor and rich, humble and eminent each to have their proper weights'.[31] These conflicts need controlling by some kind of power that is to be properly exercised. So, says Yao, 'Chinese philosophy does not in general object to hierarchy. Most philosophers tend to believe a reasonably structured hierarchy is natural, like heaven above and the earth below – you can't just move it around and say the earth will be above.'

However, the Confucian can turn the criticism into a challenge against the critic. Could it not be that one of the problems of the contemporary West is that it has come to see hierarchy as a dirty word and has failed to appreciate how social harmony requires fair, just hierarchies? An academic workshop on the issue persuaded me that this was in large part true.[32]

It doesn't take much reflection to realise that we wouldn't want to eliminate all hierarchies. We need managers and directors for practical reasons. We also want to be treated by experienced doctors not trainees, have our hair cut by senior stylists not apprentices, get our wiring checked by qualified electricians not handy persons. Eliminating hierarchies of expertise and experience would entail the absurd pretence that everyone knows the same and has the same skills as everyone else.

Western suspicion of hierarchy is built on two pillars. One is a justice-based rejection of oppressive political structures such as feudalism and absolute monarchy. The other is an embrace of the Enlightenment ideal of the autonomous, free rational agent. This was expressed in Kant's seminal essay 'What is Enlightenment?', in which he implored readers, 'Have the courage to use your *own* understanding.' Only this would bring humanity out of its 'self-incurred immaturity', as characterised by 'the inability to use one's own understanding without the guidance of another'.[33]

Such ideals give rise to a radical egalitarianism in which no one stands above or below anyone else and everyone decides for themselves. This ideal comes in both realistic and unrealistic forms. The ideal of equality, for example, makes perfect sense if it is an equality of value which grants equal rights before the law. It is an absurdity, however, if it is interpreted as an equality of skills, ability or knowledge. We are obviously not equal in this sense.

Second, the idea of rational autonomy is perfectly sensible if it means that ultimately we have to decide what to believe for ourselves. In a sense this is just a tautology: no one else can make up our minds for us. But again the view flips into absurdity if it means that we don't require the wisdom, knowledge and expertise of others to help us to make decisions. Only I can decide whether to follow my doctor's advice. But I need the doctor to give me that advice to be as informed as I can be to make that choice.

The ideal of the autonomous, free rational agent is therefore not absolutely opposed to all hierarchies. Rather, it rejects hierarchies that give unjust political powers or rights to groups on the basis of heredity or patronage, or that give experts or authorities the ultimate right to make decisions that undermine reasonable autonomy. This leaves plenty of room for what we might call just hierarchies, which have three key features.

First, they are domain-specific. In medicine, a doctor's views carry more weight than mine, but no one need defer to their surgeon in matters of politics or sport.

Second, they are dynamic. Someone's place in the hierarchy is determined by merit or experience, which means that others might acquire such expertise and move up the hierarchy, or lose it and slip down. Hierarchies become unjust when they are ossified and movement is impossible: think of rulers who are fairly elected but then cling on to power after they lose their mandate, or parents who try to maintain their authority over their children after those children have grown up.

Third, they are empowering. What ultimately justifies the superior position of the teacher over the student is that the student can benefit from this relationship to acquire some of the teacher's skills and knowledge. If the teacher is not teaching, then their position is not merited and the hierarchical relationship loses its purpose. Likewise, a parent's authority over a child is only justified to the extent to which that parent helps to bring up that child. An abusive or neglectful parent has no superior status to the child.

Arguably, all of these features should be found in the hierarchical relationships promoted by Confucian harmony at its best. Harmony is empowering because it allows everyone to function to their fullest capabilities. Where there is no harmony, no one can fulfil their potential. Confucianism also promotes domain-specific hierarchies because relations are defined by particular roles. So the ruler stands above the subject in that relation, but below an elder brother or a father in a family hierarchy. Finally, harmony is dynamic because relations change over time: the son becomes a father, the subject a ruler. Furthermore, Confucian ethics puts a strong emphasis on virtue, as we'll shortly see, which means that a person's suitability for holding power is based on their qualities, not their greater popularity or accidents of birth. Confucian hierarchy is therefore not democratic, but nor is it based on hereditary privilege, as reflected in China's competitive Imperial Examinations system for the civil service, which lasted more than thirteen centuries until its abolition in 1905.[34] The system ensured appointments were made on merit, an ethos that largely endures, with a modified version of the system still operating in Taiwan.

It would be too optimistic to suggest that traditional Confucian harmony perfectly delivers the sorts of just hierarchies we would nowadays wish to promote. Even if it did, in the view of Xu Zhiyuan hierarchy has become divorced from its wider Confucian context and turned into a kind of habit in its own right. Market forces have combined with a form of social Darwinism in which the new hierarchies are of rich and poor. There is surely some truth in this, but the fact that hierarchies can be and have been abused does not mean that the framework of hierarchical harmony is not fully compatible with justice. As Li reminds us, 'Embracing an ideal does not imply a consensus regarding its application.'[35] An ideal is not invalidated by its misapplication. Indeed, one Confucian test of any hierarchy is whether it promotes harmony (remembering that this is not the same question as 'Does it keep everyone quiet?' or 'Does it eliminate disagreement?'). If the new hierarchies of rich and poor in China are producing disharmony, as many critics claim, they flunk that test.

Most people would agree that hierarchy leads to too much deference to authority in East Asian cultures. However, an excess of deference is not inevitable. For example, while I was in Japan its then prime minister, Shinzō Abe, was visiting the UK, where several journalists commented on the extraordinarily subservient deference the Japanese press corps showed him, never challenging at all. I wondered if this was a deep-rooted aspect of Japanese culture. But the philosopher Nakajima Takahiro told me that 'before Abe the press asked very tough questioning to the politicians' and that the problem was not perennial obeisance but a particular government 'intervening in media production process'. The centrality of harmony as a value might make East Asian cultures more vulnerable to excessive obedience, but it does not make this unavoidable.

The classical Chinese texts don't sanction deference. We've already seen how sons are obliged to challenge their fathers when they are wrong. In fact, everyone's obligation to do what is right is greater than their duty to obey people further up the hierarchy. Mencius thought it wrong to obey bad rulers. 'If I were to bend my principles and follow these princes, of what kind would my conduct be?' he wrote. 'Never has a man who has bent himself been able to make others straight.'[36] Mencius is shown to follow this principle, openly challenging many of the powerful people who sought his advice. King Hûi of Liang greeted him by saying, 'I presume you are provided with counsels to profit my kingdom?' Mencius immediately challenged him, 'Why must your majesty use that word "profit"? What I am provided with are counsels to benefit benevolence and righteousness, and these are my only topics.'[37] Obsequious subservience was neither practised nor preached by the Confucian masters.

The idea that harmony requires difference and lack of deference has an application to the practice of intercultural dialogue. Everyone agrees that this requires showing due respect, but we tend to have a rather po-faced idea of what respect for other cultures requires. Stephen Muecke argues that as a result laughter is something anthropologists tend to ignore. In contrast, his indigenous friends taught him 'not to take things too seriously or rather that laughter has got a good place to play in knowledge production'.

I doubt there are many laughs in this book, but I hope there is not excessive reverence either. Too often it is assumed that respect for other traditions precludes criticism. But as the highly respectful comparative philosopher Charles Moore says, 'Understanding does not involve approval or acceptance: it may lead to exactly the opposite.'[38] Excessive deference leads not to dialogue but to what Bruce Janz calls 'dialit', the mere exchange of texts accompanied by approving, polite nods and smiles.[39] Real dialogue requires careful listening but also mutual examination and questioning . I would go so far as to say that to refuse to criticise in all circumstances is in itself disrespectful, since it treats 'other' philosophies as more fragile and less able to stand up to scrutiny than our own. Criticism and disagreement are only disrespectful when they come from a combination of arrogance and ignorance.

Another feature of harmony which is increasingly attractive today is its environmental dimension. In the West 'harmony with nature' is often a rose-tinted vision of bucolic fields and lambs lying with lions. Chinese harmony, however, is 'not always rosy and pretty', as Li says. Harmony in nature might include a balance of predators and prey.[40] Although Confucians emphasised harmony in human relations more than with nature, the two are never entirely separate. Li sees a link in Xunzi, who maintains that 'social disharmonies lead to the detrimental treatment of nature, which results in shortage of resources; a shortage of resources in turn creates more disharmonies in society.'[41] In this analysis, social inequality is the result of environmental degradation caused by social disharmonies. For example, when water supply is good, everyone gets a decent share, but water shortages create tensions between those who can afford to buy in supplies and those who can't. This suggests that harmony promotes equality rather than that equality promotes harmony, or at least that harmony is a prerequisite for equality and that trying to achieve greater equality in the absence of harmony is going to be a difficult, if not impossible, task.

This is more evident when we look beyond Confucianism to

Daoism, where harmony is also a virtue, but manifested in slightly different ways. Whereas Confucian harmony is defined in terms of relations between humans, Daoism emphasises the harmony of humanity with nature. As Li sees it, Daoists seek for humans to 'harmonise *with* the world', while Confucians seek to 'harmonise the world' for the sake of humans.[42] The two interchangeable modern Chinese words for ethics and morality demonstrate this difference. *Daode* literally means 'the way and its power', while *lunli* means 'the patterns in human kinship and relations'. Robin Wang argues that this gives them different connotations. 'Following the pattern of the world is *daode*', which is more Daoist, 'whereas to keep human relationships orderly is *lunli*', which is more Confucian.[43]

For example, the Daoist Zhuangzi's statement that 'Virtue is the cultivation of complete harmony' sounds like it could easily have come straight from a Confucian text.[44] But when he spells out what this means, it becomes clear that his Daoist harmony is to be found not so much in ordering the world as in detaching from it. He praises people who have gone beyond care, people who 'have given up' and 'forgotten other people, and by forgetting other people they have become people of Heaven. You can honour them and they won't be pleased. You can despise them and they won't be mad. Only those who have identified with Heaven's harmony are like this.'[45]

Daoist harmony is more centred on the individual than in Confucianism, which emphasises the social. Joel Kupperman says that a harmonious Daoist self is created when there is 'an accord between words and behaviour, on the one hand, and inner impulses, on the other, so that there is an absence of inner conflicts'. The meanings of 'harmony' and 'naturalness' converge, and in Daoism involve 'spontaneity in behaviour, simplicity in social life, and harmony with the fundamental tendencies of the universe'.[46]

Daoism portrays the current state of humanity in terms of a fall from a golden age of the *Dao*, when we followed our natural state without the need for thought or concepts. The original harmony of the *Dao* was a kind of effortless naturalness. Laozi urges us to try to return to this.[47]

> The earth models itself on heaven.
> Heaven models itself on the Way.
> The Way models itself on what is natural.[48]

To achieve the harmony of the *Dao* we must go beyond the limiting categories of thought and language. 'The Way is hidden and without name.'[49] 'An excess of speech will lead to exhaustion.'[50] One curious feature of this view is that the categories of virtue and vice only emerge when the perfect unity and harmony of nature are disrupted. As Kupperman puts it, 'Once virtue concepts are originated [...] the logical space (so to speak) for vices has also been created – the real vices will not be far behind.'[51] Hence, the *Daodejing* says, 'When the great way is abandoned, there are benevolence and righteousness. When wisdom and intelligence come forth, there is great hypocrisy.'[52]

It's a bit like the Christian fall, in which the idyll of Eden has no room for distinctions of good and bad. The fall described in the *Daodejing* is more complicated in that it involves four levels of degeneration:

> When the Way was lost there was Virtue;
> When Virtue was lost there was benevolence;
> When benevolence was lost there was righteousness;
> When righteousness was lost there were the rites.[53]

The way back is to abandon the artificial constructs of book-learning and morality and return to something purer. 'Cut off sageliness, abandon wisdom, and the people will benefit one-hundred-fold. Cut off benevolence, abandon righteousness, and the people will return to being filial and kind.'[54]

Harmony in Daoism is most obviously articulated in the balance of *yin* and *yang*. 'The myriad creatures shoulder *yin* and embrace *yang*, and by blending these *qi*, they attain harmony.'[55] Although most associated with Daoism, the concepts of *yin* and *yang* have become 'the common ground for the intermingling of the divergent philosophical schools' of China.[56] In her definitive study of *yinyang* thinking, the contemporary Daoist philosopher Robin Wang deliberately uses the word '*yinyang*' rather than '*yin-yang*' or '*yin* and *yang*' when talking of both together, reflecting the Chinese usage in which the terms 'are directly set together and would not be linked by a conjunction', a subtle but important point.[57] In the popular Western imagination, '*yin* and *yang*' represent the eastern embrace of opposites and contradictions, as opposed to the Western binary either/or. This misses the irony that such a description itself creates a binary pair, *yin* and *yang*. A genuine alternative to dichotomous logic would not neatly separate the two concepts but would emphasise their interdependence and interpenetration. Thinking in terms of *yinyang* helps us to remember this.

This is difficult, because on the face of it *yinyang* is full of binary distinctions. Wang lists at least thirty-five pairs of opposites in the *Daodejing*, such as beautiful/ugly, good/not good, presence/nonpresence, difficult/easy.[58] And yet she insists that 'the distinction of oppositions like *yin* and *yang* is not a matter of seeing reality through a dualistic or atomistic lens'. The very word for 'things' in Chinese, *wu*, does not mean 'entities in isolation', says Wang. *Wu* are better seen as 'phenomena, events, and even histories' which have stages and 'are always becoming'.[59] In Chinese thought, the principle is not so much 'the whole is greater than the sum of its parts' as 'parts become less when artificially isolated from the wholes to which they belong'. When a thing is only what it is when it is in relation to others, no items in any list of pairs can be seen as mutually exclusive or discrete.

Key to overcoming an excessive duality is seeing that *yin* and *yang* are not things or fixed essences of things. Whether something is *yin* or *yang* varies according to the context and relationship between things. This is suggested by the origins of the words themselves, which first referred to the sunny (*yang*) and shady (*yin*) sides of a hill, which would change as the sun moved across the sky.[60] To give a clear example of the dynamism of *ying* and *yan* offered by Alfred Forke, although the left hand is *yang* and the right *yin*, when hands are raised both are *yang*, when put down *yin*, and whether up or down, left or right, both hands are *yang* when hot and *yin* when cold.[61] That something can be *yin* and *yang* at the same time in different ways is not paradoxical. The same is true of any relational property: something can be to the left of one thing, to the right of another; above one thing, below another; hotter than one thing, cooler than another. *Yinyang* shares this dependence on context because it is inherently concerned with relationships. According to Wang, these relationships can take six forms: contradiction and opposition (*maodun*); interdependence (*xiangyi*); mutual inclusion (*huhan*); interaction or resonance (*jiogan*); complementarity or mutual support (*hubu*); change and transformation (*zhuanhua*).

The main function of *yinyang* is not to describe the world in some kind of pseudo- or proto-scientific way, even if at times that is precisely what some thinkers have tried to do with it. Rather, it is to enable us to live well in it. It is inherently practical. 'Yinyang is a *shu*,' says Wang, 'a strategy or technique that enables one to function effectively in any given circumstance.'[62] This is captured succinctly in the seventh-century-BCE classic the *Guanzi*, which poses the question, 'What is *yinyang*?' and answers, 'Timing.'[63] In other words, *yinyang* responds appropriately to the precise situation as it is now, not as it was or will be. A wise action today could be a foolish one tomorrow. By attending to the relationships between things one is able to respond to them in such a way that the desired outcome flows naturally from the situation.[64] This is true in virtually every aspect of human life, including sex. A man's penis is called *yangjiu* (*yang* equipment) and a woman's vagina *yinhu* (*yin* house). In skilful sex, the *yangjiu* picks up *yin* energy from the *yinhu*, without its own *yang* energy being extinguished too early or too fast. 'This sexual intercourse is sometimes called *caiyinshu*, the art of picking *yin*.'[65]

Yinyang is part of a wider *qi* cosmology. *Qi* is usually described as a kind of energy, a fundamental force in nature, often now dismissed as unscientific. While there is and has been a lot of pseudoscience around *qi*, it is as much a mindset as it is a theory. To think in terms of *qi* and *yinyang* today is not to think of supplements or rivals to Newtonian physics or quantum mechanics. It is, rather, a practical way of thinking about how to ensure that things flow, stand in the right relation to others and achieve a frictionless harmony.

That harmony is the central and most distinctive value in Chinese culture and thought should be uncontroversial. More contentious is how this ideal plays out politically. Other nations may talk more about freedom and rights, but no one wants a *disharmonious* society. However, all over the world, harmony has been used to justify unjust status quos. In 1770, the chancellor of the French judiciary, Antoine-Louis Séguier, denounced the radical Enlightenment thinkers as criminals who intended to 'destroy the close harmony' between the social orders.[66] Throughout Chinese history, oppression has always been justified under the name of 'harmony'.[67] 'China has a history of appropriating its own tradition, with very different figures each claiming to be true to the original values of Confucius,' Andrew Lambert told me. 'It's a strategy for gaining legitimacy.' Most obviously, the Chinese government set a 'harmonious society' (*hexie shehui*) as its goal under the leadership of Hu Jintao, from

2002 to 2012. But for many this was a kind of double-speak, since what it in fact sought was uniformity.[68] 'Harmonisation' becomes a euphemism for the elimination of dissent. For instance, dissident writer Xu Zhiyuan writes about the 'Great Firewall of China', the state censorship of the Internet which blocks out any 'inharmonious information'.[69] Confucians themselves have been well aware of this danger of distortion. 'To harmonise with others in what is good is called "proper compliance",' says Mencius, but to 'harmonise with others in what is bad is called "toadying"'.[70]

Xu suggests that people talk the language of harmony as a kind of cultural habit even though it bears no relation at all to what is actually going on today. 'People say I'm looking for harmony but actually society is not harmonious,' he told me. 'There's lots of anger and coldness, even in families.' For him, the core of the problem is a lack of respect for individual rights, trampled upon in the name of 'harmony'.

Interestingly, Xu also gives an example of how dissidents can embody the virtue of harmony. The human rights lawyer Zhiyuan Xu fights his battles not by antagonism but, as he himself said in a lecture, by working 'towards unity, consensus, participation and dedication'.[71] In addition, the very fact that the Chinese government speaks the language of harmony tells us something about how central a value it is, just as the need for every prospective president of the USA to talk about freedom tells us how much that is valued in America, irrespective of whether their policies will increase it or not. Nor should we assume that 'harmony' is now a mere weasel word. Much as democrats might dislike the idea, objective surveys suggest that there is a high degree of satisfaction with politics in China. Daniel Bell points to the highly respected Asian Barometer Survey, which showed that 'Chinese citizens trust their political institutions more than in any of the eight societies surveyed, including democratic Japan, South Korea, the Philippines, and Taiwan.'[72]

One of the most controversial political applications of harmony today is China's treatment of its ethnic minorities. The country often boasts of a proud history of embracing its minorities, reflected in the extensive space the Shanghai Museum devotes to its Kadoorie Gallery of Chinese Minority Nationalities' Art. The promotion of harmony in society can follow the key principle that 'difference precedes unity', as Chenyang Li puts it. This is not a celebration of difference for difference's sake. 'Not all differences are good and should be promoted', says Li, such as 'when people clearly act in ways contrary to the generally accepted standards of humanity'. Some differences should be celebrated, while others can and should be accepted even if they do not meet our personal approval.[73] Such a vision of pluralism without anarchy is just what we need in a complex, diverse world which calls out for 'a mentality of harmony rather than a mentality of confrontation or hegemony'.[74]

The darker side of this, however, is that difference is only respected if it reflects unity. While I was in Beijing I visited an exhibition at the National Art Gallery called 'The Great Unity of China'. Although it was a celebration of the minorities' 'picturesque homelands and colourful national customs', its message was how 'people of all nationalities in China unite as one'. This emphasis on unity places an absolute limit on how much autonomy any of China's ethnic groups or regions can be allowed. China may celebrate its Tibetan minority, for example, but only if it remains committed to its Chinese ties, even at the price of the region becoming overwhelmed by Han immigrants diluting the local culture. In recent years, this has become a significant issue, with the current Chinese government reinforcing the conflation of Chinese and Han identity, the ethnic group that makes up 92 per cent of mainland China's population.[75] Uniform homogenisation has been promoted in the name of Confucian harmony.

Irrespective of how harmonious China actually is today, we have a lot to learn about how harmony should be manifested in the political domain. Confucian thought has some interesting ideas about how important the glowing example of a good ruler is for creating harmony. Confucian virtue ethics places great importance on the moral exemplar over enforcing laws. It is not that Confucians don't see laws as important. Mencius approved of the old saying, 'Virtue alone is not sufficient for the exercise of government; laws alone cannot carry themselves into practice.'[76] There has to be a balance of law and virtue, and if a law has to be enforced it already shows that harmony has broken down. It is therefore better to govern in such a way that the force of law never has to be used. 'When it comes to hearing civil litigation, I am as good as anyone else,' said Confucius in the *Analects*. 'What is necessary, though, is to bring it about that there is no civil litigation at all.'[77] The flipside is when laws are applied with a heavy hand, creating disharmony. 'If you try to guide the common people with coercive regulations and keep them in line with punishments, the common people will become evasive and will have no sense of shame.'[78]

Ideally, the leader behaves in such a way that harmony will follow without coercion. For instance, Mencius said that when people have parcels of land adjacent to one another, they 'render all friendly offices to one another in their going out and coming in, aid one another in keeping watch and ward, and sustain one another in sickness'.[79]

Even in Daosim, which exalts the natural state, the *Daodejing* says, 'In government, the good lies in orderliness.'[80] The Daoists take the idea of the natural flow of harmony even further, suggesting that when government is working at its best, it does as little as possible: 'The more dull and depressed the government, the more honest and agreeable the people. The more active and searching the government, the more deformed and deficient the people.'[81] In a metaphor that would delight modern-day libertarians, the *Daodejing* says, 'Ruling a great state is like cooking a small fish.'[82] In other words, the more you meddle, the more it falls apart.

Although it might sound desirable to keep the law out of day-to-day affairs as much as possible, it is an ideal that can conflict with the tradition of rule of law, which guarantees the equal treatment of all by insisting that the law, not rulers or their agents, has the final say. The Confucian value of equity, which Li describes as 'a kind of flexibility or amenability in applying a law in a special situation', directly challenges this.[83] Take the one-child policy, which did not apply to China's ethnic minorities. Since they make up a small proportion, and harmony is required across society, it makes sense to grant them special privileges.[84] Jin Li tells an even more striking story about a Muslim friend of her family whom they called 'Uncle'. Starting the late 1950s and through the Cultural Revolution, every family was allocated a pound of pork per person per month. But because Muslims do not eat pork, Uncle's family was allocated more than a pound of beef.

The Confucian principle behind this making of exceptions is *quan*, weighing or discretional action, derived from the idea of something carrying weight.[85] Such is the importance of this that the Chinese word for rights is *quan li*, where *li* means 'benefit' or 'interest'. This isn't just an etymological curio: rights involve weighing because which rights apply is always dependent on context.[86] Although this would appear to directly contradict the Western tradition of rights as invariable and inviolable, context also matters in the West to some degree. Even the right to life is not absolute.

Aristotle recognised something like the principle of *quan* when he wrote, 'Where a thing is indefinite, the rule by which it is measured is also indefinite.'[87] Aristotle was a staunch defender of the rule of law, arguing that one of the main problems with democracy was that the majority ruled, not the law. This suggests that we should not think of a stark choice between the rigid rule of law and executive caprice, but could rather think of a middle way in which discretion is exercised under a law which is clear but flexible. Some countries like Britain imagine their systems to operate in this way. The ideas of 'common sense' and 'discretion' are part of the popular imagination. It is – or at least was – widely believed that British policemen would not simply apply the law blindly but would let people go with a caution or a telling-off if they thought the misdemeanour was not serious. This culture of flexibility has declined for understandable reasons. When rules are not explicitly stated and followed, no one really knows what they ought to do to stay on the right side of the law. In a passage that sounds a little sinister to modern ears, the *Daodejing* states, 'In ancient times, those good at practicing the Way did not use it to enlighten the people, but rather to keep them in the dark.'[88] The other main problem with discretion is that it is only as good as the judgement of the person exercising it. In practice, this results in 'discretion' often meaning people whose face fit are treated leniently while those with the wrong skin colour or accents are given no benefit of the doubt.

Both rigidity and flexibility have their pros and cons. The ideal balance is, I would suggest, a transparent *quan* in which discretion is saved from abuse by being completely open. A legal system could sanction the use of reasonable judgement, accepting that this would mean not everyone would reach the same conclusion. The law would be applied with some variability but not so much as to threaten the necessary equality. Flexibility of this kind is already built into some laws, but perhaps not enough.

Finally, mention should be made of the Chinese legalist tradition, which emerged during the Warring States period of around 475 to 221 BCE. Although not as influential in the long run as Confucianism or Daosim, it has nonetheless had an enduring influence as a counterweight to both. The legalists were dismissive of the view that harmony can be achieved by virtue and good example. As Han Feizi, the pre-eminent philosopher of the school, put it, 'The sage does not work on his Virtue, he works on his laws.'[89]

Clear laws make everything work well: 'When handing out rewards, it is best to make them substantial and dependable, so that the people will prize them; when assigning penalties, it is best to make them heavy and inescapable, so that the people will fear them; when framing laws, it is best to make them unequivocal and fixed, so that the people will understand them.'[90]

Paradoxically, Han also thought that a ruler needs to be as enigmatic and as unpredictable as his laws are clear and transparent. The 'Way of the Ruler' is to be an enigma, whose wishes are not clearly known, to keep everyone on their toes. 'When an enlightened ruler practices nonaction above, the assembled ministers will be anxious and fearful below,' he says, and that is a good thing. 'See others, but do not allow yourself to be seen; hear others but do not allow yourself to be known.'[91] The rationale is that if people know the ruler's likes and dislikes they will try to pander to them and so their true nature will not be known. 'Thus it is said, "Get rid of likes and dislikes and the true character of the assembled ministers will be plain. And when the true character of the assembled ministers is plain, the ruler of men cannot be deceived."'[92]

Han is clear that a ruler needs to be ruthless and powerful. 'If the ruler of men loses his power to punish and grant favours and allows his ministers to use them, then the ruler instead will be controlled by his ministers.' Han spells out what this means: 'To kill or execute – this is what is meant by "punishment".'[93] Punishment is one the 'two handles', the other being favour. However, Han prefers the stick over the carrot: 'In a stern household there are no impertinent servants, but a compassionate mother will often have spoiled children. By this I know that might and the power of position can be used to put an end to violence, while even the most profound Virtue is not enough to stop disorder.'[94]

There have always been periods in Chinese history when the ideals of the virtuous ruler and natural harmony have been rejected in favour of stern leadership and ersatz 'harmonisation'. The ideal of 'harmony', however, has served for centuries as a centre of social and political gravity. All rulers must justify themselves in terms of harmony. The use and abuse of this ideal is something that all societies could potentially learn from.

Perhaps most have already. Thaddeus Metz has observed the striking similarities between African and Chinese harmony and quotes some words of Archbishop Desmond Tutu that reflect how embedded it is in the culture: 'Social harmony is for us the *summum bonum* – the greatest good.'[95] Harmony is linked with the value of *ubuntu*, which emphasises the bonds of humanity between us. This leads to a way of dealing with social problems which is very different from the Western legalistic, rule-based system which has become the global default. Rules are readily discarded if they are seen to create more problems than they solve. As Pieter Boele van Hensbroek explains, 'Why are you going to apply some general principle when you see with your eyes that the practical result is creating animosity? So then they would say maybe the principle can be a bit less a principle and we're going to bend and work with this to come to a kind of settlement.' For traditions that value the rule of law, this looks like compromising justice. But bending of the rules in Africa is often rooted in commitment to a deep moral principle and is not always corruption.

Daniel Bell claims that harmony is a more universal value than even freedom. You see harmony in the Confucian-influenced East Asian societies, across much of Africa, in indigenous Latin American societies, in the idea of *tawḥīd* in Islamic philosophy.[96] The twelfth of the famous stone edicts of the Buddhist emperor Aśoka, who ruled most of India during the third century BCE, stated, 'Concord alone is meritorious.' Arguably, harmony already is and has usually been the pre-eminent global political value.

VIRTUE

Comparative philosophy reveals interesting contrasts and differences, and occasionally uncovers even more striking similarities. Arguably the most amazing of these is the remarkable congruence in the way in which classical Greek and Chinese philosophers, especially Aristotle and Confucius, put virtue at the heart of their ethics. This is even more incredible when you consider that there is no evidence that the two traditions learned from each other. Pretty much the exact same idea emerged independently at around the same time, 5,000 miles apart.

In Western philosophy, virtue ethics is most associated with Aristotle. Its central idea is that to live well we need to cultivate the right habits and dispositions, more than to follow moral codes or principles. A good person has a good character and this is what inclines them to act well. A person of bad character is always going to be inclined to behave badly, no matter what moral principles they officially subscribe to.

When people describe their moral values, they usually do so in terms of the rules and principles of their tradition, often religious.

When praising moral values, however, we tend to point to the people we believe exemplify them. People around the world admire the likes of Nelson Mandela, Mahātmā Gandhi and the Dalai Lama even though they belong to three religious traditions with very different beliefs. Their exceptional moral character matters more than the specifics of their beliefs. Similarly, pollsters repeatedly claim that elections often hinge upon questions of character more than they do on the specific policies being advocated.

Although the idea of virtue ethics lives on today, the word 'virtue' sounds increasingly anachronistic, used mostly in old idioms such as 'patience is a virtue'. In contemporary everyday usage it has strongly moralistic overtones. It is often used either ironically or mockingly to suggest an excessive puritanism. Someone who chooses a piece of fruit rather than a biscuit is being 'virtuous'. In ancient Greece, however, virtue (*arete*) had none of these moralistic associations, which is why some prefer to translate *arete* as 'excellence'. A virtue is an excellence because it is a skill or trained disposition that enables us to live well, meaning not just that we do the right thing by others but that we ourselves flourish as individuals.

The kind of virtue Aristotle is most concerned with is *ethike arete*, which is usually translated as 'moral virtue', although this is somewhat misleading. As Aristotle himself points out, *ethike* is 'formed by a slight variation from the word *ethos* (habit)'.[1] So we should talk not of 'moral virtue' but of 'ethical excellence', the kinds of habits and dispositions that enable us to live well. Virtue is not some sort of inner state but is constituted by right action. 'To virtue belongs virtuous activity,' wrote Aristotle, saying that 'the good for man is an activity of soul in accordance with virtue'.[2]

It is often said that Aristotle thought virtue led to happiness, but 'happiness' is a poor translation of the Greek *eudaimonia*. Happiness is generally conceived of today as an affective state of mind, something that we feel. *Eudaimonia* is better translated as 'flourishing'. To flourish as a human being is to live fully in accordance with your nature. Feeling good is often a consequence, but that is more of a side effect than the main purpose of *ethike arete*. When we are flourishing we have a satisfaction that we are living good lives, irrespective of whether we are often or ever in a good mood. Such satisfaction is arguably a deeper source of contentment than the kind of cheerful happiness that comes and goes. Conversely, someone might be happy much of the time but not truly be flourishing because their pleasure is shallow, the kind of thing that an animal could just as easily experience.

Compare an artist like Vincent van Gogh and a *bon viveur* like the film director Michael Winner. There is no reason to doubt that Winner had a good life. He enjoyed success and enjoyed himself, despite by all accounts often being difficult to be with or work with. Van Gogh, on the other hand, had a troubled life and died young of syphilis. If we ask which life was more pleasant Winner's is the clear winner. But if we ask which life contained more 'flourishing' many would choose van Gogh's. Any number of his paintings achieved an excellence far greater than Winner's magnum opus, *Death Wish*. From a third-person perspective, we might say that van Gogh had the better life. If we were to ask which life we would prefer for ourselves, I suspect we'd get different answers. Many assume that happiness is the highest goal and would choose to walk Winner's road. But many others would think it better to flourish, even at the price of happiness. John Stuart Mill's famous claim that it was 'Better to be Socrates dissatisfied than a fool satisfied' would be a tad harsh applied to Winner, but it captures the basic point well.[3]

Fortunately, Aristotle believed that a person of moral virtue would be unlikely to be as troubled as van Gogh, who exemplifies artistic *arete* not *ethike arete*. He knew how to paint, not how to live, and so flourished in only one limited domain. Generally speaking, to follow the path of virtue increases, not decreases, your chances of being happy, as long as you do not confuse happiness with transient fun or pleasure. Considering van Gogh's life highlights the distinction between happiness and flourishing by pushing it to unusual extremes.

Because virtue is a matter of having the right habits and dispositions (*hexis*), it must be cultivated and nurtured by right actions. Self-cultivation is also emphasised in Confucianism. 'There are many charges, but the charge of one's self is the root of all others,' said Mencius.[4] Similarly, 'The sovereign may not neglect the cultivation of his own character.'[5] Mencius repeats almost verbatim a line in *The Doctrine of the Mean* which says that we should be like the archer who, when he 'misses the centre of the target[,] he turns round and seeks for the cause of his failure in himself'.[6]

Xunzi has perhaps the most concise and memorable guide to the principles of self-cultivation, in a chapter devoted to this theme: 'When you observe goodness in others, then inspect yourself, desirous of studying it. When you observe badness in others, then examine yourself, fearful of discovering it. If you find goodness in your person, then approve of yourself, desirous of holding firm to it. If you find badness in your person, then reproach yourself, regarding it as calamity.'[7]

Most agree that it requires effort to become virtuous but Confucians believe it is within the reach of everyone. 'What kind of man was Shun?' asked Confucius of the great sage-king. 'What kind of man am I? He who exerts himself will also become such as he was.'[8] Those who claim it is too much for them just aren't trying hard enough. One disciple is reported to have told Confucius, 'It is not that I do not delight in your Way, Master, it is simply that my strength is insufficient.' Confucius was not impressed with this apparently humble confession. 'Someone whose strength is genuinely insufficient collapses somewhere along the Way,' he replied. 'As for you, you deliberately draw the line.'[9]

Although self-cultivation was important for all the classical Confucians, they disagreed about the extent to which the self being cultivated is intrinsically good or bad. Confucius did not take a clear position on the intrinsic goodness of human beings. Mencius, in contrast, came out on the side of those who thought human beings were essentially good and only became corrupted by bad societies. 'Benevolence is the distinguishing characteristic of man,' he wrote.[10] This comes out in the story of his discussion with King Xuan of Qi, who asked Mencius, 'What must one's virtue be like so that one can become a king?' Mencius told him that he must care for the people and the King wondered if he was capable of this. Mencius replied by reminding him of a time when he spared an ox from slaughter, replacing it with a sheep instead. The people thought he was being miserly, but his motivation was that he could not bear to witness its fright. Mencius argued that this showed the King had the seeds of benevolence within him, and needed to extend this from animals in sight to people out of sight. Indeed, the fact that he could feel compassion for an ox showed he was more than able to show it for his people.[11]

For Mencius, self-cultivation follows the grain of human nature. He rejects the metaphor of the philosopher Kâo that 'Man's nature is like the ch'î-willow and righteousness is like a cup or bowl.' Mencius objects, 'If you must do violence and injury to the willow in order to make cups and bowls with it, on your principles you must in the same way do violence and injury to humanity in order to fashion from it benevolence and righteousness! Your words, alas! would certainly lead all men to reckon benevolence and righteousness to be calamities.'[12]

Although human nature, being good, is not a blank slate, it still requires nurturing. The innate goodness of humankind needs to be developed, but gently. This lesson is most famously given in Mencius's story of the man from Song (a stock idiot figure) who tried to help his sprouts grow by pulling on them, thus killing them: 'Those who abandon it, thinking it will not help, are those who do not weed their grain. Those who help it grow are those who pull on the grain. Not only does this not help, but it even harms it.'[13]

The Neo-Confucians largely sided with Mencius, while also stressing theories and practices of self-cultivation.[14] Xunzi took the opposite view, claiming that 'people's nature is bad' and that 'their goodness is a matter of deliberate effort. [. . .] Without ritual and the standards of righteousness, they will be unruly, chaotic, and not well ordered.' We become good by our 'deliberate efforts', not through what is in our nature.[15] 'The nature of the gentleman is one and the same as that of the petty man.'[16]

Aristotle took a typically moderate stance in this debate, arguing that virtues 'are engendered in us neither *by* nor *contrary to* nature; we are constituted by nature to receive them, but their full development in us is due to habit'. Virtue could not be something 'engendered by nature' because moral goodness is cultivated by good habits and 'nothing that is what it is by nature can be made to behave differently by habituation'.[17]

This classical debate echoes the modern one about whether we are the products of nature or nurture, our genes or our environment. Most would agree this is now settled, in favour of Aristotle. We do indeed inherit a great deal, but except in a few examples, such as eye colour, our genes set a range of possibilities rather than a determinate outcome. Nurture makes actual what nature makes possible.

Although it would seem to matter a great deal which of Mencius, Xunzi or Aristotle was correct, it is less important than you might think, since in practice all virtue theorists end up advocating the same thing: only by the practice of virtue can people be virtuous, either by avoiding the slide into vice or by pulling themselves out of the default of vice:

If you do not accumulate little steps,
You will have no way to go a thousand li.
If you do not accumulate small streams,
You will have no way to form river or sea.[18]

Either way human nature requires cultivating. As Xunzi himself put it, 'If there were no human nature, then there would be nothing for deliberate effort to be applied to. If there were no deliberate effort, then human nature would not be able to beautify itself.'[19]

Talk of self-cultivation is notable only by its absence in Western philosophy today. 'There is little discussion in contemporary practical ethics of changing oneself, the one part of the universe that one has some actual control over,' laments Owen Flanagan.[20] Such an omission would seem bizarre to the classical Chinese thinkers. Even in Daosim, where the goal is effortless natural action, cultivation is essential. The name of its central text suggests this: *Daodejing* literally means the classic of *de* (virtue) and *dao* (the way). Zhuangzi says, 'Virtue is the cultivation of complete harmony,'[21] while in the *Daodejing* it is written:

Cultivate it in yourself and its [the Way's] Virtue will
be genuine.
Cultivate it in one's family and its Virtue will be more
than enough.[22]

Nevertheless, there is a resistance to the idea of cultivation in Daoism since in nature goodness just *is*, so the need to cultivate virtue is a sign that things have gone wrong. This relates to the Daoist emphasis on the somewhat paradoxical concept of *wu-wei*, a kind of effortless action that we achieve only through years of long practice, like the skills of master butcher Ding. That we need to try so hard to recover what is so effortless is another sign of our fall from nature.

The need for virtue to be cultivated helps outsiders to make sense of one of the more curious features of Confucian ethics: its emphasis on ritual. Ritual is essential for the cultivation of virtue. 'If you are respectful but lack ritual you will become exasperating; if you are careful but lack ritual you will become timid; if you are courageous but lack ritual you will become unruly; and if you are upright but lack ritual you will become inflexible.'[23] Ritual is also important for nurturing social harmony.

Once again translation creates problems for understanding this properly. *Li* is usually translated as 'ritual' but is by no means restricted to the kind of formal ceremonies that modern Westerners think of as rituals. 'Originally it meant rituals and rites,' explains Yao Xinzhong, 'but Confucius expanded it to moral codes, codes of conduct. It's become both the external rules that you should follow and the internal senses you should cultivate.'

Another translation is 'propriety', which although better in some ways makes *li* appear to be little more than etiquette. The hybrid translation 'ritual propriety' captures the broader meaning a little better, but it might be best to think of *li* simply as the right way of conducting one's interactions with others. Chenyang Li calls *li* 'cultural grammar', making it far less mysterious and exotic because every culture has such a grammar which you need to know to interact seamlessly with others.[24] Shaking hands when greeting, for example, is part of the *li* of many cultures. Although trivial in some ways, if it isn't done when or how it should be, serious offence can be caused. The handshakes of Donald Trump as he first met other world leaders were scrupulously analysed and various video compilations can be found online. The one he offered French president Emmanuel Macron was described by a journalist as a 'screw you, in handshake form'.[25] The British prime minister, Theresa May, faced accusations of being too friendly with the divisive president when they were seen briefly holding hands as they walked down the White House's colonnade. This is *li* in the twenty-first-century

West. Similarly, *li* in China today is best exemplified in day-to-day manners, such as greeting the oldest people in a group first or receiving and giving gifts with both hands.

If such quotidian details seem trivial it is perhaps because we have forgotten how important the micro-interactions of daily life are for building good character, courtesy and respect. Forgotten, because we did once know: Ram-Prasad says, 'The English saying "manners maketh man", is really a Confucian principle.'[26] *Li* is the means of training the self, to nurture the habits of the virtuous person. 'By nature people are similar; they diverge as the result of practice,' says Confucius, adding that only the very wisest and most stupid cannot be changed by practice.[27] Xunzi similarly says, 'Know well that ritual, the standards of righteousness, good form, and proper order are the way to nurture one's dispositions. [...] If a person puts even one measure of effort into following ritual and the standards of righteousness, he will get back twice as much.'[28]

Li is only of use when done in the right spirit, as captured in Confucius's poetic saying 'When we say, "the rites, the rites," are we speaking merely of jade and silk? When we say "music, music," are we speaking merely of bells and drums?'[29] Similarly, Mencius says, 'If there be honouring and respecting without the reality of them, a superior man may not be retained by such empty demonstrations.'[30] And the *Xunzi* says in its concluding words, 'Follow the Way, not your lord. Follow righteousness, not your father.'[31]

Ritual has no value in itself. 'The filial piety of now-a-days means the support of one's parents,' writes Confucius. 'But dogs and horses likewise are able to do something in the way of support; – if you are not respectful, what is there to distinguish the one support given from the other?'[32] At the heart of ritual is a positive attitude towards others. 'Character is to be cultivated by his treading in the ways of duty,' says Confucius, 'and the treading of those ways of duty is to be cultivated by the cherishing of benevolence.'[33]

There can be too much as well as too little emphasis on *li*:

'When native substance overwhelms cultural refinement, the result is a crude rustic. When cultural refinement overwhelms native substance, the result is a foppish pedant. Only when culture and native substance are perfectly mixed and balanced do you have a gentleman [*junzi*].'[34] One form of excess is rigidity, which is routinely criticised. 'As long as one does not transgress the bounds when it comes to important Virtues, it is permissible to cross the line here and there when it comes to minor Virtues,' says the *Analects*.[35] Sometimes it seems even major virtues can be suspended. 'The gentleman is true, but not rigidly trustworthy,' says Confucius, suggesting that sometimes it is even necessary to betray a trust.[36]

Mencius further developed this resistance to rigidity. Van Norden describes his approach as 'particularist', 'emphasising the context-sensitivity of virtue'.[37] Mencius discusses Shun, the great sage-king, who did not tell his parents that he was going to marry, a great neglect of filial duty. But Mencius defended him, saying, 'If he had informed them, he would not have been able to marry. That male and female should dwell together is the greatest of human relations. If Shun had informed his parents, he must have made void this greatest of human relations, thereby incurring their resentment. On this account, he did not inform them.'[38]

Sometimes it is more important to eat than to obey the rules of propriety, but that does not mean that eating is in general more important. 'Gold is heavier than feathers; – but does that saying have reference, on the one hand, to a single clasp of gold, and on the other, to a wagon-load of feathers?'[39]

Perhaps the best example of the flexibility of *li* is that although it is against propriety for men and women to touch, Mencius said, 'To not pull your sister-in-law out when she is drowning is to be a beast.' The prohibition is *li*, but it is trumped by the need for 'discretion'.[40]

Li is often assumed to require a blind perpetuation of old customs, although Confucius explicitly says that this is not the case. Sometimes change is to be embraced, sometimes not. 'A ceremonial cap made of linen is prescribed by the rites, but these days people use silk. This is frugal, and I follow the majority. To bow before ascending the stairs is what is prescribed by the rites, but these days people bow after ascending. This is arrogant and – though it goes against the majority – I continue to bow before ascending.'[41]

Rituals continue to evolve today. Take the Chinese New Year, which centres on the reunion dinner in which several generations of the family gather together to eat. This *li* is important for strengthening and honouring familial ties. The precise form of the ritual has changed in recent years, with people buying rather than making the *fu* ('good fortune') signs to paste on their doors and staying up all night watching China Central Television New Year's Gala (with 700 million others) rather than waiting for the arrival of the lunar new year while chatting around the fire. Even the oldest customs change their clothes.

Li fits neatly with the Aristotelian ideal of *hexis* or habit. In both Confucius and Aristotle, by repeatedly doing the right things one becomes a more virtuous person. 'Wear the clothes of Yâo, repeat the words of Yâo, and do the actions of Yâo, and you will just be a Yâo,' writes Mencius.[42] As with Aristotle, once practice has been embedded, good actions become almost automatic. 'The great man does not think beforehand of his words that they may be sincere, nor of his actions that they may be resolute; – he simply speaks and does what is right.'[43]

Virtue ethics can never result in rigid rules because the good person cultivates the wisdom and sensitivity to judge each case on its merits. There can be no prescription for the right proportions of fear, confidence, desire, anger or pain, says Aristotle. The 'mark of virtue' is 'to have these feelings at the right times on the right grounds towards the right people for the right motive and in the right way'.[44] Aristotle frequently made such lists of 'rights' unaccompanied by any algorithm to determine what 'right' is. For critics of virtue ethics, this is a weakness. We are never told what is right, merely that good people know it when they see it, and more importantly do it. If we don't know what right actions are, how do we know who the good people choosing to do them are? Virtue ethicists shrug their shoulders, objecting that critics demand clear rules when there are none. As Aristotle said, 'It is the mark of the trained mind never to expect more precision in the treatment of any subject than the nature of that subject permits.'[45]

In the Western world, this virtue tradition declined after Aristotle, with rule- and principle-based ethics dominating, until its revival by scholars in the later twentieth century. This has recently started to permeate the wider culture, most notably with the renewed concern for character education in schools. However, there were flickers of virtue ethics during this interregnum. 'Habit is another powerful means of reforming the mind, and implanting in it good dispositions and inclinations,' wrote David Hume in the eighteenth century, lines which could have come straight from Confucius or Aristotle. Like them, he also saw that changing habits required perseverance and effort to bear fruit: 'Where one is thoroughly convinced that the virtuous course of life is preferable; if he have but resolution enough, for some time, to impose a violence on himself; his reformation needs not be despaired of.' What Hume noticed that many of his predecessors missed was that one has to be at least half good already to want to be better. 'This conviction and this resolution never can have place,' he wrote, 'unless a man be, before-hand, tolerably virtuous.'[46]

Although virtue traditions emphasise habitual behaviour over abstract principles, they very much believe in the importance of the intellect. For Aristotle, the capacity to reason is what distinguishes us from other animals. Contemplation is the highest human activity because it is the most human activity.[47] The *Xunzi* broadly agrees: 'To pursue [learning] is to be human, to give it up to be a beast.'[48]

The cultivation of the intellect is necessary to guide the culti-vation of good habits. Aristotle commends to people the rational part of the soul 'because it urges them in the right direction and encourages them to take the best course'.[49] Without an educated mind, even the virtues can become clouded. In the absence of learning, Confucius warns, love of being benevolent leads to 'a foolish simplicity'; love of knowing leads to 'dissipation of mind', love of being sincere leads to 'an injurious disregard of conse-quences', love of straightforwardness leads to 'rudeness', boldness to 'insubordination', firmness to 'extravagant conduct'.[50]

These warnings show that even what is good can become bad if taken to extremes. Virtue requires a balance between deficiency and excess, which is another of the remarkably similar ideas found in both Confucius and Aristotle. Indeed, the name of the idea came to be identical: the Doctrine of the Mean. Aristotle defines the mean as the virtue which stands 'between two vices, that which depends on excess and that which depends on defect'. So generosity is the mean that falls between the excess of profligacy and the deficiency of meanness. Bravery is the mean between the deficiency of cowardice and the excess of rashness. 'Vices respectively fall short of or exceed what is right in both passions and actions, while virtue both finds and chooses that which is intermediate.'

The mean is a powerful and simple idea which counters the tendency we have to resort to dualistic thinking in ethics, where virtue and vice are opposites. It takes a realistic view of human dispositions in which they are always exhibited to a certain degree, sometimes too little and sometimes too much.

The mean in Confucianism is pretty much identical. It's illus-trated in the *Analects* by the story of Tsze-kung asking which of Shih or Shang was the superior man. Confucius did not answer the question directly, but said, 'Shih goes beyond the due mean, and Shang does not come up to it.' Tsze-kung concluded that 'the superiority is with Shih, I suppose'. Confucius corrected him: 'To go beyond is as wrong as to fall short.'[51]

The mean is dependent on context. What might be brave in one situation could be rash in another. It is also person-specific. So whereas a mathematical mean is equidistant between two extremes, the mean in relation to us, says Aristotle, is 'not one and the same for all'.[52] Just as the right amount of protein-packed, energy-rich food for a bodybuilder is too much for a desk-bound writer, the right amount of courage for a racing driver would be too much rashness for a taxi driver. It is particularly important to consider idiosyncratic factors when working to develop our characters. In the *Analects*, for example, Zihua protested that when Zilu asked whether or not one should immediately take care of something upon learning of it, Confucius told him he shouldn't, as long as he had family. But when Ran Qiu asked the same question, Confucius said he should. 'I am confused and humbly ask to have this explained to me,' he replied, understandably. Confucius told him, 'Ran Qiu is overly cautious, and so I wished to urge him on. Zilu, on the other hand, is too impetuous, and so I sought to hold him back.'[53] To train ourselves to act well, we need to err on the opposite side of where we tend to err, pushing towards an excess when we tend to be deficient or towards a deficiency when we tend to excess. Aristotle said something more or less identical: 'We must notice the errors into which we ourselves are liable to fall [. . .] and we must drag ourselves in the contrary direction; for we shall arrive at the mean by pressing well away from our failing – just like somebody straightening a warped piece of wood.'[54]

The Doctrine of the Mean is connected to broader ideas of harmony and equilibrium. This is explicit in the text *The Doctrine of the Mean*, which was said to have been passed down orally in the Confucian tradition until Tse-sze wrote it down for Mencius. Complete equilibrium, it states, is only possible 'while there are no stirrings of pleasure, anger, sorrow, or joy' in the mind. However, once stirred, as long as they 'act in their due degree, there ensues what may be called the state of Harmony. This equilibrium is the great root from which grow all the human actings in the world, and this harmony is the universal path which they all should pursue.'[55]

In practice our task is often to bring things that are off-balance back to the centre. Xunzi writes, 'For unyielding *qi*, soften it with harmoniousness. For overly deep thinking, simplify it with easy goodness. For overly ferocious courage, reform it with proper compliance. For expedience-seeking hastiness, restrain it with regulated movements. For small-minded narrowness, broaden it with expansiveness . . .' The list goes on.[56]

One insightful passage in the *Xunzi* applies this idea to philosophy itself: 'Almost always, the problem with people is that they become fixated on one angle and are deluded about the greater order of things.' Philosophers identify something that is important and then fixate on that to the exclusion of other equally important things. All Xunzi's notable predecessors' faults and strengths are analysed using this model:

Mozi was fixated on the useful and did not understand the value of good form. [. . .] Shenzi was fixated on laws and did not understand the value of having worthy people. Shen Buhai was fixated on power and did not understand the value of having wise people. [. . .] Zhuangzi was fixated on the Heavenly and did not understand the value of the human.

All had focused simply on one aspect of the Way, but 'No one aspect is sufficient to exhibit it fully.'[57]

Mencius gave a similar analysis of the failings of the amoralist Yang Chû and the consequentialist Mozi, both successors of Confucius. Mencius objects that Yang's principle 'each one for himself' does not acknowledge the claims of the sovereign, while Mozi's principle 'to love all equally' does not acknowledge the particular affection due to a father. Both are half right and half wrong, since 'to acknowledge neither king nor father is to be in the state of a beast'.[58]

These passages suggest that it is not simply a matter of finding the right mean and sticking to it. Because the mean is a matter of balance, even the mean itself must be held lightly and flexibly. The spirit of the mean is to avoid all extremes, and to stick too rigidly to any position, even a moderate one, is extremist. 'The reason I hate holding to one point is the injury it does to the way of right principle,' wrote Mencius. 'It takes up one point and disregards a hundred others.'[59]

Although *The Doctrine of the Mean* is a Confucian text, its central idea appears throughout Chinese thought. The *Daodejing* uses quintessentially mean language when it says, 'The Way of Heaven takes from what has excess and augments what is deficient.'[60] Perhaps the more fundamental concept is that of *zhong*, usually rendered as centrality or equilibrium. Li says it is 'a stance against extremes' and it also means 'unbiased'. It has connotations of being both upright and central. In Confucian philosophy, 'centrality and harmony are mutually dependent concepts'.[61]

Yao for one believes the doctrine of the mean holds sway in contemporary China. 'The majority of Chinese do not like extremes,' he told me. 'They use the image of the pendulum. I believe this is why China is so comparatively stable. They couldn't go to extremes. When they get to a certain point they begin to return to the other side. Of course today we have extreme nationalism, extreme liberalism, extreme conservatism, but it's always a small minority. The majority of the people don't go to extremes.'

How, then, do we explain Mao's Cultural Revolution, one of the most extreme events in twentieth-century world history, in which between 500,000 and 2 million people died? It is significant that during this time the doctrine of the mean was explicitly rejected. For instance, Lin Biao, a one-time ally of Mao who was subsequently denounced as a traitor, was criticised for advocating the doctrine of the mean, 'a reactionary philosophy used by Confucius more than 2,000 years ago in stubborn defence of the slave system'.[62]

The mean was not the only traditional belief to be completely thrown out by Mao. More shocking still, children were encouraged to denounce their own parents, the very antithesis of Confucian values. Although no one claimed to be able to fully understand this, the general view among philosophers I spoke to seems to be that rare, violent changes are the price China pays for its more typical stability. One notable example is the first emperor of the Ching dynasty, who ordered the burning of many Chinese classics in 213 BCE and buried 460 Confucian scholars alive three years later. It is as though the desire to maintain harmony occasionally suppresses necessary, gradual change, creating pressure that leads to occasional big, violent eruptions.

In all traditions you see something resembling virtue. In the *Mahābhārata*, it says, 'Conduct has been said to be superior to all the branches of knowledge. It is conduct that begets righteousness, and it is righteousness that prolongs life.'[63] However, the reward of virtue in Indian philosophy is *mokṣa* (salvation). This differs significantly from Chinese and Aristotelian virtue in which living virtuously is its own reward, not the path to something else, which is why it is valued even over life itself. Aristotle said that the man of good character performs good actions for his friends and country and 'if necessary even dies for them'.[64] 'I like life, and I also like righteousness,' wrote Mencius. 'If I cannot keep the two together, I will let life go, and choose righteousness. I like life indeed, but there is that which I like more than life, and therefore, I will not seek to possess it by any improper ways.' Believing that human nature was essentially good, he thought everyone had this preference, it's just that the righteous do not lose it.[65]

I have stressed that we should never look for black and white distinctions between traditions but differences of emphasis. Virtue traditions emphasise habits, but do not completely reject rules or principles. The difference is in the function and nature of those rules. One should follow *li*, for existence, not for its own sake but to promote virtue, and if one has to choose between following ritual or being good, one should be good.

Perhaps the clearest illustration of the subtle but important role of emphasis comes in the most famous Confucian maxim of all, the Golden Rule: 'Do not impose upon others what you yourself do not desire.'[66] Often said to be a universal principle of human morality, it has variants in many traditions. 'Do to others what you would have them do to you,' said Jesus,[67] while Jains have the maxim 'One should not deliberately do harm to another person that is unwelcome to oneself.'[68] However, the differences between the wordings of each are as significant as the similarities.

The Jain wording emphasises the avoidance of harm, reflecting its central teaching of respect for all life. Its version of the Golden Rule is quite specific and restricted in its scope. Jesus is the only one of the three to present the rule in a positive form, emphasising the absolute duty we have to treat people well. He wasn't the first to do so, however. In the fourth century BCE, Mozi wrote, 'Do for others as one would do for oneself.'[69] This is a positive call to do as you would be done by, not the negative Confucian version in which we are told not to do to others what we would not want done to us. In Confucian ethics, it is enough not to treat others badly. For Mozi, we need to go further and treat people as we would be treated, with an impartial universal benevolence.

This difference is made clear in the *Analects* when Confucius is asked, 'What do you think of the saying, "requite injury with kindness"?' This is in effect a direct question about what he would make of the Christian injunction 'resist not evil: but whosoever shall smite thee on thy right cheek, turn to him the other also. And if any man will sue thee at the law, and take away thy coat, let him have thy cloak also.'[70] Confucius roundly rejects such a position as excessive. 'With what, then, would one requite kindness?' he asks. 'Requite injury with uprightness, and kindness with kindness.'[71] On another occasion he reiterated the Golden Rule when asked if there was one word that could serve as a practice for all of one's life. He replied, 'Reciprocity' (or 'Sympathetic understanding'), defining this as 'Do not impose on others what you yourself do not desire.'[72]

What such reciprocity requires, however, depends on the specifics of a situation and requires virtue to judge. Ram-Prasad explains this in terms of the Confucian emphasis on 'deference' (*shu*), not to superiors but 'to the needs and circumstances of others, as one likens oneself to others and sees the world in their terms'. The key is not emotional empathy but a more intellectual 'putting oneself in another's place and thereby coming to conclusions about what should be done in that person's place'.[73] Psychologists today call this cognitive empathy and it requires an ethical skill which cannot be reduced to mere benevolent feeling or rule-following. This reflects an idea implicit in early Indian Buddhism, which did not distinguish between good and evil but between *kuśala* and *akuśala* – 'skilful' and 'unskilful'.[74]

In Chinese culture, a measured, skilful response to others leads as much to restraint as it does to the active charity advocated by Jesus. The man of perfect virtue is 'cautious and slow in speaking', said Confucius.[75] Asked what constitutes perfect virtue, he replied, 'Restraining yourself and returning to the rites constitutes Goodness.'[76] Indeed, sometimes virtue sounds rather boring. The scholar must be 'among his friends, earnest and urgent; among his brethren, bland'.[77]

The virtue tradition fits very naturally within the intimacy orientation we have already examined. 'In the integrity orientation ethics is primarily a morality of principles,' says Tom Kasulis. 'In the intimacy orientation, however, ethics is a morality of love.'[78] Kasulis recounts the famous story of a Buddhist monk who helped a young woman across a ford, even though monks were forbidden to touch women. 'I can't believe what you did,' admonished his colleague later. 'I'll have to report you to the abbot for breaking the rules.' To which he replied, 'How tired you must be! When I got the woman across the river, I put her down. But you, you've been carrying her all this way!' Kasulis says, 'The first monk was trapped by integrity's submission to the rules whereas the second monk responded to the immediate situation out of intimacy's compassion.'[79]

In this intimacy orientation we find another twist on the Golden Rule. The Zen master Dōgen found the biblical imperative 'Thou shalt not kill' inadequate as it sets out an imperative to obey. The objective, however, is to become the kind of person who is simply no longer capable of killing. This transforms the order 'Thou shalt not kill' into a description, 'You are such a person that you will not kill.'[80] In the virtue tradition, we might seek a similar transformation of the Golden Rule. Following a principle is second best to simply being the kind of person who treats others as they ought to be treated. The Golden Rule *prescribes* the way for those who need help identifying the good, but it *describes* the way in which those who are truly good act without its guidance.

Something like this attitude to moral rules is also found in Buddhism. 'Those who don't steal don't need precepts against theft,' said the Zen master Bankei Yōtaku. 'Precepts against lying are wasted on a truthful man.'[81] The Buddha tells a parable of a man who constructs a raft to help him cross a flooded riverbank. His skill and ingenuity would turn to folly if he then concluded that the raft had been so useful that he ought to carry it on his head as he continued his journey. The Buddha said that his moral teachings, the *Dharma*, are just like the raft, 'being for the purpose of crossing over, not for the purpose of grasping. [...] When you know the *Dharma* to be similar to a raft, you should abandon even the teachings.'[82]

Perhaps the most striking and surprising aspect of the virtue tradition is that its focus is not on great evils and great acts of goodness but on everyday life. The cultivation of virtue requires attending to small things. The best, pithy encapsulation of this, however, comes not from China or Greece but also from Buddhism: 'Think not lightly of evil saying that "it will not come near me". Even a water-pot is filled by the falling of drops of water. A fool becomes evil even if he gathers it little by little.'[83]

Moral exemplars

Hanging above the entrance to the Forbidden City on Tiananmen Gate is a massive portrait of Mao Tse-tung. In a mausoleum in Moscow's Red Square, visitors still pay their respects to the preserved body of Vladimir Lenin. In many South American countries, political leaders claim the legacy of Simón Bolívar, the Venezuelan who played a prominent role in the liberation of not only his own country but Bolivia, Colombia, Ecuador, Peru and Panama.

The elevation of individuals such as these to almost living gods is often derided as a form of personality cult. But although the devotion may be excessive, the impulse to admire exceptional people is a cultural universal. The uncharitable explanation for this is that we feel the need for heroes and saviours. There is surely something to this, but we have another, more realistic need for moral exemplars. The likes of Martin Luther King Jr, Mother Teresa, Mahātmā Gandhi and Nelson Mandela are not simply admired, they are taken to be people worthy of emulation.

The idea that great people provide at least as much moral guidance as rules and principles is a natural corollary of the virtue traditions' emphasis on character. It is no accident that *New York*

Times columnist David Brooks's bestseller *The Road to Character*, which helped revive the virtue tradition, was structured around eight biographical sketches.[1]

In China, the moral exemplar is captured in the ideal of the *junzi*. This word originally described a gentleman, a member of the ruling upper classes. Confucius transformed it into an ideal of the nearly perfect person, morally advanced and virtuous. Such a person displays the highest virtue, *jen*, translated variously as 'righteousness', 'benevolence' and 'perfect virtue', among innumerable others. The plurality of translations suggests that it is one of those words that has no single accurate English equivalent. It is related to *yi*, justice. '*Jen* is the inside, to try to make yourself be a good person,' explained Yao Xinzhong, 'but *yi* is how you treat other people, appropriately. When you treat people well and in a proper way you also demonstrate virtue.' *Jen* can be understood as an inner moral force which keeps us in balance. We might call it being of good character.

Today *junzi* is usually translated as 'exemplary person', 'superior person' or 'person of excellence', but sometimes still as 'gentleman'. Confucius said he never expected to meet a true *junzi* in his life, but in time the term became increasingly used, with less rigorous criteria. The change from 'gentleman' to 'exemplary person' was part of a move towards meritocracy which remains strong in China today. Although Yao says that hypocrisy and corruption mean the ideal is more honoured in the breach than in the observance, the idea that people should hold positions of authority on the basis of how they behave remains strong. For instance, Singapore's prime minister, Lee Hsien Loong, once said:

> Many Confucian ideals are still relevant to us. An example is the concept of government by honourable men (*junzi*), who have a duty to do right for the people, and who have the trust and respect of the population. That fits us better than the Western

concept that a government should be given as limited powers as possible, and always be treated with suspicion, unless proven otherwise. [2]

The *junzi* exemplifies an idea of exceptional individuals as paradigms or models for others to follow that recurs in several traditions. The *junzi* achieves the Chinese ideal of 'sageliness within and kingliness without', an inner goodness that radiates outwards.[3] This idea of the good person as a beacon for others has recurred all over the world in intellectual history. Akeel Bilgrami sees something like this in the philosophy of Mahātmā Gandhi, who wrote, 'When one chooses for oneself, one sets an example to everyone.' Peter Adamson also notes, ' Muḥammad is identified in the Qur'ān as a paradigm to be emulated by other Muslims.'[4] In the *Bhagavad Gītā*, it says, 'Whatsoever a great man does, the same is done by others as well. Whatever standard he sets, the world follows.'[5] The *Mahābhārata* says, 'If the king regards it, righteousness becomes regarded everywhere.'[6] And Radhakrishnan and Moore say, 'The Buddha is not so much a saviour as an example.'[7]

The emphasis on individuals as moral exemplars goes against the grain of ethical systems based on reason and principles. In such systems, it is never relevant to point to an individual's actions to advance a moral argument. You argue for or against positions, not people. You 'play the ball not the man'. To do otherwise is to commit the ad hominem fallacy. But where moral exemplars are valued, the real fallacy is to ignore the person and focus only on the principles they argue for.

The middle position gives due weight to both what is said and who is saying it. Aristotle, for instance, remarked that the arguments of Eudoxus that pleasure is the highest good 'were accepted more for the excellence of his character than of their own account'. Aristotle did not think this missed the point because Eudoxus's moral excellence showed that 'he did not state this view because he was a pleasure-lover, but that the facts were really so'.[8] This may not be decisive for assessing his position but it is relevant data.

Where virtue traditions are strong, people become even more important than principles as sources of moral guidance. This is the case not only in Confucianism but in Daoism. The *Daodejing* says, 'Sages embrace the One and serve as models for the whole world', but they do not parade themselves as models, as that would be self-defeating. 'They do not make a display of themselves and so are illustrious.'[9] The idea of the moral exemplar pre-dates Confucianism. Mencius quotes the ancient *Odes*: 'He set an example for his wife, It extended to his brothers, And so he controlled his family and state.'[10]

Setting an example is especially important for rulers. 'Go before the people with your example, and be laborious in their affairs,' Confucius advised them.[11] The other side of this coin is that *junzi* should participate in ruling. The scholar should be active in public life to serve as an example and anyone in public life needs to be a scholar to demonstrate their worthiness to be an exemplar. Chan Wing-Tsit points out that 'from Tung Chung-Shu (c. 176–104 BC) through Chi Hsi down to K'ang Yu-wei (1857–1927), with only a few exceptions, all prominent scholars have been active public figures'.[12] Similarly, many public figures have also been keen to show themselves to be scholars. Mao published several works on philosophy, while the Chinese president at the time of writing, Xi Jinping, has explicitly talked about Marxist political philosophy. In 2016 he hosted a symposium on philosophy and the social sciences at which he gave a 100-minute speech stressing their 'irreplaceable role' in 'building socialism with Chinese characteristics'.[13]

Because the exemplary ruler is so important, recent corruption scandals have been particularly damaging to the Chinese Communist Party (CCP). In the first five years of the anti-corruption drive launched at the 18th National Congress of the CPC in 2012, the Central Commission for Discipline Inspection registered over a million cases and took disciplinary actions against 1.2 million people. The vast majority of these are low-ranking officials referred to as 'flies', with only 240 senior 'tigers' prosecuted.[14] Between them they are accused of stealing over 6.3 billion yuan (around $1 billion).[15]

Yao doesn't believe the Chinese people hold unrealistic views about the purity of their leaders. Corrupt people are tolerated if they are capable and move things forward and are deemed preferable to nice, gentle people who couldn't achieve anything. Virtue which bears no fruits is useless, and anything that bears fruits is at least in part virtuous. However, the scale of corruption that has been exposed is so great that 'people wonder: is there any kind of good person in the Communist Party, or in the government? This has shaken people's confidence in the government. People just don't believe any more what they say.'

In Chinese thought, it is not simply that *junzi* serve as models to be copied. Rather, their goodness radiates in such a way as to make people behave better, a kind of positive moral contagion against which vice would be powerless. Discussing the 'rude' wild tribes of the east, Confucius said, 'If a *junzi* dwelt among them, what rudeness would there be?'[16] That's why Philip Ivanhoe suggests 'moral charisma' as an alternative to 'virtue' as a translation of *de*.[17] 'The flowing progress of virtue is more rapid than the transmission of royal orders by stages and couriers,' said Confucius.[18] A *junzi* is like the wind, the people are like the grass. When the wind blows over the grass, the grass will bend. This has a clear and explicit political implication. Good rulers do not need to be coercive, since their virtuous rule will naturally lead to content subjects willing to obey them. Confucius expressed this idea colourfully in two of his most famous sayings: 'One who rules through the power of Virtue is analogous to the Pole Star: it simply remains in place and receives the homage of myriad lesser stars'[19] and 'Raise up the straight and apply them to the crooked, and the people will submit to you. If you raise up the crooked and apply them to the straight, the people will never submit.'[20]

Gandhi took a similar view, saying, 'If we do our duty, others also will do theirs some day. We have a saying to the effect: If we ourselves are good, the whole world will be good.'[21] But not all advocates of moral exemplars are as sanguine about the tendency of the masses to automatically follow the virtuous. Buddhism emphasises the need for an inner transformation before one can be receptive to external teachings or examples. The *Dhammapada* puts it elegantly: 'If a fool be associated with a wise man even all his life, he will not perceive the truth even as the spoon does not perceive the taste of soup. But if a thoughtful man be associated with a wise man even for a minute, he will soon perceive the truth even as the tongue perceives the taste of soup.'[22] In China the emphasis is on right conduct first, from which all else follows, whereas Buddhism strives for an inner transformation which leads to better action.

More sceptical, cynical even, is the third-century-BCE Chinese legalist philosopher Han Feizi. 'Everyone in the land within the four seas was pleased by his benevolence and praised him for his righteousness,' he said of Confucius, 'but those who followed him numbered only seventy men.' What's more, 'Duke Ai acted as Confucius's ruler despite his inferiority as a ruler. Confucius did not yield to the Duke's righteousness, he submitted to the power of the duke's superior position.'[23] Talk of virtuous rulers sounds noble but reality is harsher. 'If one says that achieving good order requires both worthiness, which cannot be forbidden, and the power of position, which has nothing it cannot forbid, this is just like saying one has both all-penetrating spears and impenetrable shields. Hence, the fact that worthiness and the power of position are incompatible should be abundantly clear.'[24] Han would consider laughably naive Mencius's view that 'The benevolent has no enemy.'[25]

Han Feizi was hardly a fan of so-called wise sages at the best of times. 'What the world calls "wise" is language that is subtle and mysterious,' he mocked.[26] We don't even know what the great thinkers really believed and instead rely on dubious received versions of their doctrines. And even if we did reliably know their thoughts, if they were so wise, why did they all disagree with each other? 'Those who depend on the teachings of former kings and are absolutely sure about the Way of Yao and Shun are either fools or charlatans.'[27]

Han, however, is the exception. Most classical Chinese philosophers praise virtue in the ruler and make it central to good governance. Perhaps it sounds a little idealistic, as though the good ruler doesn't have to govern well but merely set a good example to be copied. But of course to set a good example he must rule well, enacting fair laws and ensuring that the people are well served. As Confucius put it, 'Good government obtains, when those who are near are made happy, and those who are far off are attracted.'[28] This rings true. Think of the societies that are most admired today, such as the Nordic nations, with comparatively contented populations and admirers overseas who are constantly asking how to successfully emulate their success.

These old ideas have received support from contemporary social psychology, which has shown that there are many ways in which our behaviour is influenced by that of those around us, even that of a single person. Perhaps the clearest example is the well-studied bystander effect. If someone appears to be in need and there is only one person close by, that person will usually offer help. But if there are several people, often none will. No one makes the first move, unsure whether it is appropriate, which in turn indicates to others that helping out is not socially mandated. But if one person breaks ranks and goes to help, others will often join them.

Chinese moral thought appreciates that ethics has a strong social dimension much more than mainstream Western philosophy, which emphasises the duties, rights and responsibilities of the individual. Once we recognise the role our social environment plays in our own ethical development and formation, we have to take seriously the idea that it matters a great deal who we choose to associate with. 'If one does not choose to dwell among those who are Good, how will one obtain wisdom?' asked Confucius.[29] That is perhaps also why 'Virtue is never solitary; it always has neighbours.'[30] Or as Aristotle said, citing the poet Theognis, 'A sort of training in virtue may result from associating with good people.'[31]

This entails that the good person will sometimes need to withdraw from society if it becomes too corrupted to be able to live in it ethically. 'When good government prevails in his State the superior man is to be found in office. When bad government prevails, he can roll his principles up, and keep them in his breast.'[32] It is striking how many of the people held up as moral exemplars today have been unable to function in the societies they seek to reform and have either been imprisoned or had to flee into exile. The Dalai Lama, for example, lives in exile from Tibet, while Nelson Mandela's legend grew during his twenty-seven years in prison.

The good person must choose their friends carefully. 'Befriending the upright, those who are true to their word, or those of broad learning – these are the beneficial types of friendship,' says Confucius. 'Befriending clever flatterers, skilful dissemblers, or the smoothly glib – these are the harmful types of friendship.'[33] Xunzi goes so far as to value friendship more than even *li*. 'In learning, nothing is more expedient than to draw near the right person. Rituals and music provide proper models but give no precepts. [. . .] Of the paths to learning, none is quicker than to like the right person, and exalting ritual comes second.'[34] Once again, Aristotle sings from the same hymn sheet: 'The friendship of the good is good, and increases in goodness because of their association. They seem even to become better men by exercising their friendship and improving each other; for the traits that they admire in each other get transferred to themselves.'[35]

That friendship is an ethical issue at all says a lot about the virtue tradition. When morality is a matter of rules and precepts, friendship is irrelevant to living well. But when it is about being a good person and living in harmony, friends are vital. It is no surprise then that Aristotle devotes many pages to the subject. For Aristotle, 'Perfect friendship is the friendship of men who are good, and alike in virtue.' Whatever the differences between them, such friends are equal in regards to virtue and share a mutual 'friendship of the good'. This is practically identical to the advice of Mencius, who said, 'Friendship should be maintained without any presumption on the ground of one's superior age, or station, or the circumstances of his relatives. Friendship with a man is a friendship with his virtue, and does not admit of assumptions of superiority.'[36]

The problem with focusing on individuals rather than on principles as moral ideals is that it can be difficult to pin down exactly what being good actually involves. We've already seen that perfect virtue in Confucianism is *jen* – 'righteousness' or 'benevolence' – but that doesn't fill out the details of what righteousness is. In both Chinese and Greek thought, the virtuous man (it was, alas, always a man) is usually somewhat detached from worldly cares and concerns. 'The superior man has three things in which he delights, and to be ruler over the kingdom is not one of them,' says Mencius. Those three are having no cause for anxiety over parents and brothers, feeling no shame before heaven or men, and teaching and nourishing the most talented of the kingdom.[37] As such the good person is able to face the world with a kind of equanimity. 'The superior man does not murmur against Heaven, nor grudge against men.'[38] Similarly, the *Analects* tell us that 'there were four things from which the Master was entirely free. He had no foregone conclusions, no arbitrary predeterminations, no obstinacy, and no egoism.'[39] The Master himself agreed on the ideal but believed that not even he was up to it. 'The way of the superior man is threefold, but I am not equal to it. Virtuous, he is free from anxieties; wise, he is free from perplexities; bold, he is free from fear.'[40] This theme was continued by the Neo-Confucian Dunyi Zhou, who said that the sage 'regards tranquillity as fundamental. Having no desire, he will be tranquil.'[41]

This ideal of being beyond care recurs even in traditions that are explicitly anti-Confucian. Throughout Chinese thought, virtue is associated with a kind of detachment. The Daoist Zhuangzi says, 'Betting for tiles, you're good. Betting for buckles, you worry. Betting for gold, you panic. Your skill is the same, but you care, so you value what is on the outside. Those who value what is on the outside are clumsy on the inside.'[42]

Aristotle describes 'the crown of the virtues' – magnanimity or 'greatness of soul' (*megalopsuchia*) – in strikingly similar terms. For the magnanimous man 'there are few things he values highly' and 'nothing is great in his eyes'. He 'does not care for personal conversation' nor 'to be complimented himself' or 'compliment others'. He is the last to complain about unavoidable or minor troubles 'because such an attitude would imply that he took them seriously'.[43] If this form of detachment seems to verge on the haughty, that is probably because *megalopsuchia* was a distinctively aristocratic virtue.

Virtue is largely a matter of desiring the right things rather than the wrong ones, which means not having too many desires in the first place. 'To nourish the mind there is nothing better than to make the desires few,' says Mencius. 'Here is a man whose desires are few: – in some things he may not be able to keep his heart, but they will be few. Here is a man whose desires are many: in some things he may be able to keep his heart, but they will be few.'[44]

Virtue entails a low regard for worldly goods such as wealth and fame. 'A scholar who has his heart set on the Way but who is still ashamed of having shabby clothes or meagre rations is not worth engaging in discussion,' said Confucius.[45] And 'to live in obscurity, and yet practise wonders, in order to be mentioned with honour in future ages: – this is what I do not do.'[46] Not that Confucius is against people receiving proper recognition. Strikingly, he says, 'The superior man dislikes the thought of his name not being mentioned after his death.'[47] Aristotle echoes this, saying that 'magnanimous people are concerned with honour, because it is honour above all that they claim as their due, and deservedly'.[48] It is good to receive honour when it is due, but one should focus on doing what is rightly honoured rather than pursue honour for its own sake. Honour can be a sign that you are doing the right thing, but it is not the goal or purpose of right action.

Like recognition, material wealth is not bad in itself but not something the good person strives for. 'Wealth and social eminence are things that all people desire, and yet unless they are acquired in the proper way I will not abide them,' said Confucius. 'Poverty and disgrace are things that all people hate, and yet unless they are avoided in the proper way I will not despise them.'[49] Whether it is good or bad to be rich or poor very much depends on the context and how you arrived at your situation. 'When a country is well-governed, poverty and a mean condition are things to be ashamed of. When a country is ill-governed, riches and honour are things to be ashamed of.'[50] In a well-functioning welfare state like Norway, no one need be destitute. But in a corrupt, oil-rich state like Equatorial Guinea, wealth is a sure sign of complicity in the theft of the nation's natural resources.

In the virtue traditions there is nothing bad about wealth in itself. Indeed, Aristotle believed that 'it is difficult if not impossible to do fine deeds without any resources'.[51] Taking a swipe at Plato, he says, 'Those who maintain that, provided he is good, a man is happy on the rack or surrounded by great disasters, are talking nonsense.'[52] Mencius took a similar view, arguing that unless the people are materially comfortable, they cannot be expected to be good. 'To lack a constant livelihood, and yet to have a constant heart – only a scholar is capable of this. As for the people, if they lack a constant livelihood, it follows that they will lack a constant heart.'[53] Good governance means enabling people to gain material comfort. Advising King Hsüan of Ch'î, he said, 'If your majesty loves wealth, give the people power to gratify the same feeling, and what difficulty will there be in your attaining the royal sway?'[54]

Asceticism for its own sake is frowned upon. Confucius confided, 'I once engaged in thought for an entire day without eating and an entire night without sleeping, but it did no good. It would have been better for me to have spent that time in learning.'[55] We can have too much and too little concern for worldly comforts, and each comes at its own price: 'Extravagance leads to insubordination, and parsimony to meanness.' One price, however, is higher: 'It is better to be mean than to be insubordinate.'[56] It certainly seems to be true that, even in the materialist contemporary world, our moral exemplars tend to favour simple living, from Mao to Mandela, Gandhi to Mother Teresa.

The risk with moral exemplars is that they cannot live up to the unrealistically high standards they are seen to embody. Such was the case with Aung San Suu Kyi, the Burmese leader who was adored for decades, even awarded the Nobel Peace Prize, before disillusioning millions by her seeming complicity with the persecution of the minority Muslim Rohingya in Myanmar. Mother Teresa has suffered a similar backlash from critics who argue her concern with salvation in the next world led her to almost wallow in the poverty of this one.

The desire to bring our heroes down to earth, however, can be as pathological as the one to elevate them to the heavens. Recognising that some people are indeed morally better than us is both humbling and a spur to try to become better. Acknowledging their human frailties should not be a tool to drag them down to our level but a reminder that human beings do not need to be perfect to be at their wonderful best. Perhaps the most useful function of such role models is that they show us that character is more important than sectarian allegiance to a religion or a moral philosophy. Moral exemplars are sometimes used to divide people, but when their virtues are genuine they are a means of uniting us.

LIBERATION

'It is relatively clear that, over time, classical Indian philosophy comes to acknowledge *mokṣa* – liberation from the conditions of life in the world – as the supreme good.'[1] This simple statement by the scholar Chakravarthi Ram-Prasad sums up the standard view found in almost all introductions to Indian thought. *Mokṣa* is 'a common *Summum Bonum* of all the different systems of Hindu philosophy, Buddhism, and Jainism,' agrees S. K. Saksena.[2] It's also a view that seems to come directly from the *Vedas*. In the *Upaniṣads*, for example, there is a passage listing what the virtuous person does: learns the *Veda*, continues to study the *Veda* in a clean place, produces sons and pupils, concentrates all his senses on the self, harms nothing. The consequence of this is clear: 'He, indeed, who lives this throughout his length of life, reaches the *Brahmā*-world and does not return hither again – yea, he does not return hither again!'[3]

The idea that Indian philosophy is essentially about *mokṣa* nonetheless provokes howls of outrage by those who think this a gross simplification which can either romanticise or condescend by playing up the idea that 'India is spiritual'. Daniel Raveh is one such dissenter. 'There was an interest in *moksa*, but there was also interest in so many other things,' he told me. 'There are texts about philosophical argumentation, mathematics, architecture, politics, society. But somehow the *moksa* texts were always highlighted and the other texts were always marginalised.'

Raveh's teacher Daya Krishna was one of the leading opponents of the reduction of Indian philosophy to the pursuit of *moksa*. 'Indian philosophy, on the very first page of any book dealing with the subject, is proclaimed to be something dealing with the final and ultimate liberation of the spirit, or what is technically known as *moksa*,' he correctly points out in order to demur.[4] On closer examination, however, Krishna's objections look much more like important qualifications. Krishna identifies the source of interest in *moksa* as the so-called *Śramana* traditions of Sāṃkhya, Buddhism and Jainism which stood outside the mainstream. Only then did ideas of *moksa* became incorporated into the orthodox Vedic trad-itions.[5] But since we're talking here of innovations that took place between 900 and 600 BCE, it is hardly misleading to talk now of *moksa* being deeply rooted in Indian classical philosophy. As he himself acknowledges, 'The idea of *moksa* as the highest ideal for man was accepted in India as early as the time of the *Upanisads* and the Buddha.'[6]

What Krishna and Raveh most object to is not the simple observation that *moksa* has long been a central concern of Indian philosophy but the stronger suggestion that it is 'the focal concern around which the whole of Indian philosophy is woven'.[7] When Krishna says *moksa* 'is not the exclusive concern of Indian phil-osophy', he is undeniably correct, as he is when he points out that Indians are not the only ones concerned with *moksa*.[8] But when he says, 'Nor is it the predominant concern either,' he is on shakier ground.[9] At the very least, it is an unorthodox view since he himself accepts that the idea that *mokṣa* is the central concern of Indian philosophy is 'widely shared by experts and laymen alike'.[10] The one exception is, as usual, Cārvāka, which sees pleasure in this life as the only goal.

What, though, is *mokṣa* and how is it attained? For Radhakrishnan and Moore, *mokṣa* in its most general sense and its Buddhist counterpart *nirvāṇa* have the same essential meaning, namely 'emancipation or liberation from turmoil and suffering, and freedom from rebirth'. This follows from the schools' endorsement of the same essential metaphysics of *karma* that we looked at earlier in which human beings are caught in *saṃsāra* (the cycle of birth and rebirth).[11]

Dig down to the detail, however, and there are many differences, which point to the wisdom of heeding Daya Krishna's warnings of oversimplification. 'There is no one *mokṣa*,' says Raveh, 'and there are many means of *mokṣa*.'

The main ways in which *mokṣa* can be achieved, depending on the tradition, are by the cessation of the activity that fuels the cycle of rebirth and by the attainment of salvific knowledge, or some combination of the two. Jainism emphasises the first path, arguing that by adopting ascetic practices one can stop the accumulation of *karma* and escape *saṃsāra*. Omniscience is a consequence of this, rather than a cause.

It is more common, however, for salvation to come from enlightenment. Gautama's *Nyāya Sūtra* succinctly describes the process by which the removal of false knowledge leads to liberation: 'Pain, birth, activity, faults and misapprehension – on the successful annihilation of these in reverse order, there follows release.'[12] First, we rid ourselves of our mistaken view of the world. This leads to moral improvement, as all wrong action is based on ignorance of the true nature of reality. This ultimately results in no action at all, which prevents rebirth and thus also pain and suffering. This basic sequence is found with some variations in almost all schools.

In all Vedānta schools, *mokṣa* is the result of knowledge of the identity between *Brahman* (the divine principle) and *ātman* (the individual self), overcoming the false identification of *jīva* (the enduring self) with the body. In the non-dualism of Śaṅkara, *mokṣa* is a kind of release which can be achieved even before death: 'The person who has reached true knowledge is free from his body even while still alive.'[13] Release is a kind of union with *Brahman*. Śaṅkara quotes the *Upaniṣads*: 'As the flowing rivers disappear into the sea, having lost their name and their form, thus a wise man freed from name and form goes to the divine Person who is greater than the great.'[14] Śaṅkara explains that 'The passage means to say only that on the self departing from the body all specific cognition vanishes, not that the Self is destroyed.'[15] This is destruction of the individual self, but not of the higher self.

The Viśiṣṭādvaita Vedānta school also stresses the way in which knowledge is the route to liberation: 'Knowing *Brahman*, he becomes *Brahman*.'[16] Again, the true view allows us to realise – in the sense of both intellectually recognising and actually becoming – the essential oneness of reality: 'The proper form of the soul is free from all differentiations consisting in the distinctions that are brought about by the natural evolution of *pakṛti* [materiality] into the bodies of gods, men, etc.'[17] Similarly, in Yoga, it is knowledge of the distinction between ordinary awareness (*citta*) and the true consciousness of the seer (*puruṣa*) that leads to spiritual liberation.'[18]

The link between knowledge and salvation is identified by many commentators as a central feature of Indian philosophy. 'Philosophising, in the sense of attempting to understand the nature of whatever it is one is focusing on, is directly associated with one's personal destiny,' says Sue Hamilton. 'So philosophy is seen not in terms of a professional intellectual pursuit that can be set aside at the end of the working day, but as an attempt to understand the true nature of reality in terms of an inner or spiritual quest.'[19] Ram-Prasad says that in India 'all schools share the conviction that knowledge that things are really such and such actually transforms the knower, altering consciousness and the very conditions of existence'.[20] Similarly, Joel Kupperman says that Western philosophy operates with a 'split screen' dividing the moral and non-moral, whereas Indian philosophy offers 'a unified approach to all of life's decisions'.[21] This connects with what we have already seen about religion and philosophy not being neatly separable. It also suggests that the highest good is not abstract truth and that in a sense the good is more important than the true. 'It is always proper to speak the truth,' says the *Mahābhārata*, but, 'It is better again to speak what is beneficial than to speak what is true.'[22]

In Buddhism, both the (in-)active and contemplative paths to salvation can be found, reflected in the two key types of meditation practised. *Samatha* meditation aims at stilling the mind and the cessation of activity, while *vipassana* meditation aims at insight. Whether these should be considered two completely separate activities or part of the same essential practice is much debated. Many texts emphasise the end of activity. 'What is the Noble Truth of the cessation of suffering?' asks the *Majjhima-nikāya*. 'It is the utter and passionless cessation of this same craving – the abandonment and rejection of craving, deliverance from craving, and aversion from craving.'[23] But is it the end of *saṃsāra* that puts an end to craving or the end of craving that allows us to escape *saṃsāra*? And is it knowledge that brings us *nirvāṇa* or does *nirvāṇa* bring with it knowledge? Different thinkers offer different answers, or problematise the question.

The ambiguity extends to the nature of *nirvāṇa* itself. *Nirvāṇa* often looks like a kind of extinction, which is what the word itself literally means, deriving from the Sanskrit words 'to blow' (*nis*) and 'out' (*va*). In Buddhist texts the enlightened sage is sometimes compared to a flame blown out by the wind. Salvation is paradoxically also extinction: '*Nirvāṇa* is, but not the man who seeks it.

The path exists, but not the traveller on it.'[24] The resolution of this paradox comes from the Buddhist conception of self as lacking essence. What is extinguished when we become enlightened is not the self but an illusion of self. Liberation is freedom from such illusions and so entails the end of the illusory, conventional self.

There is also a debate about when *nirvāṇa* is achieved, with a spectrum of options ranging from a time after death to the here and now. In the earlier Theravāda tradition, the Buddha is liberated at the moment of enlightenment. The later Mahāyāna tradition argues that the enlightened *bodhisattva* must wait for the rest of the world to join him before his liberation is complete, something sometimes called *parinirvāṇa*, or final liberation. An analogy for this is that enlightenment is like taking a pot off the fire, but final freedom only comes when it has eventually lost all its heat.[25] This waiting, however, is also presented as a choice: the *bodhisattva* postpones ultimate liberation in order to help the rest of the world.[26]

A further complication is that for Mahāyāna, which includes Tibetan and Zen Buddhism, there is a sense in which *nirvāṇa* is *saṃsāra* and *saṃsāra* is *nirvāṇa*.[27] 'Nirvāṇa in the Mahāyāna sense,' says Abe Masao, 'is simply the realisation of *saṃsāra* as really *saṃsāra*, no more, no less, by a thoroughgoing return to *saṃsāra* itself. This is why, in Mahāyāna Buddhism, it is often said of true *nirvāṇa* that "*saṃsāra*-as-it-is is *nirvāṇa*".'[28] Similarly, Karaki Junzō writes, 'We should not think that the impermanence of birth-and-death is followed by the permanence of *nirvāṇa*. Rather, impermanence is *nirvāṇa*; birth-and-death is *nirvāṇa*.'[29] *Nirvāṇa* in this sense is not a place or a state we achieve after death. It is, as Ram-Prasad puts it, 'simply (!) a switch in our perspective on ourselves and the world'.[30] This kind of *nirvāṇa* is more comprehensible from a naturalistic viewpoint than the prospect of escaping the cycles of rebirth. The idea that a full realisation of the impermanence and emptiness of self provides some kind of liberation can be understood in broadly secular terms.

Ideas of *nirvāṇa* are not confined to academics and scholars but are part of the popular Indian imagination. 'Even today, when these traditional philosophical beliefs have dimmed in the stress and strife of modern life,' according to S. K. Saksena, 'it is difficult to say that an Indian goes through his daily life of birth, marriage and death unimpressed and unaffected by these beliefs, the truth of which he seems to feel in his very bones.'[31] He wrote these words in 1957, but they are arguably as true today as they were sixty years ago and probably will be for a long time to come. But what difference do these ideas of *saṃsāra*, *nirvāṇa* and *mokṣa* make to how people actually live? We've already seen how the metaphysics of *karma* can foster some acceptance of one's lot in this life, and a certain degree of detachment from life and worldly concerns. In Indian philosophy, this is not usually manifested as a positive antipathy to worldly goods or wealth, as long as they are kept in their place. 'Emancipation does not exist in poverty; nor is bondage to be found in affluence,' says the *Mahābhārata*. 'One attains to emancipation through knowledge alone, whether one is indigent or affluent.'[32]

Physical and material prosperity is not bad but irrelevant: 'When one reflects properly [. . .] one comes to know that the things of this world are as valueless as straw.'[33] This is similar to the view of the ancient Greek and Roman Stoics, who argued that wealth was an 'indifferent' that we should not be afraid to make use of but should not fret about not having either. 'No one has sentenced wisdom to poverty,' said the (very wealthy) Seneca. Epictetus suggested we treat wealth like we treat good things at a symposium: 'Something is being passed round and comes to you: put out your hand and take your share politely. It goes by: do not detain it. It has not yet come: do not stretch your desire out towards it, but wait till it comes to you.'[34]

This moderate position, however, is not always maintained in Indian philosophy. Sometimes more value appears to be placed on worldly goods. *Artha*, or material advantage/prosperity, is on most of the lists of legitimate goals of human effort (*purusa-arthas*) found in orthodox texts, alongside pleasure (*kama*), ethicality or virtue (*dharma*) and on some lists *moksa*.[35] In the *Artha-Śāstra*, written between the second century BCE and the third century CE, it takes on primary importance.

At the same time, worldly goods are often dismissed along with all attachments, including to people. The *Mahābhārata* says that 'attachment to world objects is productive of evil. Relatives, sons, spouses, the body itself, and all one's possessions stored with care, are substantial and prove of no service in the next world.'[36] Of no service because they just won't be there, according to *The Laws of Manu*: 'For in the next world neither father, nor mother, nor wife, nor sons, nor relations stay to be his companions; spiritual merit alone remains (with him).'[37]

Similarly, the *Bhagavad Gītā* warns that 'When a man dwells in his mind on the objects of sense, attachment to them is produced. From attachment springs desire, and from desire comes anger. From anger arises bewilderment, from bewilderment loss of memory, from loss of memory the destruction of intelligence, and from the destruction of intelligence he perishes.' Only 'a man of disciplined mind' who moves in the world 'with the senses under control and free from attachment and aversion' can attain 'purity of spirit'.[38]

These attitudes have been maintained in the heterodox schools. Jains, for example, are told, 'Laymen ought to make love to their wives without even being attached.'[39] Buddhism is perhaps best known for its advocacy of non-attachment, which often expresses itself in quite extreme terms. 'He whose passions are destroyed, who is indifferent to food, who has perceived the nature of release and unconditioned freedom, his path is difficult to understand like that of birds through the sky. Even the gods envy him whose senses are subdued like horses well tamed by the charioteer,'[40] says the *Dhammapāda*, adding, 'Do not be a friend of the world.'[41]

The emphasis on detachment in Buddhism has created a historical tension between a compassionate active social engagement and a retreat from the world that is often said to be required to achieve *nirvāṇa*. An early Pali text, the *Rhinoceros Sūtra*, stresses the need for social isolation and offers a vivid warning against the dangers of getting too close to people:

> One whose mind
> is enmeshed in sympathy
> for friends and companions,
> neglects the true goal.
> Seeing this danger in intimacy,
> wander alone
> like a rhinoceros.[42]

Sometimes this indifference to the world and a desire to detach from it morph into real disgust. The *Dhammapāda* invites us to 'Look at this beautified body' as 'a nesting ground for disease' and 'a mass of sores propped up, full of illness, the object of many plans, with nothing stable or lasting'. It reminds us that 'When life ends in death, this putrid body dissolves' and that the city is 'built of bones, plastered with blood and flesh'.[43]

In this, Buddhism was merely continuing a theme found in the orthodox Indian schools. Take this striking passage from the *Upaniṣads*:

> in this ill-smelling, unsubstantial body, which is a
> conglomeration of bone, skin, muscle, marrow, flesh, semen,
> blood, mucus, tears, rheum, faeces, urine, wind, bile, and
> phlegm, what is the good of enjoyment of desires? In this
> body, which is afflicted with desire, anger, covetousness,
> delusion, fear, despondency, envy, separation from the
> desirable, union with the undesirable, hunger, thirst, senility,

death, diseases, sorrow, and the like, what is the good of
enjoyment of desires?
And we see that this whole world is decaying, as these gnats,
mosquitos, and the like, the grass, and the trees that arise and
perish [. . .]
In this sort of cycle of existence (*saṁsāra*) what is the good of
enjoyment of desires, when after a man has fed on them there
is seen repeatedly his return here to earth?
Be pleased to deliver me. In this cycle of existence I am like a
frog in a waterless well.[44]

Once again, though, it is possible to find many more moderate
passages that commend neither excessive desire nor repulsion. The
first discourse of the Buddha in the Pali canon explicitly advocates
avoiding extremes of sensual indulgence and vexatious asceticism.
Avoiding both is required to follow the 'middle way', which 'gives
rise to vision, which gives rise to knowledge, and leads to peace,
to direct knowledge, to enlightenment, to *Nibbāna* [*nirvāṇa*]'.[45]
Similarly, an early (Hīnayāna) Buddhist text describes two her-
esies 'by which some fall short of the truth, and some outrun the
truth'. Those who fall short 'delight in existence, take pleasure in
existence, rejoice in existence, so that when the doctrine for the
cessation of existence is preached to them their minds do not leap
toward it, are not favourably disposed toward it, do not rest in it,
do not adopt it.' But those who outrun the truth 'are distressed at,
ashamed of, and loathe existence, and welcome the thought of non-
existence'. The right path is a more neutral 'absence of passion' for
things and a cessation of yearning.[46]

The right attitude to wealth is in part determined by your
role in society, reflected in the Hindu idea of the four stages of
life: the student (*brahmacarya*), the householder (*gārhasthya*),
the forest-dweller (*vānaprastha*) and the wandering ascetic (*sun-
nyāsa*). During the second of these, it is entirely appropriate to

accumulate wealth in order to provide for your family. On the arrival of the first grandchild, however, it is time to focus more on reflection and spiritual development in the forest. Finally, at the end of life, all wealth should be renounced in preparation for departure from the world and its cares. Although few people follow these stages strictly, it represents a powerfully persistent ideal which explains and justifies differing attitudes to material prosperity at different times of life. But even when it is appropriate to earn, it is never right to become too attached to this world, as that blocks the path to ultimate liberation from its cycle of rebirth and suffering.

The range of attitudes towards worldly goods, from complete renunciation to acceptance as a legitimate goal of life, all context-dependent, is reflected in contemporary India, where ascetics are revered but the wealthy are not despised and often admired. Neither wealth nor poverty is good or bad in itself; it all depends on how and why one is in a certain material condition. This helps explain why so many gurus are not automatically ruined by stories of their huge personal wealth. Many 'guru-entrepreneurs' have even featured in *The Economist* as a result of their business acumen. The firm MSG (Messenger of God), run by Gurmeet Ram Rahim Singh, makes Bollywood-style films and has over 150 consumer products. A yoga teacher called Ramdev has a range of 'ayurvedic' drugs and beauty products and has been diversifying into foods and detergents. In one week his Patanjali brand had 17,000 television adverts, making it the top spender in January 2017.[47] As long as the gurus are seen as doing humanitarian work with a good part of their huge profits, it doesn't seem shocking that they should make them.

The fabled 'spirituality' of India is perhaps much more rooted in earthly life than stereotypes suggest. *Mokṣa* seems to point to other-worldly concerns, but it is achieved by right action in this life. Since everything we do has karmic consequences, that means ethics is everywhere and our own self-interest is never separable from the interests of others. It is perhaps not fanciful to suppose that this world view has deep roots in the Indian psyche and generates an ever-present sense of the spiritual and the ethical.

TRANSIENCE

It's not unusual to see a group of people all looking at the same thing in an art gallery. But there is not an artwork to be seen where these silent watchers at the Idemitsu Museum in Tokyo are gathered. They sit outside the exhibition space on benches in front of a window overlooking the parks of the Imperial Palace. Having just spent time looking at paintings largely of nature scenes, they are now contemplating a patch of nature itself, in the heart of the city.

Japanese sensitivity to nature and especially to the passage of the seasons is more than just a quaint stereotype. Its nature and significance, however, are elusive. It is not a distinct, discrete characteristic of their world view, a kind of bolt-on that could be attached to any tradition. It is rooted in a whole way of relating to the world that represents a radical alternative to most other traditions.

I first had inklings of this when I was talking to Kobayashi Yasuo about what makes Japanese philosophy distinctive. 'I have a tendency to think that in Japanese history and culture we can find something like philosophy,' he told me, but it's 'not a conceptual reconstruction of the world' like that of, say, Plato and Aristotle. It is, rather, 'based upon a kind of aesthetic reaction' located in the 'interface between the human being and the world'. It's 'very sensitive', experiential, touching the 'very nearest thing'. This is both the 'problem' and the 'charm of Japanese philosophical thought'.

I struggled to understand what this meant at the time (and to some extent still do), and it was only much later that I saw the connection with something another philosopher, Kazashi Nobuo, had said about traditional Japanese thought. 'There is no clear-cut separation between the aesthetic, the moral and the religious.' To give a clear example, in Shintō, the indigenous religion/philosophy, 'there is no clear moral code, like the ten commandments. It is an aesthetic appreciation of nature and human relationships.'

One problem I as a Westerner have understanding this is that the primary connotations of 'aesthetic' for me concern art, with appreciation of natural beauty as a secondary consideration. But the original, broader meaning of aesthetic is 'relating to felt experience', from the Greek *aisthēta* (perceptible things) and *aisthesthai* (perceive). It was only later in the nineteenth century that the meaning 'concerned with beauty' became common. To say that Japanese philosophy is aesthetic rather than conceptual is not primarily to say that it is concerned with appreciation of beauty – artistic, natural or otherwise – but that it centred on the experiential.

When I first drafted that last sentence I wrote 'the experiential rather than the intellectual' and then almost added 'based on feeling rather than thinking'. That was a mistake, and an instructive one. Psychology and philosophy have traditionally distinguished between the affective, which concerns the emotions, and the cognitive, which concerns intellection. But there is no sharp division between the two, as the work of psychologist Antonio Damasio has helped to demonstrate.[1] Our emotional responses often involve judgements, such as when we are afraid because we judge implicitly that something is dangerous, or we feel upset because we judge we have been let down. Also, our reasoning is often driven by emotion, such as when we convince ourselves we know more about a subject than we do to avoid embarrassment.

Japanese philosophy also challenges the division between feeling and thinking. The kind of aesthetic sensibility that Kobayashi and Kazashi describe is not an unthinking gut reaction. It is a kind of reflective sensitivity, one that attempts to understand by attending carefully to what is being experienced. This is thinking but not primarily with concepts. 'The important thing is to feel, not to conceptualise,' says Kobayashi, a philosopher whose business it is to think.

For Kobayashi, this entails getting close to things. That's what he means when he says that Japanese philosophy is 'touching'. He mixes spatial and temporal images to express this, saying that 'the most important thing happens not over there but in this present'. If we can achieve this closeness, it generates real understanding of a kind that is hard to define.

Take, for example, the sense of the transience and imperfection of all things. Every philosophy has in some way recognised this, but most also posit some kind of unchanging real world behind the world of appearances. Plato, for instance, thought of this life as a kind of fleeting illusion. But as Abe Masao points out, he 'held onto an idea of an immutable realm' of changeless forms beyond this world.[2] In Buddhist-influenced societies, impermanence is more thoroughgoing and has frequently been expressed through words, for instance in Ikkyū's famous poem *Skeletons*:

> Vanity of vanities
> the form of one
> I saw this morning
> Has become the smoky cloud
> Of the evening sky.

In every culture you can find examples of *memento mori*, reminders of the fragility of life and the inevitability of death. Buddhism's sense of the 'mutability of this world' goes much deeper than this commonplace acceptance of mortality. 'To the eye of illusion it appears that though the body dies, the soul does not,' says Ikkyū in prose. 'This is a terrible mistake. The enlightened man declares that both perish together.'

In Buddhist philosophy, transience has been analysed in terms of emptiness (*śūnyatā* in Sanskrit, *mu* in Japanese). But even in these traditions, it is more important to really feel what emptiness, impermanence or nothingness means than to define it or analyse it conceptually. As a merely abstract idea, it is almost useless. Anyone can intellectually understand that everything passes. But for this idea to affect how you live, you need to feel it. This is what the Japanese do. When crowds gather to watch the cherry blossoms as they disappear, blown away by the wind, they appreciate a beauty that is of its nature fleeting, not eternal. 'Cherry blossoms are very beautiful, the wind blows up and there is nothing, there are no flowers any more and we see this kind of emptiness but we admire this,' says Kobayashi. 'It's a very unique and special moment.' Although most salient in Japan, this is something shared across the Far East. Crowds gather to see the spring cherry blossoms in Yuyuantan Park in Beijing and along Yeouiseo-ro in Seoul, just as they do in Maruyama Park in Kyoto.

Emptiness is here first and foremost an aspect of experience that is only subsequently analysed philosophically. It is not a philosophical concept that we then take and apply to our experience. The same is true of time. 'Time is always present to us,' says Kobayashi, not as a concept but as a feeling. In the *hanami* festival, the annual ritual of going out to eat, drink and sing under the cherry blossoms for the brief period before they fall, 'We find out the truth of time.' The problem for Kobayashi, as a philosopher, is that 'we can't conceptualise this aesthetics'.

The aesthetic nature of Japanese thought fosters a sensitivity to the passage of time and impermanence. However, it goes much beyond this. As Kazashi intimated, ethics itself is rooted in the aesthetic. At the heart of Japanese aesthetics are the values of 'purity, wholeheartedness, straightforwardness', as Kazashi puts it. This manifests itself in art: in a haiku every syllable is carefully chosen, in a painting not a stroke is wasted. But these values are also clearly ethical values. So, for example, at the table no food is wasted, in contrast to China, where waste and even messy tables (to Japanese eyes) are almost positives. I noticed this in China myself, especially when staying at a hotel as a guest of a commissioning magazine. The manager there joined me for many of my meals, always ordering much more than we could eat and never finishing anything she herself took. (I heard it said that this is beginning to cause problems in Japan as increasing numbers of Chinese tourists offend local sensitivities.)

These values of 'purity, wholeheartedness, straightforwardness' also seem to be behind ethical qualities observed by the Bengali poet Rabindranath Tagore during his visit to Japan in 1916. 'The Japanese do not waste their energy in useless screaming and quarrelling,' he observed, 'and because there is no waste of energy, it is not found wanting when required. The calmness and fortitude of body and mind is part of their national self-realisation.'[3]

This relationship between the aesthetic and the ethical challenges one of the key dogmas of modern Western philosophy, the so-called 'is/ought gap'. Often attributed to David Hume, this is the idea that nothing about how the world *is* can tell us about how it *ought to be* or how we ought to act. Facts are facts, values are values, and you cannot logically transform one into another. However, that does not stop many people making just that leap. When reading any system of morality, Hume remarked there would always come a point when 'all of a sudden I am surprised to find, that instead of the usual copulations of propositions, *is*, and *is not*, I meet with no proposition that is not connected with an *ought*, or an *ought not*. This change is imperceptible; but is however, of the last consequence.[4] Some of the most egregious examples of this fallacy are found when people leap from the (alleged) fact that a certain kind of human behaviour is natural to its being morally right, or unnatural to its being morally wrong. But the fact that the desire for revenge is natural does not morally justify taking it, any more than the unnaturalness of flush toilets makes their use immoral.

Superficially, an ethics based on an aesthetic attention to the natural order makes the same mistake, jumping to conclusions about what is right on the basis of what we take nature to be like. In fact, the connection between is and ought is very different in this context, not least because there is no logical inference being made at all, and hence no logical fallacy to be made. The whole point of the aesthetic approach is to replace rational deduction with aesthetic sensibility.

Take attitudes to impermanence. There is no deduction here, from the premise 'everything is impermanent' to the conclusion 'therefore one should live in such and such a way'. Rather, one comes to see the best way to live by understanding the nature of impermanence and how it relates to our existence. Our attitudes develop in response to our awareness, not as a simple logical consequence of them. Or to put it another way, we come to appreciate more deeply the significance of impermanence itself, not what follows logically from it.

To give another example, we could take our awareness of the suffering of others as a kind of premise in a rational argument. But that would risk the is/ought fallacy: 'such an action causes suffering therefore I ought not to do it' is not a valid logical deduction because an ought is stated in the conclusion that does not appear in the premises. However, when we modify our behaviour to others in response to a recognition of their suffering, we are committing no such fallacy because our response is an affective, not a logical one. To stress again, however, that does not make it unthinking. Thinking is not to be found solely in rational deduction. Thinking also involves paying attention, noticing, attending to what matters most.

If it is true that there are serious forms of thinking that are not about following chains of logical reasoning, it would not be possible to grasp this simply by reading the kind of systematic account I'm attempting to set out here. To appreciate the centrality of the aesthetic in Japanese philosophy, it is necessary to cultivate something of the same sensitivity. The most useful text I have found for helping us to do this is *The Book of Tea*, written by Okakura Kakuzō in 1906. In some ways, it is a romantic work, celebrating the culture of a tea ceremony which was already in decline when the book was written and which is extremely marginal in Japanese society today. The people I met had either not participated in one for many years or, in the case of some of the younger ones, never done so at all.

However, Okakura captures beautifully sensibilities behind the tea ceremony which endure beyond it. He shows the aesthetic rather than the intellectual appreciation of emptiness and impermanence in action. 'Teaism,' he says, 'is a cult founded on the adoration of the beautiful among the sordid facts of everyday existence. [. . .] It is essentially a worship of the imperfect, as it is a tender attempt to accomplish something possible in this impossible thing we know as life.'[5] The ephemerality of tea is a reminder of the ephemerality of life, and the vanity of thinking its value lies in anything transcendent or eternal: 'When we consider how small after all the cup of human enjoyment is, how soon overflowed with tears, how easily drained to the dregs in our quenchless thirst for infinity, we shall not blame ourselves for making so much of the tea-cup.'[6] Humans are exceptional not because they have risen above the natural world but because they have come to see it as more than just a meaningless, functional system. Primeval *Homo sapiens* became fully human for Okakura by 'rising above the crude necessities of nature. He entered the realm of art when he perceived the subtle use of the useless.'[7]

The Japanese call this sensitivity to imperfection and imper-manence *mono no aware*. It has an ethical dimension, since it fosters a kind of modesty that makes us more open to the value of things beyond ourselves. 'Those who cannot feel the littleness of great things in themselves are apt to overlook the greatness of little things in others,' says Okakura.[8] This attitude also generates a self-deprecating humour. 'Teaism,' says Okakura, 'is the noble secret of laughing at yourself, calmly yet thoroughly, and is thus humour itself – the smile of philosophy.'[9]

The stereotype of the Japanese is of disciplined, sober workers, formal and keeping face. As I found in Japan, however, the reality is much gentler. Warm smiles are common, as is laughter. The Zen tradition in particular reflects this. Many stories speak of Zen masters roaring with laughter (at least when they are not beating their novices). The aesthetic principle *wabi-sabi* is concerned with capturing the bitter-sweet pathos of things, and that sweetness is never overpowered by the sour.

Japan exerts a particular fascination for many in the West. On the one hand, it seems so modern, so Western in its infrastruc-ture, and on the other, it seems utterly exotic, alien in its cultural superstructure. Yet for all its otherness, it has in many ways a philosophical tradition that is easier to learn and borrow from than many others. It is not tied to any particular religious metaphysics but is essentially rooted in an appreciation of and attention to the immanent world of nature. It is reflective but not purely or even mainly in a logical, analytic way. Its philosophy offers an oppor-tunity to deepen and enrich other systems of philosophy without requiring them to give up anything essential of their own.

IMPARTIALITY

Most of us think that anyone who donates one of their kidneys to a complete stranger is a special kind of altruist. But for Zell Kravinsky, the most problematic option was not giving an organ. He worked out that if he donated his kidney, his risk of dying as a donor was one in 4,000. Without a donated kidney, the probability of the potential recipient dying was one. As a good mathematician, Kravinsky concluded that not giving his kidney would mean that he valued his own life 4,000 times more than that of the recipient. Since all human lives are in fact of equal worth, that would be obscene. So Kravinsky, already a philanthropist, added to cash donations with his kidney.

Some think he is mad, but Kravinsky says he doesn't feel crazy. 'I am looking for the moral life,' he explains. 'This means I cannot have wealth, or the use of two kidneys, when others have none. I cannot value myself and my life higher than others.'[1]

Kravinsky did not come to this conclusion on the basis of any moral philosophy, but the logic he followed matches that of utilitarianism, a moral philosophy created by Jeremy Bentham in the late eighteenth century and further developed by his godson John Stuart Mill. One of the world's leading contemporary utilitarians, Peter Singer, uses Kravinsky as an example of his theories in action. For utilitarians, morally right actions are those that promote the greatest overall 'utility' and morally wrong actions decrease it. Utility is defined variously by different theorists in terms of happiness, pleasure, welfare or preference satisfaction. So, for example, if you have a choice between giving £1,000 to charity to save three lives or to pay for a guide dog for one blind person for a few months, you give to save lives.

In such summary terms, utilitarianism can sound sensible and appealing. However, take it to its logical conclusion and it is extremely demanding. Say you're wondering where to read the next chapter of this book. You could go and sit in a nice café and spend a few pounds on a flat white. Or you could put that money in a charity jar instead and read the book at home. Give to the right charity and that money will provide much more benefit to someone else than you would have got from your coffee. There are people living on a dollar a day for whom that cash could make the difference between going to sleep hungry or not. But that is true of everything you buy that is not a strict necessity. To maximise utility, you need to give away every penny above what you need to keep yourself tolerably well and comfortable.

When describing utilitarianism, textbooks tend to emphasise how it focuses on consequences. This supposedly is what distinguishes it from the other major traditions in Western moral philosophy: deontological ethics, which focuses on duties, and virtue ethics, which focuses on character. But it seems to me that what really distinguishes utilitarianism, not just from these systems but from other moral frameworks around the world, is its absolute impartiality. It demands that we treat everyone's interests equally, irrespective of how we are related to them. Other moral theories typically say that we have more duties towards some than to others, most obviously our families.

Take Indian philosophies. While many do promote a kind of universal benevolence or compassion, this is not a duty to maximise overall total welfare. The primary focus is on the karmic consequences of action for the actor, not the practical benefits for others. No matter how well you treat others, you cannot give them the ultimate good – *mokṣa* or *nirvāṇa*, release from the cycle of rebirth. The greatest good of the greatest number is out of our control and so it would be absurd to place it at the heart of ethics.

In the virtue tradition, absolute impartiality is rejected even more overtly. Roger Ames describes Confucianism as a form of 'role ethics' precisely because it says that your obligations differ depending on your role in society.[2] The moral responsibilities of fathers and sons, husbands and wives, rulers and ruled all differ. The same is true in African Akan society, where Pieter H. Coetzee says that rights are all role-rights. 'To be a rights bearer requires a place in a social structure, and so rights can only be awarded to, and exercised by, persons occupying specific social roles.'[3] Most, if not all, traditional societies share this approach. What makes utilitarianism so challenging is that it utterly rejects role ethics, arguing that we should consider the welfare of distant strangers as much as we should that of kith and kin.

The implications are staggering. Kravinsky believed 'that a refusal to give a kidney to a person who would otherwise die is the same as murder – you are responsible for their death'. This meant that when his wife objected to his donation, he would have been wrong to take this into account. Indeed, he even said that 'my wife's refusal to let me donate was like murder'. This was not an off-the-cuff overstatement. A friend once asked him, 'Do you mean that anybody who is not donating a kidney is taking someone's life?' Kravinsky said yes. The friend did not like the implication. 'So, by your terms, I'm a murderer?' he asked. Kravinsky didn't blink. We are all – me, probably you, almost everyone you know – murderers in this utilitarian view. Even giving a kidney wouldn't let you off:

unless you have given away almost all of your wealth, you have chosen to spend money on non-essentials for yourself, friends or families that could have saved lives. In the utilitarian calculus, the vast majority of people in developed countries are serial killers.

Kravinsky did subsequently soften up, accepting that he was too harsh on his wife. 'Now I realise that she is entitled to her own feelings and her own opinions,' he has said. But at most this seems like a realistic acceptance of the limits of human compassion. He hasn't changed his principles; he's just less inclined to spell out their logical consequences, accepting that they are too demanding for most people to follow.

The philosophical history of absolute impartiality is an interesting one, because it emerged independently in at least two traditions but only really thrived in one. Its earliest flowering was in fifth-century-BCE China in the philosophy of Mozi. His key maxim was 'The business of a benevolent person is to promote what is beneficial to the world and eliminate what is harmful.' This is remarkably similar to John Stuart Mill's nineteenth-century Principle of Utility: 'actions are right in proportion as they tend to promote happiness, wrong as they tend to produce the reverse of happiness.'[4] Mozi, however, is a more austere kind of utilitarian whose idea of what is beneficial to society seems to exclude such frivolities as pleasure. His utilitarianism leaves no place for musical performances, at least not those that require fine instruments and time for practice. If rulers employ people to make music, that means they can't plough, plant, weave or sew. Musical performances 'divert such vast resources that could be used to produce food and clothing for the people'.[5] Very similar arguments are heard today by those who object to state subsidies for the arts when health and education services are in such dire need.

The other main difference with Mill is that Mozi more clearly presented his philosophy as an attack on partiality, which is the subject of many of his most memorable lines. 'It is those who are partial in their dealings with others who are the real cause of all the great harms in the world,' he said. 'Impartiality gives rise to all the great benefits in the world and impartiality gives rise to all the great harms in the world.' And most pithily: 'Replace partiality with impartiality.'[6]

Interestingly, Mozi does not see this impartiality as conflicting with the traditional duties assigned to people according to their roles. 'There are rulers who are not kind, ministers who are not loyal, fathers who are not loving, and children who are not filial,' he observes. 'These too are some of the harms being done in their world.' This would seem to endorse the idea that we ought to be partial in our care and affection. But Mozi argues that anyone who is truly filial, for instance, has to ultimately endorse impartiality. The idea is that we would all be better off if we extended our filial concern to other families too: 'According to the very meaning of filial piety, he must want other people to care for and benefit his parents.'[7] His argument for this is a clever one:

> To whom would one entrust the well-being of one's parents, wife, and children? Would one prefer that they be in the care of an impartial person or would one prefer that they be in the care of a partial person? I believe that under such circumstances, there are no fools in all the world. Even though one may not advocate impartiality, one would certainly want to entrust one's family to the person who is impartial. But this is to condemn impartiality in word but prefer it in deed.[8]

I'm not convinced that Mozi's impartiality really does preserve values such as filial piety. His claim that it does appears to be a kind of rhetorical ploy to appeal to the Chinese he sought to convert, an attempt to redefine what filial duty means. You believe children should care for their parents, he says. If that's what you want, then surely it would be better if all children cared for all parents equally? But this completely transforms the meaning of filial piety while claiming to preserve it. Whatever treating all parents equally means, it is not fulfilling a special duty of a child. Nor is what one would want when entrusting the care of a family member to a stranger any indication of what dutiful children would want in normal circumstances, which is to look after them themselves.

Mozi's argumentative strategy exploits the fact that almost everyone agrees with impartiality in one sense. To be ethical requires us to be consistent. To complain that someone has done wrong when you have done just the same is hypocritical, unless there are important differences in circumstances. But in most moral systems, one of the things that justifies differences in actions is our relationship to others. To favour one's own children is not to be unjust to other children. The only kind of impartiality we require in such cases is to judge how others treat their children by the same standard as how we treat ours; it is not to insist that we should treat each other's children equally. That kind of absolute impartiality fails to respect the 'separateness of persons': the fact that we each have an individual identity and relationship to others and so when thinking about how we treat others we have to think about who they are in particular and not just treat them as though they were interchangeable with anyone else.

Mohism never became dominant in Chinese society, but it did leave a legacy, exerting an influence on the other major strand of classical Chinese philosophy to embrace absolute impartiality, legalism. The legalists believed that society needed strict and clear rules to function and that to rely on the virtue of leaders was naive and dangerous. 'If one abandons the power of position, turns one's back on the law, and waits for a Yao or Shun, then when a Yao or Shun arrives there will indeed be order, but it will only be one generation of order in a thousand generations of disorder,' said the greatest legalist philosopher, Han Feizi. 'On the other hand, if one holds to the law, relies on the power of position, and waits for a Jie or a Zhou, then when a Jie or a Zhou comes there will indeed be disorder, but it will only be one generation of disorder in a thousand generations of order.' He advised the monarch, 'If Your Majesty would only attend to the law everything would be fine.'[9]

Han employed several colourful images to illustrate this basic idea. In one, he claimed that saying we should wait for great virtuous leaders 'is like saying that one should hold out for fine grain and meat in order to save oneself from starvation'.[10] In another, he compares those who place their trust in good leadership to the idiot farmer from Song who, after seeing a rabbit run into a stump and break its neck, set out to catch rabbits by waiting for them to run into stumps.[11]

For Han, the need to stick to rules is absolute. He tells the story of how the Steward of Caps covered Marquis Zhao of Han one night when he fell asleep drunk, worried that he would be cold. When the Marquis discovered this he punished the steward because he felt the man had overstepped the limits of his position. 'It was not that the Marquis did not dislike the cold, but rather that he felt that the harm that comes from ministers encroaching on each other's office is even greater than the harm that comes from being cold. If someone oversteps the boundaries of his office, he should die.'[12]

Like Mohism, legalism never supplanted the dominant Confucianism. However, its rigidity and emphasis on rules have resurfaced whenever there have been reactions against Confucianism, notably after the communist revolution. Insisting on absolute impartiality was one way of signalling an end to old-fashioned and hierarchical Confucianism. Jung Chang gives an all too clear example of this in her family memoir *Wild Swans*. Chang's father was a senior official in the Communist Party when her mother had her second child. It had been a problematic birth and she had to spend several days in hospital. All this time, her husband was in the countryside rallying support for the collectivisation programme.

After a week, a colleague of her father sent a car to the hospital to bring her home, in keeping with the accepted practice that the Party would take care of officials' wives if their husbands were away. But when her husband returned he severely reprimanded the colleague. The rule stipulated that she could only ride in an official car when her husband was in it. The exceptional circumstances of her illness and his absence were irrelevant. A rule is a rule. Chang says this kind of 'puritanical rigidity' was common and something her mother found hard to take.[13] That is not surprising, because it flies in the face of not only an almost universal special concern for family but also thousands of years of Chinese culture.

In China, this absolute impartiality was a temporary, historical aberration. For most of its history, Chinese ethics has embraced some partiality as natural and right. Confucius's maxim that a son should not testify against his father, for example, was extended in the T'ang dynasty so that a prosecutor could not even ask any member of a family household to stand as a witness. Simply making an accusation against your parents became a capital offence, whereas during the Cultural Revolution it became a civic duty.[14]

In the West, however, a more tempered form of impartiality has become the default mode of thinking about ethics. In the modern era, its first and most explicit expression came with utilitarianism – Britain's Mohism – in the nineteenth century. Its founders had clear, snappy slogans to capture its essence. Jeremy Bentham summed up its central maxim as 'Create all the happiness you are able to create: remove all the misery you are able to remove.'[15]

The key feature of this system is not, however, its focus on happiness. Utilitarians since have sometimes disagreed that this is the ultimate good and have instead urged us to maximise welfare or preference satisfaction. They all agree, however, that actions are right and wrong solely on account of whether they increase the ultimate good. Crucially, the criterion here is the overall *total* good, not *your* good or the good of friends and family. The moral goal here is entirely impersonal, the basic principle rigorously impartial, captured in Bentham's dictum 'everybody to count for one, nobody for more than one.'[16]

This absolute impartiality did not appear in a vacuum. As we have seen, Western philosophy has in various ways long emphasised objectivity, and ethical impartiality is another side of the same coin. Kant, for example, argued that the ultimate principle in morality was 'I ought never to act except in such a way that I could also will that my maxim should become a universal law.'[17] This 'categorical imperative' requires a high degree of impartiality. It requires us to consider right and good only those actions that we think everyone else would also be entitled to do in relevantly similar circumstances.

Another example of the emphasis on impartiality is Adam Smith's idea of the 'impartial spectator'. Smith argued that to examine our own moral conduct, it is essential to imagine how it would look to an external judge, a disinterested spectator.[18] Again, the assumption here is that only from an absolutely impartial point of view can actions be truly judged right or wrong.

This assumption recurs again and again, with political ramifications. One of the most influential political philosophers of the twentieth century, John Rawls, put absolute impartiality at the core of his theory of justice. According to Rawls, the way in which we should decide what is just is to imagine which rules we would establish for a society if we were behind a 'veil of ignorance', not knowing what position in society we would occupy and so ensuring that partiality cannot infect the process. If we don't know whether we would be winners or losers, lucky or unlucky, we have to decide what is fair in a way that considers the interests of everyone equally.

Although absolute impartiality is most obviously associated with utilitarian philosophies that aim to maximise the general good, it is equally central to another, often conflicting, belief in individual rights and liberty. These came to the fore during the

Enlightenment. A leading historian of that period, Jonathan Israel, lists the key principles of the Enlightenment as 'democracy; racial and sexual equality; individual liberty of lifestyle; full freedom of thought, expression, and the press; eradication of religious authority from the legislative process and education; and a full separation of church and state.'[19] These are most commonly seen first and foremost as aspects of individual liberty, but could equally be seen as facets of impartiality. Read through the list again and you'll see that each item essentially concerns the elimination of all partiality in the treatment of citizens.

One curious feature is that although principles of universal rights appear to have the general good at heart, when someone insists on their rights, they are often not at all concerned about whether exercising that right improves the lot of others. Hence the strong strand in Western society opposed to large-scale state intervention. In this view, governments do not have a utilitarian duty to maximise the general welfare of all. Rather, their role is to defend the rights of all, and if that leads to inequalities, so be it. This still involves a notion of absolute impartiality, namely that we all of us have the same rights, irrespective of our social position, wealth, education and so on. Impartiality when it comes to rights means respecting the rights of everyone to keep the fruits of their own labour, so to take from the rich to give to the poor, for example, is to treat the wealthy with unjust partiality.

The fact that the ideal of impartiality can be used to justify both government intervention and a laissez-faire, libertarian state illustrates how pervasive it is. There is no clearer evidence that a philosophical assumption is deeply embedded in a society than the observation that people with very different substantive views all feel the need to justify their positions by reference to it.

The emphasis on impartiality can be seen as another aspect of Kasulis's characterisation of integrity cultures. In integrity cultures, the grounds of all knowledge are transparent and open, not based on personal experience. Hence the stress on categorical imperatives, veils of ignorance and impartial spectators, all means of arriving at the truth from a neutral point of view.

Because it is in tension with deeply held family values, in practice it is as though in the West absolute impartiality stops at the front door. In the civic domain, impartiality rules, while in the home, we can be as partial as we please. But even in the privacy of our living rooms, the imperative of impartiality is felt. Many people feel the need to acknowledge that the interests of others are as important as their own. Charitable giving and voluntary work are both highly valued and the more people have, the more they are expected to give. Although we do not always feel obliged to act according to an absolutely impartial perspective, it is there in the background, a kind of cultural superego nagging at us for not taking the welfare of others into sufficient consideration.

The tension between civic partiality and domestic partiality sometimes explodes when politicians mix home and work. The 2017 French presidential bid of François Fillon was scuppered when he was accused of employing his wife as his parliamentary assistant, paying her handsomely for more work than she actually did. His poll ranks slumped even though no wrongdoing had actually been proved, because, it seems, the public felt there was something wrong about this arrangement even if the rules had been followed. If Fillon was aggrieved by this, he had some reason. Such arrangements have been extremely common and he was taken by surprise when public opinion seemed to decide it should not be. Several British Members of Parliament were also caught out when it emerged as part of a wider expenses scandal in 2009 that they were employing members of their own family. In both France and Britain, the tension between civic impartiality and family partiality became no longer sustainable, in both cases because the demands of civic impartiality trumped the right to family partiality.

Look for manifestations of truly absolute impartiality in Western societies and you'll come back empty-handed. It has always been an impossibly inhuman ideal, and even its advocates admit as much. Peter Singer, for example, was accused of being a hypocrite when it emerged that he had helped pay for the care of his mother when she was suffering from Alzheimer's disease. From a utilitarian point of view this was an unjustified allocation of a lot of resources for the benefit of one person when the same money could have helped many more. When pressed on this, Singer accepted that it was 'probably not the best use you could make of my money'. It didn't change his mind, it simply made it clearer to him how demanding his version of impartiality was. 'I think this has made me see how the issues of someone with these kinds of problems are really very difficult,' he told the journalist Michael Specter. 'Perhaps it is more difficult than I thought before, because it is different when it's your mother.'[20] Most would say his experience pointed to a deeper truth. 'No sensible person should want to live in a world in which all moral problems are solved by or justified by impersonal principles,' says Owen Flanagan. 'There are reasons of love, friendship, communal solidarity, which are not impersonal.'[21]

Nonetheless, assumptions of the value of absolute impartiality inform almost every ethical debate in the West. It is the invisible thread that links the twin ideals of equality and freedom. To treat people equally, you need to treat them impartially. In order to guarantee the freedoms of all, their rights have to be granted impartially. The problem for Westerners, however, is that they know at some level that impartiality has its limits, that the particular ties we have to community, family and friends matter and should make a difference to how we behave. Arguably an excessive emphasis on impartiality has created a lot of discontent. The political direction of Europe in particular has been directed by a vision in which it doesn't matter whether you're Greek, German, British or Dutch; Christian, Jew, atheist, Muslim or Hindu; working class, middle class or aristocratic. The free movement of people requires an absolute impartiality that grants the same rights to all. One consequence of this has been a sense of dislocation, a lack of belonging. What held communities together was not what made humans all fundamentally the same, it was what made us contingently different. And so people rebelled against a kind of impartiality that broke down precisely those partial ties of identity that made people feel at home.

The solution, if there is one, cannot be to abandon all ideals of impartiality. Equal rights and a political sense of the equal interests of all are vital for a fair and just society. At the same time, this should be compatible with granting people the rights to their partial attachments.

CONCLUSION

It is easy to treat the world's philosophies as offerings in a global supermarket of ideas, putting anything that takes your fancy in your basket. Picking and mixing, however, doesn't work when it plucks fruit off the plant which it needs to grow. Ideas are parts of living ecosystems and when you try to move them to a strange context they can wither and die. If we transplant them carefully, though, grafting them onto robust local trunks, sometimes they can flourish abroad. 'Concepts can travel,' says Bruce Janz, 'but not intact.'[1]

The most helpful metaphor I can offer for cross-cultural learning about values is that of the mixing desk. In the studio, producers record each instrument as an individual track, playing them back through separate channels. By sliding controls up or down, the volume of each track can be increased or decreased.

The moral mixing desk works in much the same way. Almost everywhere in the world you'll find the same channels: impartiality, rules, consequences, virtue, God, society, autonomy, actions, intentions, harmony, community, belonging and so on. The differences between cultures is largely a matter of how much each is

314

turned up or down. It is unusual for any channel to be completely turned off, but sometimes – God, for instance – it isn't in the mix at all. Cross-cultural thinking requires a good ethical ear and this is hard to develop if you are not attuned to the whole range of moral concepts. It also requires the wisdom to realise that it is impossible to turn everything up to ten: some values clash with others, at least when they are at equal volume. Similarly, when some values are turned down low they become inaudible, which may be the price to pay for a harmonious overall balance.

The metaphor of the mixing desk makes sense of moral pluralism: the idea that there is more than one good way to live and that emphasising certain values might require neglecting others. Pluralism is often mistaken for laissez-faire relativism, but just as in the recording studio, it simply isn't the case that anything goes. More than one moral mix can work but many more than one won't.

Listening to the moral music of others can help us to reconsider the quality of our own. Admiring harmony, for example, we might wonder whether we have allowed it to be drowned out in our own tradition. Seeing impartiality used more sparingly we might find that ours is an overpowering, incessant beat in comparison. Valuing the fruits of autonomy we might conclude our own moral rhythm is too restrictive. The goal is not to come up with a mix that will be the favourite of everyone in the world but to make our own the best it can be.

PART FIVE

Concluding Thoughts

I've talked in this book about how buildings like those in the Alhambra, the Athenian Agora and the Forbidden City reflect philosophical values. Reading the *Shanghai Daily* in a hotel surrounded by high-rises on land that was used for farming just two decades ago, I came across a columnist who agreed in principle, but added an important caveat: those values are disappearing. 'China's ancient residences were conceived and executed according to principles that are now widely forgotten,' wrote Wan Lixin. 'In the past, for instance, buildings were scrupulously judged on their harmonious relationship with the surrounding, natural environment. By contrast, modern buildings are conceived in disdain for such considerations. Indeed, our modern urban buildings are celebrations of individualism.'[1]

Wan raises a question that goes to the heart of this book. Can the historical values and philosophies of a culture really reveal anything about the fast-changing world of today? Can we really find Confucius on the streets of Qufu or Aristotle in the Athenian supermarket? I can see many reasons to be sceptical. Just before finishing this book I happened to be enjoying *ravioles du Dauphiné* with a glass of Crozes-Hermitage at Le Procope, the oldest café in Paris, where the likes of Voltaire, Victor Hugo and the *encyclopédistes* thrashed out the principles of the Enlightenment. But there are no *philosophes* here now, unless I presume to count myself. Nor are there many French customers. The brasserie, as it is today, is selling us the nostalgia of smart but stern waiters and rich old-school French food that the Parisians themselves have all but abandoned. In the rapidly globalising world, national traditions seem to be conserved only for the benefit of visitors such as myself and the group of Chinese tourists at the table opposite me. Why should national philosophies be any more resilient?

Signs of the overturning of old orders are everywhere. 'For nearly 2,000 years the family has been the organising principle of Chinese society,' said *The Economist* in a special report on how that society is changing. It concluded that two millennia of tradition were coming to an abrupt end: 'Notions of family and identity have struggled to keep up with the country's accelerated modernisation.'[2] Similar things are said about the decline of belief in *karma* and caste in India, about the threat to the ethic of *ubuntu* in Africa, about the loss of connection with the land as traditional societies become urbanised and so on.

However, in the course of writing this book I have spoken with dozens of people who are experts on the philosophies of the countries in which they live. Without exception they have seen deep connections between philosophy and culture. I've also seen plenty of evidence for this myself, be it the everyday references to harmony in China, resistance to secularisation in the Islamic world, assumptions of rebirth in India or the evident individualism of the West. Cultures have deep roots and sometimes the most obvious changes are also the most superficial. Tokyoites (*Edokko*) and New Yorkers both wear cotton slacks and use the subway, but the evident differences in how they behave while riding it show that, though the material worlds they inhabit are virtually indistinguishable, their ways of being are not. Outside Le Procope, whether they know it or not, the Parisians celebrating the annual LGBT Pride festival are living the humanistic, individualistic principles of the Enlightenment philosophers.

What we cannot know, however, is whether the constant tugging of globalised modernity on these roots will eventually pull them up and, if that happens, how long it will take. Nor do we know whether traditions might evolve and mutate through cross-pollination so as to become unrecognisable. Should either of these things occur, we would have all the more reason to retain an appreciation of what has been lost so that we are ready to relearn the valuable lessons the history of global philosophy has taught us. Philosophy may cease to be a window into culture as it is and become rather a source of images of what culture could become.

No matter how tightly connected the philosophies and cultures of the world are, there clearly are identifiable global philosophical traditions with their own distinctive characteristics. Ideas within these traditions do not stand in isolation. They form parts of wider wholes, networks of beliefs that mutually sustain and support each other, while sometimes also being in tension. It is this overall shape that gives each system its general character, one that becomes easier to discern after you have looked carefully at some of its main details. Now is therefore the time to sketch out a broad summary of the dominant features of the world's philosophical landscapes.

It bears repeating that these do not capture all or everything. They are generalisations that have many exceptions, just as a mountainous country may have its plains or a serious person might be capable of great laughter. These pen portraits capture only what is most dominant in the thinking of each region of the world.

How the world thinks

We begin in East Asia, home to nearly a quarter of the world's population, the vast majority in China and most of the rest in Taiwan, Japan and Korea. The ideas and ideals found in classical Chinese philosophy still resonate across the region today. Prime among these is harmony, a belief that the highest good is an ordered world in which families, villages and states all stand in the right relationship to each other. Harmony cannot be achieved if all differences are eradicated or if they are so marked as to make common purpose impossible.

Because harmony requires each person to fulfil his or her own role, society is inherently hierarchical. However, this should not be a hierarchy in which those at the top serve their own interests. Hierarchy should be to the benefit of all, the ruled benefited by good rule, students benefited by good teaching, filial children benefited by good parents. The openness of many civic hierarchies is reflected in the meritocratic tradition of civil service examinations in which positions are awarded to those who perform best.

Virtue enables a person to live well, promoting harmony in all their relationships. Virtue is having good character, and what it means to be good cannot be set down in a manual. It is more of a skill than a list of moral maxims. The virtuous person must become good at *quan*: weighing up the merits of each case and making discretionary choices about what ought to be done. There is no algorithm to do this, not least because the right thing to do is always dependent on the precise context. *Quan* requires sensitivity to the proper mean: the appropriate point between two extremes, such as rashness and cowardice, meanness and profligacy, and servility and unruliness.

Virtue is achieved by self-cultivation. The main means of this is *li*, ritual: formal and informal kinds of appropriate social behaviour. By following *li*, one internalises habits of virtuous action so that being good becomes second nature. The *junzi*, the exemplary person who succeeds in this, becomes a kind of moral paradigm, leading others to act well by example.

Ethical self-cultivation reflects a broader emphasis on practice and habit in achieving excellence. It is not primarily by learning but by doing that one becomes good at anything. The end result is *wu-wei*, a kind of effortless action that nonetheless requires years of conscious effort before it becomes instinctive. It is not possible to express in words what the person who exhibits *wu-wei* knows and indeed much of the deepest knowledge we have is ineffable. Language is an imperfect net in which to catch the world and practice is more important than theory.

The region's thought is characterised by a kind of metaphysical agnosticism. We can't know the nature of ultimate reality and that doesn't really matter. The tradition is more way-seeking than truth-seeking, interested primarily in what we need to live well, not in achieving knowledge of ultimate things for its own sake. To the extent that there is a metaphysics it is one of change and dynamism. *Yinyang* reflects the sense that everything is in active interrelation, creating a dynamic system in which nothing is ever settled for long. The concept of *qi* captures this sense that everything is flowing, that energy is constantly moving, and it requires skill to channel it and use it well.

The religious impulse finds its expression not in gods and heaven but in a sense of reverence for ancestors and for nature, as well as in an ideal of personal change that could be seen as a kind of spiritual transformation. The focus is very much on this world. *Tian*, heaven, is not another realm we might move on to after death but a kind of principle that regulates the physical world and is immanent in it.

The absence of any idea of final salvation links with a view of time that sees our golden age in the past rather than in the future. Maintaining tradition is important because it keeps alive the wisdom of the great sages. There may be material and technological progress, but morality and ethics are more likely to regress.

There are several characteristic features of East Asian philosophy that find their clearest expression in Japanese thought. Prime among these is the idea of the relational self, that we are who we are because of how we stand to others. There is no atomic self that can exist in complete isolation from the world. Self is empty, not least because there is a sense in which everything is empty. The world is impermanent, everything in it transient, devoid of any unchanging, inherent essence. Hence proper understanding of the world and ourselves is found as much in the spaces between things as it is in the things themselves, as the relations are more fundamental than the items related. That explains why experiments show that while Americans attend almost exclusively to foreground items in pictures and videos, East Asians see backgrounds as equally important.

Ideas of emptiness and impermanence are reflected in a sensitivity to the passing of the seasons, which can be seen as almost a kind of religious observance. The watching of the cherry blossom also reflects an ideal of harmony with nature, as something that stands not in contrast to human culture but at the heart of it. We are as close to nature when we use computers as we are when we walk along the coast because nature is as much in silicon and steel as it is in sand and sea.

The primary way of relating to the world is aesthetic rather than intellectual. We are more likely to *see* truth by direct, attentive experience of the world than we are to conceptualise it by detached reasoning. In such experience the distinction between subject and the world disappears.

Another quarter of the world's population inhabits the Indian subcontinent, which has again been shaped by its classical philosophy. More than any other tradition, for better or for worse, it has drawn on the full arsenal of philosophical tools: insight, revealed scriptures, a highly developed logic, tradition, observation. These are captured in the traditional taxonomy of *pramāṇas* (valid sources of knowledge): *pratyakṣa* (perception), *anumāna* (inference), *upamāna* (comparison and analogy), *arthāpatti* (postulation, derivation from circumstances), *anupalabdhi* (non-perception, negative/cognitive proof) and *śabda* (word, testimony of reliable experts).

If there is a first among equals, it is *pratyakṣa*, the direct perception of reality, often by a kind of trained intuition. This is reflected in the traditional word for philosophy in India, *darśana*, which literally means 'to look at' or 'to see'. Reason only leads us so far before we need *pratyakṣa* to show us how things really are. Since we are not all capable of this, the *pratyakṣa* and *śabda* of *ṛṣis* are highly valued, as well as those of great teachers. This creates a culture of deference which many outsiders perceive as excessive.

Both orthodox and heterodox schools mostly take some key texts to be sources of revealed knowledge, the orthodox supposedly distinguished by a fidelity to the *Vedas* which is in reality not always that unconditional. Indian philosophy is so intertwined with Indian religion that it does not even make sense to separate the two. Philosophers almost invariably see themselves as carrying the torch of a tradition, where their role is not to come up with new ideas but to better explain old ones. The glory of Indian philosophy, however, is that commentators have interpreted old texts with such ingenuity and creativity that there has never been a shortage of originality and innovation.

A key characteristic of Indian philosophy is its soteriological focus. Every school has its conception of what *mokṣa* (salvation) is and how to achieve it. A common theme is that the world of appearances is not the world of ultimate reality and we are led astray by our senses. By practices of meditation we can still our minds, silence our senses, attend more carefully and see things as they really are. This is often as much a bodily discipline as an intellectual one: posture and breathing are all-important if we are to get into the right state of mind to see through illusion.

One problem with writing about ultimate truth is that it is beyond not just language but any rational understanding. Language is itself a framing of experience which, like the senses, packages it up into units that we can get a hold of, but in so doing language transforms and distorts it. What we can say, however, is that conventional reality has an appearance of solidity even though it is really impermanent and in flux.

The most important example of this is the self. All schools agree that the conventional self, the way we normally think of ourselves and others, is illusory. That self is merely a stream of experiences, a bundle of perceptions that has no persisting essence. Most orthodox schools believe that our true self is *Brahman*, the one universal self of which we are just part. Buddhists, in contrast, believe that there is no *Brahman* either. Arguably, however, their agreement on the illusory nature of the common-sense self is more distinctive of the Indian tradition than their disagreement about what the truth really is.

Indian philosophy is cosmogonic, meaning that everything is rooted in a conception of how the universe is fundamentally structured. That is why each school offers a holistic vision of reality in which ethics, metaphysics and epistemology combine into an all-encompassing system of explanation. A key feature of almost all cosmologies is a principle of *karma* in which actions, thoughts or both (depending on the school) generate good or bad consequences for the agent, either in this life or in a life to come, since belief in rebirth is also widespread.

The belief in the illusion of the material world and a liberation to come fosters an ethics of detachment. While material prosperity is not always bad in itself and often deemed appropriate at certain times in life, it is never good to place too much importance on wealth or fleeting pleasures. Those who achieve *mokṣa* or *nirvāṇa* move beyond such cares – indeed, beyond all cares or attachments.

Nearly a quarter of the world's population is Muslim. The cultures of majority-Muslim countries, however, vary considerably, with populations found in the Arab world, North Africa, the Indian subcontinent and South East Asia, home to Indonesia, the country with the largest Muslim population in the world. 'Whatever, in a given culture, did not contradict a tenet of Islam was integrated into the religious substrate of that culture,' writes Tariq Ramadan, 'so much so that it has always been extremely difficult to distinguish between religion and culture.'[1] It is therefore difficult to generalise about the influence of classical Islamic philosophy, which was centred in the Middle East and al-Andalus, on the entire Muslim world.

Islamic philosophy has for the most part been impossible to divorce from theology. The idea that the battle between 'philosophy' (*falsafa*) and 'theology' (*kalām*) led to the victory of theology over philosophy understates the extent to which *kalām* has engaged with philosophy and plays down the extent to which those *falāsifa* also had unshakable religious views. It also conflates philosophy in general with the particular revival of ancient Greek thought by the *falāsifa*. It is more accurate to see the debate as one played out within Islamic philosophy about how large a role independent reasoning, *itjihād*, was permitted to play.

Reason has tight limits in Islamic philosophy because of the unity and completeness of Islam. The Qur'ān, being the complete and final revelation of God to humankind has an authority that no secular reason can challenge. Philosophical speculation about the nature of God is limited, for instance, because we can only know of God what God chooses to reveal of himself to us. God's control is such that nothing happens unless he wills it, which results in a strong strand of belief in predestination.

For the devout Muslim, religion impacts on every aspect of life. The notion of secular ethics barely makes sense: morality comes from God. Ethics is inherently religious. Even the self is primarily defined by its relation to God. 'Human selfhood is based upon a dynamic relationship with the Creator, grounded in gratitude and reciprocal love,' as Asma Afsaruddin puts it. To deny this relationship by disbelief is to do an injustice to oneself.[2]

Reading this summary, it would be easy to think that Islamic philosophy is a closed, dogmatic system. At times it has indeed been true that an orthodoxy has taken hold which has shut down any dissent. However, many periods of intellectual diversity and flourishing have demonstrated that there is nothing inevitable about such stasis. The Qur'ān may be the last word of God but it is silent or ambiguous on many things and always requires interpretation. Most obviously, the Qur'ān is said to have been revealed gradually over twenty-three years, the earlier passages being dictated to Muḥammad in Mecca, the later ones in Medina. Many of the Medinan passages in particular appear to offer guidance specific to the situation of the early Muslim community there, meaning that it is a difficult task to know how to apply them in the here and now.[3]

This long tradition of interpretation cautions against taking any statement of what Islamic philosophy must definitively uphold with a pinch of salt. Non-Muslims need to be aware that the tradition has a proven capacity to evolve and accept the fruits of secular knowledge, but that God and the Qur'ān will always be at its heart.

Between them, East Asia, India and the Islamic countries are much more populous than Europe and North America. For several centuries, however, what we call the Western world has for reasons noble and ignoble been the dominant force around the globe. Many believe that this era will soon come to an end. Western Europe and North America together house less than 12 per cent of the world's population. Even adding Central and South America, where European-origin immigrants have dominated the culture, only takes that proportion up to less than 20 per cent. The West, which has become so used to seeing its culture as the default global one, needs not only to understand the rest of the world better but to recognise what makes it distinctive, even unusual.

Western philosophy is essentially truth-seeking and cosmogonic. That is to say, it starts with the assumption that our primary task is to understand the world as it really is. It upholds the 'autonomy of reason', valuing truth and knowledge for their own sake. Reason's autonomy also means it is secular, working without supernatural assistance to deliver us understanding of the world and ourselves. It can do this because the natural world is taken to be scrutable and the way that it operates can be described by laws which require no assumption of divine agency. These assumptions are shared by both major branches of Western philosophy: empiricism, which is based on careful observation of the world, and rationalism, based on reasoning from first principles of logic.

Its primary mode of reasoning is based in logic. Philosophy in this mode is *aporetic*: it identifies contradictions generated by our imperfect understanding and attempts to remove them. It does this by seeking precise definitions and measurements, then proceeding to draw out their implications by sound steps of reasoning. This had led to many achievements, but it is a method which tends to result in adversarial either/or debates. It also focuses attention away from that which is unclear or ambiguous and tends to encourage a tidying up of reality to make the world as amenable to clear explanation as possible. One major manifestation of this approach is the reductionist tendency to understand things by breaking them down to their smallest possible units and to see these, rather than the wholes to which they belong, as the fundamental foci of explanation.

Ethically, this has tended to generate rule- and principle-based ethics which have impartiality as a central value. This has given ethics, like all Western philosophy, an aura of placeless universalism, so much so that the qualifier 'Western' is hardly even used. Philosophy is just philosophy, even though what comes under its umbrella is clearly geographically and historically located in one corner of the globe. Its universalist aspiration has actually made it unwittingly parochial. This has sometimes been exacerbated by a belief in progress which conveniently puts the Western world at its vanguard.

The reductionist tendency, combined with a belief in the autonomy of reason, has generated a conception of free, rational, autonomous selves which is individualistic and atomistic. Individuals are not primarily parts of societies, societies are collections of individuals. This has led to an egalitarian and democratic ethos, but it has also arguably contributed to the fragmentation of society and a decline of respect for legitimate hierarchies of expertise or seniority.

Like all traditions, Western philosophy has its internal variations. One of the least appreciated is how distinctive American philosophy is. Far from being the prime exemplar of Western philosophy, it is if anything an outlier. American pragmatists were less worried about establishing truth than any of the canonical philosophers since Plato and Aristotle. Pragmatism's emphasis on what works gives it a practical orientation that is even more marked than the British empiricism from which it is descended. Its belief that truth is nothing more than what opinion converges on also gives it a democratic colour, legitimising popular beliefs, particularly religious ones, that have stood the test of time.

The world's classical philosophical literatures leave out huge swathes of the globe where the written word has only recently been embraced. Collectively, these are often called 'traditional societies', but of course what is traditional varies from place to place. Nonetheless, attempts to understand the philosophies that have been transmitted orally in such cultures have identified several ways of thinking that, although not universal, are widely shared.

Perhaps the most significant is thinking about place and time. Written philosophy is in many ways a work of abstraction and universalisation, the quest for ideas that hold for all people at all times. Whatever the merits of this, it goes hand in hand with a loss of connection with the specifics of our own local lands and cultures. Oral philosophies, in contrast, see an intimate connection between land and people, so much so that there is no real distinction between them. A vivid recent example of this was when the Whanganui River, New Zealand's third longest, was declared a legal person in March 2017. When the law recognised it as a 'living whole', it was meeting the obligations of the Treaty of Waitangi of 1840 between the British crown and the Māori who had arrived on the islands in the thirteenth century. The declaration recognised the Māori belief in the connection of land and people reflected in the proverb 'I am the river and the river is me.'[4] The land and the sea are the anchors of personal identity, more so than our personal biographies or histories. In this cosmology the linear passage of time is less important than the way in which the cycles of time return us to home.

The connection with land is conceived of as a kind of kinship, which is the relationship of primary importance. Kinship is enjoyed not just with family and tribe but also with place and the natural world. This means that nature is not something other which stands outside human culture. Nature is as much part of our human communities as children, parents, friends and fellow tribe members.

In such cultures, ethics is inherently communitarian. This does not mean that individuality isn't valued; often it very much is. It is rather that individuality is expressed within the group and no one stands outside it. As in East Asia, the self is relational. This tends to lead to a consensual rather than authoritarian or majority-will way of reaching decisions. This works because everyone recognises that ultimately no one can exist outside the group and that therefore compromise is required, and once achieved, everyone has to wholeheartedly embrace it.

The communitarian ethos could even extend to the idea of what makes a philosopher. In oral traditions there are sages who can be either defenders of tradition or challengers of it. But it can also be true that philosophy is shaped collectively by the whole people. A philosopher can be a group, not just an individual thinker.

There is one major part of the world which I have not yet mentioned at all: Russia. This would seem to be a serious lacuna, since Russia is of great geopolitical importance and philosophy is 'the key to the mystery of that country and culture', according to Lesley Chamberlain.[5] It's a gap that is hard to fill, however, as Russian philosophy is an extremely elusive subject, given some rare oxygen in recent years by Chamberlain's own magnificent book on it. In part this is due to the problem of classification. Chamberlain says that when the Russian Nikolai Lossky published his *History of Russian Philosophy* in 1953 the book's main effect was, as Isaiah Berlin put it, to persuade 'the entire anglophone world that Russia had no philosophers, only magi of the steppes'.[6]

The problem of identifying what constitutes Russian philosophy, however, is also an indigenous one, with historical disagreements about what to include under the rubric. It is telling that Isaiah Berlin's famous book is called *Russian Thinkers*, a broader and more inclusive category which avoids the issue of what counts as philosophy. What is generally agreed is that philosophy only really emerged in Russia at the end of the eighteenth century and its main inspirations have been Orthodox Christianity and German idealism.

Russian philosophy has self-consciously stood as a kind of a bridge between Europe and Asia while not belonging to either. 'We have never walked alongside other peoples,' wrote Pyotr Chaadaev in the nineteenth century. 'We don't belong to any of the great families of the human race; we are neither of the West nor the East.'[7] Its scholarly engagement has been primarily with Western texts, if only to reject them. For Chamberlain, this can be summed up in 'its startlingly consistent rejection of Descartes and the value of "I think, I am"'.[8] Descartes's *cogito* gave primacy to the individual as an autonomous, thinking subject. This goes strongly against the Orthodox ideal of *kenosis*, a self-emptying necessary to make oneself ready to receive God. *Kenosis* entails the belief that the individual does not have the resources to reach ultimate truth and that to attempt to do so alone and by reason is hubristic. The self is therefore not to be elevated but chopped down to size. 'One must wholly annihilate one's personal ego,' wrote Mikhail Bakunin, after Johann Gottlieb Fichte, 'annihilate everything that forms its life, its hopes and its personal beliefs.'[9]

The place of rationality in the Cartesian system was taken in Russian philosophy by intuition. Truth is not so much understood as felt. 'Really to know the world we have to simplify ourselves intellectually and revert to a mode of immediate apprehension,' wrote Aleksei Khomiakov. 'By this intuitive knowledge we can distinguish between the real and our mind's fantasy.'[10] Hence philosophy is continuous with literature and poetry. Solzhenitsyn, for example, is a philosopher in his native land but a novelist and historian in the international eyes of reference books like the *Encyclopaedia Britannica*. That is also why poets and artists have been considered so dangerous by Russian rulers. 'Only in Russia is poetry respected,' says Osip Mandelstam. 'It gets people killed.'[11] The same emotionalism that the West saw as a weakness in Russian thinking was seen domestically as a strength.

At the same time the place of the individual was taken by the collective. Russia embraced the myth of the *obshchina*, a peaceful, harmonious peasant community of souls that was wilfully naive so as to avoid the corrupting atheism, competition and individualism that Western rationality had unleashed. Apart from their official godlessness, the communists took this ideal on lock, stock and barrel. Soviet art and propaganda is full of images of happy, defiant peasants and labourers, working together, while Westerners were portrayed as soulless, selfish materialists.

However, the centrality of social harmony seems rooted as much in fear for what Russia could lose as it is in pride for what it sees as its moral superiority. When I met Chamberlain, the first thing she mentioned about Russian philosophy was the striking claim by the contemporary philosopher A. S. Akhiezer that the need to hold society together has been the prime mover of Russian thought. 'The practical pathos of Russian philosophy is directed at preventing the falling away of the part from the whole,' he wrote.[12] This has been a preoccupation of Russian intellectuals for centuries. Hence Russian harmony is not Confucian harmony: it craves uniformity and sees dissent as a threat.

For Chamberlain, the rejection of the self and rationality is a kind of postmodernism *avant la lettre*. It's certainly the case that Russian philosophy seems unconcerned with traditional notions of truth. It is telling that not many dissidents during the communist era were philosophers; indeed, philosophers generally seemed happy to provide intellectual support for the status quo. Even the Russian language helps maintain the elasticity of truth, for which it has two words. *Istina* is natural truth, the truth of the universe, and is immutable. *Pravda*, in contrast, describes the human world and is a human construction. That helps explain why it was not evidently outrageous when in 1931 the Communist Party declared itself the final arbiter of philosophical truth.[13]

A permissive attitude to truth, a rejection of decadent Western values, a sense of national exceptionalism, the prime importance of holding the nation together, the unimportance of the individual compared to the collective destiny: the connections between these ideas and the actions of Russian political leaders of all stripes is plain to see. That makes it all the more disappointing that so little critical attention has been paid to Russian philosophy, at home and abroad. It is a gap I hope others better qualified than me will fill.

A SENSE OF PLACE

It is well known that the literal meaning of the word 'utopia', etymologically speaking, is 'no-place'. This is of much more than passing interest when talking about the utopia of philosophy. The Western tradition I was trained in overtly strives for an objectivity that transcends any particular time or place. Although extreme in this, most traditions claim to be speaking of what is true for humankind, not only for their own nationals.

Should such universal wisdom be the ultimate goal of comparative philosophy? The title of the book *Comparative Philosophy without Borders* seems to suggest this. Its editors, Arindam Chakrabati and Ralph Weber, want to 'throw away the ladder of comparison' and just do 'global combative cooperative critical creative philosophy'.[1]

There are many who share this aspiration. 'I make use of Japanese philosophers but I also make use of Western philosophers,' says John Krummel. 'That's a natural ideal: we're all philosophers doing philosophy.' His colleague Leah Kalmanson hopes that if philosophers around the world genuinely work together it will lead us out of our local silos. There would be something a little insincere about working together, all the while intending to remain in our niches, as if we believed we could learn from each other, but only up to a point.

There are those who are suspicious of the very possibility of a truly universal philosophy, because they believe it is hubris to think we can detach ourselves from the particularities of time and place. One weakness of Western philosophy is often said to be that it has what Owen Flanagan calls a 'transcendentally pretentious' goal of 'identifying what is really good or right independently of history and culture'.[2] Any philosophy which aspires to objectivity is caught in a perennial tension: the attempt to transcend the par-ticularities of the individual thinker and their time and place can only be made by specific individuals in specific times and places. We have to give up the idea of the view from nowhere and accept that a view is always from somewhere.

That, however, does not condemn us to parochial subjectivism. By becoming philosophical explorers, we can build a more com-plete picture of the world and a more objective understanding of it by taking *multiple* perspectives. The metaphor of views helps here. Rather than trying to create a comprehensive, single map, we can view a terrain from various places: from within it, from the sky, from a distance and so on. Rather than a view from nowhere, we seek views from everywhere, or at least everywhere that is accessible.

There are three ways in which taking multiple perspectives can give us a better understanding. The first is when different per-spectives combine to give us more information than any one could provide alone. 'Moral traditions inevitably involve selective vision and sensitivity,' warns Joel Kupperman, so 'we should worry about the possibility that we do not see, or are insensitive to something that is important'.[3]

Consider the parable of the blind men and the elephant, which is found in various forms in Indian philosophy, one of the earliest being in the *Udāna*, part of the Buddhist Pali canon. Those who felt the elephant's ear proclaimed the beast to be 'just like a winnowing basket', those who felt the tusk said it was 'just like plowshare', those who touched the trunk concluded it was 'just like the pole of a plow', those who had been shown the tuft at the end of the elephant's tail said it was 'just like a broom' and so on.[4] Each has one aspect of the truth but it requires bringing all their perspectives together to see the whole truth. The Jains use the parable to illustrate their doctrine of *anekāntavāda*, which asserts that ultimate truth always has a multidimensional character. We don't need to go the whole way with Jainism to accept that different philosophical traditions of the world may each have stumbled upon parts of the truth but none have discovered all of it. The most complete picture we can form is therefore like a cubist painting, which combines perspectives that could not all be seen from one point of view on the same canvas. Call this the *cubist perspective*.

The second way multiple perspectives can be illuminating is when they reveal that there is in fact more than one issue at stake. I think this is the best way to think about the question of what it means to be a person or a self. It is easy to think there is a single question here. In fact, it disguises myriad questions, such as: What is the self made of? Is the self permanent? How do relations to others fashion the self? What gives us our sense of identity? In different traditions 'the problem' of the self is likely to involve only one or some of these questions and others are set aside. Seeing multiple perspectives allows us to achieve a more objective understanding by 'disaggregating' problems, breaking down apparently simple questions into their more complex parts. Call this the *disaggregating perspective*.

A third benefit of taking multiple perspectives is when we realise that there is more than one legitimate way of either understanding the world or constructing norms. We see this pluralism most clearly when it comes to visions of the good life, personally and politically. Values of autonomy, harmony, community and individuality all have a legitimacy, but there is no way to live that allows us to maximise all of them. There is more than one way for humans to flourish and trade-offs are inevitable. Sometimes we can borrow a value and it can flourish in our native soil, just as the Japanese privet has thrived in Britain. Sometimes, however, values struggle outside their native environments, just as you can't grow coffee or cocoa in England. This is the *pluralist perspective*.

To accept that there are many different possible values and combinations of values is not to say that anything goes. As Isaiah Berlin argued, pluralism is not relativism.[5] It is rather a matter of objective truth that people differ and circumstances vary according to time and place. The social world is not an abstract given, the same for everyone regardless of time or place. From this it follows that no concepts concerning the social world can be taken as given either, which means that morality and politics must adjust to circumstances.

The taxonomy of cubist, disaggregating and pluralist perspectives is intended to be suggestive rather than definitive. It points to the main ways in which looking at philosophy from a variety of global perspectives need not lead us to give up our quest for a more objective understanding but could enrich our understanding of what objectivity itself is. The cubist perspective enables us to see the whole, single picture better by taking a variety of views of it. The disaggregating perspective enables us to see that what we first assumed was a single issue is in fact made up of several distinct ones. The pluralist perspective enables us to see that, when it comes to ethics and politics, no one master value or set of values can fit every time and place.

Inattention to the peculiarities of a philosophy's own place and to philosophy in other places confuses the admirable aspiration for greater objectivity with a misguided ideal of placeless universality. Ideas are neither tightly tethered to specific cultures nor free-floating, universal and placeless. Like people, they are formed by a culture but can travel. If we truly aspire to a more objective understanding of the world, we have to make use of the advantages to be gained by occupying different intellectual places. Doing so with reverence but not deference to the past and present of other cultures could help us transform our own philosophical landscapes.

NOTES

Introduction

1 Maurice Merleau-Ponty, *Phenomenology of Perception*, trans. Colin Smith (Routledge, 2002 [1945]), p. 459. Thanks to Yves Vende for the pointer.
2 This possibly apocryphal quote is cited in Alasdair MacIntyre, *A Short History of Ethics* (Routledge, 1976), p. 182.
3 Jonathan Israel, *A Revolution of the Mind* (Princeton University Press, 2010), p. 224.
4 Ibid., p. 37.
5 Thomas P. Kasulis, *Intimacy or Integrity: Philosophy and Cultural Difference* (University of Hawai'i Press, 2002), p. 17.
6 Xu Zhiyuan, *Paper Tiger: Inside the Real China* (Head of Zeus, 2015), p. 146.
7 Kasulis, *Intimacy or Integrity*, p. 140.
8 Ibid., p. 17.
9 See Robert E. Carter, *The Kyoto School: An Introduction* (SUNY Press, 2013), p. xi.
10 Xu, *Paper Tiger*, p. xi.

Prologue:
A historical overview from the Axial to the Information Age

1 See Karl Jaspers, *The Origin and Goal of History*, trans. Michael Bullock (Routledge & Kegan Paul, 1953 [1949]).
2 See Julian Baggini, *The Edge of Reason* (Yale University Press, 2016).

3 Sarvepalli Radhakrishnan and Charles A. Moore (eds.), *A Sourcebook in Indian Philosophy* (Princeton University Press, 1957), p. xviii.

4 Ibid.

5 Plato, *The Republic*, trans. Robin Waterfield (Oxford University Press, 1994), p. 90.

6 Joel Kupperman, *Learning from Asian Philosophy* (Oxford University Press, 1999), p. 157.

7 Ibid., p. 350.

8 See 'Women in Philosophy in the UK: A Report by the British Philosophical Association and the Society for Women in Philosophy UK' (2011), www.bpa.ac.uk/uploads/2011/02/BPA_Report_Women_In_Philosophy.pdf, and Eric Schwitzgebel and Carolyn Dicey Jennings, 'Women in Philosophy: Quantitative Analyses of Specialization, Prevalence, Visibility, and Generational Change', *Public Affairs Quarterly*, 31 (2017), pp. 83–105.

9 Thomas P. Kasulis, *Intimacy or Integrity: Philosophy and Cultural Difference* (University of Hawai'i Press, 2002), p. 18.

10 Richard Rorty, 'Philosophy as a Kind of Writing', in *Consequences of Pragmatism: Essays 1972–1980* (University of Minnesota Press, 1982), p. 92.

11 Kwame Anthony Appiah, *In My Father's House: Africa in the Philosophy of Culture* (Oxford University Press, 1993), pp. 26, 91.

12 Mogobe B. Ramose, 'The Philosophy of *Ubuntu* and *Ubuntu* as a Philosophy', in P. H. Coetzee and A. P. J. Roux (eds.), *The African Philosophy Reader*, 2nd edn (Routledge, 2003), p. 230.

13 'Generalisation is a necessary part of organisation. A generalisation is not the same as a universal qualifier: a generalisation cannot be refuted by a simple counterexample', Kasulis, *Intimacy or Integrity*, p. 8.

14 Ibid., p. 20.

15 Ibid., pp. 154–6.

16 See Carmel S. Saad, Rodica Damian, Verónica Benet-Martínez, Wesley G. Moons and Richard R. Robins, 'Multiculturalism and Creativity: Effects of Cultural Context, Bicultural Identity, and Ideational Fluency', *Social Psychological and Personality Science*, 4 (2013), pp. 369–75.

1 Insight

1 James Mill, *The History of British India*, 3rd edn (Baldwin, Cradock and Joy, 1826), Vol. 1, Book I, Chapter 1, p. 3, and Book II, Chapter 6, p. 286.

2 Immanuel Kant, 'Physical Geography', in Emmanuel Chukwudi Eze (ed.), *Race and the Enlightenment: A Reader* (Wiley-Blackwell, 1997), p. 63.

3 David Hume, 'Of National Characters' (1753).

4 Sarvepalli Radhakrishnan and Charles A. Moore (eds.), *A Sourcebook in Indian Philosophy* (Princeton University Press, 1957), p. xxv.

5 Sue Hamilton, *Indian Philosophy: A Very Short Introduction* (Oxford University Press, 2001), p. 9.

6 Ibid., p. 69, and (*sākṣāt-kāra*) Dhirendra Mohan Datta, 'Epistemological Methods in Indian Philosophy', in Charles A. Moore (ed.), *The Indian Mind* (University of Hawai'i Press, 1967), p. 124.

7 Radhakrishnan and Moore (eds.), *A Sourcebook in Indian Philosophy*, p. 356.

8 *Katha Upaniṣad*, II.23, III.12, ibid., pp. 46–7.

9 *Muṇḍaka Upaniṣad*, III.8, ibid., p. 54.

10 Ibid., pp. 353–4.

11 Ibid., p. 355.

12 S. K. Saksena, 'Relation of Philosophical Theories to the Practical Affairs of Men', in Moore (ed.), *The Indian Mind*, pp. 13–14.

13 *Nyāya Sūtra*, 7, in Radhakrishnan and Moore (eds.), *A Sourcebook in Indian Philosophy*, p. 359.

14 Deepak Sarma (ed.), *Classical Indian Philosophy: A Reader* (Columbia University Press, 2011), p. 141.

15 Chakravarthi Ram-Prasad, *Eastern Philosophy* (Weidenfeld & Nicolson, 2005), p. 140.

16 *The Vedānta Sūtras with commentary by Śaṅkarākārya*, II.i.5, in Radhakrishnan and Moore (eds.), *A Sourcebook in Indian Philosophy*, p. 524.

17 Ibid., p. 37.

18 *The Laws of Manu*, II.201, ibid., p. 178.

19 *Vaiśeṣika Sūtra*, IX.2.13, ibid., p. 397.

20 Uddyotakara's *Nyāya-Vārttika*, in Sarma (ed.), *Classical Indian Philosophy*, p. 136.

21 Haribhadra, *Ṣaḍdarśana-samuccaya*, ibid., p. 3.

22 The *Sarvadarśanasaṁgraha*, in Radhakrishnan and Moore (eds.), *A Sourcebook in Indian Philosophy*, p. 234.

23 *The Vedānta Sūtras with commentary by Śaṅkarākārya*, II.i.5, ibid., p. 522.

24 *Yoga Sūtra*, 4.1, in Sarma (ed.), *Classical Indian Philosophy*, p. 192.

25 *Vaiśeṣika Sūtra*, IX.2.13, in Radhakrishnan and Moore (eds.), *A Sourcebook in Indian Philosophy*, p. 397.

26 *Chāndogya Upaniṣad*, VII.vi.1, in ibid., p. 70.

27 Sue Hamilton, *Indian Philosophy: A Very Short Introduction* (Oxford University Press, 2001), p. 10.

28 *Yoga Sūtra*, 1.1–2, in Sarma (ed.), *Classical Indian Philosophy*, p. 180.

29 Hamilton, *Indian Philosophy*, p. 107.

30 *Kauṣītaki Upaniṣads*, VI.18, in Radhakrishnan and Moore (eds.), *A Sourcebook in Indian Philosophy*, p. 96.

31 *Bhagavad Gītā*, 6.11–16, ibid., p. 124.

32 *Yoga Sūtra*, 3.23–28, 30, 41, in Sarma (ed.), *Classical Indian Philosophy*, pp. 189–90.

33 C. D. Sebastian, '*Ajñāna*: Retrospectives and Prospects from G. R. Malkani, Rasvihary Das and T. R. V. Murti', paper given at the 90th Session of the Indian Philosophical Congress, Magadh University, Bodh Gaya, 1–4 February 2016.

34 L. N. Sharma, 'The Indian Quest', Presidential Address at the 90th Session of the Indian Philosophical Congress, Magadh University, Bodh Gaya, 1–4 February 2016.

35 Sarvepalli Radhakrishnan, 'The Indian Approach to the Religious Problem', in Moore (ed.), *The Indian Mind*, p. 177.

36 Charles A. Moore, Introduction, ibid., p. 8.

37 Sarvepalli Radhakrishnan and Charles A. Moore, ibid., p. 351.

38 Ibid., p. 506.

39 *The Vedānta Sūtras with commentary by Śaṅkarākārya*, II.i.5, ibid., pp. 512–13.

40 Ibid., p. 516.

41 Aristotle, *Nicomachean Ethics*, 1143b11–14, trans. J. A. K. Thomson (Penguin, 1996), p. 220.

42 Owen Flanagan, *The Geography of Morals* (Oxford University Press, 2017), p. 254.

43 René Descartes, *Meditations on First Philosophy*, 2nd Meditation, Section 25, trans. John Cottingham (Cambridge University Press, 1986 [1641]), p. 17.

44 Robert E. Carter, *The Kyoto School: An Introduction* (SUNY Press, 2013), p. 7.

45 Ibid., p. 32.

46 Nishida Kitarō, 'Pure Experience', in James W. Heisig, Thomas P. Kasulis and John C. Maraldo (eds.), *Japanese Philosophy: A Sourcebook* (University of Hawai'i Press, 2011), pp. 647–8.

47 Carter, *The Kyoto School*, p. 27.

48 Ibid., p. 23.

49 Quoted by Takeuchi Yoshinori, 'The Philosophy of Nishida', *Japanese Religions*, III:4 (1963), pp. 1–32, reprinted in Frederick Franck (ed.), *The Buddha Eye: An Anthology of the Kyoto School and Its Contemporaries* (World Wisdom, 2004), p. 190.

50 Hakuin Ekaku, 'Meditation', in Heisig, Kasulis and Maraldo (eds.), *Japanese Philosophy*, p. 209.

51 D. T. Suzuki, 'What Is the "I"?', *Eastern Buddhist*, IV:1 (1971), pp. 13–27, reprinted in Franck (ed.), *The Buddha Eye*, p. 25.

52 Edward Slingerland, *Trying Not to Try* (Canongate, 2014), p. 153.

53 D. T. Suzuki, 'Self the Unattainable', *Eastern Buddhist*, III:2 (1970), pp. 1–8, reprinted in Franck (ed.), *The Buddha Eye*, p. 7.

54 Suzuki, 'What Is the "I"?', reprinted ibid., pp. 31–2.

55 Carter, *The Kyoto School*, p. 31.

56 See ibid., p. 28.

57 Tanabe Hajime, 'Philosophy as Metanoetics', in Heisig, Kasulis and Maraldo (eds.), *Japanese Philosophy*, p. 689.

58 See Carter, *The Kyoto School*, pp. 67ff.
59 Thomas P. Kasulis in Heisig, Kasulis and Maraldo (eds.), *Japanese Philosophy*, pp. 135–6.

2 The ineffable

1 *Daodejing*, 1.41, in Philip J. Ivanhoe and Bryan W. Van Norden (eds.), *Readings in Classical Chinese Philosophy*, 2nd edn (Hackett, 2005), p. 183.
2 Ibid., 1.71, p. 198.
3 Ibid., 1.38, p. 181.
4 Robin R. Wang, *Yinyang: The Way of Heaven and Earth in Chinese Thought and Culture* (Cambridge University Press, 2012), p. 48.
5 *Daodejing*, 25, in Ivanhoe and Van Norden (eds.), *Readings in Classical Chinese Philosophy*, p. 175.
6 Ibid., 1.56, p. 190.
7 Joel Kupperman, *Learning from Asian Philosophy* (Oxford University Press, 1999), p. 183.
8 *Zhuangzi*, 26, in Ivanhoe and Van Norden (eds.), *Readings in Classical Chinese Philosophy*, p. 250.
9 Ibid., 13, p. 245.
10 *Analects*, XVII.ix.3, in James Legge, *The Chinese Classics*, Vol. 1 (Clarendon Press, 1893), p. 326.
11 Chakravarthi Ram-Prasad, *Eastern Philosophy* (Weidenfeld & Nicolson, 2005), p. 146.
12 Kamo No Mabuchi, 'The Meaning of Our Country', in James W. Heisig, Thomas P. Kasulis and John C. Maraldo (eds.), *Japanese Philosophy: A Sourcebook* (University of Hawai'i Press, 2011), p. 468.
13 Fujitani Mitsue, 'On *Kotodama*', ibid., p. 501.
14 Ibid., p. 160.
15 Nāgārjuna's *Vigrahavyāvartanī*, Part 2.29, in Deepak Sarma (ed.), *Classical Indian Philosophy: A Reader* (Columbia University Press, 2011), p. 44.
16 *Shurangama Sūtra*, 2, www.fodian.net/world/shurangama.html.
17 Shidō Bunan, 'This Very Mind Is Buddha', in Heisig, Kasulis and Maraldo (eds.), *Japanese Philosophy*, p. 191.
18 D. T. Suzuki, 'Self the Unattainable', *Eastern Buddhist*, III:2 (1970), pp. 1–8, reprinted in Frederick Franck (ed.), *The Buddha Eye: An Anthology of the Kyoto School and Its Contemporaries*, pp. 6–7.
19 Robert E. Carter, *The Kyoto School: An Introduction* (SUNY Press, 2013), p. 19.
20 Suzuki, 'Self the Unattainable', reprinted in Franck (ed.), *The Buddha Eye*, pp. 3–4.
21 Musō Soseki, 'Dialogues in a Dream', in Heisig, Kasulis and Maraldo (eds.), *Japanese Philosophy*, p. 171.

22 Quoted in Barney Jopson, 'A Pilgrim's Progress', *FT Magazine* Japan supplement, 10–11 September 2016, pp. 16–21.

23 *Kena Upaniṣad*, I.1–3, in Sarvepalli Radhakrishnan and Charles A. Moore (eds.), *A Sourcebook in Indian Philosophy* (Princeton University Press, 1957), p. 42.

24 *Bṛhadāraṇyaka Upaniṣad*, III.iv, ibid., p. 84.

25 *Maitri Upaniṣad*, VI.17, ibid., p. 95.

26 *Taittirīya Upaniṣad*, II.8, ibid., p. 60.

27 Ram-Prasad, *Eastern Philosophy*, pp. 168–9.

28 Rabindranath Tagore, 'Fireflies' (177), at www.tagoreweb.in.

29 See Emilie Reas, 'Small Animals Live in a Slow-Motion World', *Scientific American*, 1 July 2014.

30 The Encyclopedia of Diderot & d'Alembert: Collaborative Translation Project, hosted by Michigan Publishing, https://quod.lib.umich.edu/d/did/, d'Alembert, 'Preliminary Discourse', https://goo.gl/LmG5Qa.

3 Theology or philosophy?

1 John Locke, 'A Letter Concerning Toleration' (1689), www.constitution.org/jl/tolerati.htm.

2 Omar Saif Ghobash, *Letter to a Young Muslim* (Picador, 2017), p. 168.

3 Peter Adamson, *Philosophy in the Islamic World: A Very Short Introduction* (Oxford University Press, 2015), p. 31.

4 Al-Ghazālī, *The Incoherence of the Philosophers*, 'The First Discussion', in Jon McGinnis and David C. Reisman (eds.), *Classical Arabic Philosophy: An Anthology of Sources* (Hackett, 2007), p. 241.

5 Al-Kindī, 'The Explanation of the Proximate Efficient Cause for Generation and Corruption', ibid., p. 1.

6 Al-Kindī, 'On Divine Unity and the Finitude of the World's Body', ibid., p. 22.

7 Qur'ān, 59:2.

8 Ibn Rushd, *The Decisive Treatise*, Chapter 1, in McGinnis and Reisman (eds.), *Classical Arabic Philosophy*, p. 309.

9 Ibid., p. 312.

10 Ibid., Chapter 2, pp. 318–19.

11 Ibid., Chapter 3, p. 323.

12 Christopher de Bellaigue, *The Islamic Enlightenment* (The Bodley Head, 2017), p. xxiii.

13 Ibid., p. 25.

14 Robert E. Carter, *The Kyoto School: An Introduction* (SUNY Press, 2013), p. 6.

15 Tanabe Hajime, 'The Philosophy of Dōgen', in James W. Heisig, Thomas P. Kasulis and John C. Maraldo (eds.), *Japanese Philosophy: A Sourcebook* (University of Hawai'i Press, 2011), p. 684.

16 Takeuchi Yoshinori, 'Buddhist Existentialism', ibid., p. 745.

17 Carter, *The Kyoto School*, p. 6.

18 Takeuchi, 'Buddhist Existentialism', in Heisig, Kasulis and Maraldo (eds.), *Japanese Philosophy*, p. 746.

19 Carter, *The Kyoto School*, p. 8.

4 Logic

1 The Encyclopedia of Diderot & d'Alembert: Collaborative Translation Project, hosted by Michigan Publishing, https://quod.lib.umich.edu/d/did/, Diderot, 'Encyclopédie', https://goo.gl/cJxiiy.

2 Ibid., d'Alembert, 'Preliminary Discourse', https://goo.gl/nTPjgv.

3 Ibid., Diderot, 'Encyclopédie', https://goo.gl/cJxiiy.

4 Thomas P. Kasulis, *Intimacy or Integrity: Philosophy and Cultural Difference* (University of Hawai'i Press, 2002), p. 148.

5 G. W. Leibniz, *New Essays on Human Understanding*, Book 4, Chapter 2, Section 1 (362), trans. and ed. Peter Remnant and Jonathan Bennett (Cambridge University Press, 1996 [1704]).

6 Aristotle, *Metaphysics*, Book 4, Part 4, trans. W. D. Ross (Dover Publications, 2018), p. 49.

7 *Daodejing*, 42, in Philip J. Ivanhoe and Bryan W. Van Norden (eds.), *Readings in Classical Chinese Philosophy*, 2nd edn (Hackett, 2005), p.184.

8 Chakravarthi Ram-Prasad, *Eastern Philosophy* (Weidenfeld & Nicolson, 2005), p. 213.

9 Gongsun Longzi, 'On the White Horse', in Ivanhoe and Van Norden (eds.), *Readings in Classical Chinese Philosophy*, p. 365.

10 Ram-Prasad, *Eastern Philosophy*, p. 228.

11 Nicholas Rescher, *Philosophical Reasoning: A Study in the Methodology of Philosophising* (Blackwell, 2001), p. 93.

12 *Nyāyakusumāñjali*, Chapter 3, Section 8, cited in Bimal Krishna Matilal, *Nyāya-Vaiśeṣika*, Vol. 6, Fasc. 2, of Jan Gonda (ed.), *A History of Indian Literature* (Otto Harrassowitz, 1977), p. 97.

13 Gautama, *Nayāya sūtra*, 1.2.42, in Deepak Sarma (ed.), *Classical Indian Philosophy: A Reader* (Columbia University Press, 2011), p. 104.

14 Ibid., 1.2.43, p. 105.

15 Ibid., 1.2.44, p. 105.

16 Ibid., 1.2.43, p. 105.

17 Ibid., 1.1.32, p. 101.

18 Mādhavācarya, *Sarvadarśana-saṃgraha*, in Sarma (ed.), *Classical Indian Philosophy*, 2011, p. 7.

19 Ram-Prasad, *Eastern Philosophy*, p. 216.

20 Gautama, *Nayāya sūtra*, 1.2.129, in Sarma (ed.), *Classical Indian Philosophy*, p. 123.

21 Ibid., 1.2.51, 53, 55, p. 107.
22 Nāgārjuna, *Vigrahavyāvartanī*, Part 2 (32), in Sarma (ed.), *Classical Indian Philosophy*, p. 45.
23 Gautama, *Nayāya sūtra*, 1.2.118–19, ibid., p. 121.
24 Ram-Prasad, *Eastern Philosophy*, p. 212.
25 *Hitopadeśa*, Introduction. A more literal translation is in Friedrich Max Müller, *The First Book of the Hitopadeśa* (Longman, Green, Longman, Roberts, and Green, 1864), pp. 6–7.

5 Secular reason

1 Stephen Hawking, *A Brief History of Time* (Bantam, 1998), p. 175.
2 Christopher de Bellaigue, *The Islamic Enlightenment* (The Bodley Head, 2017), p. xxxiii.
3 Baruch Spinoza, *Ethics*, Part 1, Axiom 3 and Proposition 8, in *The Ethics and Selected Letters*, trans. Samuel Shirley (Hackett, 1982 [1677]), pp. 32, 34.
4 René Descartes, *Meditations on First Philosophy*, 3rd Meditation, Section 40, trans. John Cottingham (Cambridge University Press, 1986 [1641]), p. 28.
5 David Hume, *An Enquiry Concerning Human Understanding* (1748), Section VII, Part I.
6 *Mozi*, 35, in Philip J. Ivanhoe and Bryan W. Van Norden (eds.), *Readings in Classical Chinese Philosophy*, 2nd edn (Hackett, 2005), p.111.
7 Henri Poincaré, quoted in 'The French University Conflict', *The Nation*, 97 (11 September 1913), p. 231.
8 Seyyed Hossein Nasr, *Islam in the Modern World* (HarperOne, 2012), pp. 191–2.
9 William Jennings Bryan, *Bryan's Last Speech* (Sunlight Publishing Society, 1925).
10 Winston Churchill, speech to the Royal College of Physicians, 10 July 1951.
11 Fritjof Capra, *The Turning Point* (Bantam, 1983), p. 87.
12 Arthur C. Clarke, *Voices from the Sky: Previews of the Coming Space Age* (Pyramid Books, 1967), p. 156.

6 Pragmatism

1 WIN/Gallup International End of Year Survey 2016, www.wingia.com/web/files/news/370/file/370.pdf.
2 William James, 'Philosophical Conceptions and Practical Results', in Robert B. Talisse and Scott F. Aikin (eds.), *The Pragmatism Reader: From Peirce through the Present* (Princeton University Press, 2011), p. 76.
3 Charles Sanders Peirce, *The Collected Papers of Charles Sanders Peirce: Volumes V and VI*, ed. Charles Hartshorne and Paul Weiss (Harvard University Press, 1931–58), p. 293.

4 John Dewey, 'The Need for a Recovery of Philosophy', in Talisse and Aikin (eds.), *The Pragmatism Reader*, p. 129.

5 Ibid., p. 132.

6 William James, 'Pragmatism's Conception of Truth', in Talisse and Aikin (eds.), *The Pragmatism Reader*, p. 80.

7 Charles Sanders Peirce, 'How to Make Our Ideas Clear', ibid., pp. 55–6.

8 James, 'Philosophical Conceptions and Practical Results', ibid., p. 66.

9 John Dewey, 'The Influence of Darwinism on Philosophy', ibid., p. 148.

10 James, 'Philosophical Conceptions and Practical Results', ibid., p. 78.

11 Peirce, 'How to Make Our Ideas Clear', ibid., p. 61.

12 Dewey, 'The Need for a Recovery of Philosophy', ibid., p. 138.

13 Charles Sanders Peirce, 'Some Consequences of Four Incapacities', ibid., p. 12.

14 Dewey, 'The Influence of Darwinism on Philosophy', ibid., p. 148.

15 Robert E. Carter, *The Kyoto School: An Introduction* (SUNY Press, 2013), pp. 18–19.

16 Dewey, 'The Need for a Recovery of Philosophy', in Talisse and Aikin (eds.), *The Pragmatism Reader* (Princeton University Press, 2011), p. 132.

17 Peirce, 'How to Make Our Ideas Clear', ibid., p. 63.

18 Peirce, 'Some Consequences of Four Incapacities', ibid., p. 13.

19 Richard Rorty, 'Solidarity or Objectivity?', ibid., p. 369.

20 James, 'Pragmatism's Conception of Truth', ibid., p. 87.

21 Rorty, 'Solidarity or Objectivity?', ibid., p. 370.

22 Peirce, 'How to Make Our Ideas Clear', ibid., p. 65.

23 Rorty, 'Solidarity or Objectivity?', ibid., p. 370.

24 James, 'Pragmatism's Conception of Truth', ibid., p. 81.

25 Dewey, 'The Need for a Recovery of Philosophy', ibid., p. 136.

26 James, 'Pragmatism's Conception of Truth', ibid., p. 80.

27 Peirce, 'Some Consequences of Four Incapacities', ibid., p. 13.

28 Carlin Romano, *America the Philosophical* (Vintage, 2013), p. 65.

29 James, 'Philosophical Conceptions and Practical Results', Talisse and Aikin (eds.), *The Pragmatism Reader*, p. 74.

30 William James, 'Will to Believe', ibid., pp. 104–5.

31 Rorty, 'Solidarity or Objectivity?', ibid., p. 373.

7 Tradition

1 Charles A. Moore, 'Introduction: The Humanistic Chinese Mind', in Charles A. Moore (ed.), *The Chinese Mind* (University of Hawai'i Press, 1967), p. 3.

2 *Analects*, VII.ii, in James Legge, *The Chinese Classics*, Vol. 1 (Clarendon Press, 1893), p. 195.

3 Chan Wing-Tsit, 'Syntheses in Chinese Metaphysics', in Moore (ed.), *The Chinese Mind*, p. 144.

4 Chan Wing-Tsit, 'Chinese Theory and Practice, with Special Reference to Humanism', ibid., p. 12.

5 John C. H. Wu, 'Chinese Legal and Political Philosophy', ibid., p. 233.

6 Shimomura Toratarō, 'The Logic of Absolute Nothingness', in James W. Heisig, Thomas P. Kasulis and John C. Maraldo (eds.), *Japanese Philosophy: A Sourcebook* (University of Hawai'i Press, 2011), p. 734.

7 Both cited in Mogobe B. Ramose, 'The Struggle for Reason in Africa', in P. H. Coetzee and A. P. J. Roux (eds.), *The African Philosophy Reader*, 2nd edn (Routledge, 2003), pp. 13–14. See also Walter J. Ong, *Orality and Literacy* (Routledge, 1982).

8 Ibid., p. 6.

9 Moya Deacon, 'The Status of Father Tempels and Ethnophilosophy in the Discourse of African Philosophy', in Coetzee and Roux (eds.), *The African Philosophy Reader*, p. 98.

10 Placide Tempels, *Bantu Philosophy* (Presence Africaine, 1959), p. 36.

11 Quoted in Deacon, 'The Status of Father Tempels and Ethnophilosophy in the Discourse of African Philosophy', in Coetzee and Roux (eds.), *The African Philosophy Reader*, p. 108.

12 H. Odera Oruka, *Sage Philosophy: Indigenous Thinkers and Modern Debate on African Philosophy* (African Center for Technological Studies, 1991), p. 150.

8 Conclusion to Part One

1 *Cūla-Māluṅkya Sutta*, MN 63, quoted in Rupert Gethin, *Sayings of the Buddha: New Translations from the Pali Nikayas* (Oxford World's Classics, 2008), p. 172.

2 Chenyang Li, *The Confucian Philosophy of Harmony* (Routledge, 2014), pp. 20–21.

3 Robin R. Wang, *Yinyang: The Way of Heaven and Earth in Chinese Thought and Culture* (Cambridge University Press, 2012), pp. 120, 123.

4 Ibid., p. 125.

5 Owen Flanagan, *The Geography of Morals* (Oxford University Press, 2017), p. 12.

6 Edward Slingerland, *Trying Not to Try* (Canongate, 2014), p. 214.

7 Chakravarthi Ram-Prasad, *Eastern Philosophy* (Weidenfeld & Nicolson, 2005), p. 145.

8 Ibid., p. 153.

9 Charles A. Moore, 'Introduction: The Comprehensive Indian Mind', in Charles A. Moore (ed.), *The Indian Mind* (University of Hawai'i Press, 1967), p. 1.

10 Chakravarthi Ram-Prasad, *Eastern Philosophy* (Weidenfeld & Nicolson, 2005), p. 179.

9 Time

1 Book of Revelation 22:13 (King James Version).
2 Sarvepalli Radhakrishnan and Charles A. Moore (eds.), *A Sourcebook in Indian Philosophy* (Princeton University Press, 1957), p. 354.
3 *Ṛg Veda*, I.185, ibid., p. 11.
4 *Zhuangzi*, 18, in Philip J. Ivanhoe and Bryan W. Van Norden (eds.), *Readings in Classical Chinese Philosophy*, 2nd edn (Hackett, 2005), p. 247.
5 James Legge, *The Chinese Classics*, Vol. 1 (Clarendon Press, 1893), p. 95.
6 *Mencius*, Book 4, Part 1, Chapter 1.2, in Legge, *The Chinese Classics*, Vol. 2 (Clarendon Press, 1895), p. 289.
7 Ibid., Book 7, Part 2, Chapter 37.13, p. 501.
8 Seyyed Hossein Nasr, *Islam in the Modern World* (HarperOne, 2012), p. 120.
9 See David Maybury-Lewis, *Millennium* (Viking, 1992).
10 Stephen Muecke, *Ancient & Modern: Time, Culture and Indigenous Philosophy* (UNSW Press, 2004), p. 2, and see p. 15.
11 Ibid., p. 118.
12 Ibid., p. 174.
13 Ibid., p. 172.
14 Ibid., p. 63.
15 Ibid., p. 104.
16 David Goodhart, *The Road to Somewhere* (C. Hurst & Co., 2017), p. 36.
17 Kwame Anthony Appiah, *In My Father's House: Africa in the Philosophy of Culture* (Oxford University Press, 1993), p. 58.
18 Jay L. Garfield and Bryan W. Van Norden, 'If Philosophy Won't Diversify, Let's Call It What It Really Is', *The Stone*, 11 May 2016, www.nytimes.com/2016/05/11/opinion/if-philosophy-wont-diversify-lets-call-it-what-it-really-is.html.
19 A point made by Thomas P. Kasulis, *Intimacy or Integrity: Philosophy and Cultural Difference* (University of Hawai'i Press, 2002), pp. 7, 16.
20 Cited in Appiah, *In My Father's House*, p. 58.
21 Gandhi, *Young India*, 1 June 1921, p. 170.
22 Anthony Kenny, *The Enlightenment: A Very Brief History* (SPCK Publishing, 2017), pp. 125–6.
23 John Gray, *Gray's Anatomy* (Allen Lane, 2009), pp. 298–9.
24 Jonathan Israel, *A Revolution of the Mind* (Princeton University Press, 2010), p. 3.
25 In the introduction to the 1874 edition of *The Gilded Age: A Tale of Today*, which he co-wrote with his neighbour Charles Dudley Warner.

10 *Karma*

1 Sue Hamilton, *Indian Philosophy: A Very Short Introduction* (Oxford University Press, 2001), p. 11.
2 Ibid., p. 12.
3 Deepak Sarma (ed.), *Classical Indian Philosophy: A Reader* (Columbia University Press, 2011), p. 51.
4 *Dhammapada*, I.1, in Sarvepalli Radhakrishnan and Charles A. Moore (eds.), *A Sourcebook in Indian Philosophy* (Princeton University Press, 1957), p. 292.
5 *The Laws of Manu*, XII.9, ibid., p. 173.
6 Galatians 6:7 (King James Version).
7 *Mozi*, 26, in Philip J. Ivanhoe and Bryan W. Van Norden (eds.), *Readings in Classical Chinese Philosophy*, 2nd edn (Hackett, 2005), p. 92.
8 S. K. Saksena, 'Relation of Philosophical Theories to the Practical Affairs of Men', in Charles A. Moore (ed.), *The Indian Mind* (University of Hawai'i Press, 1967), p. 38.
9 *The Laws of Manu*, X.1–4, in Radhakrishnan and Moore (eds.), *A Sourcebook in Indian Philosophy*, p. 176.
10 Ibid., VIII, p. 177.
11 *The Laws of Manu*, II.168, www.sacred-texts.com/hin/manu/manu02.htm.
12 Ibid., X.65, www.sacred-texts.com/hin/manu/manu10.htm.
13 Analabha Basu, Neeta Sarkar-Roy and Partha P. Majumder, 'Genomic Reconstruction of the History of Extant Populations of India Reveals Five Distinct Ancestral Components and a Complex Structure', *Proceedings of the National Academy of Sciences*, 113:6 (9 February 2016), pp. 1594–9, reported in Subodh Varma and Sharon Fernandes, '70 Generations Ago, Caste Stopped People Inter-mixing', *Times of India*, 5 February 2016.
14 See Somini Sengupta, *The End of Karma: Hope and Fury Among India's Young* (Norton, 2016).

11 Emptiness

1 'Enduring Power', *The Economist*, 11 March 2017, p. 88.
2 Robert E. Carter, *The Kyoto School: An Introduction* (SUNY Press, 2013), p. 47.
3 Dōgen, 'Temporality', in James W. Heisig, Thomas P. Kasulis and John C. Maraldo (eds.), *Japanese Philosophy: A Sourcebook* (University of Hawai'i Press, 2011), p. 149.
4 Takuan Sōhō, 'Undisturbed Wisdom', ibid., p. 180.
5 *Chāndogya Upaniṣad*, IV.x.4–5, in Sarvepalli Radhakrishnan and Charles A. Moore (eds.), *A Sourcebook in Indian Philosophy* (Princeton University Press, 1957), p. 66.

6 Sue Hamilton, *Indian Philosophy: A Very Short Introduction* (Oxford University Press, 2001), pp. 73, 76.

7 S. K. Saksena, 'Philosophical Theories and the Affairs of Men', in Charles A. Moore (ed.), *The Indian Mind* (University of Hawai'i Press, 1967), p. 129.

8 David Ross Komito, *Nāgārjuna's Seventy Stanzas* (Snow Lion Publications, 1987), Stanza 3, p. 79.

9 Ibid., Stanza 35, p. 88.

10 Ibid., p. 148.

11 Ibid., Stanza 29, p. 86.

12 Ibid., Stanza 50, p. 91.

13 Nāgārjuna, *Vigrahavyāvartanī*, Part 2 (22), in Deepak Sarma (ed.), *Classical Indian Philosophy: A Reader* (Columbia University Press, 2011), p. 44.

14 *Aṅguttara-nikāya*, III.134, in Radhakrishnan and Moore (eds.), *A Sourcebook in Indian Philosophy* (Princeton University Press, 1957), p. 273.

15 Komito, *Nāgārjuna's Seventy Stanzas*, Stanza 73, p. 95.

16 Thanks to Wen Haiming for drawing my attention to this.

17 D. T. Suzuki, 'The Buddhist Conception of Reality', *Eastern Buddhist*, VII:7 (1974), pp. 1–21, reprinted in Frederick Franck (ed.), *The Buddha Eye: An Anthology of the Kyoto School and Its Contemporaries* (World Wisdom, 2004), p. 98.

18 Ibid., p. 86.

19 Matsuo Bashō, *Narrow Road to the Interior*, trans. Sam Hamill (Shambhala, 1991), pp. 35–6.

20 Carter, *The Kyoto School: An Introduction*, p. 130.

12 Naturalism

1 Joel Kupperman, *Learning from Asian Philosophy* (Oxford University Press, 1999), p. 61.

2 Charles A. Moore, 'Introduction: The Humanistic Chinese Mind', in Charles A. Moore (ed.), *The Chinese Mind* (University of Hawai'i Press, 1967), p. 1.

3 *Mencius*, Book 4, Part 2, Chapter 26.1, in James Legge, *The Chinese Classics*, Vol. 2 (Clarendon Press, 1895), p. 331.

4 Yao Xinzhong's insights inform a lot of this section.

5 Philip J. Ivanhoe and Bryan W. Van Norden (eds.), *Readings in Classical Chinese Philosophy*, 2nd edn (Hackett, 2005), p. 392.

6 *The Doctrine of the Mean*, 14.4, in Legge, *The Chinese Classics*, Vol. 1 (Clarendon Press, 1893), p. 396.

7 *Xunzi*, 17, in Ivanhoe and Van Norden (eds.), *Readings in Classical Chinese Philosophy*, p. 272.

8 Chan Wing-Tsit, 'Chinese Theory and Practice, with Special Reference to Humanism', in Moore (ed.), *The Chinese Mind*, p. 20.

9 Y. P. Mei , 'The Status of the Individual in Chinese Ethics', ibid., p. 325.

10 Legge, *The Chinese Classics*, Vol. 1, p. 97.

11 *Analects*, 5.13, in Ivanhoe and Van Norden (eds.), *Readings in Classical Chinese Philosophy*, p. 15.

12 *Analects*, XI.xi, in Legge, *The Chinese Classics*, Vol. 1, pp. 240–41.

13 *Xunzi*, 9, in Ivanhoe and Norden (eds.), *Readings in Classical Chinese Philosophy*, pp. 270–71.

14 *Xunzi*, 8, ibid., p. 267.

15 Ibid., 17, p. 273.

16 Stephen C. Angle and Justin Tiwald, *Neo-Confucianism: A Philosophical Introduction* (Polity, 2017), p. 71.

17 Chakravarthi Ram-Prasad, *Eastern Philosophy* (Weidenfeld & Nicolson, 2005), p. 72.

18 Ibid., pp. 13, 15, 16.

19 *Zhuangzi*, 6, in Ivanhoe and Van Norden (eds.), *Readings in Classical Chinese Philosophy*, p. 236.

20 Robin R. Wang, *Yinyang: The Way of Heaven and Earth in Chinese Thought and Culture* (Cambridge University Press, 2012), p. 59.

21 *Zhuangzi*, 3, in Ivanhoe and Van Norden (eds.), *Readings in Classical Chinese Philosophy*, p. 225.

22 Ibid., p. 228.

23 Ibid., 2, p. 224.

24 Ibid., p. 223.

25 Thomas P. Kasulis, *Shinto: The Way Home* (University of Hawai'i Press, 2004), p. 43.

26 Stephen Muecke, *Ancient & Modern: Time, Culture and Indigenous Philosophy* (UNSW Press, 2004), p. 49.

27 Kasulis, *Shinto*, p. 54.

28 Ibid., p. 43.

29 Lebisa J. Teffo and Abraham P. J. Roux, 'Themes in African Metaphysics', in P. H. Coetzee and A. P. J. Roux (eds.), *The African Philosophy Reader*, 2nd edn (Routledge, 2003), p. 168.

30 See 'Realistic Monism: Why Physicalism Entails Panpsychism', in Galen Strawson, *Real Materialism and Other Essays* (Oxford University Press, 2008).

31 Mādhavācarya, *Sarvadarśana-saṃgraha*, in Deepak Sarma (ed.), *Classical Indian Philosophy: A Reader* (Columbia University Press, 2011), pp. 5–6.

13 Unity

1 Robert Irwin, *The Alhambra* (Profile, 2005), p. 20.

2 Seyyed Hossein Nasr, *Islam in the Modern World* (HarperOne, 2012), p. 246.

3 Ibid., p. 217.

4 Irwin, *The Alhambra*, p. 88.
5 Nasr, *Islam in the Modern World*, p. 213.
6 Irwin, *The Alhambra*, p. 114.
7 Ibid., p. 99.
8 John Renard (ed.), *Islamic Theological Themes: A Primary Source Reader* (University of California Press, 2014), p. 135. See also p. 4.
9 Nasr, *Islam in the Modern World*, p. 167.
10 *Īśā Upaniṣad*, 1.4–5, in Sarvepalli Radhakrishnan and Charles A. Moore (eds.), *A Sourcebook in Indian Philosophy* (Princeton University Press, 1957), p. 40.
11 *Chāndogya Upaniṣad*, VI.ix.4, ibid., p. 69.
12 *Bṛhadāraṇyaka Upaniṣad*, IV.v.15, ibid., pp. 88–9.
13 Ibid., II.iv.14, p. 82.
14 Sue Hamilton, *Indian Philosophy: A Very Short Introduction* (Oxford University Press, 2001), pp. 64–5, and Dhirendra Mohan Datta, 'Indian Political, Legal, and Economic Thought', in Charles A. Moore (ed.), *The Indian Mind* (University of Hawai'i Press, 1967), p. 286.
15 *Zhuangzi*, 2, in Philip J. Ivanhoe and Bryan W. Van Norden (eds.), *Readings in Classical Chinese Philosophy*, 2nd edn (Hackett, 2005), p. 218.
16 *Analects*, 4.15, ibid., p. 12. See also 15.3, p. 44.
17 *Analects*, VII.viii, in James Legge, *The Chinese Classics*, Vol. 1 (Clarendon Press, 1893), p. 197.
18 'Al-Ghazālī, Ash'ari Creed', in Renard (ed.), *Islamic Theological Themes*, p. 109.
19 Jon McGinnis and David C. Reisman (eds.), *Classical Arabic Philosophy: An Anthology of Sources* (Hackett, 2007), pp. xxvi–xxvii.
20 Peter Adamson, *Philosophy in the Islamic World: A Very Short Introduction* (Oxford University Press, 2015), p. 6.
21 Ibid., p. 47.
22 Ibid., p. 58.
23 'Al-Ghazālī, Ash'ari Creed', in Renard (ed.), *Islamic Theological Themes*, p. 112.
24 Nasr, *Islam in the Modern World*, p. 130.
25 Ibid., p. 4.
26 Ibid., p. 38.
27 Tariq Ramadan, *Islam: The Essentials* (Penguin Random House, 2017), p. 61.
28 Ibn Rushd, *The Decisive Treatise*, Chapter 2, in McGinnis and Reisman (eds.), *Classical Arabic Philosophy*, p. 313.
29 Ibid.
30 Letter of the Pontifical Biblical Commission to the Archbishop of Paris, 1948.
31 Nasr, *Islam in the Modern World*, p. 200.
32 Ibid., p. 265.
33 Qur'ān 49:12, trans. M. A. S. Abdel Haleem (Oxford University Press, 2010), p. 339.
34 *Al-Mustadrak 'ala as-Saheehain*, 8198.

35 Nasr, *Islam in the Modern World*, pp. 152, 155.
36 Ibid., p. 183.
37 Ibid., pp. 141–2.
38 Al-Ghazālī, 'Concerning That on Which True Demonstration Is Based', in McGinnis and Reisman (eds.), *Classical Arabic Philosophy*, p. 239.
39 Nasr, *Islam in the Modern World*, p. 6.
40 Ibid., pp. 177–8.
41 Ibid., p. 72.
42 Ramadan, *Islam*, p. 225.
43 An-Nawawi, *Forty Hadith*, Hadith 4, quoted in Renard (ed.), *Islamic Theological Themes*, p. 14.
44 *Sahih Muslim Book of Destiny*, Vol. 6, Book 33, Hadith 6392, https://muflihun.com/muslim/33/6392.
45 Qur'ān 13:27, trans. Haleem, p. 155.
46 Ibid., 61:5, p. 370.
47 Ibid., 14:27, p. 160.
48 B. K. Paul and M. Nadiruzzaman, 'Religious Interpretations for the Causes of the 2004 Indian Ocean Tsunami', *Asian Profile*, 41:1 (2013), pp. 67–77.
49 Qur'ān 7:96–9, as translated on Islam21C.com.
50 Shaikh Haitham Al-Haddad, 'Reasons behind the Japanese Tsunami', 15 March 2011, www.islam21c.com/islamic-thought/2387-reasons-behind-the-japanese-tsunami/.
51 Sanā'ī, 'On the Intimate/Experiential Knowledge [of God, ma'rifat]', in Renard (ed.), *Islamic Theological Themes*, p. 273.
52 Adamson, *Philosophy in the Islamic World*, p. 42.
53 Ibid., p. 89.
54 Ibid., p. 91.
55 Nasr, *Islam in the Modern World*, p. 140.
56 Ramadan, *Islam*, p. 196.
57 See Christopher de Bellaigue, *The Islamic Enlightenment* (The Bodley Head, 2017).
58 Ramadan, *Islam*, pp. 90, 253.

14 Reductionism

1 Thomas P. Kasulis, *Intimacy or Integrity: Philosophy and Cultural Difference* (University of Hawai'i Press, 2002), p. 95.
2 The Encyclopedia of Diderot & d'Alembert: Collaborative Translation Project, hosted by Michigan Publishing, https://quod.lib.umich.edu/d/did/, d'Alembert, 'Preliminary Discourse', https://goo.gl/nTPjgv.
3 Harry G. Frankfurt, 'On Bullshit', in his *The Importance of What We Care About: Philosophical Essays* (Cambridge University Press, 1998), p. 117.

4 This is in Chapter IV of *An Introduction to the Principles of Morals and Legislation* (1781), called 'Value of a Lot of Pleasure or Pain, How to be Measured'.

5 See, for example, E. H. Rosch, 'Natural Categories', *Cognitive Psychology*, 4:3 (1973), pp. 328–50.

6 Janet Radcliffe Richards, *Human Nature after Darwin* (Routledge, 2000), p. 179.

7 Ibid., p. 180.

15 Conclusion to Part Two

1 Talk at Google European Zeitgeist conference, www.youtube.com/watch?v=r4TO1iLZmcw.

2 Karl Popper, 'Replies to My Critics', in Paul Arthur Schilpp (ed.), *The Philosophy of Rudolf Carnap* (Open Court, 1963), p. 980.

3 Immanuel Kant, *Prolegomena to Any Future Metaphysics*, 4:367, trans. Gary Hatfield (Cambridge University Press, 2004), p. 118.

16 No-self

1 *Chāndogya Upaniṣad*, III.xiv.2, 4, in Sarvepalli Radhakrishnan and Charles A. Moore (eds.), *A Sourcebook in Indian Philosophy* (Princeton University Press, 1957), p. 65.

2 L. N. Sharma, 'The Indian Quest', Presidential Address at the 90th Session of the Indian Philosophical Congress, Magadh University, Bodh Gaya, 1–4 February 2016.

3 *Padārthadharmasaṁgraha*, Chapter 5, III.i.19, III.ii.1, in Radhakrishnan and Moore (eds.), *A Sourcebook in Indian Philosophy*, pp. 405, 406.

4 Deepak Sarma (ed.), *Classical Indian Philosophy: A Reader* (Columbia University Press, 2011), p. 141.

5 *Sāṃkhya-Kārikā*, LXIV, in Radhakrishnan and Moore (eds.), *A Sourcebook in Indian Philosophy*, p. 444.

6 Gautama, *Nayāya sūtra*, 1.1.19, in Sarma (ed.), *Classical Indian Philosophy*, p. 100.

7 Sarma (ed.), *Classical Indian Philosophy*, pp. 179–80.

8 Patañjali, *Yoga Sūtras*, I.51, in Sarma (ed.), *Classical Indian Philosophy*, p. 184.

9 John Locke, *An Essay Concerning Human Understanding* (1689), Book II, Chapter XXVII, Para. 9.

10 Chakravarthi Ram-Prasad, *Eastern Philosophy* (Weidenfeld & Nicolson, 2005), pp. 57–8.

11 Ibid., p. 133.

12 Sarma (ed.), *Classical Indian Philosophy*, p. 21.

13 *Milindapañha*, 251, in Radhakrishnan and Moore (eds.), *A Sourcebook in Indian Philosophy*, p. 284.

14 *Dhammapada*, Verse 80, ibid., p. 298.

15 *Visuddhi-magga*, XVI, ibid., p. 289.

16 *Dhammapada*, Verses 15–16, ibid., p. 293.

17 http://info-buddhism.com/13th_Dalai_Lama_Tubten_Gyatso_Tsering_Shakya.html.

18 Quoted in Melvyn C. Goldstein, *A History of Modern Tibet, Volume 2: The Calm Before the Storm: 1951–1955* (University of California Press, 2007), p. 200. Interview in English.

19 Ram-Prasad, *Eastern Philosophy*, pp. 84–5.

20 See Chenyang Li, *The Confucian Philosophy of Harmony* (Routledge, 2014), p. 18.

21 Maulana Jalalu-'d-din Muhammad Rumi, *The Masnavi I Ma'navi*, abridged and trans. E. H. Whinfield (1898), Book V, Story III, 'The Sage and the Peacock', www.sacred-texts.com/isl/masnavi/.

22 Alison Gopnik, 'How an 18th-Century Philosopher Helped Solve My Midlife Crisis', *The Atlantic*, October 2015.

23 John Locke, *An Essay Concerning Human Understanding* (1689), Book II, Chapter XXVII, Para. 13.

24 David Hume, *A Treatise of Human Nature* (1739), Book I, Part IV, Section VI.

25 See, for example, Todd E. Feinberg, *Altered Egos: How the Brain Creates the Self* (Oxford University Press, 2001), and *From Axons to Identity: Neurological Explorations of the Nature of the Self* (W. W. Norton, 2009).

26 See Bruce Hood, *The Self Illusion* (Oxford University Press, 2012), and Thomas Metzinger, *The Ego Tunnel* (Basic Books, 2009).

27 YouGov survey https://goo.gl/yKiuJh.

17 The relational self

1 Robert E. Carter, *The Kyoto School: An Introduction* (SUNY Press, 2013), p. 139.

2 Thomas P. Kasulis, *Zen Action, Zen Person* (University of Hawai'i Press, 1986), p. 7.

3 Ibid., p. 8.

4 Carter, *The Kyoto School*, p. 141.

5 Ibid., p. 147.

6 Ibid., p. 149.

7 Ibid., pp. 130–31.

8 Kuki Shuzō, 'Regarding the Japanese Character', unpublished translation by Leah Kalmanson.

9 Carter, *The Kyoto School*, p. 51.

10 Ibid., pp. 121–2.

11 Ibid., pp. 130–31.
12 Takeuchi Yoshinori, 'The Philosophy of Nishida', *Japanese Religions*, III:4 (1963), pp. 1–32, reprinted in Frederick Franck (ed.), *The Buddha Eye: An Anthology of the Kyoto School and Its Contemporaries* (World Wisdom, 2004), p. 193.
13 Nishitani Keiji, 'Nihility and Nothingness', in James W. Heisig, Thomas P. Kasulis and John C. Maraldo (eds.), *Japanese Philosophy: A Sourcebook* (University of Hawai'i Press, 2011), p. 725.
14 See Chan Wing-Tsit, 'Chinese Theory and Practice, with Special Reference to Humanism', in Charles A. Moore (ed.), *The Chinese Mind* (University of Hawai'i Press, 1967), p. 59.
15 Hsieh Yu-Wei, 'The Status of the Individual in Chinese Ethics', ibid., p. 318.
16 Confucius, *The Great Learning*, Verse 6, trans. Y. P. Mei, in William T. de Bary (ed.), Sources of Chinese Tradition (Columbia University Press, 1960), p. 129.
17 Quotes from Chico Harlan, 'After Ferry Disaster, a Katrina-like Reckoning in South Korea', *Washington Post*, 27 April 2014.
18 Stephen Muecke, *Ancient & Modern: Time, Culture and Indigenous Philosophy* (UNSW Press, 2004), p. 98.
19 Ibid., p. 70.
20 'Māori Resistance Results in Te Urewera Gaining Legal Personality', Environmental Justice Atlas, https://goo.gl/V51Pm4.
21 See Lebisa J. Teffo and Abraham P. J. Roux, 'Themes in African Metaphysics', in P. H. Coetzee and A. P. J. Roux (eds.), *The African Philosophy Reader*, 2nd edn (Routledge, 2003), p. 171.
22 Segun Gbadegesin, 'The Yoruba Concept of a Person', ibid., p. 191.
23 Kwame Gyeke, 'Person and Community in African Thought', ibid., p. 300.
24 Michael Onyebuchi Eze, *Intellectual History in Contemporary South Africa* (Palgrave Macmillan, 2010), pp. 190–91.
25 This point is stressed in several contributions to Coetzee and Roux (eds.), *The African Philosophy Reader*. See, for example, Mogobe B. Ramose, 'Globalisation and *Ubuntu*', p. 643.
26 See Kwasi Wiredu, 'The Moral Foundations of an African Culture', ibid., p. 295.

18 The atomised self

1 Plato, *Phaedo*, 79c–84a, in *The Last Days of Socrates*, trans. Hugh Tredennick (Penguin, 1959), pp. 132–7.
2 René Descartes, *Meditations on First Philosophy*, 6th Meditation, Sections 78 and 85, trans. John Cottingham (Cambridge University Press, 1986 [1641]), pp. 54, 59.
3 David Hume, *A Treatise of Human Nature* (1739), Book I, Part IV, Section VI.

4 See Anthony Giddens, *The Third Way: The Renewal of Social Democracy* (Polity, 1998), p. 65.

5 Jean-Paul Sartre, 'Existentialism and Humanism', in Stephen Priest (ed.), *Jean-Paul Sartre: Basic Writings*, (Routledge, 2001 [1945]), p. 24.

6 See Julian Baggini, 'Our Common Creed: The Myth of Self-Authorship', Theos, 31 January 2017, http://www.theosthinktank.co.uk/comment/2017/01/31/common-creed-the-myth-of-self-authorship.

7 Owen Flanagan, *The Geography of Morals* (Oxford University Press, 2017), pp. 230–31.

8 P. Cross, 'Not Can but Will College Teaching Be Improved?', *New Directions for Higher Education*, 17 (1977), pp. 1–15.

9 Aristotle, *Nicomachean Ethics*, 1169b11–35, trans. J. A. K. Thomson (Penguin, 1996), p. 304.

10 Ibid., 1094a22–b12, p. 64.

11 Leif Wenar, *Blood Oil* (Oxford University Press, 2016), p. 221.

19 Conclusion to Part Three

1 Thomas P. Kasulis, *Intimacy or Integrity: Philosophy and Cultural Difference* (University of Hawai'i Press, 2002), p. 99.

2 Ibid., p. 37.

3 Ibid., p. 38.

4 Ibid., pp. 97–8.

5 Ibid., pp. 103–4.

6 Ibid., p. 4.

7 Ibid., p. 57.

8 Ibid., p. 35.

9 Ibid., p. 50.

10 Ludi Simpson and Nissa Finney, 'How Mobile Are Immigrants, After Arriving in the UK?', in *Understanding Society: Findings 2012*, p. 19, www.understandingsociety.ac.uk/research/publications/findings/2012: cited in David Goodhart, *The Road to Somewhere* (C. Hurst & Co., 2017), p. 38.

Part Four: How the World Lives

1 Adrian Wooldridge, 'The Service Economy', *1843*, October/November 2016.

20 Harmony

1 Anthony White, *The Forbidden City* (Great Wall Publishing, 2002), p. 2.

2 Chenyang Li, *The Confucian Philosophy of Harmony* (Routledge, 2014), p. 1.

3 John C. H. Wu, 'Chinese Legal and Political Philosophy', in Charles A.

Moore (ed.), *The Chinese Mind* (University of Hawai'i Press, 1967), p. 226.

4 *Mencius*, Book 3, Part 1, Chapter 4.8, in James Legge, *The Chinese Classics*, Vol. 2 (Clarendon Press, 1895), p. 252.

5 James Legge, *The Chinese Classics*, Vol. 1 (Clarendon Press, 1893), p. 102.

6 Li, *The Confucian Philosophy of Harmony*, p. 12.

7 Ibid., p. 25.

8 Ibid., p. 22.

9 Ibid., p. 1.

10 Ibid., p. 8.

11 Ibid., p. 37.

12 Philip J. Ivanhoe and Bryan W. Van Norden (eds.), *Readings in Classical Chinese Philosophy*, 2nd edn (Hackett, 2005), p. 60.

13 Li, *The Confucian Philosophy of Harmony*, p. 1.

14 Ibid., pp. 29–30.

15 See Dhirendra Mohan Datta, 'Indian Political, Legal, and Economic Thought', in Charles A. Moore (ed.), *The Indian Mind* (University of Hawai'i Press, 1967), p. 286.

16 Li, *The Confucian Philosophy of Harmony*, p. 27.

17 Aristotle, *Nicomachean Ethics*, 1155a24–b8, trans. J. A. K. Thomson (Penguin, 1996), p. 259.

18 Li, *The Confucian Philosophy of Harmony*, p. 27.

19 Lin Yutang, 'The Chinese People', *The China Critic*, IV:15 (9 April 1931), pp. 343–7.

20 Aristotle, *Nicomachean Ethics*, 1163b7–28, p. 285.

21 Li, *The Confucian Philosophy of Harmony*, p. 106.

22 Chakravarthi Ram-Prasad, *Eastern Philosophy* (Weidenfeld & Nicolson, 2005), p. 102.

23 Li, *The Confucian Philosophy of Harmony*, p. 107.

24 Hsieh Yu-Wei, 'The Status of the Individual in Chinese Ethics', Moore (ed.), *The Chinese Mind*, p. 185.

25 *Mencius*, Book 1, Part 1, Chapter 7.24, in Legge, *The Chinese Classics*, Vol. 2, p. 149.

26 Friedrich Nietzsche, *On the Genealogy of Morals*, Third Essay, Section 7, in Friedrich Nietzsche, *On the Genealogy of Morals/Ecce Homo*, trans. Walter Kaufmann (Vintage, 1969), p. 107.

27 Plato, *Phaedo*, 117a–118a, in *The Last Days of Socrates*, trans. Hugh Tredennick (Penguin, 1959), p. 183.

28 Li, *The Confucian Philosophy of Harmony*, pp. 101–3.

29 Ibid., p. 109.

30 Ibid., p. 112.

31 *Xunzi*, 19, in Ivanhoe and Van Norden (eds.), *Readings in Classical Chinese Philosophy*, pp. 274–5.

32 Berggruen Institute Worskhop on Hierarchy and Equality, Stanford, California, 11–12 March 2016. See 'In Defence of Hierarchy' by workshop participants Stephen Angle, Kwame Anthony Appiah, Julian Baggini, Daniel Bell, Nicolas Berggruen, Mark Bevir, Joseph Chan, Carlos Fraenkel, Stephen Macedo, Michael Puett, Jiang Qian, Mathias Risse, Carlin Romano, Justin Tiwald and Robin Wang, *Aeon*, 22 March 2017, https://aeon.co/essays/hierarchies-have-a-place-even-in-societies-built-on-equality.

33 Immanuel Kant, *An Answer to the Question: What is Enlightenment?* (Penguin, 2009 [1784]), p. 1.

34 Legge, *The Chinese Classics*, Vol. 1, p. 93.

35 Li, *The Confucian Philosophy of Harmony*, p. 166.

36 *Mencius*, Book 3, Part 2, Chapter 1.5, in Legge, *The Chinese Classics*, Vol. 2, p. 264.

37 Ibid., Book 1, Part 1, Chapter 1.3, p. 126.

38 Charles A. Moore, 'Introduction: The Comprehensive Indian Mind', in Moore (ed.), *The Indian Mind*, p. 3.

39 Bruce B. Janz, 'Philosophy-in-Place and the Provenance of Dialogue', *South African Journal of Philosophy*, 34:4 (2015), pp. 480–90, DOI: 10.1080/02580136.2015.1105507.

40 Li, *The Confucian Philosophy of Harmony*, p. 13.

41 Ibid., p. 157.

42 Ibid., p. 36.

43 Robin R. Wang, *Yinyang: The Way of Heaven and Earth in Chinese Thought and Culture* (Cambridge University Press, 2012), p. 129.

44 *Zhuangzi*, 3, in Ivanhoe and Van Norden (eds.), *Readings in Classical Chinese Philosophy*, p. 234.

45 Ibid., 23, p. 249.

46 Joel Kupperman, *Learning from Asian Philosophy* (Oxford University Press, 1999), pp. 28–9.

47 See Ivanhoe and Van Norden (eds.), *Readings in Classical Chinese Philosophy*, p.162.

48 *Daodejing*, 1.25, ibid., p. 175.

49 Ibid., 1.41, p. 183.

50 Ibid., 1.5, p. 165.

51 Kupperman, *Learning from Asian Philosophy*, p. 63.

52 *Daodejing*, 1.18, in Ivanhoe and Van Norden (eds.), *Readings in Classical Chinese Philosophy*, p. 171.

53 Ibid., 1.5, p. 165.

54 Ibid., 1.19, p. 171.

55 Ibid., 1.42, p. 183.

56 Chan Wing-Tsit, 'Chinese Theory and Practice, with Special Reference to Humanism', in Moore (ed.), *The Chinese Mind*, p. 51.

57 Wang, *Yinyang*, p. 6.
58 Ibid., p. 30.
59 Ibid., p. 49.
60 Ibid., p. 24.
61 Ibid., p. 7.
62 Ibid., pp. 120, 123.
63 Ibid., p. 139.
64 Ibid., p. 137.
65 Ibid., p. 160.
66 Ibid., p. 103.
67 Li, *The Confucian Philosophy of Harmony*, p. 167.
68 Wang, *Yinyang*, p. 15.
69 Xu Zhiyuan, *Paper Tiger: Inside the Real China* (Head of Zeus, 2015), p. 46.
70 *Xunzi*, 2, in Ivanhoe and Van Norden (eds.), *Readings in Classical Chinese Philosophy*, p. 262.
71 Xu, *Paper Tiger*, p. 196.
72 Daniel Bell, The China Model (Princeton University Press, 2015), p. 137.
73 Li, *The Confucian Philosophy of Harmony*, pp. 144–5.
74 Ibid., p. 147.
75 See 'The Upper Han', *The Economist*, 19 November 2016.
76 *Mencius*, Book 4, Part 1, Chapter 1.3, in Legge, *The Chinese Classics*, Vol. 2, p. 289.
77 *Analects*, 12.13, in Ivanhoe and Van Norden (eds.), *Readings in Classical Chinese Philosophy*, p. 36.
78 Ibid., 2.3, p. 5.
79 *Mencius*, Book 3, Part 1, Chapter 3.18, in Legge, *The Chinese Classics*, Vol. 2, p. 245.
80 *Daodejing*, 1.7, in Ivanhoe and Van Norden (eds.), *Readings in Classical Chinese Philosophy*, p. 166.
81 Ibid., 1.60, p. 192.
82 Ibid., 1.41, p. 183.
83 Li, *The Confucian Philosophy of Harmony*, pp. 120–21.
84 Ibid., p. 124.
85 Ibid., p. 128.
86 Ibid., pp. 132–3.
87 Ibid., pp. 120–21. See also Aristotle, *Nicomachean Ethics*, 1137b, trans. Martin Oswald (The Bobbs-Merrill Company, 1962), p. 142.
88 *Daodejing*, 2.65, in Ivanhoe and Van Norden (eds.), *Readings in Classical Chinese Philosophy*, p. 195.
89 *Han Feizi*, 50, ibid., p. 357.
90 Ibid., 49, p. 343.
91 Ibid., 5, p. 315.

92 Ibid., 7, p. 327.
93 Ibid., 7, p. 323.
94 Ibid., 50, p. 357.
95 Thaddeus Metz, 'Harmonising Global Ethics in the Future: A Proposal to Add South and East to West', *Journal of Global Ethics*, 1:2 (2014), pp. 146–55, quoting Desmond Tutu, *No Future Without Forgiveness* (Random House, 1999), p. 35.
96 Bell, *The China Model*, pp. 55–6.

21 Virtue

1 Aristotle, *Nicomachean Ethics*, 1103a14, trans. J. A. K. Thomson (Penguin, 1996), p. 91.
2 Ibid., 1098a15, p. 76.
3 John Stuart Mill, *Utilitarianism* (1863), Chapter 2.
4 *Mencius*, Book 4, Part 1, Chapter 19.2, in James Legge, *The Chinese Classics*, Vol. 2 (Clarendon University Press, 1895), p. 309.
5 *The Doctrine of the Mean*, 20.7, in James Legge, *The Chinese Classics*, Vol. 1 (Clarendon Press, 1893). p. 406.
6 Ibid., 14.5, p. 396; *Mencius*, Book 2, Part 1, Chapter 7.5, ibid., p. 205.
7 *Xunzi*, 2, in Philip J. Ivanhoe and Bryan W. Van Norden (eds.), *Readings in Classical Chinese Philosophy*, 2nd edn (Hackett, 2005), p. 261.
8 *Mencius*, Book 3, Part 1, Chapter 1.4, in Legge, *The Chinese Classics*, Vol. 2, p. 235.
9 *Analects*, 6.2, in Ivanhoe and Van Norden (eds.), *Readings in Classical Chinese Philosophy*, p. 50.
10 *Mencius*, Book 7, Part 2, Chapter 16, in Legge, *The Chinese Classics*, Vol. 2, p. 485.
11 *Mencius*, Book 1, Part 1, Chapter 7, in Ivanhoe and Van Norden (eds.), *Readings in Classical Chinese Philosophy*, pp. 120–21.
12 *Mencius*, Book 6, Part 1, Chapter 1.2, in Legge, *The Chinese Classics*, Vol. 2, p. 395.
13 *Mencius*, Book 2, Part 1, Chapter 2, in Ivanhoe and Van Norden (eds.), *Readings in Classical Chinese Philosophy*, p. 127.
14 Stephen C. Angle and Justin Tiwald, *Neo-Confucianism: A Philosophical Introduction* (Polity, 2017), pp. 50–51, 133.
15 *Xunzi*, 23, in Ivanhoe and Van Norden (eds.), *Readings in Classical Chinese Philosophy*, pp. 298–9.
16 Ibid., 23, p. 303.
17 Aristotle, *Nicomachean Ethics*, 1103a14–b1, trans. Thomson, p. 91.
18 *Xunzi*, 1, in Ivanhoe and Van Norden (eds.), *Readings in Classical Chinese Philosophy*, p. 257.

19 Ibid., 19, p. 281.
20 Owen Flanagan, *The Geography of Morals* (Oxford University Press, 2017), p. 11.
21 *Zhuangzi*, 5, in Ivanhoe and Van Norden (eds.), *Readings in Classical Chinese Philosophy*, p. 234.
22 *Daodejing*, 1.54, ibid., p. 188.
23 *Analects*, 8.2, ibid., p. 24.
24 Chenyang Li, *The Confucian Philosophy of Harmony* (Routledge, 2014), p. 66.
25 Comment by a colleague of BBC News Europe producer Piers Scholfield, reported on his Twitter feed @inglesi, 25 May 2017.
26 Chakravarthi Ram-Prasad, *Eastern Philosophy* (Weidenfeld & Nicolson, 2005), p. 91.
27 *Analects*, 17.2, in Ivanhoe and Van Norden (eds.), *Readings in Classical Chinese Philosophy*, p. 48.
28 *Xunzi*, 19, ibid., p. 275.
29 *Analects*, 17.11, ibid., p. 49.
30 *Mencius*, Book 7, Part 1, Chapter 37.3, in Legge, *The Chinese Classics*, Vol. 2, pp. 471–2.
31 *Xunzi*, 29, in Ivanhoe and Van Norden (eds.), *Readings in Classical Chinese Philosophy*, 2005), p. 307.
32 *Analects*, XXVI, in Legge, *The Chinese Classics*, Vol. 1, p. 148.
33 *The Doctrine of the Mean*, 20.4, ibid., p. 405.
34 *Analects*, 6.18, in Ivanhoe and Van Norden (eds.), *Readings in Classical Chinese Philosophy*, p. 18.
35 Ibid., 19.11, p. 54.
36 Ibid., 15.37, p. 46.
37 Ivanhoe and Van Norden (eds.), *Readings in Classical Chinese Philosophy*, p. 117.
38 *Mencius*, Book 5, Part 1, Chapter 2.1, in Legge, *The Chinese Classics*, Vol. 2, p. 346.
39 Ibid., Book 6, Part 2, Chapter 1.6, p. 423.
40 Ibid., Book 4, Part 1, Chapter 17, in Ivanhoe and Van Norden (eds.), *Readings in Classical Chinese Philosophy*, p. 138
41 *Analects*, 9.3, in Ivanhoe and Van Norden (eds.), *Readings in Classical Chinese Philosophy*, p. 25.
42 *Mencius*, Book 6, Part 2, Chapter 2.5, in Legge, *The Chinese Classics*, Vol. 2, p. 426.
43 Ibid., Book 4, Part 2, Chapter 11, pp. 321–2.
44 Aristotle, *Nicomachean Ethics*, 1106b9–1107a1, trans. Thomson, p. 101.
45 Ibid., 1094b1–20, p. 65.
46 David Hume, 'The Sceptic' (1742), www.econlib.org/library/LFBooks/Hume/hmMPL18.html.
47 See Aristotle, *Nicomachean Ethics*, 1138b35–1139a16 and b1178b7–29, trans. Thomson, pp. 204, 333.

48 *Xunzi*, 1, in Ivanhoe and Van Norden (eds.), *Readings in Classical Chinese Philosophy*, p. 258.

49 Aristotle, *Nicomachean Ethics*, 1102b15, trans. Thomson, p. 89.

50 *Analects*, XVII.viii.3, in Legge, *The Chinese Classics*, Vol. 1, p. 322.

51 Ibid., XI.xv, p. 242

52 Aristotle, *Nicomachean Ethics*, 1106a20–b9, trans. Thomson, p. 100.

53 *Analects*, 11.22, in Ivanhoe and Van Norden (eds.), *Readings in Classical Chinese Philosophy*, p. 31.

54 Aristotle, *Nichomachean Ethics*, 1109a25-b15, trans. Thomson, p. 109.

55 *The Doctrine of the Mean*, 1.4, in Legge, *The Chinese Classics*, Vol. 1, p. 384.

56 *Xunzi*, 2, in Ivanhoe and Van Norden (eds.), *Readings in Classical Chinese Philosophy*, p. 263.

57 Ibid., 21, p. 287.

58 *Mencius*, Book 3, Part 2, Chapter 9.9, in Legge, *The Chinese Classics*, Vol. 2, p. 282.

59 Ibid., Book 7, Part 1, Chapter 26.3-4, p. 465.

60 *Daodejing*, 1.73, in Ivanhoe and Van Norden (eds.), *Readings in Classical Chinese Philosophy*, p. 200.

61 Li, *The Confucian Philosophy of Harmony*, pp. 72–3.

62 Chiang Yu-ping, 'The Philosophy of the Communist Party Is the Philosophy of Struggle', *Peking Review*, 12, 22 March 1974.

63 *Anuśāsanaparva*, 104.155–7, in Sarvepalli Radhakrishnan and Charles A. Moore (eds.), *A Sourcebook in Indian Philosophy* (Princeton University Press, 1957), p. 167.

64 Aristotle, *Nicomachean Ethics*, 1168b32–1169a23, trans. Thomson, p. 302.

65 *Mencius*, Book 6, Part 1, Chapter 10.2–5, in Legge, *The Chinese Classics*, Vol. 1, pp. 411–12.

66 *Analects*, 12.2 and 15.24, in Ivanhoe and Van Norden (eds.), *Readings in Classical Chinese Philosophy*, pp. 34, 45–6.

67 Matthew 7:12 (New International Version).

68 Hemacandra, *Yogaśāstra*, Chapter 2 (20), in Deepak Sarma (ed.), *Classical Indian Philosophy: A Reader* (Columbia University Press, 2011), p. 61.

69 *Mozi*, 16, in Ivanhoe and Van Norden (eds.), *Readings in Classical Chinese Philosophy*, p. 68.

70 Matthew 5:39–40 (King James Version).

71 *Analects*, 14.34, in Ivanhoe and Van Norden (eds.), *Readings in Classical Chinese Philosophy*, p. 43.

72 Ibid., 15.24, p. 46.

73 Ram-Prasad, *Eastern Philosophy*, pp. 116, 119.

74 Thomas P. Kasulis, *Intimacy or Integrity: Philosophy and Cultural Difference* (University of Hawai'i Press, 2002), p. 118.

75 *Analects*, XII.iii, in Legge, *The Chinese Classics*, Vol. 1, p. 252.

76 *Analects*, 12.1, in Ivanhoe and Van Norden (eds.), *Readings in Classical Chinese Philosophy*, p. 34.

77 *Analects*, XIII.xxvii, in Legge, *The Chinese Classics*, Vol. 1, p. 274.

78 Kasulis, *Intimacy or Integrity*, p. 120.

79 Ibid., p. 119.

80 Thomas P. Kasulis, *Zen Action, Zen Person* (University of Hawai'i Press, 1986), p. 96.

81 Bankei Yōtaku, 'The Unborn', in James W. Heisig, Thomas P. Kasulis and John C. Maraldo (eds.), *Japanese Philosophy: A Sourcebook* (University of Hawai'i Press, 2011), p. 199.

82 *Majjhima Nikāya*, 22, https://suttacentral.net/mn.

83 *Dhammapada*, IX.6, in Radhakrishnan and Moore (eds.), *A Sourcebook in Indian Philosophy*, p. 301.

22 Moral exemplars

1 See David Brooks, *The Road to Character* (Random House, 2015).

2 In Daniel Bell, *The China Model* (Princeton University Press, 2015), p. 32, quoting Edwin Lee, *Singapore: The Unexpected Nation* (ISEAS, 2008), p. 547.

3 See Charles E. Moore, 'Introduction: The Humanistic Chinese Mind', in Charles A. Moore (ed.), *The Chinese Mind* (University of Hawai'i Press, 1967), p. 5.

4 Peter Adamson, *Philosophy in the Islamic World: A Very Short Introduction* (Oxford University Press, 2015), p. 2.

5 *Bhagavad Gītā*, 3.21, in Sarvepalli Radhakrishnan and Charles A. Moore (eds.), *A Sourcebook in Indian Philosophy* (Princeton University Press, 1957), p. 114.

6 *Mahābhārata*, Book 12: Santi Parva, Section 75, www.sacred-texts.com/hin/m12/m12a074.htm.

7 Radhakrishnan and Moore (eds.), *A Sourcebook in Indian Philosophy*, p. 273.

8 Aristotle, *Nicomachean Ethics*, 1172b1–23, trans. J. A. K. Thomson (Penguin, 1996), p. 313.

9 *Daodejing*, 1.22, in Philip J. Ivanhoe and Bryan W. Van Norden (eds.), *Readings in Classical Chinese Philosophy*, 2nd edn (Hackett, 2005), p. 173.

10 *Mencius*, Book 1, Part 1, Chapter 7, ibid., p. 121.

11 *Analects*, XIII.i.1, in James Legge, *The Chinese Classics*, Vol. 1 (Clarendon Press, 1893), p. 262.

12 Chan Wing-Tsit, 'Chinese Theory and Practice, with Special Reference to Humanism', in Moore (ed.), *The Chinese Mind*, p. 17.

13 Wu Jiao, 'Xi Says It's Time for Philosophy to Flourish', *China Daily*, 18 May 2016, www.chinadaily.com.cn/china/2016-05/18/content_25333404.htm.

14 'Factbox: Seven Facts of China's Anti-corruption Campaign', XinhuaNet, 4 July 2017, http://news.xinhuanet.com/english/2017-07/04/c_136416939.htm.

15 'Portrait of a Purge', *The Economist*, 13 February 2016.

16 *Analects*, IX.xiii.2, in Legge, *The Chinese Classics*, Vol. 1, p. 221.

17 Chenyang Li, *The Confucian Philosophy of Harmony* (Routledge, 2014), p. 137.

18 *Mencius*, Book 2, Part 1, Chapter 1.12, in James Legge, *The Chinese Classics*, Vol. 2 (Clarendon Press, 1895), p. 184.

19 *Analects*, 2.1, in Philip J. Ivanhoe and Bryan W. Van Norden (eds.), *Readings in Classical Chinese Philosophy*, 2nd edition (Hackett, 2005), p. 5.

20 Ibid., 2.19, p. 7.

21 Mahātmā Gandhi, 'Letter to Ramachandra Kahre', 11 February 1932, cited in *Collected Works of Mahatma Gandhi*, Vol. 55. Thanks to Akeel Bilgrami.

22 *Dhammapada*, V.5–6, in Radhakrishnan and Moore (eds.), *A Sourcebook in Indian Philosophy*, p. 297.

23 *Han Feizi*, 49, in Ivanhoe and Van Norden (eds.), *Readings in Classical Chinese Philosophy*, p. 342.

24 Ibid., 8, p. 330.

25 *Mencius*, Book 1. Part 1, Chapter 5.6, in Legge, *The Chinese Classics*, Vol. 2, p. 136.

26 *Han Feizi*, 49, in Ivanhoe and Van Norden (eds.), *Readings in Classical Chinese Philosophy*, p. 345.

27 Ibid., 50, p. 352.

28 *Analects*, XIII.xvi.2, in Legge, *The Chinese Classics*, Vol. 1, p. 269.

29 *Analects*, 4.1, in Ivanhoe and Van Norden (eds.), *Readings in Classical Chinese Philosophy*, p. 10.

30 Ibid., 4.25, p. 13.

31 Aristotle, *Nicomachean Ethics*, 1169b35–1170a24, trans. Thomson, p. 305.

32 *Analects*, XV.vi.2, in Legge, *The Chinese Classics*, Vol. 1, p. 296.

33 *Analects*, 16.4, in Ivanhoe and Van Norden (eds.), *Readings in Classical Chinese Philosophy*, p. 47.

34 *Xunzi*, 1, ibid., p. 259.

35 Aristotle, *Nicomachean Ethics*, 1172a6–15, trans. Thomson, p. 311.

36 *Mencius*, Book 5, Part 2, Chapter 3.1, in Legge, *The Chinese Classics*, Vol. 2, p. 376.

37 Ibid., Book 7, Part 1, Chapter 20.1–4, pp. 458–9.

38 Ibid., Book 2, Part 2, Chapter 13.1, p. 232.

39 *Analects*, XIX.iv, in Legge, *The Chinese Classics*, Vol. 1, p. 217.

40 Ibid., XIV.xxx.1, p. 286.

41 Stephen C. Angle and Justin Tiwald, *Neo-Confucianism: A Philosophical Introduction* (Polity, 2017), p. 96.

42 *Zhuangzi*, 19, in Ivanhoe and Van Norden (eds.), *Readings in Classical Chinese Philosophy*, p. 248.

43 Aristotle, *Nicomachean Ethics*, 1123b35–1125a20, trans. Thomson, pp.155–8.
44 *Mencius*, Book 7, Part 2, Chapter 35, in Legge, *The Chinese Classics*, Vol. 2, p. 497.
45 *Analects*, 4.9, in Ivanhoe and Van Norden (eds.), *Readings in Classical Chinese Philosophy*, p. 11.
46 *The Doctrine of the Mean*, 11.1, in Legge, *The Chinese Classics*, Vol. 1, p. 391.
47 *Analects*, XV.xix, in Legge, *The Chinese Classics*, Vol. 1, p. 300.
48 Aristotle, *Nicomachean Ethics*, 1123b13–35, trans. Thomson, p. 154.
49 *Analects*, 4.5, in Ivanhoe and Van Norden (eds.), *Readings in Classical Chinese Philosophy*, p. 11.
50 *Analects*, VIII.xiii.3, in Legge, *The Chinese Classics*, Vol. 1, p. 212.
51 Aristotle, *Nicomachean Ethics*, 1099a32, trans. Thomson, p. 80.
52 Ibid., 1153b11–35, p. 254.
53 *Mencius*, Book 1, Part 1, Chapter 7, in Ivanhoe and Van Norden (eds.), *Readings in Classical Chinese Philosophy*, p. 122.
54 *Mencius* Book 1, Part 2, Chapter 5.4, in Legge, *The Chinese Classics*, Vol. 2, p. 163.
55 *Analects*, 15.31, in Ivanhoe and Van Norden (eds.), *Readings in Classical Chinese Philosophy*, p. 46.
56 *Analects*, V.xxxv, in Legge, *The Chinese Classics*, Vol. 1, p. 207.

23 Liberation

1 Chakravarthi Ram-Prasad, *Eastern Philosophy* (Weidenfeld & Nicolson, 2005), p. 132.
2 S. K. Saksena, 'Philosophical Theories and the Affairs of Men', in Charles A. Moore (ed.), *The Indian Mind* (University of Hawai'i Press, 1967), p. 30.
3 *Chāndogya Upaniṣad*, VIII.15, in Sarvepalli Radhakrishnan and Charles A. Moore (eds.), *A Sourcebook in Indian Philosophy* (Princeton University Press, 1957), p. 77.
4 Daya Krishna, *Indian Philosophy: A Counter Perspective* (Oxford University Press, 1996), p. 16.
5 Ibid., p. 6.
6 Ibid., p. 26.
7 Ibid., p. 16.
8 Ibid., p. 48.
9 Ibid., p. 32.
10 Ibid., p. 16.
11 Radhakrishnan and Moore (eds.), *A Sourcebook in Indian Philosophy*, p. xxviii.
12 Gautama, *Nayāya sūtra*, 1.1.2, in Deepak Sarma (ed.), *Classical Indian Philosophy: A Reader* (Columbia University Press, 2011), p. 96.
13 *The Vedānta Sūtras with commentary by Śaṅkarākārya*, XXIV, in

Radhakrishnan and Moore (eds.), *A Sourcebook in Indian Philosophy*, pp. 512–13.

14 Ibid., p. 517.

15 Ibid., p. 519.

16 Rāmānujācārya, *Vedārthasaṃgraha*, Section 144, in Sarma (ed.), *Classical Indian Philosophy*, p. 221.

17 Ibid., Sections 4–5, p. 216.

18 Patañjali, *Yoga Sūtras*, III.55, ibid., p. 192.

19 Sue Hamilton, *Indian Philosophy: A Very Short Introduction* (Oxford University Presss, 2001), p. 1.

20 Ram-Prasad, *Eastern Philosophy*, p. 180.

21 Joel Kupperman, *Learning from Asian Philosophy* (Oxford University Press, 1999), p. 124.

22 *Śāntiparva*, 329.13, in Radhakrishnan and Moore (eds.), *A Sourcebook in Indian Philosophy*, p. 166.

23 *Majjhima-nikāya*, II.248–52, ibid., p. 275.

24 *Visuddhi-magga*, XVI, ibid., p. 289.

25 Ram-Prasad, *Eastern Philosophy*, p. 129.

26 Ibid., p. 128.

27 Robert E. Carter, *The Kyoto School: An Introduction* (SUNY Press, 2013), p. 57.

28 Abe Masao, 'God, Emptiness, and the True Self', *Eastern Buddhist*, II:2 (1969), pp. 15–30, reprinted in Frederick Franck (ed.), *The Buddha Eye: An Anthology of the Kyoto School and Its Contemporaries* (World Wisdom, 2004), p. 59.

29 Karaki Junzō, 'Metaphysical Impermanence', in James W. Heisig, Thomas P. Kasulis and John C. Maraldo (eds.), *Japanese Philosophy: A Sourcebook* (University of Hawai'i Press, 2011), p. 231.

30 Ram-Prasad, *Eastern Philosophy*, p. 130.

31 Saksena, 'Philosophical Theories and the Affairs of Men', in Moore (ed.), *The Indian Mind*, p. 36.

32 *Śāntiparva*, 321.50, in Radhakrishnan and Moore (ds.), *A Sourcebook in Indian Philosophy*, p. 169.

33 Ibid., 174.4, p. 170.

34 Epictetus, *Handbook*, Section 15, in Epictetus, *The Discourses, The Handbook, Fragments*, ed. Christopher Gill (Everyman, 1995), pp. 291–2.

35 Ram-Prasad, *Eastern Philosophy*, p. 112.

36 *Śāntiparva*, 329.29, 32, in Radhakrishnan and Moore (eds.), *A Sourcebook in Indian Philosophy*, p. 167.

37 *The Laws of Manu*, IV.239, ibid., p. 174.

38 *Bhagavad Gītā*, 2.62–4, ibid., p. 111.

39 Hemacandra, *Yogaśāstra*, Chapter 2 (93), in Sarma (ed.), *Classical Indian Philosophy*, p. 67.

40 *Dhammapada*, VII.4–5, in Radhakrishnan and Moore (eds.), *A Sourcebook in Indian Philosophy*, p. 305.
41 Ibid., XIII.1, p. 29.
42 www.hermitary.com/solitude/rhinoceros.html.
43 *Dhammapāda*, 11, trans. Gil Fronsdal (Shambhala, 2005), pp. 39–40.
44 *Kauṣītaki Upaniṣad*, I.3–4, in Radhakrishnan and Moore (eds.), *A Sourcebook in Indian Philosophy*, p. 93.
45 *Dhammacakkappavattana Sutta*, part of *Saṃyutta Nikāya*, 56.11, in Bikkhu Bodhi (ed.), *In the Buddha's Words: An Anthology of Discources from the Pāli Canon* (Wisdom Publications, 2005), p. 75.
46 *Visuddhi-magga*, XVIII, in Radhakrishnan and Moore (eds.), *A Sourcebook in Indian Philosophy*, p. 285.
47 'Holy Noodle', *The Economist*, 12 March 2016, p. 56.

24 Transience

1 See Antonio Damasio, *Descartes' Error: Emotion, Reason, and the Human Brain* (Putnam Publishing, 1994).
2 Abe Masao, '*Śūnyatā* as Formless Form', in James W. Heisig, Thomas P. Kasulis and John C. Maraldo (eds.), *Japanese Philosophy: A Sourcebook* (University of Hawai'i Press, 2011), pp. 754–5.
3 Rabindranath Tagore, *A Tagore Reader*, ed. Amiya Chakravarty (Macmillan, 1961), p. 4.
4 David Hume, *A Treatise of Human Nature* (1739), Book II, Part I, Section I.
5 Okakura Kakuzō, *The Book of Tea* (Penguin, 2016 [1906]), pp. 3–4.
6 Ibid., p. 4.
7 Ibid., p. 85.
8 Ibid., p. 5.
9 Ibid., p. 12.

25 Impartiality

1 Charles Laurence, 'I Feel Better for Giving Everything – Whether My Money or My Organs', *Daily Telegraph*, 8 August 2004.
2 See Roger T. Ames, *Confucian Role Ethics* (University of Hawai'i Press, 2011).
3 Pieter H. Coetzee, 'Particularity in Morality and Its Relation to Community', in P. H. Coetzee and A. P. J. Roux (eds.), *The African Philosophy Reader*, 2nd edn (Routledge, 2003), p. 277.
4 John Stuart Mill, Utilitarianism (1861), Chapter 2.
5 *Mozi*, 632, in Philip J. Ivanhoe and Bryan W. Van Norden (eds.), *Readings in Classical Chinese Philosophy*, 2nd edn (Hackett, 2005), pp. 105–7.
6 Ibid., 16, p. 68.

7 Ibid., p. 74.
8 Ibid., p. 70.
9 *Han Feizi*, 6, ibid., p. 319.
10 Ibid., 8, p. 331.
11 Ibid., 49, p. 340.
12 Ibid., 7, p. 325
13 Jung Chang, *Wild Swans* (HarperCollins, 1991), p. 193.
14 John C. H. Wu, in Sarvepalli Radhakrishnan and Charles A. Moore (eds.), *A Sourcebook in Indian Philosophy* (Princeton University Press, 1957), p. 347.
15 Jeremy Bentham, 'Advice to a Young Girl', 22 June 1830.
16 Attributed to Bentham by John Stuart Mill in *Utilitarianism* (1863), Chapter 5.
17 Immanuel Kant, *Groundwork of the Metaphysics of Morals*, trans. Mary Gregor (Cambridge University Press, 1993 [1785]), p. 15.
18 See Adam Smith, *The Theory of Moral Sentiments* (1759), Part III, Chapter 1.6.
19 Jonathan Israel, *A Revolution of the Mind* (Princeton University Press, 2010), p. viii.
20 Michael Specter, 'The Dangerous Philosopher', *New Yorker*, 6 September 1999.
21 Owen Flanagan, *The Geography of Morals* (Oxford University Press, 2017), p. 53.

26 Conclusion to Part Four

1 Remark at the 2016 East-West Philosophers' Conference.

Part Five:
Concluding thoughts

1 Wan Lixin, 'Intangible Culture Key to Modern Identity', *Shanghai Daily*, 20 January 2016, p. A7.
2 'Chinese Society', *The Economist* Special Report, 9 July 2016, p. 6.

27 How the world thinks

1 Tariq Ramadan, *Islam: The Essentials* (Penguin Random House, 2017), p. 24.
2 Asma Afsaruddin, 'The Qur'ān and Human Flourishing: Self, God-Consciousness and the Good Society from an Islamic Perspective', unpublished paper.
3 See Ramadan, *Islam*, pp. 33–4.
4 'Try Me a River', *The Economist*, 25 March 2017.
5 Lesley Chamberlain, *Motherland: A Philosophical History of Russia* (Atlantic Books, 2004), p. x.

6 Ibid., p. 92.
7 Ibid., p. 17.
8 Ibid., p. xiv.
9 Ibid., p. 116.
10 Ibid., p. 41.
11 Eimear McBride, 'Stalin and the Poets', *New Statesman*, 5–11 May 2017.
12 Chamberlain, *Motherland*, p. 166.
13 Ibid., p. 203.

28 A sense of place

1 Arindam Chakrabati and Ralph Weber, 'Afterword/Afterwards', in Arindam Chakrabati and Ralph Weber (eds.), *Comparative Philosophy without Borders* (Bloomsbury, 2015), p. 238.
2 Owen Flanagan, *The Geography of Morals* (Oxford University Press, 2017), p. 7.
3 Joel Kupperman, *Learning from Asian Philosophy* (Oxford University Press, 1999). p. 138.
4 *Udāna*, 6.4, *Tittha Sutta*, trans. Thanissaro Bhikkhu, www.accesstoinsight. org/lib/authors/thanissaro/udana.pdf.
5 Isaiah Berlin, 'My Intellectual Path', in *The Power of Ideas* (Princeton University Press, 2001), pp. 1–23.

FURTHER READING

There are so many intellectual journeys that could start from this book. The following is a very selective list of some of the best guidebooks that have helped me. Other works used are cited in the notes.

ANTHOLOGIES OF PRIMARY SOURCES

Coetzee, P. H., and Roux, A. P. J. (eds.), *The African Philosophy Reader*, 2nd edn (Routledge, 2003)

Cooper, David E., and Fosl, Peter S., *Philosophy: The Classic Readings* (Wiley-Blackwell, 2009)

Franck, Frederick (ed.), *The Buddha Eye: An Anthology of the Kyoto School and Its Contemporaries* (World Wisdom, 2004)

Heisig, James W., Kasulis, Thomas P., and Maraldo, John C. (eds.), *Japanese Philosophy: A Sourcebook* (University of Hawai'i Press, 2011)

Ivanhoe, Philip J., and Van Norden, Bryan W. (eds.), *Readings in Classical Chinese Philosophy*, 2nd edn (Hackett, 2005)

McGinnis, Jon, and Reisman, David C. (eds.),
  Classical Arabic Philosophy: An Anthology of Sources
  (Hackett, 2007)

Radhakrishnan, Sarvepalli, and Moore, Charles A. (eds.), *A
  Sourcebook in Indian Philosophy* (Princeton University
  Press, 1957)

Renard, John (ed.), *Islamic Theological Themes: A Primary Source
  Reader* (University of California Press, 2014)

Sarma, Deepak (ed.), *Classical Indian Philosophy: A Reader*
  (Columbia University Press, 2011)

Talisse, Robert B., and Aikin, Scott F. (eds.), *The Pragmatism
  Reader* (Princeton University Press, 2011)

Secondary sources

Adamson, Peter, *Philosophy in the Islamic World: A Very Short
  Introduction* (Oxford University Press, 2015)

Angle, Stephen C., and Tiwald, Justin, *Neo-Confucianism: A
  Philosophical Introduction* (Polity, 2017)

Chamberlain, Lesley, *Motherland: A Philosophical History of
  Russia* (Atlantic Books, 2004)

Cooper, David E., *World Philosophies: An Historical Introduction*,
  2nd edn (Blackwell, 2003)

Flanagan, Owen, *The Geography of Morals* (Oxford University
  Press, 2017)

Hamilton, Sue, *Indian Philosophy: A Very Short Introduction*
  (Oxford University Press, 2001)

Israel, Jonathan, *A Revolution of the Mind* (Princeton University
  Press, 2010)

Kasulis, Thomas P., *Zen Action, Zen Person* (University of Hawai'i
  Press, 1986)

Kasulis, Thomas P., *Intimacy or Integrity: Philosophy and Cultural
  Difference* (University of Hawai'i Press, 2002)

Krishna, Daya, *Indian Philosophy: A Counter Perspective* (Oxford University Press, 1996)

Kupperman, Joel, *Learning from Asian Philosophy* (Oxford University Press, 1999)

Li, Chenyang, *The Confucian Philosophy of Harmony* (Routledge, 2014)

Muecke, Stephen, *Ancient & Modern: Time, Culture and Indigenous Philosophy* (UNSW Press, 2004)

Slingerland, Edward, *Trying Not to Try* (Canongate, 2014)

Wang, Robin R., *Yinyang: The Way of Heaven and Earth in Chinese Thought and Culture* (Cambridge University Press, 2012)

ACKNOWLEDGEMENTS

I could not have written this book without the generosity of numerous experts who took time to be interviewed, respond to emails and read draft material. For this I am extremely grateful to Asma Afsaruddin, Roger Ames, Meera Baindur, Nicholas Bunnin, Lesley Chamberlain, P. Chinnaiah, David E. Cooper, P. George Victor, Frank Griffel, Dimitri Gutas, Bruce Janz, Hirini Kaa, Leah Kalmanson, Tom Kasulis, Kazashi Nobuo, John Krummel, Andrew Lambert, Jin Lee, Luis Xavier Lopez-Farjeat, Yahya Michot, Stephen Muecke, Chandrakala Padia, Daniel Raveh, Carlin Romano, R. C. Sinha, Takahiro Nakajima, Joram Tarusarira, Richard Taylor, Pieter Boele Van Hensbroek, Yves Vende, Wen Haiming, David Wong, Xu Zhiyuan, Yao Xinzhong and Yasuo Kobayashi.

I also learned a great deal from the participants in three workshops organised by the Berggruen Institute at Stanford University, with the support of Margaret Levi. These include many of the above and also Stephen Angle, Kwame Anthony Appiah, Pico Ayer, Nicolas Berggruen, Rajeev Bhargava, Mark Bevir, Akeel Bilgrami, Joseph Chan, Carlos Fraenkel, Rebecca Newberger Goldstein,

Alexander Görlach, Peter Hershock, Ganeri Jonardon, Anton Koch, Haiyan Lee, Stephen Macedo, Thaddeus Metz, Pankaj Mishra, Jay Ogilvy, Philip Pettit, Michael Puett, Jiang Qian, Mathias Risse, Thomas Sheehan, Edward Slingerland, Anna Sun, Sigridur Thorgeirsdottir, Justin Tiwald, Robin Wang, Yunxiang Yan and Taisu Zhang.

Producing podcasts and other resources for the Berggruen Institute also enabled me to take my research further and I am extremely grateful for the travel support the institute offered me. Thanks to Nicolas Berggruen, Jenny Bourne and Dawn Nakagawa.

Thanks also to Mark Jones and Cathy Adams from *Discovery* magazine for helping to get me to China.

The book was made possible and improved by my editor, Bella Lacey, with the support of everyone at Granta Books, especially Iain Chapple, Lamorna Elmer, Helen James, Christine Lo, Angela Rose, Pru Rowlandson, Natalie Shaw and Sarah Wasley, copy editor Lesley Levene and proofreader Kate Shearman. Thanks to my agent, Lizzy Kremer, I only need worry about doing the best job of writing the book I can.

This book depended on the help of so many people that I am sure I have neglected to thank at least some of them. I am as apologetic as I am grateful to them.

Last of all, thanks to the centre of my world, Antonia Macaro.

INDEX